Zion

216 · 464-6500

26201

216 283-8500

6025 Kruse

*The Life and Adventures*
*of Thomas Coryate*

# AN EXPLICATION OF THE EMBLEMES OF
## THE FRONTISPICE

A. First, th'Author here glutteth Sea, Haddocke and Whiting
With spuing, and after the world with his writing.          [*p.* 17]

B. Though our Author for's Venerie felt no whips smart,
Yet see here he rides in a Picardie Cart.          [*p.* 20]

C. His love to strange horses he sorteth out prettilie,
He rides them in France, and lies with them in Italie.          [*pp.* 26, 61]

D. Here up the Alpes (not so plaine as to Dunstable)
Hee's carried like a Cripple, from Constable to Constable.          [*p.* 28]

E. A Punke here pelts him with egs. How so?
For he did but kisse her, and so let her go.          [*p.* 51]

F. Religiously here he bids, row from the stewes,
He will expiate this sinne with converting the Jewes.          [*p.* 53]

G. Thy Cortizan clipt thee, ware Tom, I advise thee,
And flie from the Jewes, lest they circumcise thee.          [*p.* 53]

H. Here, by a Boore too, hee's like to be beaten,
For Grapes he had gather'd before they were eaten.          [*p.* 84]

I. Old Hat here, torne Hose, with Shoes full of gravell,
And louse-dropping Case, are the Armes of his travell.          [*p.* 114]

K. Here, finer then comming from his Punke you him see,
*F. shews what he was, K. what he will bee.          [*p.* 123]

L. Here France, and Italy both to him shed
Their hornes, and Germany pukes on his head.          [*p.* 75]

M. And here he disdain'd not, in a forraine land,
To lie at Livory, while the Horses did stand.          [*p.* 61]

N. But here, neither trusting his hands, nor his legs,
Beeing in feare to be rob'd, he most learnedly begs.          [*p.* 79]

---

* *Not meaning by F. and K. as the vulgar may peevishly and wittingly mistake, but that he was then comming from his Courtesan a Freshman, and now having seen their fashions, and written a description of them, he will shortly be reputed a knowing, proper, and well traveld scholer, as by his starch'd beard and printed ruffe may be as properly insinuated.*

1. Title page of *Coryat's Crudities*, 1611, engraved by William Hole. The explanatory couplets are by Ben Jonson except A, B, C and G, which are by Laurence Whitaker. The page numbers after the couplets refer to passages in *The Life and Adventures of Thomas Coryate*.

# THE LIFE AND ADVENTURES
## OF
# *Thomas Coryate*

## MICHAEL STRACHAN

LONDON
OXFORD UNIVERSITY PRESS
NEW YORK TORONTO
1962

*Oxford University Press, Amen House, London E.C.4*

GLASGOW NEW YORK TORONTO MELBOURNE WELLINGTON
BOMBAY CALCUTTA MADRAS KARACHI LAHORE DACCA
CAPE TOWN SALISBURY NAIROBI IBADAN ACCRA
KUALA LUMPUR HONG KONG

PRINTED IN GREAT BRITAIN

# Contents

# List of Illustrations

## LIST OF MAPS

# *Foreword*

ONE Spring day some years ago I was trying to keep pace
with my friend Enoch Powell during a walk from Shrews-
bury to Hereford when he added point to remarks about
my shortcomings as a pedestrian by asking whether I had ever
heard of the Englishman who walked to India. To cure my ignorance and satisfy my curiosity he lent me Sir William Foster's
*Early Travels in India* containing Coryate's letters written from
the Court of the Great Mogul. Thus began a chain of events
which has resulted in the publication of this book.

As my investigations progressed I became convinced that
Coryate deserved fuller and fairer treatment than he has hitherto
received. I also came to admire his many good qualities, not least
of which is his ability to write fine, vigorous prose. I have therefore not hesitated to let Coryate tell his own story whenever it
seemed appropriate; his own words convey the man and his
period more vividly than any paraphrase. The original spelling
has generally been maintained, except that the letters i, j, u, and v
have been modernised and obvious printers' errors have been
corrected. References to the *Crudities* are to the 1905 edition, as
being the most accessible.

In preparing this volume my greatest debt is to Dr. Esmond
S. de Beer who has made freely available to me the resources of
his astounding scholarship and has suggested numerous additions
and improvements. Without his most liberal help the book would
have been very much more imperfect than it is.

I am indebted to Professor William A. Jackson for much information and many useful suggestions concerning the bibliographical aspects of the work; to Mr. J. W. Gladwell for indispensable assistance in unravelling the complexities of Coryate's
lawsuit, and to Mr. Michael R. E. Gough for help and advice in
connexion with the description of Alexandria Troas. The Rev.
H. P. Cromie went to great trouble on my behalf in searching for
Coryate's tomb at Surat and Suvali.

Many others have helped me in numerous ways. I would like to thank particularly Mr. John H. Harvey, Archivist to Winchester College, Mr. Ivor P. Collis, Somerset County Archivist and Mr. Boies Penrose. Mr. K. R. Potter has kindly helped me with some translations from Latin. I remember with gratitude the help and encouragement of the late Rev. H. D. Owen-Brown, Rector of Odcombe.

In identifying the members of Coryate's circle I have received generous assistance from Professor Franklin B. Williams, Jr., who has allowed me to use material from his *Index of Dedications and Commendatory Verses*. I have also been greatly helped by the writings of Dr. Leslie Hotson and Mr. I. A. Shapiro, both of whom have kindly spared time to correspond with me on various queries.

My task has been made much easier by the resources and facilities of the London Library. I also wish to record my gratitude to the staff of the National Library of Scotland, in particular to Mr. D. M. Lloyd, Mr. A. Rodger, Dr. M. A. Pegg, Miss M. Deas and Miss A. Young; to Mr. D. G. Neill and the staff of the Bodleian Library; to Mr. E. R. S. Fifoot of Edinburgh University Library, and to the staffs of the British Museum Library and Edinburgh Public Library.

I have throughout received splendid assistance from Miss V. J. Ledger, who has most competently and enthusiastically carried out many hours of research for me in London.

Finally, the book could not have been written without the co-operation and forbearance of my dear wife.

M. F. S.

*Edinburgh, April* 1962.

# CHAPTER I

## *Early Life*

THOMAS CORYATE, writer, eccentric, wit, and one of the most tireless, inquisitive, and courageous of all English travellers, was born when Shakespeare was a boy of thirteen, and died in 1617, the year after Shakespeare, at the age of forty. His connexion with the Prince of Wales's household made him known to King James and the other members of the Royal Family. He was acquainted with Ben Jonson, Inigo Jones, John Donne, Sir Thomas Roe, and many other celebrities of his time. He attended meetings of the Mermaid Tavern Club—indeed he provides the only indisputable contemporary evidence of its existence. The account of his European tour, *Coryat's Crudities*, published in 1611 when he was thirty-five, has earned its author a place in the history of English literature, but he deserves to be remembered for much more than his literary achievement. He was, for example, the first English traveller to take a scholarly interest in the classical sites of the Trojan Plain; the first Englishman ever to visit India purely out of curiosity; the first European (and to this day the last) to *walk*, with no resources except his own faith and courage, from the eastern shores of the Mediterranean, through Persia and Afghanistan into the heart of the Mogul Empire. This astounding feat would be better known if his early death in India had not prevented him from writing another great book. Nevertheless, his surviving notes and letters give a splendidly vivid picture of Constantinople, the Levant of the Ottoman Empire, and the Court of the Great Mogul. Yet he has been strangely neglected by biographers, and the story of his life and adventures has never before been fully related.

The foreign travels all took place during the last ten years of his short life. Childhood and much of his early manhood were spent in the Somerset village of Odcombe. This was his home and here were his roots; he liked to call himself 'The Peregrine of Odcombe' or 'The Odcombian Leg-stretcher'.

Odcombe today is a straggling village with groups of cottages and farm houses perched on steep slopes and linked by narrow, high-banked lanes. It cannot be greatly different from what it was in Coryate's day. On the highest point in the village stands the church. Thence one can look down into Yeovil, three miles away to the east, and catch a glimpse of Montacute at the foot of the hill, a mile away to the west; northwards stretches the rich, rolling Somerset countryside, to the south one can see into the heart of Dorset.

Here in the parsonage house, which in Elizabethan times stood near the church, Thomas Coryate was born, the only son of the Rev. George Coryate, rector of Odcombe, by his wife Gertrude. There is some evidence that she was George Coryate's second wife and that he had two or even three daughters by his first marriage.[1] In his writings Thomas makes no mention of half-sisters, which may mean that they died in infancy. Thomas was proud to claim that he was a fourth cousin of the Earl of Essex. It is not known whether this remote relationship existed on his father's side or through the family of his mother, whose maiden name was almost certainly Williams.[2] Nothing else is known about his mother's background and early life except that she was some years younger than her husband, being perhaps seventeen or eighteen when she married.

We know much more about Thomas's father, George Coryate (1545 ?–1607), whose family came from Salisbury. He was admitted to Winchester College at the age of twelve, and after three years there went on to New College, Oxford, where he was elected a perpetual fellow in 1562. Anthony à Wood says that he was much commended in his time for his fine fancy in Latin poetry.[3]

---

[1] According to *Antiquitates Sarisburienses*, 1771, pp. 226–7, George Coryate was born in St. Thomas's Parish, Salisbury, and received the rudiments of learning for some time in the Free School of the city; he is said to have married Henrietta Cooper of Salisbury by whom he had one son named Thomas, and three daughters. But it is clear from Thomas's letters that Henrietta Cooper was not his mother. 'R' (? Abraham Rees), who wrote the article on Thomas in *Biographia Britannica*, London, 1789, vol. IV, p. 273, states that there were two daughters, but gives no source for this information.

[2] In Letter No. 6 from India Thomas speaks of his Uncle Williams, q.v. Williams p. 292 below.

[3] *Athenae Oxonienses*, London, 1721 edn., vol. I, p. 335.

One of the earliest examples of this discriminating talent, written
when he was nineteen, was a poem addressed to Queen Elizabeth
when she was thirty years of age, exhorting her to marry without
delay. This piece of impertinence did not prevent his being
chosen two years later, when the Queen visited New College, to
receive Her Majesty and to pronounce a Latin oration, for which
he received great praise and a handsome purse of gold.[1] The
money was no doubt quite as welcome as the congratulations,
for it seems that George Coryate was never a rich man. He became a Bachelor of Divinity in 1562, and continued at Oxford
until he was appointed Rector of Odcombe eight years later.

Such literary promise as he showed at Oxford did not develop
when he reached maturer years. Some of his verses were published
as an act of filial piety by his son in an appendix to the *Crudities*.
This selection includes the lines recommending the Queen to
marry, and mention is made of a large work—no less than a
description of England, Scotland, and Ireland in Latin verse.
That this was never published is probably no disappointment to
others besides Welshmen. He also translated the complete Book
of Psalms into Latin verse, but of this only the Preface dedicated
to the Queen has survived.

For a period he obtained some acquaintance with the influential
world by his appointment as Chaplain to Henry, second Earl of
Pembroke, Lord Lieutenant of Somerset, and a nobleman of
importance at Court. However, this did not set him on the ladder
to high preferment. After twenty-five years at Odcombe he became a Prebendary of York, with a moiety of the rectory of
Axminster in Devon.[2] Neither forceful nor ambitious, he seems
to have gone on quietly leading the life of a country parson,
attending to his pastoral duties at Odcombe for thirty-seven
years until he died.

The date of Thomas's birth presents us with an enigma. The
parish records for this period no longer exist, and the earliest
evidence is contained in the records of Winchester College,
whither Thomas followed in his father's footsteps. The entry in
the original Register of Scholars shows that he was elected in
August 1590, though he did not obtain a place until eleven
months later, and implies that his birthday fell some time between

---

[1] *History of the University of Oxford*, 1773, p. 226.
[2] Joseph Foster, *Alumni Oxonienses 1500–1714*, 1891.

25 June and 29 September 1579. That he was born in 1579 is corroborated by an entry in the College's Register of Oaths, 1576–1639, f. 73ᵛ. It was the custom of the College to make pupils take the oath to the Statutes of Scholars very soon after they 'came of age' at fifteen. At the swearing in, which took place in the College Chapel on 29 September 1594, Thomas Coryate was the first of the boys sworn, and the year of birth of all the other nine, checked with the Register of Scholars, is in every case 1579.

Yet it is impossible to reconcile this apparently conclusive evidence with information available from other sources clearly indicating that Coryate was born in 1577. Wood states that he became a Commoner of Gloucester Hall, Oxford, 'in the beginning of the year 1596 aged 19', while Coryate himself says that he reaped more benefit from his European travels in 1608 than he did 'all the dayes of my life before in England which contayned two and thirty years'.[1] Finally there is his portrait, which Coryate commissioned William Hole to draw for the title page of the *Crudities*. This shows the author at the age of 35, and if we assume that he was born in 1577, this gives Coryate's age in the year his book was published. Acceptance of 1579 implies that Coryate was unaware of his true date of birth, and went through life believing that he was two years older than he was. An alternative solution would seem to be that the decision to send him to Winchester[2] was made somewhat belatedly and, in order to secure a place for him, his age was deliberately misrepresented by two years. The hitherto accepted year of birth has been 1577 with a query, and as 1577 accords with the evidence supplied by Coryate himself, it seems best to leave it at that, although the Winchester College records serve to emphasize the query.

He would therefore have been nineteen when he went up to Gloucester Hall, now Exeter College, Oxford. This was older than normal; the usual age of entry as an undergraduate in Elizabethan times was from thirteen to sixteen, and the course generally lasted some seven years. Coryate was there for only

---

[1] *Crudities*, vol. I, p. 9.

[2] T. F. Kirby, *Annals of Winchester College*, 1892, p. 294, and other writers state that he was removed from Winchester at an early age, and sent to Westminster School, but there is no evidence whatever to support this. The earliest occurrence of this error that I have found is in Croker's edition of *Boswell's Johnson*, 1831, vol. II, p. 170, n. In other respects Croker's note correctly revises Dr. Johnson's not entirely accurate knowledge of Coryate.

about three, and left without taking a degree, though in those days this meant little more than that he had decided not to take holy orders. Logic was the basic subject taught, and in this Wood says 'he attained by the help of a great memory to some competency . . . but more by far in the Greek Tongue, and in humane learning.'[1] Humane learning included Latin and of course Rhetoric. Coryate never claimed to be more than an amateur scholar, but in fact his knowledge of classical literature and history was both thorough and extensive. He was never at a loss for an apt quotation and knew long passages of many authors, particularly Virgil, by heart. Rhetoric was his speciality. His studies at Oxford were based on the works of Quintilian, Hermogenes and Cicero, and later he applied this knowledge when composing the many fancifully ornate orations which he made before kings, princes, ambassadors, and lesser beings whenever he got the chance.

For several years after leaving Oxford he seems to have lived at home in Odcombe. It is impossible to conceive that a man as active and inquisitive as Coryate should have remained idle. He may have held some teaching post locally, but this is mere speculation. He certainly became well known throughout the district, and was acquainted with the Phelipses of Montacute, the Pouletts of Hinton St. George, the Speakes of Ilminster, and the Sydenhams of Brympton, all influential families living in fine houses within walking distance of Odcombe.

He was at Odcombe in 1606, for we have his own account[2] of a novel form of church-ale, an early example of the village pageant in aid of church funds, which he devised and organized, and in which he played the leading part: 'It hapned in the yeare 1606 that the Church stocke of my natalitiall Parish of Odcombe being exhausted and spent, saving sixteene shillings, some of my frends of the Parish, amongst the rest the Churchwardens, sollicited me to set abroach my wits, and invent some conceited and plausible matter, to the end to draw some great company of good fellowes together for the benefit of our Church of Odcombe, seeing they knew that I was well acquainted in the countrye. Hereupon I resolved to muster up out of the Parish one hundred choise and able men, as were fit to beare armes in the field, and by a time limited, even the Whitson day following, about sixe

---

[1] *Op. cit.*, vol. I, p. 422.  [2] *Coryat's Crambe*, sig. D4.

of the clocke in the morning appointed them to meete me at
Odcombe Crosse. Which they did according to my appointment,
being furnished with convenient munition for a kinde of warfare.
For some of them had muskets, others Calivers, some Partizans,
some Halberts, with diversity of other weapons. Likewise we had
good Martiall Musicke and military officers. I myselfe being their
Captaine, was mounted upon a goodly milk-white steed . . .'

It will be noted that the day chosen for the entertainment was
Sunday, and that a start was made at 6 a.m. People began and
ended their day early, and it is possible that before Coryate's
troops appeared on parade, they had already attended Morning
Prayer, though this was generally held from 7 to 8 a.m. Attendance at church was of course compulsory, but otherwise Sunday
was treated as a happy holiday except in districts where the dismal
influence of Puritanism was already strong.

Having put his 'whole centurie in to a convenient order',
Coryate 'marched forward with them towards the towne of Evill
[Yeovil], three miles distant from Odcombe, being met by the
way by the Oppidanes of Evill, that consisted of two cohorts, one
Masculine, and another Foeminine, which incountred us like a
company of Amazones, & after there had bene some two or three
volleys of shot discharged on both sides with a prettie kinde of
velitation or light skirmish, we descended a hill called Henford
and entred the towne'.

The opposing armies made their way to the market place where
at least two thousand people from Yeovil and surrounding villages
had congregated to see the fun. If it should be thought surprising
that such a throng should gather, or indeed that the little village
of Odcombe could produce a hundred able-bodied men, it must
be remembered that although the total population of England and
Wales was only about five millions, Somerset was at this period
more densely populated than any of the southern counties except
Gloucestershire.[1]

Here in the market place a final skirmish took place around the
Cross; then Coryate climbed on to a platform surmounted by a
canopy, the martial musicians sounded a fanfare, and Coryate,
brandishing his sword, treated the astonished country folk to an
Oration—the first of a number which he preserved among his
writings. He made no concessions to the limited education of

[1] A. L. Rowse, *The England of Elizabeth*, 1953 edn., pp. 250-1.

most members of his audience, but gave them a history of the
evolution of church-ales, or their equivalent, from the days of
Greek orgies and Roman saturnalia, liberally seasoned with
allusions to Homer, Xenophon, and Livy. Such functions, he said,
too often bear a close resemblance to these pagan feasts, whereas
they should be modelled on the feasts of charity held by the early
Christian Church. When they are conducted soberly they are
valuable 'First for the breeding of love betwixt neighbours, and
secondly for the raising of a stocke for the supporting and maintenance of our Church, and the Church affairs: so that I do most
confidently beleeve that the good and religious use of Church-ales
may be well retained, if the abuses thereof be utterly banished,
and exterminated out of a Christian Commonwealth, as drunkennesse, gluttonie, swearing, lasciviousnesse, with many more,
which indeed I must needs confesse seeme to be the inseparable
accidents and individuale adjuncts of Church-ales.'

It seems unlikely that Coryate's hearers understood more than
a fraction of what he said and even less probable that they paid
heed to his homily on behaviour, but no doubt when the oration
was over there was much merrymaking that day to the benefit of
the Yeovil Church funds.

It will be recollected, however, that the primary object of the
expedition was the replenishment of the parish purse of Odcombe. Coryate had worked on the sage principle of using an
Odcombe sprat to catch a Yeovil mackerel, and in due course
the people of Yeovil made their return visit to Odcombe. This
gave him the opportunity of making another oration: 'Deere
Associates', he began, 'we entertaine you with a whole volley[1] of
most heartie thankes, partly for the bountifull and magnificent
entertainment yee lately affoorded us at your towne, and partly for
that yee have satisfied our expectation by revisiting us according
to your faithfull promises, for the reliefe of our Church. Truly we
ingenuously confesse that yee Evillians have justly merited our
everlasting love, in that ye being oppidanes (that is, townesmen)
borne, brought up and dwelling in a rich, populous, and fertile
towne, . . . doe vouchsafe us your poore confederates the
Odcombians of this favour, as to visite us with such a troope of
the most selected persons of your towne; us I say the Od-

---

[1] At the pronouncing of this word, a volley of shot was discharged by twenty
Musketeers [Coryate's footnote].

combians, being a rurall and mountainous people, dwelling upon
a hilly and sterill countrie, and wanting many comfortable helpes
of life, which both Nature and Art have most abundantly powred
out upon you. Neverthelesse . . . pardon me I pray you though
I speake somewhat in commendation of this little parish Odcombe, being my native soyle, the smoake whereof (according
as another Author[1] saith of a mans native countery) is more deare
unto me, then the fire of a forraine place . . .'

Odcombe, said the orator, was famous for five things: its
wholesome and pleasant air; its wool; its Church 'being erected
upon so loftie a place that it overprieth and overtoppeth the whole
countrie round about', its sweet springs of water, and finally and
most important, the love and unity of its inhabitants, 'for we all
from the verie highest to the lowest are most firmly knit together
in an indissoluble knot of friendship'.

Later, when Coryate was travelling in far-off lands, his many
friends who lived in and around Odcombe were often in his mind,
and he frequently recalled memories of his beloved Somerset
countryside. These recurring thoughts of home were not simply
the sentimental nostalgia of the traveller. Before ever he left
home he had conceived a deep affection for Odcombe, born of the
happy years he spent there in his youth.

In March the following year, 1607, the death of Coryate's
father caused an upheaval in the family. He was sixty-two, a ripe
age in those days. Nevertheless death may have taken the parson
by surprise, for he left no will. Alternatively he may have possessed so little property that a will was not worth making.[2]
Thomas was at home and took charge of the funeral arrangements,
which were so peculiar that they are more likely to be truth than
fiction. George Coryate died on 4 March, 'whereupon his son
Tom, upon some design, preserving his body from stench above
ground, till the 14th April following, was then buried in the
Chancel of the Church at Odcombe'.[3]

There is a legend that Thomas did not embalm or preserve the
body in any way, and that he laid it to await burial in one of the
caves on the road from Odcombe to Montacute, but this story is

---

[1] Lucian in his Treatise intituled 'Encomium patriae' . . . [Coryate's footnote].

[2] F. A. Crisp, *Abstracts of Somersetshire Wills, Etc.*, First Series, 1887, vol. I, p. 33,
where it is recorded that letters of administration were granted to his widow on
28 April. The year is given incorrectly as 1606.

[3] Wood, *op. cit.*

chiefly of interest because it is still current in the village of
Odcombe at this day, over three and a half centuries after the
event.

Casting about for an explanation of this extraordinary episode,
one may guess that Thomas had set his mind on certain special
arrangements in connexion with the funeral which took some
six weeks to accomplish, and with characteristic determination he
persuaded his mother to leave her husband's body unburied until
they were. The nobility and gentry spent much money on funerals,
and we read that the body of one indigent Elizabethan noble lay
unburied for many weeks since nobody could be found to support
the expense of an honourable funeral in keeping with his rank.[1]
Money was certainly short in the Coryate family, but the amount
involved in giving a country parson fitting burial cannot have
been large unless Thomas had ideas above his station.

Another possible explanation is that Thomas had set his heart
on some particular person conducting the funeral or being
present at it. We know, as it happens, that the funeral service,
when it eventually took place, was conducted by the new incumbent, the Rev. Gibbs Gollop[2] of Gloucester Hall, Thomas's
old college at Oxford, but there is no obvious reason why the
burial of his predecessor should have thus been delayed until his
arrival.

The advent of Mr. Gollop meant the Coryates' removal from the
parsonage. Gertrude Coryate continued to live in Odcombe,
but at this time, if not before, Thomas would seem to have left
home for London.

The church at Odcombe still stands on the summit of the high
ground where it 'overprieth and overtoppeth the whole countrie
round about', as Coryate described it. There is no trace now of the
tombs in the chancel in which the remains of George Coryate
and, many years later, those of his wife were laid. Very little of the
fabric of the church has escaped the renovators, but the font with
its Norman bowl and fifteenth-century cover is the one in which
Coryate was baptized.

He was christened Thomas after his godfather, Thomas Phelips,
squire of Montacute, who died when his godson was about nine.

---

[1] The Marquis of Northampton; eventually the Queen herself paid up, and he was
fitly buried, see *The Black Book of Warwick*, ed. T. Kemp, pp. 51–55.
[2] Wood, *op. cit.* Wood calls him Gallop.

Thomas Phelips left Montacute to his youngest and favourite son, Edward, who immediately began to build the splendid mansion which is one of the finest surviving examples of Elizabethan domestic architecture. The golden stone for the new house came from the quarries only two miles from Odcombe, on Hamdon Hill. This famous hill forms the western buttress of the same high ridge on the eastern extremity of which stands Odcombe Church. As a boy Coryate must have seen the great blocks of stone being dragged by horses down the hill to Montacute. After the house was finished in 1601 he was a frequent visitor; he thought it one of the finest buildings in the world, and on several occasions used it as a basis for favourable comparison with the architectural splendours which he saw on his travels. When he visited Venice he thought that the Piazza San Marco, paved with brick, 'made a shew fair enough'; but had it been paved with diamond pavier of freestone like that to be seen at Montacute House 'it would have made the whole Piazza much more glorious and resplendent then it is'. The Archbishop of Cologne's palace at Bonn was, he conceded, 'a most magnificent and princely building. But . . . there is one in mine own county of Somersetshire, even the magnificent house of my most worthy and right Worshipful neighbour . . . Sir Edward Philippes . . . in the towne of Montacute, so stately adorned with the statues of the nine Worthies,[1] that may bee at the least equally ranked with this of Bonna, if not something preferred before it'.

The owner, Edward Phelips, spent much of his time in London. He was an able and ambitious man who, having achieved success as a lawyer, went into politics. His son, Robert, several years younger than Coryate, followed in his father's footsteps, and was also elected to Parliament. It cannot often have happened that a father and son should both have been created knights in the same year, but both Edward and Robert Phelips received their title in 1603. This was after the accession of James I, who in a very short time made himself ridiculous and brought knighthood into dis-

---

[1] Eight Worthies occupy the niches between the top floor windows while the ninth accentuates the central gable-like circle which tops the porch parapet. All nine, from Hector to Charlemagne, irrespective of race, creed, or period, are clothed in renaissance classical garb. To generations of local people they have been known as the Master Mason and his Eight Sons. See H. Avray Tipping, *The Story of Montacute and its House*, London, 1956, p. 11, and J. J. Hooper, *Proceedings of the Somerset Archaeological & Natural History Society*, 1871, vol. XVII, p. 83.

2. Odcombe Church.

3. Montacute House. The east façade, showing the statues of the
Nine Worthies in their niches.

4. Henry, Prince of Wales, and Robert Devereux, 3rd Earl of Essex, hunting. From a painting by an unknown artist at Hampton Court. *Reproduced by gracious permission of Her Majesty The Queen.*

repute by the number of new knights whom he created, and the fees he took for the bestowal of the honour. While neither Edward nor young Robert can escape the suspicion of being 'thirty-pound knights', they were both far superior in birth, merit, and ability to those at whom the authors of *Eastward Hoe* were tilting.[1] Edward Phelips was elected Speaker of the House of Commons the following year; Robert, who had been one of Queen Elizabeth's pages, continued at Court after her death and became one of the Gentlemen of the Privy Chamber Extraordinary in the household of Prince Henry, James I's elder son.[2]

When we hear that Coryate on leaving home was himself received into Prince Henry's family, it is not therefore difficult to surmise whence the influence came to secure him this favour. The surmise is virtually a certainty since Coryate refers both to Sir Edward and to Sir Robert on separate occasions as his Maecenas,[3] a description which does not apply to anyone else.

King James had set up a separate household for his nine-year-old son and six-year-old daughter, Princess Elizabeth, in the summer of 1603. Initially it was a modest establishment at Oatlands Palace near Weybridge, with seventy servants. But the King augmented it twice before the year was out, and soon three standing houses were being maintained for the royal children at Richmond, St. James's, and Queen Elizabeth's favourite palace of Nonesuch at Cheam in Surrey. In addition to spending some time at each palace they paid occasional visits to their parents wherever they might be at the time. The household continued to increase until the official and unofficial attendants numbered slightly under five hundred, 'many of them young gentlemen born to great fortunes, in the prime of their years when their appetites were strong, their reason weak and their experience little. But his [Prince Henry's] judgement, and the gravity of his princely aspect and his own example were sufficient restraints upon them'.[4]

In view of the Prince's extreme youth one might discount the last sentence, were it not for impartial contemporary evidence of

---

[1] Chapman, Marston, and Jonson, the co-authors, raised a double laugh against the new knights and against the influx of Scotsmen with the line, 'I ken the man weel, he's one of my thirty-pound knights'.

[2] Thomas Birch, *Life of Prince Henry*, London, 1760, p. 450.

[3] *Crudities*, vol. I, p. 5, vol. II, p. 310, and Letter No. 2.

[4] Birch, *op. cit.*, p. 394.

his precocious wisdom and strength of character. Writing in 1606 the French Ambassador reported as follows: 'None of his pleasures savour the least of a child. He is a particular lover of horses & what belongs to them; he is not fond of hunting; when he goes to it, it is rather for the pleasure of galloping, than that which the dogs give him. He plays willingly enough at Tennis, & at another Scots diversion very like mall [i.e. golf]; but this always with persons older than himself, as if he despised those of his own age. He studies two hours a day, and employs the rest of his time in tossing the pike, or leaping, or shooting with the bow, or throwing the bar, or vaulting, or some other exercise of that kind, and he is never idle . . . besides his exerting his whole strength to compass what he desires, he is already feared by those, who have the management of affairs, and especially the Earl of Salisbury, who appears to be greatly apprehensive of the Prince's ascendant; as the Prince on the other hand, shews little esteem for his Lordship'.[1]

Later in the same letter the Ambassador remarked that his mother had not so much affection for him as for his younger brother, the Duke of York, which the Prince seemed to have discovered, and that the King often showed that he was not pleased to see him advance so fast.

Despite the French Ambassador's assertion that Prince Henry kept his tutor busy for only two hours a day, he could write French, had a growing knowledge of Latin and Greek, and was an amateur as well as being a patron of the arts, particularly literature. He took his religious instruction and his devotions extremely seriously. Swearing he regarded with abhorrence, and he had boxes installed at his various establishments to receive the fines exacted from anyone caught in an oath. In organizing his household he not only gave the orders but himself saw that they were carried out. He was rarely at a loss for the name of any of his numerous domestic staff. It is a relief to hear that such a paragon had at least two minor childish weaknesses: the Treasurer of his Household reports that he had an excessive fondness for fruit and that he occasionally teased Princess Elizabeth and the Duke of York.[2]

[1] Birch, *op. cit.*, pp. 75–76.
[2] Sir Charles Cornwallis, *A Discourse of the . . . late Prince of Wales*, Harleian Miscellany, vol. IV, pp. 323–4. Princess Elizabeth married Frederick V, Elector Palatine in 1613, and became Queen of Bohemia. She was the mother of Prince Rupert and grandmother of George I. The Duke of York became Charles I.

Coryate's position in the household is uncertain. Thomas Fuller, who belonged to a generation younger than Coryate and was probably not writing from first-hand knowledge, says that 'Prince Henry allowed him a pension and kept him for his servant'.[1] There is no evidence to support the first part of this statement; as for the second, Coryate does not appear in either of the lists of the Prince's Household drawn up in 1603 or 1610.[2] His position seems to have been that of an unofficial court jester. According to Fuller 'sweetmeats and Coryate made up the last course at all court entertainments. Indeed he was the courtiers' anvil to try their wits upon; and sometimes this anvil returned the hammers as hard knocks as it received, his bluntness repaying their abusiveness'. It seems that he was driven to adopt the role of a court fool by his overweaning desire to attract attention. He had neither wealth nor social eminence to help him make his way; his chief endowments were courage, a ready tongue, a retentive memory well stored with the fruits of much reading, and, above all, a very strong urge to make a name for himself. As Fuller admits, 'few would be found to call him fool might none do it save such who had as much learning as himself'. He loved people to take notice of him, and to laugh at the jokes he made, but he could not bear being mocked, and quickly became incensed at those who found humour where none was intended. A jester who wishes to entertain at one moment and to be taken seriously the next is doomed to hurt feelings.

While at Court Coryate did not come into contact solely with well-born, wealthy, young courtiers. The Prince took an eager interest in land and sea warfare and in voyages overseas. He liked listening to soldiers, sailors, and gentlemen adventurers. The English Ambassadors at Paris, Madrid, Venice, and Brussels, all corresponded with him and came to see him when they arrived home. There were, naturally, frequent visits from foreign diplomats who came to observe and report on the heir apparent to the British throne.

It is easy to understand how Coryate's horizon was suddenly lifted by seeing, hearing, and sometimes talking to the many strange and colourful characters who thronged round the Prince, and how his imagination was fired with the idea of himself

[1] *The Worthies of England—Somersetshire*, ed. John Freeman, 1952, p. 502.
[2] Birch, *op. cit.*, pp. 35 and 449.

embarking on an adventure. He could have elected to see something of the world as a soldier or seaman, but neither of these alternatives in the least appealed to him. Not that he feared danger or hardship, but his interests were civilized, historical, and scholarly, far removed from the boredom, interspersed with occasional hectic excitements, of campaigning, or the enforced constriction and monotony of life at sea. Above all, he wished to be his own master. Maybe for that reason he shunned the idea of travelling in the suite of some rich man, and resolved to be a solitary wanderer. If he was no man's servant his freedom was assured, within the limits imposed by a light purse. Even that important handicap could be mitigated by simple tastes, reliance on two strong legs, and abundant courage. Using one's eyes and ears cost little or nothing in any country.

The goal which he set himself to reach was one of the most celebrated cities in the civilized world. Coryate's thoughts may have been first directed towards Venice by reading, or by conversations with those who had seen its glories. Perhaps he attended a performance of *Volpone* or one of several other plays set in this fabulous city, still immensely powerful and now at the zenith of its decorative beauty. He would travel to Venice overland through France and Italy, and return by way of Switzerland, Germany, and the Netherlands, observing for himself some of the wonders he had heard and read about, taking notes of all he saw, so that on his return he could write a book the like of which had never been seen in the world before.

# CHAPTER II

## France and Savoy

I T had for some time been usual for travellers to stake money
prior to their departure abroad on condition that, should they
return safely, they were to receive from two to ten times the
amount deposited. Before leaving for Jerusalem in 1595 Henry
Moryson, brother of the famous Fynes, laid out no less than
four hundred pounds, and would have received twelve hundred
if he had reached home again. Fynes Moryson staked one hundred
for three hundred on the same journey, though he admitted that
the practice was no longer genteel, being resorted to by bank-
rupts, stage players, and men of base condition, while courtiers
and gentlemen considered such transactions beneath them.

Coryate aspired to gentility, but was too poor to let slip this
opportunity of improving his financial position, and entered
into at least one such bargain which later, as we shall see, involved
him in a troublesome lawsuit. He deposited £40 with Joseph
Starre, a Yeovil linen-draper, and received in exchange Starre's
bond—the equivalent of a post-dated cheque—for 200 marks
(£133. 6s. 8d.).[1] The exact terms of the contract are unknown, but
they were embodied in a bill of adventure, which suggests that
conditions of a commercial nature may have been included.
Perhaps Coryate was to execute some commissions or deliver
some goods. Part of a letter which his friend Richard Martin wrote
to introduce Coryate to the English Ambassador in Venice gives
a hint that there may have been a business aspect to the journey:
'if any of your Intelligencers should give advisement of any
traffiquing or merchandising used by this Gentleman at Naples

---

[1] The mark was primarily a denomination of weight, usually 8 oz., employed
chiefly for gold and silver throughout western Europe. Hence it became a money
of account, originally representing the value of a mark weight of pure silver. In
England, after the Conquest, the ratio of twenty sterling pennies to an ounce was
the basis of computation, and thus the value of the mark became fixed at 160 pence
—13s. 4d.

[which Coryate never visited], your Lordship would rather interpret it as done collaterally by way of entertainement, then finally for any gaine'.[1]

Before Coryate could leave the country a travelling licence had to be obtained either from the King or from the Privy Council. This document was a requisite for anyone leaving the country, though not a passport abroad, since it was surrendered at the port of embarkation. It usually specified the period of validity, the amount of money which the traveller might take with him, and the number of his servants and horses, if any. Thus a young nobleman was granted a licence to 'travel for three years with his tutor, two servants, two horses and sixty pounds in money',[2] that is, cash. Besides cash a traveller might take with him drafts or letters of credit. Dallington in his *Method for Travel* (1605) estimated that an English gentleman travelling on the Continent without a servant required eighty pounds a year to cover his living and travelling expenses. Coryate's intended rate of expenditure was probably considerably lower. He had neither servants nor horses, and was resolved to travel extremely frugally. Apart from letters of introduction and writing materials, his personal luggage amounted to little more than the clothes he stood up in.

By early May 1608 his preparations were complete, and on Saturday 14 May (24 May according to the modern calendar) he sailed from Dover to Calais. The fare between these two ports seems to have remained invariably five shillings for many years before and after 1600, though this did not include the cost of small boats, or of porters wading out, to assist passengers to embark and land.[3] It did include the second and subsequent attempts to reach the other side if the first was frustrated by a change of wind or weather. On this occasion there seems to have been no delay, and the crossing was made at the first attempt in seven hours. He gives no details of the ship in which he sailed, apart from the illustration on the title page of the *Crudities* which makes it look absurdly small. The usual passage boats were about sixty feet long with a single deck, beneath which the passengers might find shelter if the cargo left them room.[4] Coryate, as the

---

[1] *Crudities*, vol. I, p. 378.

[2] The wording of the licence issued in 1599 to Peregrine Bertie, younger son of Lord Willoughby of Eresby: *Land Travel*, by Charles Hughes in *Shakespeare's England*, vol. I, p. 212.

[3] E. S. Bates, *Touring in 1600*, London, 1911, p. 328.     [4] *Ibid*, p. 64.

illustration shows, spent most of his time on deck and 'varnished the exterior parts of the ship with the excrementall ebullitions of my tumultuous stomach, as desiring to satiate the gormandizing paunches of the hungry Haddocks'.

It was fifty years since France had recaptured Calais after two centuries of English rule, but no chances were taken with potential foreign spies or mischief-makers, nor was any opportunity lost of gaining intelligence from overseas visitors. All strangers arriving in Calais had to wait upon the Deputy Governor in order to register their names and tell him the reason for their journey. In dealing with Coryate and his fellow travellers the Deputy Governor treated them very affably, and asked many questions concerning King James I and the news from Ireland.[1]

Strangers were not allowed in certain parts of the town, notably in the vicinity of the Citadel and the Fortress. This Fortress stood outside the town in the midst of quicksands on the sea shore and was known as the Rice Bank. Coryate recounts how it earned this name when Calais was in English hands. About 1540 an English sea captain captured and brought into Calais a barque from Dunkirk laden with rice. The Governor of Calais took half the cargo for himself and gave the other half to the sea captain as a reward for his prize. The Governor then graciously enabled the captain to translate his share into cash by arranging for him to receive the victualling money normally paid to the ordinary soldiers in the Fortress in return for issuing them day after day with rice until the barque's cargo was exhausted. 'Whereupon the said little Fort hath ever since been called the Rice-banke, of the abundance of Rice, buttered and boiled in Pottage, which at that time was eaten in it.'

It is not surprising that Coryate should from the outset have been particularly struck by the difference in religious observance. Henri IV having forsaken the religion of his party to secure the crown and restore the unity of his kingdom, Catholicism was now in the ascendant in France. Catholic observances were bound to be looked upon with dislike and suspicion by the devout and staunchly Protestant son of a Church of England parson. Never-

---

[1] Perhaps news had already reached France of the rebellion of Sir Cahir O'Dogherty who on 19 April 1608 surprised Culmore Castle, and early the next morning captured, sacked, and burnt the town of Derry. The rebellion was not put down until O'Dogherty was brought to battle and slain on 5 July.

theless his strict Protestant views did not blunt his inquisitiveness nor did they hinder him from reporting faithfully all he saw. His prejudices are apparent in his comments, but they seldom distort his vision.

The day following his arrival being Whit Sunday, he went to church and 'saw their mutilated Sacrament, whereof I much heard before. For I saw the Priest minister the Sacrament to the lay people under one kind only, namely that of bread, defrauding them of the Wine, contrary to the holy institution of Christ and his Apostles, and the auncient practise of the Primitive Church . . . about the middle of their Masse there was an extreme crackling noise from a certain hollow place in the vault of the middle of the Church . . . After the noyse there was powred downe a great deale of water, immediately after the water ensued a great multitude of Wafer-cakes, both white, redde and yellow: which ceremony was done to put them in minde of the cloven tongues, that appeared that day of Pentecost to the Apostles in Hierusalem'.

Leaving Calais on foot on Whit Monday he reached Boulogne the same evening and here saw the first monks that he had ever set eyes on. Three days later in Amiens he first saw nuns when, with characteristic thrustfulness, he walked up to the Carmelite Nunnery and tried to gain admittance. He was told by the two nuns who kept the door that no man was ever admitted, but this only made him more curious to observe some of these strange beings more closely. That afternoon, therefore, he went into the church of the Franciscan Nunnery, 'the Nunnes being then at their Vespers, in a higher loft or chappell, into the which I could not have accesse. But I saw them at service sitting in two rowes opposite to each other. They wore white vailes about their heades, and black over the same which covered their whole body to their feete: one of these was a very beautifull woman.'

Thirteen years of peace and reconstruction under Henri IV had still not repaired the appalling ravages of the religious Civil Wars with which France had been torn for over three decades. Scenes of devastation caused by war were totally new to Coryate, and he was shocked to see ruined churches and monasteries and a whole village which had been ransacked and deserted. At Mont Faucon he inspected with interest 'the fayrest Gallowes that ever I saw, built upon a little hillocke called Mount Falcon, which consisteth of fourteene fair pillars of free-stone: this gallowes was made in the time of the Guisian massacre, to hang the Admiral of France, Chatillion, who was a Protestant, Anno Dom. 1572.' In fact, Châtillon was never executed. Wounded some days previously, he was murdered in the Louvre where the King had given him sanctuary. His head was sent to the Pope, and it was only what was left of his body, after it had been dragged through the streets of Paris for three days, that was hung by the feet at Mont Faucon.[1]

Places of execution and the methods by which punishment was carried out held a fascination for Coryate. There were plenty of gloomy sights to attract his attention on the way through France. Between Boulogne and Montreuil he noticed a gallows consisting of 'two goodly faire pillers of free-stone where there is no cross beame as upon our English gallowes, but that cross beame is erected when they are hanged, and taken down againe immediately after the execution'. At Clermont a gibbet was erected in the middle of the street from which was suspended a picture of an unapprehended criminal together with a description of his offence. A few days later he passed a 'very ruefull and tragicall object: ten men hanging in their clothes upon a goodly gallows made from freestone . . . whose bodies were consumed to nothing, onely their bones and the ragged fitters of their clothes remained.'

Near Montreuil he saw 'a place of execution made of timber, at the toppe whereof there is a wheele whereon the bodies of murderers only are tormented and broken in pieces with certaine yron instruments'. This horrible practice was unknown in England, though there is a record of a murderer being so executed in Edinburgh in 1604. It persisted in France until the Revolution, and in Germany until the nineteenth century. 'They breake their armes first, then their legs and thighes and after their breast: If they are favoured their breast is first broken. That blow on their

---

[1] There had been a gallows on this site since the thirteenth or fourteenth century. R. de Lasteyrie in *Voyage à Paris de Th. Coryate* (*Mémoires de la Société de l'Histoire de Paris et de l'Ile de France*), Paris 1880, vol. VI, p. 28, cites various authorities to prove that there were sixteen pillars, not fourteen. M. de Lasteyrie's work is a carefully annotated translation of pp. 167 to 195 (1905 edn.) of the *Crudities* which cover the journey from Amiens to Paris, and Coryate's description of Paris, Saint Denis, and Fontainebleau. In his prefatory remarks M. de Lasteyrie writes: 'la relation de Coryate contient sur le Louvre, sur les Tuileries, sur l'abbaye de Saint-Denis, sur le palais de Fontainebleau, plusieurs menus détails que jen 'ai pas trouvés dans d'autres auteurs. Ces détails paraissent exacts pour la plupart. Ça et là cependant on voit que l'auteur a écrit de souvenir, où qu'il a mal compris les renseignements qu'il avait recueillis.'

breast is called the blow of mercy, because it doth quickly bereave them of their life. This torment of the wheele I find in Aristotle to have been used amongst the ancient Grecians also'.

In England walking was still the usual means of travel for poor men, including students and scholars, and Coryate excelled at walking. Perhaps for novelty's sake he did, however, have himself conveyed for two stretches of his journey to Paris. From Montreuil to Abbeville he was carried in a two-wheeled country cart, a form of passenger transport sufficiently unusual in England to warrant the inclusion of a picture of the author seated therein on the title page of the *Crudities*. From Amiens he rode towards Paris in a coach, still quite a rarity in England. The new vehicle appears to have originated in Hungary at the end of the fifteenth century, whence it spread gradually across Europe. It reached England in Elizabeth's reign, and was becoming increasingly popular as a private conveyance for the rich. Hired coaches, known by detractors, such as the Thames watermen who saw their livelihood threatened, as 'Hackney Hell Carts', appeared early in the seventeenth century, but were not allowed to ply for hire in the streets until 1634. Stage coaches were unknown in England until some years after Coryate's death. The type of public conveyance with which he was familiar at home was the great lumbering stage-waggon, or long-waggon. This clumsy vehicle drawn by horses or oxen in file, carried goods and passengers ten to fifteen miles a day along the main highways. In France, however, regular coach services had been running for nearly forty years, and it seems to have been in such a coach that Coryate rode from Amiens.[1] Progress was neither rapid nor comfortable. Having lurched and jolted some fourteen miles in five hours, without being able to see much of the countryside, he resumed his journey on foot.

On the seventh day after leaving Calais he crossed the Oise by ferry at St. Leu and walked thence the last few miles into Paris. Here the country was rich and thriving, with sumptuous houses on either side of the road, many of which, as he was told, belonged to the lawyers of the city.

[1] For information about the Hungarian origin of coaches I am indebted to Dr. E. S. de Beer. For the subject of road transport in England, see Joan Parkes, *Travel in England in the seventeenth century*, Oxford, 1925. The introduction of regular coach services in France in 1571 is recorded by Gilles Corrozet, *Les antiquitez . . . de Paris*, Paris, 1586, f. 190.

His first impression of Paris, shared by several contemporaries, was that it was even filthier and more smelly than London: 'Many of the streetes are the durtiest, and so consequently the most stinking of all that ever I saw in any citie in my life.' He lodged, for the week he was there, not in the centre of the city but in the more open and salubrious suburb of St. Germain, at the house of a certain Monsieur de la Roy, a Protestant who had fought against the Papists in the Civil Wars, and was proud to show Coryate the grievous wounds he had received in battle.

Nearby lived another Protestant, whom it had long been Coryate's ambition to meet, Isaac Casaubon, the most renowned classical scholar of his day. At this time he was in his fiftieth year, with most of his work behind him, broken in health but indomitable in spirit and still writing. 'I enjoyed one thing in Paris,' says Coryate, 'which I most desired above all other things, and often times wished for before I saw the citie, even the sight and company of that rare ornament of learning Isaac Casaubonus,[1] with whom I had much familiar conversation at his house, near unto St. Germans gate within the citie.' It seems that Coryate did most of the talking. He knew how to pay compliments, and Casaubon had an appetite for flattery. 'I found him very affable and courteous, and learned in his discourses, and by so much the more willing to give me entertainment, by how much the more I made relation to him of his learned workes, whereof some I have read.' Casaubon made two observations: that it was a great pity that no learned Englishman had yet written a biography of Queen Elizabeth, and that Coryate ought the next morning to see the profane and superstitious ceremony with which the Papists celebrated Corpus Christi Day.

Accordingly the next day at nine o'clock in the morning he went to Notre Dame and watched the grand procession set out on its way through the principal streets. The procession lasted two hours and was followed by a service in Notre Dame, a 'very long and tedious devotion, for the space of two houres, with much excellent singing, and two or three solemne Masses, acted by the Bishops owne person . . . a proper and comly man as any I saw in all the city, of some five and thirty yeares old'.[2] Catholic

---

[1] Two years later, after the death of Henri IV, whose librarian he had been, Casaubon fled to England, and Coryate saw him there once more before he died in 1614.  [2] Henri de Gondi, Bishop of Paris from 1589 to 1622.

worship could not be other than 'tedious' to him, yet his honesty as an observer compelled him to admit that he was charmed by the singing, and to pay the youthful Bishop a compliment on his appearance and bearing.

His remarks on Paris, and indeed on all he saw in France, are less full than those which he amassed about other European cities and territories. This, as he infers in the Epistle Dedicatorie of the *Crudities*, was partly because he had not yet learnt to pursue his enquiries regardless of all dissuasions and distractions, and partly because he was only gradually, with time and practice, acquiring the habit of regularly and meticulously writing up his notes.

He was disappointed with Notre Dame and compared it unfavourably with Amiens cathedral which he had much admired a few days previously. He was, however, much impressed by the exterior grandeur and interior sumptuousness of the Louvre and the Tuileries. Two hundred masons were labouring to complete the gallery connecting the Tuileries to the Louvre. The fish pond in the Tuileries Gardens attracted his attention 'wherein there is not yet either fish or water . . . there I saw great preparations of conduits of lead, wherein the water shall be conveighed to that pond'.[1] Building operations were not confined to the royal palaces; work was nearing completion on the approaches to the Pont Neuf (the bridge itself had been finished in 1603), and he much admired the white free-stone construction of this fine new bridge over the Seine. In contrast to the brick and timber, or wattle and daub houses of London, he noticed that the majority of buildings in Paris were built of 'faire white free-stone . . . for the whole citie . . . is situate upon a quarre of free stone which doth extend it selfe to a great part of the territorie round about the citie, and ministreth that inexhausted plenty of stone for their houses'.

One day was devoted to an excursion to St. Denis to see the regalia, the tombs of the Kings, and the skull of the Saint himself 'inclosed in a wonderful rich helmet, beset with exceeding abundance of pretious stones: but the skull itselfe I saw not plainly only the forepart of it I beheld through a pretty crystall glasse by the light of a waxen candle'.

[1] R. de Lasteyrie, *op. cit.*, p. 36, n, points out that Coryate's account is the only existing record which gives an exact date to the pond's construction.

On Saturday, 27 May, he left Paris on a post horse about one o'clock in the afternoon for Fontainebleau, where Henri IV then held his court. 'A little after I was past the last stage saving one . . . there happened this chance. My horse began to be so tiry, that he would not stirre one foot out of the way, though I did even excarnificate his sides with my often spurring of him . . . whereupon a Gentleman of my company, one Master I.H. tooke great paines with him to lash him: at last when he saw he was so dul that he could hardly make him go with whipping, he drew out his Rapier and ranne him into his buttocke near to his funda- ment, about a foote deep very neare. The Guide perceived not this before he came to the next stage, neither there before we were going away. My friend lingred with me somewhat behinde our company, and in a certain poole very diligently washed the horses wound with his bare handes; thinking thereby to have stopped his bleeding; but he lost his labour, as much as he did that washed the Aethiopian: for the bloud ranne out a fresh notwithstanding all his laborious washing. Now when the guide perceived it, he grew so extreame cholericke, that . . . in the end Mr. I.H. being much perplexed, and finding that there was no remedy but that he must needes grow to some composition with him, unless he would sustaine some great disgrace, gave him sixe French crownes [about thirty-six shillings] to stop his mouth.' In the absence of any remark to the contrary, we must assume that Coryate did not feel himself bound to make any contribution, over and above the normal hire, towards this expensive settlement.

On arrival at Fontainebleau he had no difficulty in gaining admittance to the palace grounds, where he wandered around taking notes of everything he saw. The royal hunters in their stables: 'were fine and faire geldings and nagges, but neither for finesse of shape comparable to our Kings hunting horses, nor as I take it for swiftnesse'. He was allowed to pass through into the aviary which contained, besides storks and many varieties of pheasants, three specimens of a species which he had never seen before. 'Their neckes are much longer than Cranes . . . having none or little feathers about them. They advance themselves much higher then the tallest man that ever I saw. Also their feete and legs, which are wonderfull long, are pilled and bare: and their thighes together with their hinder parts are not only bare, but also seem very raw and redde, as if they had taken some hurt, but indeed they are naturally so. Their heads are covered all with small stubbed feathers: their eies great and black: their beakes short and sharp: their feete cloven, not unlike to a hoofe ... The feathers of their wings and tailes, but especially of their tailes, are very soft and fine. In respect whereof they are much used in the fannes of Gentlewomen.' Scattered among his writings are many descriptions of birds, beasts, and insects, but none is more shrewdly drawn than this little sketch of the king's ostriches.

At length he neared the Palace itself and saw a group of guards wearing long-skirted, half-sleeved, white surcoats covered with silver spangles. He got into conversation with them and discovered that they were members of the Scots Guard, the corps d'élite of the Royal Lifeguard. This Guard, founded by Charles VII about 1428, had by its loyalty and prowess in battle acquired many extraordinary privileges. The Guard numbered one hundred men, of whom twenty-five were always on duty. Their Captain bore the title of First Captain, stood nearest to the King during his coronation, and acquired by right the King's coronation robe after the ceremony. At night, wherever the King lay, the Scots Guard took charge of the keys to the gate, and themselves had preference in the choice of billets before the three other companies of Lifeguards. While the three other companies bore on their weapons whatever colours might be chosen by the King, the weapons of the Scots Guard were traditionally fringed with silver and white silk lace, and bore the royal coat of arms. At a river crossing the Scots Guard went in advance to guard the ship appointed to receive the King, and when he was on board two of them were always posted beside him. When the King was in church they guarded the entrances as well as his person. Finally, on the death of their royal master, they alone had the honour of carrying the coffin from Paris to St. Denis, even into the vault, and no one else was permitted to touch it. All these privileges had been confirmed by an edict of Henri IV, and were described by one of the members of the Guard in a book[1] dedicated to Henry, Prince of Wales, which was published in the year of Coryate's visit.

In those days all the Guards were Scotsmen, or at any rate bore Scots names. As the years went by, Scots and French became

[1] A. Houston, *L'Escosse Françoise*, Paris, 1608.

5. Henri IV touching for the King's Evil. A Scots guard stands next to the King, two others can be seen in the right middle distance. From an engraving by H. de Grandmaison after P. Firens.

A questo modo se
Caualchano L'
instate in Italia.

6. Italian Horseman with umbrella. From *Costumes of the Times of Queen Elizabeth 1595,* an autograph album owned by Mr. Boies Penrose. *Reproduced by courtesy of the owner.*

increasingly intermingled, but the formalities were little altered. Even in the nineteenth century, on being challenged they replied in Gaelic, 'I am here.'[1] When at last the Guard disappeared with the revolution of 1830, there were still a few who could trace their descent from the members of the old Scottish families who had served their adopted king with such distinction three and four centuries earlier.

Coryate never hid his light under a bushel, and he may well have impressed the Scots Guards on duty that morning with some stories about his own position in the Stewart royal household. At all events he successfully enlisted their help and was thus able to see more at Fontainebleau than would have normally been permitted to a chance foreign visitor when the court was in residence.[2]

With the Guards he went to the Presence Chamber and watched many of the great noblemen and gentlemen of the Court assembling there to hear Mass. 'The Dolphin was expected at the Masse but I went downe before he came up, and met him accompanied with divers Noblemen of the Court, comming forth by one of the gardens . . . He was about seven yeares old . . . His face full and fat-cheeked, his haire black, his looke vigorous and couragious, which argues a bold and lively spirit. His speech quick, so that his wordes seeme to flow from him with a voluble grace. His doublet and hose were red Sattin, laced with gold lace.' Two years later this engaging boy succeeded his murdered father as Louis XIII, and the 'bold and lively spirit' became a mere marionette in the deft hands of Richelieu.

Coryate also saw the Dauphin's infant brother, the Duke of Orléans, being carried into the gardens in the arms of a gentlewoman, while another held a red taffeta fan fringed with silver lace to keep the May sun off the royal baby's face.

Towards midday his Scottish friends informed him that they regretted not being able to show him any more that day since they had to attend the marriage of a Scotswoman in the town, but if he cared to return on the morrow they could arrange for him to see

[1] William Forbes-Leith, S.J., *The Scots Men-at-Arms and Life-Guards in France*, Edinburgh, 1882, vol. I, p. 121.

[2] Cf. Paul Hentzner, *Itinerarium Germaniae, Galliae* . . ., 7 October 1598 (pp. 250–1 of the 1629 edn.); Jodocus Sincerus, *Itinerarium Galliae*, 1616, pp. 316–21; Abraham Gölnitz, *Ulysses*, 1631, pp. 165–75. Coryate's description of Fontainebleau is more detailed and vivid than any of these.

most of the principal rooms in the palace. He was tempted to stay, but eventually decided to push on as quickly as possible towards Lyons.

Starting that very evening by post horse, he rode in a westerly direction to join the main highway at La Chapelle la Reine, where he spent the night. The following day he marched southwards on foot to such good purpose that between five in the morning and six at night he covered thirty-six miles. From Briare he rode down the Loire valley to Nevers, where he stopped long enough to visit the cathedral, remark on the abundance of wooden clogs for sale at 2¼d. a pair, and be scandalized by a concourse of gypsies more numerous than he had ever seen before. 'Their men are very Ruffians & Swashbucklers, having exceeding long black haire curled, and swords or other weapons by their sides. Their women also suffer their haire to hang loosely about their shoulders, whereof some I saw dancing in the streets, and singing lascivious vaine songs; whereby they draw many flocks of the foolish citizens about them.'

He spent the night of 1 June at St. Gérand, and the following night at Tarare. Rising very early in the morning with the intention of posting the last few miles into Lyons, he discovered that owing to some mischance no post horse was available, and he had to walk six miles to get one. Then the rain came down so heavily that by the time he reached Lyons he was soaked to the skin.

There was, however, no question of riding straight to his inn and ordering his dinner. He had to pass three gates before entering the city. At the third he was asked whence he came and what was his business by the gate-keeper, who required satisfactory answers to his questions before issuing a warrant authorizing him to lodge within the city.

Coryate stayed at the 'Three Kings', a curious choice, since it was the best and most fashionable inn of the city. Perhaps, wet through and tired by long hours on the road since leaving Fontainebleau, he decided to allow himself a treat. But he was not given to self-indulgence in creature comforts, and a more likely explanation is that he knew he might meet and introduce himself to the seventeen-year-old Earl of Essex, whom he claimed as a fourth cousin. Unfortunately for Coryate the young Earl and his whole train, having spent five days at the 'Three Kings', had left the day before.

The historical and cultural eminence of Lyons was already sufficient to make a visit to it as necessary as visits to Paris, Bordeaux, and Orleans for the young English noblemen who at this time were just beginning to make the tour of France as part of their education.[1] As the best inn in what was, after Paris, the most important commercial centre in the whole of France, the 'Three Kings' had many distinguished guests. Despite, or perhaps because of, its high-born, high-living customers the innkeeper displayed a notice, which Coryate copied down: *On ne loge céans à crédit: car il est mort, les mauvais paieurs l'ont tué.* If he was disappointed at not being able to bring himself to the notice of his eminent though distant kinsman, he was able to solace himself with the sound of 'passing fine music' played during supper for the young brother of the Duke of Guise and his companions, and the view of these 'gallant lustie Gentlemen' dancing *Corantos* and *Lavoltas*[2] in the courtyard thereafter.

Another notable guest was the French Ambassador[3] to Rome on his way thither to take up his appointment. Among his followers were two Turks whom he had brought from Constantinople. 'One was a blacke Moore, who was his jester; a mad conceited fellow, and very merry. He wore no hat at all eyther in his journey (for he overtooke us upon the way riding without a hat) or when he rested in any towne, because the naturall haire which was exceeding thicke and curled, was so prettily elevated in heigth that it served him alwaies instead of a hat: the other Turk was a notable companion and a great scholler in his kinde; for he spake sixe or seven languages besides the Latin, which he spake very well.' Coryate conversed with him for some time, in Latin. This was the first of many meetings which he was to have with men of non-Christian faith, and like several of the subsequent encounters, it ended acrimoniously: 'Amongst other questions I asked him whether he were ever baptized, he tolde me, no, and said he never would be. After that wee fell into speeches of Christ, Whom he acknowledged for a great Prophet,

[1] J. W. Stoye, *English Travellers Abroad 1604–1663*, London, 1952, p. 55.

[2] The *Courante* or *Coranto* was performed in 2/4 time, while the *Volte* or *Lavolta* was a form of the *Galliard* in 3/4 time. Both were well known in England. 'They bid us to the English dancing schools, And teach lavoltas high and swift corantos.' (*Henry V*, Act III, Sc. 5, lines 32–33.)

[3] François Savary, Comte de Brèves (1560–1628), Ambassador at Constantinople, 1591–1604, and at Rome, 1608–1614.

but not for the Sonne of God, affirming that neither he nor any of his countrey men would worship Him, but the onely true God, creator of heaven and earth: and called us Christians Idolaters, because we worshipped images; a most memorable speech if it be properly applied to those kind of Christians, which deserve that imputation of Idolatry. At last I fell into some vehement argumentations with him in defence of Christ, whereupon being unwilling to answer me, he suddenly flung out of my company.'

Part of the two days spent in Lyons was taken up with arrangements for the next stage of the journey over the Mont Cenis pass into Italy. At Lyons bills of health began, 'without the which we could not be received into any of those cities that lay in our way towards Italy. For the Italians are so curious and scrupulous in many of their cities, especially those that I passed through in Lombardy, that they will admit no stranger within the wals of their citie, except he bringeth a bill of health from the last citie he came from.' Coryate decided to join a party of travellers under a conductor, or *vetturino*, who contracted for a fixed sum to act as guide and to provide food, lodging, and horses between Lyons and Turin. This was the most convenient and reliable way of crossing the mountains. Long after Coryate's day a road ran as far as Lanslebourg, where carriages were dismantled and carried in pieces down to Susa; not until Napoleon built the present road was it possible to ride all the way in a wheeled vehicle. Nevertheless the Mont Cenis route seems to have been the one most generally used by English travellers to Italy in the seventeenth century, except for the period from 1628 to 1659 when northern Italy was ravaged by war and plague. An indication of its popularity was that for the journey between Lyons and Turin there came into use a regular written contract between the *vetturino* and his client.[1]

Coryate and his companions crossed the frontier to Savoy at Pont de Beauvoisin, and were soon in difficult country. Some of the party had hired chairmen to follow them to the summit and carry them down into Chambéry. The way was so steep and rough that Coryate decided to hand over his horse and accompany the chairmen on foot, but they led him at such a pace that he could not keep up. Fearing that he would lose the way among

---

[1] E. S. Bates, *op. cit.*, pp. 331–2; J. W. Stoye, *op. cit.*, p. 155, n. A form of contract for the journey from Lyons via Geneva to Turin is given by Abraham Gölnitz, *Ulysses*, 1631, pp. 655–6.

the thick trees and winding paths, he compounded with them in desperation to carry him the last half mile to the top for eighteen pence. This sounds a very fair wage, but so severe were their exertions that their passenger asserted he would not have changed places with them for five hundred times the price.

They spent the night at Chambéry and a further two days of arduous travel brought them to Lanslebourg at nine o'clock at night. The strain of the journey was quite as much nervous as physical. Coryate was appalled by the precipices along the edge of which their path often lay. The rest of the travellers were emboldened to remain on their horses by one of the party, a merry Italian named Antonio, who kept repeating, 'Courage, courage, le diable est mort.' But Coryate, perceiving that a stumble would have meant falling four or five times the height of St. Paul's, decided to cover the last six or seven miles into Lanslebourg on foot. He did not have a head for heights and everything in Savoy was high—even the beds were so high that one had to climb up into them.

From the top of the pass the travellers followed a steep, stony, winding track which Coryate found even more wearisome than the ascent. Despite dismounting he 'continually descended headlong' and was much relieved when they had passed through the village of Novalesa, marking the frontier between Savoy and its province of Piedmont, where at last the route became more easy.

# CHAPTER III

# *Italy*

'FORKS, what be they?' asks one of Ben Jonson's characters in *The Divil is an Ass*, first performed in the autumn of 1616. 'The laudable use of forks' is the answer 'brought into custome here, as they are in Italy, to the saving of napkins'. Who brought forks to England is another question, but Coryate has a strong claim to be the first to show Englishmen how to keep their fingers out of the gravy. As soon as he arrived in Italy he observed 'a custome in all those Italian Townes and Cities through the which I passed, that is not used in any other country that I saw in my travels, neither doe I thinke that any other nation of Christendome doth use it, but only Italy. The Italian and also most strangers that are commorant in Italy, doe alwaies at their meales use a little forke when they cut their meat. For while with their knife which they hold in one hand they cut the meate out of the dish, they fasten their forke which they hold in their other hand upon the same dish, so that whatsoever he be that sitting in the company of any others at meale, should unadvisedly touch the dish of meate with his fingers from which all the table doe cut, he will give occasion of offence unto the company, as having transgressed the lawes of good manners, in so much that for his error he shall be at the least brow-beaten, if not reprehended in wordes. This forme of feeding I understand is generally used in all places of Italy, their forkes being for the most part made of yron or steele, and some of silver, but those are used only by Gentlemen. The reason of this their curiosity is, because the Italian cannot by any means indure to have his dish touched with fingers, seeing all mens fingers are not alike cleane.'

There is a passing reference to the Italian usage in Ben Jonson's Venetian comedy *Volpone* (1605),[1] but this passage from the

---

[1] 'Then must you learn the use And handling of your silver fork at meals.' Act IV Sc. 1.

*Crudities* is the first published description of the use of table forks in English literature. It is not quite clear from what Coryate says how much forks were used in Italy for carving and how much for carrying food to the mouth. There is some evidence that in France by this time they were being used much as they are today,[1] but the fashion, said to have been imported by Henri III after visiting Venice, seems to have died away later, since even Louis XIV thought a fork a superfluous luxury. Coryate's positive statement that he never saw them in any other country during his travels suggests that they were not to be seen even in France outside great men's houses. In England they were very rare and often valuable curiosities. A fruit fork of crystal is mentioned in the wardrobe account of Edward I in 1297, and Edward II had three silver forks for eating pears. Fifteenth- and sixteenth-century English wills contain instances of a testator bequeathing a single fork for eating fruit—and in one case for eating 'greene gyngour'—but before Coryate's day their use for meat at table was quite unknown.

He lost no time in acquiring a fork of his own, and 'thought good to imitate the Italian fashion not only while I was in Italy, but also in Germany, and often times in England since I came home'. Since it was a prominent member of the Mermaid Club who nicknamed Coryate *furcifer*[2] it is not too fanciful to suppose that some of these practical demonstrations of elegant eating took place at the Club's monthly dinners and that a few of his fellow members were among the first to adopt the new fashion. Yet it was a very long time before table forks came into general use. Peter Heylyn, writing in 1621, still speaks of them as a novelty which came from Italy 'taken up of late' by some of the 'spruce gallants'. Our earliest known silver table forks bear the hallmark of 1696, and until the reign of Queen Anne most Englishmen continued to use their fingers.

[1] For this and some of the succeeding statements concerning the use of forks, see E. Green, *Tom Coryate & Forks* in *Proceedings of the Somerset Archaeological & Natural History Society*, Vol. XXXII, Part II, pp. 26, 27. Compare Fynes Moryson's observations on the use of forks in Italy, *Itinerary*, Vol. IV, p. 98: 'At the Table, they touch no meate with the hand, but with a forke of silver or other metall, each man being served with his forke and spoone, and glasse to drinke. And as they serve small pieces of flesh, (not whole joints as with us), so these pieces are cut into small bits, to be taken up with the forke, and they seeth the flesh till it be very tender.'

[2] More usually a term of vituperation, generally of slaves, 'rascal', 'gallows rogue'. Applied to Coryate by Laurence Whitaker, see *Crudities*, vol. I, p. 237. For Whitaker's connexion with the Mermaid Club, see below, p. 146.

It will already have become apparent that *Coryat's Crudities* is not simply an account of the author's journey. He amplified the story of his own experiences with a mass of historical data, architectural descriptions, notes on local customs, details of prices, warnings about exchanging currency, advice on questions of food and drink, and all kinds of information likely to be useful to travellers. The *Crudities* was in fact deliberately designed to encourage the 'many noble and generous young Gallants' who graced Prince Henry's court to enrich their minds by continental travel.[1]

The advice is almost always thoroughly sensible, though in one or two instances he makes recommendations which seem scarcely sound today. His brief stay in Turin was spoilt by a painful inflammation of his face and hands. This he attributed, probably wrongly, to drinking the sweet wines of Piedmont, and he counsels his countrymen to make sure that they dilute their wine with plenty of water: unwholesome advice at any time, though it was and is customary, and particularly risky in those days when water was so easily and frequently contaminated. Italian cooking was not entirely to his liking. He decided that fried frogs 'a dish much used in many cities of Italy' were delicious, but he strongly objected to the custom of bringing most of the best dishes to the table liberally sprinkled with cheese 'which I love not so well as the Welchmen doe, whereby I was often times constrained to leese [lose] my share of much good fare to my great discontentment'.

His indisposition in Turin made him disinclined to roam the streets. On the day of his arrival he paid a brief visit to the Cathedral, but otherwise saw little of the city. The next day, still feeling far from well, he decided to continue for a stage by coach. After a night's rest at Cigliano[2] his usual energy and high spirits returned, and he set out on horseback at four in the morning towards the border between Piedmont and the Spanish Dukedom of Milan. The first town in Milanese territory was Novara, where there lived a large colony of Spaniards, whose descendants can be recognized to this day both by their appearance and by their

---

[1] *Crudities*, vol. I, p. 1.
[2] Both Coryate and Peter Mundy, who stopped there with Paul Pindar's suite in 1620, call the place 'Sian'; see *Travels of Peter Mundy*, ed. Sir Richard Carnac Temple, Hakluyt Society, 1905, vol. I, p. 109.

names. Having had his credentials checked in Novara he was allowed to ride on to Milan, where he arrived on 14 June.

The Milanese were an industrious people; Coryate notes that their silkmen were as skilled as any in the Christian world; their embroiderers were famous for their exquisite work, particularly in gold and silver, and their cutlers excelled in the making of hilts for swords and daggers. They did not see eye to eye, metaphorically or actually, with their Spanish masters, who frowned down upon them from the citadel in the Castello Sforzesco. 'There is such an extreme hatred betwixt the Milanois and the Spaniards that neither the Milanois doe at any time come into the citadel, nor the Spaniards into the city, but only in the evening.' This did not prevent Coryate from venturing into the citadel and making a thorough inspection. Here he found a self-contained community of Spaniards, carrying on their own crafts and dwelling with their families in rows of houses built round spacious grassy courts. The citadel was well equipped to withstand a long siege; its storehouses contained three years' provision of grain and oil, and there was an inexhaustible supply of water. 'The Citadell is moted round about with a broade mote of fine running water, and many other sweet rivers and delectable currents doe flow within the Citadell. In one of these rivers there are two milles, whereof the one is for grinding of corne, the other for making of gunpowder. Also whereas these rivers doe runne into the towne to the great commodity of the townesmen, the inhabitants can at all times when they list restraine the passage of them and so barre the townesmen of the use of them, to their great prejudice and discommodity; but so cannot the townesmen on the contrary side restraine the inhabitants of the Citadell. Neare to one of these Rivers I saw a pretty amorous sight; a woman naked from the middle upward sitting at her worke.'

The Citadel's armament included a large number of great pieces of ordnance, many of which were sighted so as to be able to smash the city into submission in case of insurrection. With extraordinary diligence and tactlessness Coryate bustled to and fro, counting culverins, demi-culverins, sakers, and basilisks, measuring their barrels, and noting down gossip about their ranges and bullet weights. Such behaviour was bound to lead to trouble, and if he had not made off hastily when an irate Spaniard advanced menacingly upon him, his journey might have ended abruptly in a dungeon.

Although he spent only one day in Milan he managed to visit and take notes of many of the same famous buildings which attract modern travellers. From the ancient church of St. Ambrose, the prototype of the Lombard basilica, he went to the new Biblioteca Ambrosiana, 'which is an exceeding faire place of workmanship, but it is not yet fully finished, [it was completed the following year, 1609] so that there is not one book in it'. Finally he spent some time in the Cathedral, 'an exceeding glorious and beautifull Church, as faire if not fairer than the Cathedral Church of Amiens'. He climbed the cathedral tower, but in describing the view he omits any mention of the astounding panorama of the Alps to the north. During the crossing of the Mont Cenis pass he had shown the same lack of appreciation of mountain scenery, merely remarking that Mont Roche Melon, 11,640 feet, which he could scarcely help noticing since it was towering over him, was, according to an informant, fourteen miles high. Coryate shared his contemporaries' blindness for this particular form of beauty. Travellers dependent on primitive communications found mountains vexatious, if not frightening obstacles, useless for any civilized purpose, and therefore downright ugly.

The kind of landscape which appealed to Coryate was the fertile well-tilled plain of Lombardy, 'beautified with such abundance of goodly rivers, pleasant meadowes, fruitful vineyardes, fat pastures, delectable gardens, orchards, woodes and what not, that the first view thereof did even refocillate [revive] my spirits, and tickle my senses with inward joy'. With a countryman's practised eye he noticed that wheat in Lombardy was three months more advanced than in England, and that within twenty-four hours of the first crop being harvested, the stubble was re-ploughed to take a second sowing. He saw rice and maize growing for the first time, and a great abundance of mulberry trees, mostly shorn of their leaves to feed silkworms. Vineyards were a continual source of interest to him; in France the vines were small and low, but in Piedmont and Lombardy he noticed that the main stem of each vine was trained up a maple or in some places a walnut, willow, or elm. These supporting trees grew in long orderly lines with fruit or corn between each row. Fruiting shoots from the vines were trained on to stakes set in the ground between the trees 'so that the greatest part of the grapes doe grow about these stakes, and few on the tree. Many thousands of these vines I have seene grow so high, that they have sprowted cleane above the toppe of the tree.'

Delighting in this luxuriant countryside, he proceeded at a leisurely pace by coach from Milan to Lodi, where an unpleasant surprise awaited him. Although it was only nine o'clock on a fine summer evening, the gates of Lodi were already closed. Failing to gain admittance he went back to an inn in the suburbs only to find that every bed was already occupied. He ended by spending an uncomfortable night dozing in the coach which had brought him from Milan. At daybreak he was on the road again, and reached Pizzighettone shortly after noon. Here he was befriended by a scholarly inhabitant who entertained him at his house and discoursed to him about the history of the neighbourhood. Among other curiosities he showed Coryate the room in the castle tower where a singular captive had been imprisoned over eighty years previously. The prisoner's autograph was still visible on the wall, written out twice, once in Spanish, the language of his captors, and once in his native tongue: *François Roi de France*.[1]

Coryate does not seem to have been inconvenienced by the unaccustomed heat of the climate, but he took great interest in the various methods which the Italians employed for keeping themselves cool. 'I observed that many of their women and children goe onely in their smockes and shirts in divers places of the country without any other apparell at all by reason of the extreme heat of the clymate; and many of their children which doe weare breeches, have them so made, that all the hinder parts of their bodies are naked, for the more coolenesse of the ayre.' Ventilation was, however, not the only purpose of these apertures. Fynes Moryson noticed that 'the Italians clothe very little children with doublets and breeches, but their breeches are open behind, with the shirt hanging out, that they may ease themselves without helpe'.[2]

Fans, unknown at home except as costly ornaments for grand ladies, were commonly carried and used by both men and women, 'very elegant and pretty things ... on both sides most curiously adorned with excellent pictures, either of amorous things tending to dalliance, having some witty Italian verses or fine emblemes written under them; or of some notable Italian city with a briefe

[1] François I, taken prisoner after being defeated at Pavia, 24 February 1525.
[2] Fynes Moryson, *Itinerary*, vol. IV, pp. 219-20.

description thereof.' The best could be purchased for no more than fourpence.

'Many carry other fine things ... that will cost at the least a duckat, which they commonly call in the Italian tongue umbrellaes, that is, things that minister shadow unto them for shelter against the scorching heate of the Sunne.' Coryate says that they were made of leather stretched on wooden hoops, and were used especially by horsemen, who carried them in their hand with the end of the handle fastened to their thigh. This seems to be the earliest mention of 'umbrella' in English literature, so Coryate can claim to have introduced the word into our vocabulary, though not the article into our homes. It is ironical that umbrellas should have come to England as a protection against the sun—though even sunshades were unknown in Coryate's day. It is almost incredible, in retrospect, that the English should have endured being rained on day after day for so many years before Jonas Hanway (1712–86) conceived the notion of adapting the umbrella's use to the English climate.

An afternoon walk of twelve miles at a steady four miles an hour brought him from Pizzighettone to Cremona, where he supped off fried frogs 'so curiously dressed that they did exceedingly delight my palat'. Next morning he rode to Mantua, which he was predisposed to like because of its associations with Virgil. But the reality so far exceeded his expectations that he was quite enraptured. Here seemed to be the ideal synthesis of stately, sumptuous buildings and rich vineyards, orchards, and gardens, pervaded with sweet air and all held in the silvery arm of the river Mincio. 'Truely the view of this most sweet Paradise ... did even so ravish my senses with such inward delight, that I said unto myselfe, this is the Citie which of all other places in the world, I would wish to make my habitation in, and spend the remainder of my dayes in divine Meditations amongst the sacred Muses.' However, on reflection, the religious difficulty occurred to him—the people's gross idolatry and superstitious ceremonies, which he detested—and then again if he were in Mantua he could not be in Odcombe, 'which is so deare unto me that I preferre the very smoke thereof before the fire of all other places under the sunne'. With such thoughts he reconciled himself to ride away early the following morning towards the Venetian frontier.

The Republic of Venice had already fought four exhausting

wars against the Turks and had lost a number of her overseas possessions, but her landward territories were substantially the same as they had been at the end of the fifteenth century, and indeed remained intact until Napoleon brought the Republic to an end. Padua, Treviso, Verona, Vicenza, Bergamo, and Brescia all belonged to her. Her frontiers ran from the Alps down the course of the Adda to its junction with the Po, thence along the line of the Po to the sea, and from a point near Monfalcone inland to the Carnic Alps. Her wealth and prestige were still immense.

Coryate entered the State of Venice at the fortress town of Legnago, where he had to obtain a warrant from the Prefect before he could proceed. The ride through Este to Padua was wholly delightful, 'For as Italy is the garden of the world, so is Lombardy the garden of Italy, and Venice the garden of Lombardy.'

Arrived in Padua, he put up at the Star Inn, and lost no time in starting to explore the city. In this he was greatly assisted by three Englishmen—Dr. Moore, Mr. George Rooke, and Mr. Willoughby —and a young Italian student, an acquaintance of Rooke, with whom Coryate got into conversation in a book-binder's shop. This young man impressed him no less by his classical learning than by the fact that he was able to converse in Hebrew with the numerous Jews in the city to such good effect that he claimed to have converted some of them to Christianity. Dr. Moore, a physician, was probably attached to the faculty of medicine at the University. Padua at this time was the pre-eminent medical school in the whole of Christendom. Its fame had been built up by such illustrious teachers and pioneers as Vesalius, Falloppio, and Girolamo Fabricio. Fabricio's pupil, William Harvey, discoverer of the circulation of the blood, had graduated from Padua six years previously. Coryate was told that more foreign students from France, Germany, the Netherlands, and England came to Padua than to any other Christian university, and that the total number of students was at least 1,500. By no means all were studying medicine; many came to read civil law, and still more to study mathematics at the feet of Galileo.

Rooke[1] (who was incidentally the grandfather of Admiral Rooke of Gibraltar) belonged to the retinue of the English Ambassador in Venice, to whom Coryate had letters of introduction. It is possible that the Ambassador had arranged for him to look

[1] For an account of his life, see Stoye, *op. cit.*, pp. 151-3.

after the visitor, but more likely that Rooke happened to be in Padua and struck up a chance acquaintanceship. At all events Coryate records that Rooke used him with extreme kindness both in Padua and later in Venice.

The third Englishman, Willoughby, an elderly scholar attached to the University, was certainly not introduced to Coryate with the sanction of the Ambassador. Wotton knew Willoughby and described him as 'an infectious Papist of a still and dangerous temper'.[1] As he and Coryate parted on the friendliest terms it may be concluded that they were far too busy examining the sights of the city together to enter into religious controversy.

Coryate's time was in fact so occupied with visits to the Basilica of Sant' Antonio, the Cathedral, Bishop's Palace, and Livy's reputed house, with admiring Titian's pictures, Donatello's famous statue of Gattamelata, and with noting down inscriptions, that at the end of his stay he had to reproach himself for having neglected 'that which was indeed the principalest of all'—the University. He did, however, manage to pay a brief visit to the famous herb garden attached to the faculty of medicine.

Much of his lengthy chapter on Padua is taken up with tedious details of buildings, statuary, and inscriptions, but it is leavened with the following account of the *Pietra del Vituperio* which can still be seen to this day in the Palazzo della Ragione or Senate House: 'At the West end of the hall neare to one of the corners there standeth a round stone of some three foote high . . . on the which if any banckerout doth sit with his naked buttocks three times in some public assembly, all his debts are ipso facto remited. Round about the stone are written these wordes in capitall letters:–LAPIS VITUPERII & CESSATIONIS BONORUM.[2] But belike there is a limitation of the summe that is owed . . . otherwise it were a great injustice of the Venetians to tollerate such a custome that honest creditors should be cousened and defrauded of the summe of thirty or forty thousand duckats by the impudent behaviour of some abject-minded varlet . . . Surely it is the strangest custome that ever I heard or read off, (though that which I have related of it be the very naked truth)

---

[1] Logan Pearsall Smith, *Life & letters of Sir Henry Wotton*, 1907, vol. II, p. 114.

[2] 'The seat of shame and surrender of property'. The actual inscription ends: 'CESS. BONR' = cessionis bonorum. A bankrupt had to surrender every possession except his shirt. For a full account see Ottone Brentari, *Guida di Padova*, Padua, 1891, pp. 68–69.

whereof if some of our English bankrouts should have intelligence, I thinke they would heartily wish the like might be in force in England [in which event] there would be more naked buttocks shewed in the term time before the greatest Nobility and Judges of our land in Westminster hall, then are of young punies in any Grammar Schoole of England to . . . their whipping and severely censuring Schoole-masters.'

Two things particularly struck him about the city. The first was that the inhabitants were able to walk everywhere, protected from summer sun and winter wind and rain, beneath the arcades which bordered all the streets. Secondly, apart from university students, there were astonishingly few inhabitants to take advantage of these exceptional facilities: 'For I saw so few people here, that I thinke no citie of all Italy, France or Germany, no, nor of all Christendome that countervaileth this in quantity, is less peopled. . . . It was told me, having inquired the reason of this scarcity of inhabitants, that most of the nobler Patavine families doe live out of the citie, partly in Venice and partly in their villaes and Palaces of retrait in the countrey, and doe very seldome make their aboad in Padua. But the reason why they abandon the citie, and preferre other places before it, no man told me.'

After three full days in Padua he started on the last stage of his journey to Venice. At seven in the morning he embarked on one of the boats plying regularly with passengers between the two cities. There was a local proverb about this traffic; it was said that the boat would sink when it contained neither monk, nor student, nor courtesan, the passengers being for the most part of these kinds.[1] Floating down with the current of the Brenta, he saw boats similar to his own being drawn up by horses towards Padua, and was able to admire on both banks of the river the many fair houses and palaces of pleasure belonging to the gentlemen of Venice. At Fusina on the Adriatic shore there was a sluice over which boats going back and forth between Venice and Padua were lifted by crane. Here Coryate disembarked and had his first view of Venice, five miles away across the lagoon, 'the most glorious and heavenly show upon the water that ever any mortal eye beheld'.

[1] Fynes Moryson, *Itinerary*, vol. I, p. 159.

# CHAPTER IV

## *Venice*

---

ORYATE arrived in Venice on the afternoon of Friday, 21 June 1608. Taking Odcombe as his starting point he calculated that he had travelled 952 miles, of which 762 had been covered in the five weeks which had elapsed since he left Calais. Venice was his goal, and he had been in a hurry to reach it. Having arrived he allowed himself no respite; on the contrary his quest for information was intensified, and for six weeks he devoted all his energies to observing and taking notes. He spent much longer in Venice than in any other place during his European tour, and his description of the city occupies nearly one-sixth of the *Crudities*. He correctly claimed that he had 'more particularly described ... that most glorious, renowned and Virgin Citie of Venice, the Queen of the Christian World, that Diamond set in the ring of the Adriatique gulfe ... then it hath been ever done before in our English tongue'.[1] In fact only two previous works in English dealt with any aspects of the subject: a translation of Cardinal Contarini's narrowly historical treatise, which was already more than half a century out of date, and *The historie of Italie*, by William Thomas, published in 1549.[2]

The excellence of Coryate's description of Venice—it is one of the best ever written in any language—has led at least one writer to suggest that the *Crudities* must have been frequently used by later seventeenth-century English travellers. It has also been suggested that the reason for there being few extant copies of the first edition is that most were worn to destruction in the jolting

---

[1] *Crudities*, vol. I, p. 2.

[2] Cardinal Gasparo Contarini, *The Commonwealth and Government of Venice*, translated by L. Lewknor, London, 1599, from the original work published in 1543. The translator, Sir Lewis Lewknor, contributed eulogistic verses to the *Crudities*. For William Thomas's account of Venice, see ff. 73–113ᵛ of *The Historie of Italie*; ff. 73–85ᵛ is a description of customs, life and scenes in Venice, the remainder is a short history.

saddle bags of readers who took the book with them to study during their tours. Neither of these surmises can be substantiated. There are some forty recorded copies of the first edition of the *Crudities* and there may be, perhaps, half as many again which remain unrecorded, so it is much less rare than many books of the same age. The intention of the author was to encourage his readers to travel, but the bulkiness and diffuseness of his book made it quite unsuitable as a vademecum, even for travellers who were prepared to follow Coryate's route. It is significant that, after William Thomas's *Historie*, the earliest book in English on Italy is John Raymond's *Itinerary* . . ., which was not published until 1648. Most English visitors were well able to acquire and use compact, yet comprehensive, Latin books specifically designed for the tourist, like F. Schott's *Itinerarium Italiae*, which contains over 600 beautifully printed pages but measures only about $5'' \times 3'' \times 1\frac{3}{4}''$. Coryate himself made considerable use of this little book.

Coryate visited Venice at the very beginning of a period during which she was to hold for English travellers an unrivalled position as the most attractive and fascinating city in the whole of Europe, offering all the allurements of an older and richer civilization. Her prestige as the historical Christian champion against Turkey outshone the fact that she had been worsted in the battle for power with the Ottoman Empire. The port of Venice was still the traditional trading centre for eastern treasure and the rare cargoes of the Levant; it was not yet realized that the opening of the Cape route to the Indies was beginning to sap her gigantic mercantile strength. In the previous half century artists, sculptors, and architects, Titian, Veronese, Tintoretto, Sansovino, and Palladio had crowned the glories of past centuries with masterpieces such as the world had never seen before.

English noblemen and gentlemen, who came to Venice in progressively increasing numbers, marvelled at her splendours. They took back with them paintings, sculptures, fine glass, and visions of the handsome houses which they would have built for themselves. The British Ambassador, Sir Henry Wotton, played no small part in encouraging the visitors by his own enthusiasm and discernment. Like Coryate he had been educated at Winchester and Oxford, but he was older than Coryate by nearly ten years. Today he is best known as a poet, and as the author of that unfortunate definition of an ambassador,[1] which started as a joke in a 'Visitors Book', and ended by jeopardizing his career in the King's service. Between 1604 and 1624 he spent some fourteen years as ambassador in Venice. He never had the means to form a collection of his own, but he placed his considerable knowledge at the disposal of others, and in the year of his final departure from Venice published a little book called *The Elements of Architecture*. The title is almost as misleading as the grotesquely inaccurate judgement that it is a 'jejune tract' which is no more than 'a paraphrase of Vitruvius'.[2] It is in fact primarily an essay on the building of a country house in the Palladian style, but Wotton also sets out his views on pictures, sculpture, gardens, and decorations. His remarks on painting and sculpture show that he had ideas on art far in advance of his time.

To this cultivated connoisseur, who was a diligent and successful ambassador as well as a poet and man of letters, Coryate carried two letters of introduction. One, from his friend, Laurence Whitaker, could not have been more gracefully flattering: 'My Lord, Good wine needs no bush, neither a worthy man letters commendatory, because whithersoever he comes he is his own epistle.'[3] The other from Richard Martin, lawyer, wit, and Member of Parliament, who had known Wotton at Oxford, was amusing, condescending, and double edged: '. . . if I should adde the desert of the person whom this letter presents to your Lordship, it would make me feare the lesse, calling to my remembrance how rich your Lordship did always account your selfe in the wealth of vertuous acquaintances, and well-accomplished friends. Amongst whom this bearer M. Thomas Coryate of Odcombe in Somersetshire, will easily find a place, if for my sake, and by my means your Lordship will first deigne to take notice of him. To give your Lordship an inventory of his particular qualities, were rather to paint my friend then to praise him . . . I will only say this, that looke what pleasure or contentment may be drawn from good society, liberall studies or variable discourse, are all to be found in M. Thomas Coryate. In the first,

---

[1] 'Legatus est vir bonus peregre missus ad mentiendem Reipublicae causa', which he would see translated as 'An Ambassador is an honest man sent to lie abroad for the good of his country'—Izaak Walton's *Life*, prefacing *Reliquiae Wottonianae*, London, 1651.

[2] *Dictionary of National Biography*, article on Sir Henry Wotton.

[3] Edward Terry, *A Voyage to East India*, London, 1655, p. 71 of the 1777 edn.

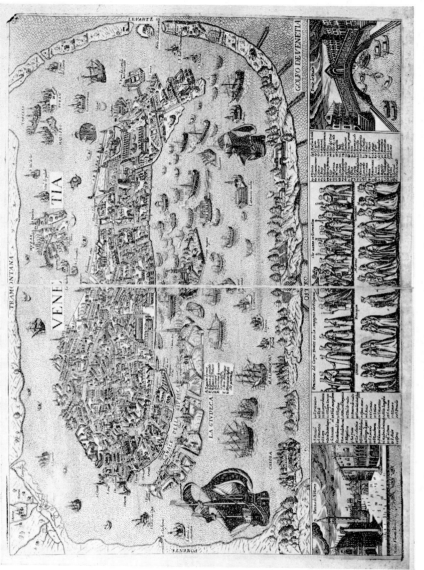

7. Venice. From an engraving by M. Florini, 1600(?), in the British Museum, press-mark 22670(13).

9. Sir Henry Wotton. By an unknown artist, dated 1620 (Bodleian Library).

8. Richard Martin. From an engraving attributed to Simon Passe, dated 1620 (Ashmolean Museum). The portrait is dedicated to Lionel Cranfield by Christopher Brooke, John Hoskins and Hugh

*in via pro vehiculo est*,[1] more pleasant than a Dutch waggon; in the second a Universall pretender; in the third amongst his friends infinite, and the last that will be wearied ... The end of his voyage (which must be first made knowen to an Ambassador) is to better himselfe by the increase of knowledge for the good of his Country, wherein he is resolved to begge wisdome among the rich, rather then wealth of riches among the learned ... Two things I have intreated him to carry with him, discretion and money, which commodities are not easily taken up by exchange upon the Rialto; he hath promised me to goe well furnished with both, of other things he hopes to be furnished by your Lordships means ...'

Although Wotton kept open house to English visitors, there is no direct evidence that the 'other things' included board and lodging during Coryate's six-week stay. In a letter written over two years later he says that he lodged in a house with other Englishmen who became worried when he sat late night after night 'scarce affoording myself an howres rest sometimes of the whole 24 in the citie of Venice by reason of my continuous writing'. Whereupon these fellow countrymen, 'observing my extreme watchings wherewith I did grievously excruciat my bodie, instantly desired me to pittie myself and not to kill myselfe with my inordinate labours'.[2] But it seems likely that Coryate would have made a point of mentioning that he had received the honour of being the Ambassador's guest whereas all he says is that Martin's letter 'was the principall occasion of purchasing me the friendship of that noble knight, which I esteeme for one of the best fortunes that hapned unto me in my travels', and that he received 'many great favours at his hands in Venice'. Despite the fact that Coryate is proud to quote Martin's letter in full, Wotton may well have gathered from its ambiguous compliments to Coryate's learning and powers of conversation that here was a poor, loquacious, worthy boor whom he would do well to keep at arms length. On the other hand there were certain solid reasons why Wotton should have felt it worth while to offer him hospitality. Martin mentioned at the end of his letter that Coryate was related, albeit distantly, to the Earl of Essex. An ambassador

[1] 'He is as good as a carriage on a journey', i.e. his society is so agreeable that he lightens the fatigue of travelling.
[2] Letter No. 1.

could not afford to omit a chance of currying favour in high places; Wotton was a regular correspondent with Prince Henry, and Coryate would no doubt himself have made the most of his position in the Prince's household, however lowly that may have been. Whatever his reception from the ambassador, Coryate formed a high opinion of Wotton's piety, scholarship, linguistic ability, and popularity with the other Christian ambassadors. Moreover, he was beholden to the ambassador, as we shall see, for rescuing him from a difficult situation.

It is a pity that nowadays so many visitors to Venice must perforce enter prosaically by way of the railway station through her back door. The city is designed to be approached across the water and should be seen for the first time as Coryate saw her, from a gondola gliding over the lagoon: 'such a shew as did even ravish me both with delight and admiration.'

Her ceremonial threshold is the gateless Piazzetta, commanded by the two famous pillars surmounted by the Lion of Venice, and the statue of the city's first patron, St. Theodore, which have stood near the water's edge since the twelfth century. Few people know that, as Coryate relates, there were originally three pillars. The first fell into the water and broke as it was being unloaded from the ship. After this mishap the architect commissioned by the Senate to erect the pillars was promised a reward of his own choosing if he should safely lift the remaining two into their places. The architect seems to have had a special zest for games of chance, which were prohibited by law, or perhaps he simply had a sense of humour. Having accomplished his task he demanded that it might be lawful for any man to play at dice between the pillars. The Senators felt bound to honour their promise, but they simultaneously decreed that this same area should henceforth be the place of execution. If this stratagem was intended to nullify the granting of the architect's request by making the spot one of ill-omen, it was unsuccessful. Coryate says that gambling between the pillars still continued, but he seems to have been misinformed since the custom appears to have been abolished in the reign of Andrea Gritti (1523–38).[1]

Coryate strongly recommends all travellers to see the view from the top of the Campanile, or St. Mark's tower as he calls it. 'For

[1] P. G. Molmenti, *Venice. The Golden Age*, trans. H. F. Brown, London, 1907, Pt. II, p. 232.

therehence may you see the whole model and forme of the citie . . . a sight that doth in my opinion farre surpasse all the shewes under the cope of heaven . . . There you may behold all their sumptuous Palaces adorned with admirable variety of beautiful pillars: the Church of S. Marke which is but a little way therehence distant, with the Dukes stately Palace adjoyning unto it, being one of the principall wonders of the Christian world, the lofty Rialto, the Piazza of Saint Stephen which is the most spacious and goodly place of the Citie except St. Markes . . . Also many fair gardens; together with their little Islands bordering about the citie wonderfully frequented . . . Also the Alps . . . the Appenines, the pleasant Euganean hils, with a little world of other most delectable objects: therefore whatsoever thou art that meanest to see Venice, in any case forget not to goe up to the top of Saint Markes tower before thou commest out of the citie. For it will cost thee but a gazet, which is not fully an English penny.'

He was able to see much of the interior of the Doge's Palace, but could not gain admittance to the Armoury, which required a special permit issued by the Council of Ten. The Great Council Hall was, he thought, 'the sumptuousest of all, exceeding spacious, and the fairest that ever I saw in my life . . . Neither do I thinke that any roome of all Christendome doth excel it in beauty. This lyeth at the South side of the Palace, and looketh towards the Sea . . . For there is assembled sometimes the whole body of the Councell, which consisteth of one thousand and sixe hundred persons: there doe they give their suffrages and voyces for the election of the Magistrates of al degrees . . . At the East end is the Duke's throne, with two pillars on both sides thereof gilt very richly . . . All this East wall where the Dukes throne standeth is most admirably painted. For there is presented paradise, with Christ and the Virgin Mary, at the top thereof, and the soules of the righteous on both sides. This workemanship, which is most curious and delectable to behold, was done by a rare painter called Tinctoretus.' Coryate is unusual for an Englishman of his time in naming painters.[1] Evidently he was unaware that this enormous picture, thirty-four feet high and seventy-two long, was

---

[1] Dr. E. S. de Beer has pointed out to me the similarity between Coryate's description and that of F. Schott, *Intinerarium Italiae* (see p. 42 of 1655 edn.). There are a number of other instances where Coryate's remarks are clearly derived or copied from Schott.

then and still is the largest on canvas by any great master, otherwise he would certainly have noted the fact in his book. He was always fascinated by any rarity and particularly anything which held a record for size, height, or age.

Compared with the vast scale of much that he saw in the Doge's Palace the Church of Saint Mark impressed him by its smallness, 'which though it be but little, yet it is exceeding rich, and so sumptuous for the statelinesse of the architecture, that I thinke very few in Christendome of the bignesse doe surpasse it . . . The inner walles of the Church are beautified with a great multitude of pictures gilt, and contrived in Mosaical worke, which is nothing else but a prety kind of picturing consisting of little peeces and very small fragments of gilt marble which are square, and halfe as broade as the naile of a mans finger . . . I never saw any of this kind of picturing before I came to Venice, nor ever either read or heard of it, of which Saint Marks Church is full in every wall and roofe.'

In no other city which Coryate described in all his travels have fewer architectural changes taken place between then and now. His accounts of many of the principal buildings, monuments, and pictures are as good as those in any modern guide book—often better because they include interesting details which are omitted in current publications. Near St. Mark's Church stands the *Pietra del Bando* (Proclamation Stone), a low pillar of red porphyry from which the laws of the Republic were promulgated to the people. Coryate describes a less well known use to which it was put: 'On this stone are laide for the space of three dayes and three nights the heads of all such as being enemies or traitors to the State, or some notorious offenders have been apprehended out of the citie, and beheaded by those that have been bountifully hired by the Senate for the same purpose. In that place do their heads remain so long, though the smell of them doth breede a very offensive and contagious annoyance. For it hath beene an auncient custome of the Venetians when soever any notorious malefactor hath for any enormous crime escaped out of the city for his security to propose a great reward to him that shal bring his head to that stone. Yea I have heard that there have beene twenty thousand duckats given to a man for bringing a traytors head to that place.'

Another important constituent of the Venetian scene, the gondola, has, in the last three hundred and fifty years, undergone some changes in appearance about the prow and stern, but is still basically the same. 'None of them are open above, but fairly covered, first with some fifteene or sixteene little round peeces of timber that reach from one end to the other, and make a pretty kinde of Arch or vault in the Gondola; then with faire blacke cloth which is turned up at both ends of the boate, to the end that if the passenger meaneth to be private, he may draw downe the same, and after row so secretly that no man can see him: in the inside the Benches are finely covered with blacke leather, and the bottomes of many of them together with the sides under the benches are very neatly garnished with fine linnen cloth, the edge whereof is laced with bonelace. The ends are beautified with two pretty and ingenuous devices . . . in the forme of a Dolphins tayle, with the fins very artificially represented, and it seemeth to be tinned over. The Water-men that row these never sit as ours do in London, but alwaies stand, and that at the farther end of the Gondola, sometimes one, but most commonly two; and in my opinion they are altogether as swift as our rowers about London. Of these Gondolas they say there are ten thousand aboute the citie, whereof six thousand are private, serving for the Gentle-men and others, and foure thousand for mercenary men, which get their living by the trade of rowing.' This comparison between Venice and London is not so far fetched as it might appear. The Thames was still London's busiest and gayest thoroughfare. John Taylor, the Water Poet, who achieved notoriety as Coryate's tormentor and who became champion of the London watermen, claimed that there were 2,000 small boats about London and that 'the number of watermen, and those that lived and were main-tained by them, and the labour of the oar and scull, betwixt the bridge of Windsor and Gravesend, could not be fewer than 40,000'.

Those gondoliers in charge of public craft, particularly those waiting under the Rialto Bridge,[1] were untrustworthy rascals. 'Therefor I counsaile all my countrimen whatsoever, Gentlemen or others that determine hereafter to see Venice, to beware of . . . these seducing and tempting Gondoleers of the Rialto bridge . . . they shall finde the iniquity of them to be such, that if the passen-ger commandeth them to carry him to any place where his serious and urgent businesse lies, . . . these impious miscreants

---

[1] Commenced in 1588 and completed three years later, it replaced an old wooden bridge and was one of the latest additions to the splendour of the city. Coryate gives a long description of it.

will either strive to carry him away, maugre his hart, to some irreligious place whether he would not goe, or at the least tempt him with their diabolicall perswasions.'

Though the buildings and the gondolas have changed so little since Coryate's visit, the outward appearance of the inhabitants was of course quite different in those days. Coryate much admired the sober dress of the Venetian gentlemen. Doublet, hose, and jerkin were generally of a seemly black, garnished with lace, over which was worn the gown appropriate to the owner's office. Members of the Council of Ten wore black gowns with long sleeves reaching almost to the ground; the Praetors' gowns were of red camlet, the Senators' crimson damask. Only the knights of Venice wore red clothes, stockings, and gloves beneath a black damask gown. All were coifed with flat black felt caps without brims.

Coryate's desire to distinguish himself from his fellows never extended to the matter of dress in which his tastes were conservative and befitting his station. In the hand-coloured plates of the copy of the *Crudities* which he presented to Prince Henry, he is shown dressed invariably in scholarly black. He found the simplicity of the Venetian gentlemen's dress to be very much in accordance with his own tastes and compared it with the exuberance to be seen in England 'for we use many more [colours] then are in the Rainbow, all the most light, garish and unseemly colours that are in the world' with 'new fangled curiosities, and ridiculous superfluities ... for we weare more phantasticall fashions than any Nation under the Sunne doth, the French onely excepted'.

On the other hand he found female Venetian fashions both shocking and ridiculous. Shocking, because, though most of the women went about veiled—black or white veils edged with lace for wives and widows, white or yellowish coloured for maidens—yet 'almost all the wives, widowes and mayds do walke abroad with their breasts all naked even almost to the middle which some do cover with a slight linnen ... a fashion me thinkes very uncivill and unseemly. For I believe unto many that have *prurientem libidinem*, they would minister a great incentive and fomentation of luxurious desires.' It is possible that the 'maidens' wearing 'yellowish' veils whom Coryate saw were actually courtesans, who were required by law to wear a yellow handkerchief, though this law was not strictly enforced. But even gentlewomen wore only little lawn or cambric ruffs which hid nothing. Gentlewomen were, however, rarely to be seen except at a wedding or a christening, or late in the evening in a gondola. The Venetian gentlemen were exceedingly jealous of their wives and daughters, and kept them close within doors. What Coryate found ridiculous was the craze for chapineys or chopines. Originally introduced because of the filthy state of the streets, they had turned into grotesque ornaments, painted or gilt, up to eighteen inches high, and worn by women indoors as well as out. Any woman who could afford to do so walked abroad leaning on a servant to prevent a fall. Coryate saw a woman take a dangerous tumble going down the steps of a bridge but refused to pity her because she wore such frivolous and ridiculous instruments, 'so uncomely a thing (in my opinion) that it is a pity this foolish custom is not cleane banished and exterminated out of the citie'.

The peculiarities of the Venetian ladies' hair style are exactly described because Coryate was privileged to watch a Venetian woman married to an Englishman dressing her hair. No pains were spared to acquire the colour and glint of gold by a combination of dyeing and bleaching. This fashion explains, incidentally, why so many women in Venetian pictures are represented with auburn tresses. 'All the women of Venice every Saturday in the afternoone doe use to annoint their haire with oyle, or some other drugs to the end to make it looke faire, that is whitish. For that colour is most affected of the Venetian Dames and Lasses. And in this manner they do it; first they put on a readen hat,[1] without any crowne at all, but brimmes of exceeding breadth . . . then they sit in some sun-shining place in a chamber . . . where having a looking glass before them they sophisticate and dye their haire with . . . drugs, and after cast it backe round upon the brimmes of the hat, till it be thoroughly dried with the heate of the sunne: and last of all they curle it up in curious locks with a frisling or crisping pinne of iron . . . the toppe whereof an both sides above their forehead is acuminated in two peakes.'

When he went to the playhouse to see a comedy he was aston-

---

[1] *Solana*. The process is described by Molmenti, *op. cit.*, Pt. II, p. 92, who also produces two contemporary illustrations of it. It was not confined to Venice; Fynes Moryson describes hairdressing in Germany: 'On Satterday . . . evening in most Cittyes the wemen sett at their dores spreading theyre hayre upon the brimmes of strawe hatts, to drye it in the Sunne, which also maketh the hayre of many very like in colour, inclyning to yeallowe': *Shakespeare's Europe*, p. 347.

ished, rather than shocked, to find that the female parts were played by women. To his surprise they acted their parts quite as well as the men. But he found the general standard of acting, the costumes, music, and the theatre itself, much inferior to what he had seen at home.

The galleries in the theatre containing the best seats were reserved entirely for courtesans. Here they sat wearing little black felt caps and short black taffeta cloaks. 'They wore double maskes upon their faces, to the end they might not be seene: one reaching from the toppe of their forehead to their chinne and under their noses. And as for their neckes round about, they were so covered and wrapped with cobweb lawne and other things, that no part of their skin could be discerned . . . I saw some men also in the Playhouse, disguised in the same manner with double vizards, those were said to be the favourites of the same Cortezans: they sit not here in galleries as we doe in London. For there is but one or two little galleries in the house, wherein the Cortezans only sit. But all the men doe sit beneath in the yard or court, every man upon his severall stoole, for the which hee payeth a gazet.'[1]

Coryate quotes a local saying:
> Vin Vicentin
> Pan Paduan
> Tripe Trevizan
> Putana Venetian

He does not specially remark on the wine of Vicenza or the bread of Padua in his observations of those cities, and he was unable to pronounce on the tripe of Treviso because he never went there, but he gives some interesting details about the Venetian courtesans whose notoriety was by no means merely local. 'Their name', he says, 'is famoused over all Christendome.' Their renown was spread mainly by word of mouth, but Coryate is wrong in claiming to be the first to write about them. William Thomas, who was in Venice some seventy years previously, has an interesting paragraph on their appearance and wealth, why they were so numerous and what became of their children.[2] Coryate's description is considerably fuller and more illuminating. According to him

---

[1] Worth a fraction less than one penny.  [2] *op. cit.*, ff. 84ᵛ–85.

Il Signior Tomaso Odcombiano     Margarita Emiliana bella
Cortesana di Venetia

Gu: Hole sculp

10. Coryate and the Venetian Courtesan. Engraving by William Hole from the *Crudities*, 1611.

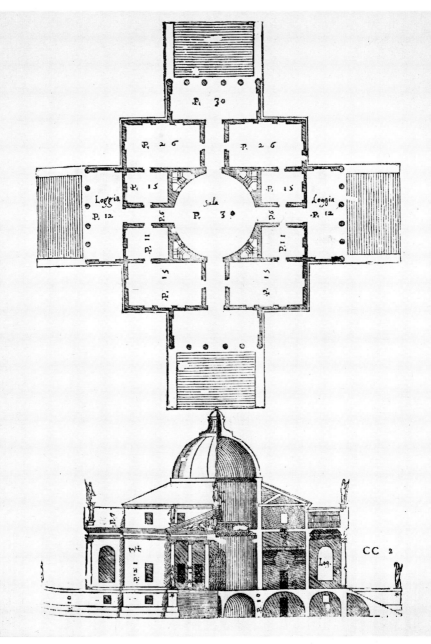

11. Villa Capra, Vicenza. Palladio's plan and elevation from *L'Architettura di Andrea Palladio*, Venice, 1642, Bk. II, p. 19.

there were estimated to be 20,000[1] courtesans in and around
Venice, Murano, and Malamocco at this time. This certainly
seems to be a high figure seeing that the total population was
less than half a million. He was told that they were tolerated primarily because the Venetians regarded them as a necessary
protection of their wives' chastity, but also because the fees they
paid to the State were sufficient to maintain a dozen galleys. The
most successful were extremely rich and lived in magnificent
palaces. If they had any children ('they have but few, for according
to the old proverbe the best carpenters make the fewest chips')
they could be brought up in a special establishment at State
expense. The boys generally entered the service of the State in the
army, the arsenal, or the galleys, and the girls often followed in
their mothers' footsteps.

In order to see for himself whether all he had heard was true,
he paid a visit to one of the foremost courtesans in her palace
and had an illustration made of her and himself 'in that forme as
we saluted each other ... When you come into one of their
Palaces (as indeed some few of the principallest of them live in
very magnificent and portly buildings fit for the entertainment of
a great Prince) you seem to enter into the Paradise of Venus. For
their fairest roomes are most glorious and glittering to behold.
The walles round about being adorned with most sumptuous
tapistry and gilt leather ... As for her selfe shee comes to thee
decked like the Queene and Goddesse of love ... For thou shalt
see her decked with many chaines of gold and orient pearl ...
divers gold rings beautified with diamonds & other costly stones,
jewels in both her eares of great worth. A gowne of damask with
a deep gold fringe ... her petticoate of red chamlet edged with
rich gold fringe, stockings of carnasion silke, her breath and her
whole body, the more to enamour thee, most fragrantly perfumed
... Moreover shee will endeavour to enchaunt thee partly with
her melodious notes that she warbles out upon her lute ... and
partly with that heart tempting harmony of her voice ... Also
thou wilt finde [her] ... a most elegant discourser, so that if she
cannot move thee with all these foresaid delights, she will assay
thy constancy with her Rhetoricall tongue. And to the end she
may minister unto thee the stronger temptations to come to her

---

[1] Molmenti thinks this is an exaggeration, though he agrees that there were over
11,000 in the first half of the sixteenth century. *Op. cit.*, Pt. II, p. 241.

lure, she will shew thee her chambers of recreation, where thou shalt see all manner of pleasing objects . . . and generally all her bedding sweetly perfumed.'

Naturally this episode was picked on by a number of the wits who wrote the introductory verses to the *Crudities*, and Inigo Jones went so far as to proclaim:

> Yet he undaunted slipt into the stewes
> For learnings cause; and in his Atticke rage
> Trod a tough hen of thirty years of age.[1]

But Coryate stoutly maintains, both in a footnote to these lines and in the text of his book, that he kept strictly to the path of virtue.

Another section of the community which Coryate investigated and reported on at length was the Jews. Their expulsion from England at the end of the thirteenth century had remained absolute ever since and there was no relaxation of the ban until Cromwell's Protectorate. No Englishman living in England therefore had any first-hand knowledge of their customs and way of life, or even of their appearance. When Coryate visited the Ghetto[2] and attended a service in one of the several synagogues he was immediately impressed by the comeliness of the worshippers: 'I observed some fewe of those Jewes especially some of the Levantines to bee such goodly and proper men, that then I said to my selfe our English proverbe: To looke like a Jew (whereby is meant sometimes a weather beaten warp-faced fellow, sometimes a phrenticke and lunaticke person, sometimes one discontented) is not true. For indeed I noted some of them to be most elegant and sweet featured persons, which gave me occasion the more to lament their religion . . . In the roome wherein they celebrate their divine service, no women sit, but have a loft or gallery proper to themselves only, where I saw many Jewish women, whereof some were as beautiful as ever I saw, and so gorgeous in their apparel, jewels, chains of gold, & rings adorned with precious stones, that some of our English Countesses do scarce exceede them . . .'

While in the Ghetto he got into conversation with a learned Rabbi who spoke good Latin. It will be remembered that he had been much impressed by the young Hebrew-speaking Italian in

---

[1] *Crudities*, vol. I, p. 64.

[2] In the Cannaregio district; the island of Giudecca was then no longer a ghetto.

Padua, who claimed to have converted Jews to the Christian faith. Regarding it perhaps as his Christian duty, or perhaps acting simply in a spirit of emulation, he took it into his head to attempt the conversion of the Rabbi. Plunging straight into religious argument, he was soon endeavouring to persuade him 'to abandon and renounce his Jewish religion and to undertake the Christian faith without the which he should be eternally damned'. The Rabbi replied that he had confidently resolved to live and die in his Jewish faith. 'In the end he seemed to be somewhat exasperated against me, because I sharply taxed their superstitious ceremonies ... After there had passed many vehement speeches to and fro betwixt us, it happened that some forty or fifty Jewes more flocked about me, and some of them beganne very insolently to swagger with me, because I durst reprehend their religion.'

The situation began to look ugly. Coryate started to edge gradually towards the bridge at the entrance to the Ghetto, talking all the time. By good fortune Sir Henry Wotton, whose house was not far away in the Rio di S. Girolamo, chanced to be passing under the bridge in his gondola. Hearing the commotion and seeing Coryate, he immediately sent his secretary to the rescue, and bore him away before any blood was spilt. The Ambassador may justifiably have admonished his countryman for his lack of discretion; perhaps it was on this occasion that Wotton told Coryate, as they slid along the canal, a long story about the four porphyry figures which stand near the entrance to the Doge's Palace, hinting that time might be better spent in examining such antiquities than in attempting to convert Jews.

In Venice the noblest families were occupied as merchants and the power of the Jews was more limited than in Ottoman territories where they played an important part in commercial life, enhanced by the Turks' contempt for all merchant business. Venice was the meeting place between West and East, and the Piazza San Marco was the market place of the world. Twice a day, between six and eleven in the morning and again after the siesta between five and eight in the evening, the Piazza was thronged with people. There 'the Venetian long gowned Gentlemen doe meete together in great troupes. For you shall not see as much as one Venetian there of the Patrician ranke without his blacke gowne and tippet. There you may see many Polonians, Slavonians, Persians, Grecians, Turks, Jews, Christians of all the famousest regions of Christendome, and each nation distinguished from another by their proper and peculiar habits.' Coryate soon learnt to pick out Greeks by their long dark hair, Turks by their white turbans; Venetian Jews wore red hats and their womenfolk a red garment: red betokening their guiltiness for Christ's blood. These distinguishing marks were not peculiar to Venice; only in Poland, thanks to the Jewish mistress of one of their kings, did the Jews have almost equal rights with Christians. Elsewhere a badge was compulsory and this was usually either red or yellow. Levantine Jews wore yellow turbans; in Mantua, where they were very powerful, the sign was merely a bit of yellow lace tacked on inside their cloaks. In Rome the distinguishing colour came to be yellow because a short-sighted cardinal mistook a red-hatted Jew for a brother cardinal and obtained a change of colour to safeguard himself against being so polite again.[1]

The Piazza San Marco was also the haunt of the mountebanks and charlatans who had the reputation of being more numerous and more eloquent than anywhere else in Italy. 'Neither doe I much doubt', says Coryate, 'but that this treatise of them will be acceptable to some readers, as being a meere novelty never before heard of (I thinke) by thousands of our English gallants.[2] Surely the principall reason that hath induced me to make mention of them is, because when I was in Venice, they often times ministred infinite pleasure unto me.' The mountebanks, as their name implies, performed upon a bench or rough stage. Twice a day, morning and afternoon, they set up five or six stages opposite the west front of the Church of St. Mark. The charlatans, poorer and stageless, had their pitches farther along towards the Doge's Palace.

'These Montebanks at one end of their stage place their trunke, which is replenished with a world of new-fangled trumperies. After the whole rabble of them is gotten up to the stage, whereof some that are women (for there are divers women also amongst them) and attyred with habits according to that person that they sustaine; after (I say) they are all upon the stage, the musicke begins. Sometimes vocall, sometimes instrumentall, and sometimes both together ... in the mean time while the musicke playes, the principall Mountebanke which is the Captaine and ringleader of all the rest, opens his truncke, and sets abroach his wares; after the musicke hath ceased, he maketh an oration to the audience of half an houre long, or almost an houre, wherein he doth most hyperbolically extoll the virtue of his drugs and confections ... though many of them are very counterfeit and false.'

Coryate, who fancied his own rhetorical abilities, was fascinated by their verve and fluency. 'For they would tell their tales with such admirable volubility and plausible grace, even extempore, and seasoned with that singular variety of elegant jests and witty conceits, that they did often strike great admiration into strangers that never heard them before: and by how much the more eloquent these Naturalists are, by so much the greater audience they draw unto them, and the more wares they sell.'

These wares consisted of 'oyles, soveraigne waters, amorous songs printed, and a common weale of other trifles'. Each mountebank had some special skill or trick to attract his customers. Coryate was particularly delighted by one who never missed a single day, morning or afternoon. He was blind and had a singular aptitude for singing extempore songs accompanied by 'a pretty kinde of musicke that he made with two bones betwixt his fingers'. Another would play with a viper's sting without receiving any hurt, a third would perform feats of juggling, while yet another would gash his arm with a knife and apply the potion he was selling, after which the amazed audience could see no trace of a wound. Wonderful bargains could be obtained and wares priced at a guinea would eventually be sold for a few pence.

On Sunday, 10 July, he attended the festival (now celebrated on the third Sunday in July) held to commemorate the deliverance of Venice from the plague of 1576, and saw the Doge walk in procession to the Church of the Redeemer, accompanied by the great men of the city. Coryate walked over the bridge of boats laid across the Grand Canal, saw the procession of all the religious orders in the city, and after the service was over, consumed his share of free wine and cakes.

A man with Coryate's energy and appetite for new experiences can do a lot in six weeks. He made an excursion to the glassworks at Murano, where he tried his hand at blowing a glass and dined off the best oysters he had ever tasted. He describes at length his-visit to the Arsenal, and we find him interceding unsuccessfully for the release from terrible hardship in the galleys of an English deserter from the Venetian army.

He devotes several pages to the Venetian monetary system which was at this time extremely complicated and full of pitfalls for the inexperienced traveller, to whom he gives some sound advice about the arranging of bills of exchange. He himself suffered substantial loss owing to lack of prior knowledge on such matters and it seems probable that he left Venice in more straitened circumstances than he had intended. This may be why he made much of the homeward journey on foot—the mode of travel to which he resorted whenever possible in all his subsequent travels.

Despite these vexatious financial losses he felt, when the time came to leave Venice and begin his homeward journey, that he had been amply repaid by all that he had seen and learnt. Indeed he went further and proclaimed that if he had been offered the choice of either seeing Venice or possessing four of the richest manors in Somerset 'I will ever say while I live, that the sight of Venice and her resplendent beauty, antiquities, and monuments, hath by many degrees more contented my minde, and satisfied my desires, then those foure Lordshippes could possibly have done.

'Thus much of the glorious citie of Venice.'

# CHAPTER V

# *Venetia*

ORYATE returned to Padua as he had come, by boat, but this time he made the journey by night, leaving Venice in the cool of the evening, and arriving in Padua at nine o'clock on the morning of 9 August.

Here he met George Rooke of the embassy staff once more. It will be remembered that Rooke had been particularly kind to Coryate during his previous visit to Padua. On this occasion Rooke seems to have been in attendance upon the seventeen-year-old Lord Wentworth[1] out from England on a visit. To Coryate's delight, and no doubt owing to Rooke's good offices, he was invited to dine at midday with the young nobleman.

After dinner Rooke volunteered to show them a curiosity. They all three sauntered to the Basilica Sant' Antonio, and there in the cloisters Rooke pointed out the tomb of Edward Courtenay, Earl of Devon,[2] who had died at Padua in suspicious circumstances half a century previously. 'Truely it strooke great compassion and remorse in me to see an Englishman so ignobly buried. For his body lieth in a poore woodden Coffin, placed upon another faire monument, having neither Epitaph nor any other thing to preserve it from oblivion.' Thus does Coryate unconsciously express his own deep yearning after fame and a measure of earthly immortality.

---

[1] Thomas, fourth Baron Wentworth of Nettlestead and first Earl of Cleveland (1591–1667), a distant kinsman of Thomas Wentworth, first Earl of Strafford, whom he attended to the scaffold. He was noted for his gallantry as a Royalist cavalry general—and for the size of his debts. In later years Cleveland ascribed his strong constitution to his habit of smoking a hundred pipes a day. See *D.N.B.* and Allan Fea, *The Loyal Wentworths*, London, 1928.

[2] Twentieth Earl of Devon (1526?–56), imprisoned and attainted after the execution of his father for high treason, he was released and restored to favour by Queen Mary. He entertained hopes of marrying Princess Elizabeth, and thus possibly succeeding to the throne. Through being implicated in Wyatt's Rebellion he was again imprisoned. On his release he went abroad and died suddenly in Padua, possibly of poison. See *D.N.B.*

Later that same afternoon Rooke walked with Coryate out of
Padua and finally bade him farewell on the road to Vicenza, which
he reached on the following morning, having spent the night at a
solitary house five miles short of the city. Here he was much
beholden to two young gentlemen, one of whom kept him company for most of the day. 'Surely many Italians are passing courteous and kinde towards strangers, of whose humanitie I made
triall in divers other cities in Italie ... Therefore I will ever
magnifie and extoll the Italian for as courteous a man to a stranger
as any man whatsoever in Christendome.'

He may have had his guides to thank for the fact that much of
his brief stay in Vicenza was occupied in examining and taking
notes of various buildings designed by Palladio, who was born in
the city and had died there thirty years previously. It is otherwise
difficult to account for Coryate's evident enthusiasm, which was
certainly not derived from anything he had seen or read at home.
He could possibly have heard of Palladio from Inigo Jones—
who, several years later, was to be responsible for introducing the
Palladian style into England. Alternatively Sir Henry Wotton,
an expert admirer of Palladio, may have advised him to pay special
attention to the great man's work.

There is much architectural description throughout the *Crudities*
and it is often difficult to decide to what extent this is based on
Coryate's own observations and how far it is borrowed from other
writers. In his report of Vicenza Coryate certainly made use of
F. Schott[1] but most of his account of Palladio's Basilica, which he
calls The Praetorium, and of the Rotonda Capra, seem to be
original. His detailed notice of the latter, to which he made a
special expedition, is of particular interest because of the extraordinary fascination which this country house exercised on European architects, who have produced a number of well-known
variations based upon it. The imitators were not Coryate's contemporaries, but late seventeenth- and eighteenth-century architects. Inigo Jones remarked merely that 'it stands very solid and
firm' and 'that a great deal of money must have been spent in
the building of this house and especially for the terraces'. On the
Continent it served as a model for the original château of Bagatelle
near Paris, and for the château of Marly le Roi, built to the design
of J. H. Mansart in 1676. The sculptor Canova also built a house

---

[1] *Itinerarium Italiae*, pp. 68–80 of the 1655 edn.

at Inverigo in Italy after the same design. The first English
derivation was Mereworth Castle, Kent, built by Colin Campbell,
the architect, in 1723. A few years later it was copied by Lord
Burlington in his villa at Chiswick, at Nuthall Temple near
Nottingham, and on a larger scale at Foots Cray Place in Kent.[1]
'The sumptuous Palace of the . . . Earle Odoricus Capra . . . is a
little mile distant from the City. It is built upon a prety eminent
hillocke, and is round (in which respect it is called in the Italian
Rotonda) having foure very beautifull fronts, which doe answere
the foure parts of the world . . . Every front hath sixe most stately
great pillars, and two paire of stairs to ascend to the same, each
contayning eighteene faire greeses. The roofe of the house is
round, and very pretily adorned partly with curious pictures, and
partly with statues.' Coryate concluded his inspection with a visit
to the 'stately celler under the Palace, the roof whereof is vaulted.
At the farther end of this cellar as you go forth of it into a faire
vineyard, this impresse is written over the dore in great letters:

> Antrum non Cumaeum
> Neque Homericum videbis,
> Sed Bacchi;
> Hospes ingredere,
> Laetior abibis;[2]

But I found not the words of the inscription true; for I went not
out more merily then I came in, because the cellarer had not the
honestie to bestowe as much as one draught of his wine upon
me.'

The following day, walking on to Verona, he noticed that most
travellers were armed and that almost every horseman carried a
loaded musket with a powder box and a pouch full of bullets
hanging at his side 'because the people of the country are so full of
villainies that they will rob, rifle and murder passengers if they
are not sufficiently provided to defend themselves'. Nevertheless
it seems that Coryate himself carried nothing more formidable
than a staff. He never mentions possessing any other weapon and

---

[1] Banister F. Fletcher, *Andrea Palladio: his life and Works*, London, 1902, p. 63.
See also John Gloag, *Guide to Western Architecture*, London, 1958; line drawings of
the Rotonda Capra and Lord Burlington's villa are given at pp. 213 and 276.

[2] 'Not the Cumaean nor Homeric cavern shalt thou see, but that of Bacchus;
enter, O Guest, more joyful shalt thou leave.'

the various illustrations in the *Crudities* all show him unarmed. Anyone carrying a weapon could be said to invite attack because the very fact suggested that he possessed something worth robbing him of. Furthermore there was the question of expense. In Italy a traveller had to give up his sword at the gate of a town and pay a man to carry it to the inn, where the host took care of it until the departure of his guest, who then had to pay again for it to be carried to the gate.

Verona had been under Venetian rule for more than two hundred years. It had always been of military importance, but now its fortifications were being continually improved by the Venetians against the possibility of further expansion from the Duchy of Milan by their arch-enemies the Spaniards. Coryate marvelled at the brick walls which in some places were forty feet high, and at the new ramparts and deep broad trenches on which work was still proceeding.

Inside the city he was principally interested in the Roman amphitheatre,[1] which he takes several pages to describe. What remained of the lower arcades were then used partly as stables and partly as poor shops and wine booths, but the interior was in process of being restored. The gentlemen of Verona who acted as his guides told him that 66,000 crowns had recently been spent mainly in providing new marble benches, and that on festival days, particularly on Shrove Tuesday, the arena was used for jousts, tournaments, and other noble exercises.

From Verona he walked to the fortress town of Peschiera and along the shores of Lake Garda, which 'yeeldeth golden sands . . . also it aboundeth with fish, especially Carpes, Troutes, and Eeles'. Having spent the night at Desenzano he marched on to Brescia. 'I heard that there are some notable antiquities and inscriptions in this citie, but I must intreat thee (gentle Reader) to pardon me although I doe not communicate them to thee. For I made so short aboad in the Citie that I could not observe halfe so much as I would have done if I had remained there but one whole day.' A

---

[1] Boies Penrose in *Urbane Travelers*, University of Pennsylvania Press, 1942, p. 82, points out that the illustration which Coryate inserted in the *Crudities*, clearly intending it to represent the amphitheatre, is in fact the Roman theatre which lies three-quarters of a mile away on the other bank of the Adige. Dr. E. S. de Beer has pointed out to me that the original view of the Roman theatre is in Torellus Saraynus, *De Origine . . . Veronae*, 1540, and that Coryate's description of the amphitheatre is an expansion of Schott, who used Torellus.

less honest writer would not have been so scrupulous, nor might
he have described so candidly the commission of a petty theft
which his acquisitive appetite for curiosities made him unable to
resist: 'It happened that the same Monday that I was in Brixia was
Barthelmew day. At what time there was a most solemne and
ceremonious dedication of a new image to the Virgin Mary with
Christ in her armes, which I saw performed in a certaine little
Chappel with many superstitious rites. For they attired the image
with a great many several robes as of sattin, taffeta, lawne, &c.
and there was a great multitude of little waxen idols brought to the
Chappel, whereof some were onely armes, some thighes, some
presented all the parts of a mans body; although these toyes were
no novelties unto me. For I saw many of them before that time in
divers Italian Cities. Yet I had a marvailous itching desire to
finger one of them, only to this end to bring it home into England,
to shew it to my friends as a token of their idolatry; but I saw
there was some difficulty in the matter. Howbeit I gave the venture
of it in this manner. I stood at one corner of the Chappel while
many women were at their divine oraizons prostrate before the
image, and very secretly conveighed my fingers into a little
basket (nobody taking notice thereof) where the images were
laid; and so purloyned one of them out, and brought him home
into England, which had it been at that time perceived, perhaps it
might have cost me the lying in the Inquisition longer then I
could willingly have endured it.'

He left Brescia at eight in the morning and walked the thirty
miles to Bergamo in eleven hours. The road was easy, but the
August sun was hot, and now and again he turned aside into one
of the many vineyards to refresh himself with fine sweet grapes—
a trespass which the Italians winked at. There were many travellers
on the road, most of them going the same way towards St.
Bartholomew's Fair in Bergamo. This fair lasted a week and was
attended by people not only from all over Lombardy, but from
other parts of Italy and from Switzerland. So great was the influx
of visitors that when he arrived in Bergamo that evening there
was not a room to be found in the town. He applied to various
inns, and raised the price he was prepared to pay for a comfortable
bed to the enormous sum of three ducats, without success. At
length, with the help of an Italian priest, he managed to obtain
leave to sleep in a stable on a pile of straw. Here, thoroughly

fatigued by his long walk, he slept as soundly as upon a bed of down.

The priest, also a traveller, and apparently more fortunate in the matter of accommodation, repaired to his own lodging, promising to meet Coryate on the morrow, to show him something of the town. But next morning he failed to arrive at the rendezvous. It would have been better for him if he had dossed down in the stable, for Coryate discovered upon enquiry that 'a certain bloudthirsty Italian', who bore him an old grudge, had sought him out in his lodging and 'shot him through the body . . . with a pewternell.'[1]

So Coryate had to make his tour of the city alone. In studying the front of the Cathedral his sharp eye detected the figures of Julius Caesar and Trajan among the statues decorating the façade. Some Italian gentlemen, who saw him making notes and enquired what he was doing, must have been taken aback when he rounded on them and told them bluntly that they had no business to allow the images of profane heathens to be erected upon their cathedral, and that while it was good to conserve such antiquities, they should be placed upon secular buildings and not upon a church where Christ was worshipped. Moreover, he told them, the inscription beneath Trajan's statue was inaccurate since it stated: 'Imperavit Annis XVIII', whereas in fact he reigned for over nineteen years. He does not record the Italian gentlemen's reaction, but in the unlikely event that they were acquainted with Trajan's dates, and his attitude towards Christians, they could scarcely have contradicted his remarks.

Being uncertain of the route from Bergamo towards Zürich, he was advised to consult a Dominican friar who had lived for some years in the Grisons. This friar warned him against taking the easier road along the shores of Lake Como where he ran the risk of falling into the hands of the Spaniards, who, so he said, would hand him over to the Inquisition as soon as they perceived that he was an Englishman. Coryate had good reason to take the warning seriously. In the previous year Lord Roos's tutor, Mr. John Molle, had been seized by the Inquisition in Rome, and even then lay in prison. Here he was to remain, despite all threats by his captors to make him recant, and attempts by his friends to exchange him for some Jesuits caught in England, until after thirty years of

[1] Variant of petronel, a large pistol or carbine.

imprisonment he died. If Coryate had not heard of that case he must certainly have known that only a few weeks previously, on 18 May, Mr. Lichefield, tutor to the young Lord Wentworth who had entertained him in Padua, had likewise been arrested in Bologna by two Dominican friars, supported by the serjeants of the town, and thrust into the prison of the Inquisition.[1] Coryate seems to have realized that this brother of the same Order who recommended him to steer clear of Lake Como had no militant designs and could be trusted: 'Truly he gave me as friendly councell as any Protestant could have done ... I am sure all kinde of Friars will not give Protestants the like Counsell to eschew the bloody Spanish carnificina [execution] ... but on the countrary side endevour rather to intrappe them therein.'

This useful discourse with the friar naturally took place in Latin. At this time Coryate spoke only Latin and Greek besides his native tongue, though he learnt Italian later in Constantinople. That he managed well enough in Latin must be ascribed to his marked linguistic facility, since many Englishmen at this time found no less difficulty in understanding Latin as spoken on the continent of Europe than in making themselves understood. An English scholar visiting J. J. Scaliger at Leyden in 1608 talked for a quarter of an hour in 'Latin' after which his perplexed host, utterly unable to comprehend, brought the interview to a close by apologizing, in perfect good faith, for his own inadequate knowledge of English.

Until he went abroad Coryate was apparently unaware that the pronunciation of Latin which he had learnt at home was peculiar to England. In the first half of the sixteenth century it had been assumed in England that the Italian method of pronouncing the vowels was right and even as late as 1542 they were still pronounced at Cambridge in the Italian manner, though in other respects there were already some differences between the English pronunciation and that practised in Italy and France. But the Reformation made it no longer necessary for the clergy to use the

---

[1] For John Molle or Mole see L. P. Smith, *op. cit.*, vol. I, p. 456; Clare Howard, *English Travellers of the Renaissance*, London 1914, p. 78, and *The Letters of Dorothy Osborne*, ed. G. C. Moore-Smith, Oxford, 1928, App. VII, pp. 300–5. The sequel to Lichefield's arrest was quite different; he at once went over to the Church of Rome, entered the Society of Jesuits and 'died a most holy death' in 1626 while filling the office of Confessor of the English College at Rome (see H. Foley, *Records of the Society of Jesus*, vol. VI, p. 257).

common language of the Roman Church, and gradually Latin came to be mispronounced as English. The mischief probably started in the grammar schools, partly to save trouble to teachers and learners, and spread thence to the universities.

Coryate was surprised to find England completely isolated in its pronunciation of the long *i*. 'The Italian when he uttereth any Latin word wherein this letter i is to be pronounced long doth alwaies pronounce it as a double e, viz as ee. As for example: he pronounceth feedes for fides: veeta for vita: ameecus for amicus, &c, but where the i is not to pronounced long he uttereth it as we doe in England, as these in wordes impius, aquila, patria, Ecclesia: not aqueela, patreea, Eccleseea. And this pronounciation is so generall in all Italy, that every man which speaketh Latin soundeth a double e for an i. Neither is it proper to Italy only, but to all other nations whatsoever in Christendome saving only England. For whereas in my travels I discoursed in Latin with Frenchmen, Germans, Spaniards, Danes, Polonians, Suecians, and divers others, I observed that every one with whom I had any conference, pronounced the i after the same manner ... Neither would some of them (amongst whom I was not a little inquisitive for the reason of this their pronunciation) sticke to affirme that Plautus, Terence, Cicero, Hortensius, Caesar, and those other selected flowers of eloquence amongst the auncient Romans, pronounced the i in that sort as they themselves doe. Whereupon having observed such a generall consent amongst them in the pronunciation of this letter I have thought good to imitate these nations herein, and to abandon my old English pronounciation ... as being utterly dissonant from the sound of all other Nations; and have determined (God willing) to retayne the same till my dying day.'

These observations are of interest because all evidence on the subject is rare. It is, however, certain that Coryate broke his lance in vain. Milton, writing in 1644, held that 'to smatter Latin with an *English* mouth, is as ill a hearing as Law-French' and recommended that the speech of boys should 'be fashion'd to a distinct and clear pronuntiation as near as may be to the Italian, especially in the vowels'. But his plea went unheeded. Half a century after Coryate a Scotsman, Lauder of Fountainhall, studying in France remarked that the difference in pronunciation of Latin often made it difficult for him either to understand or be understood, but he concluded with stubborn insularity that the French have 'a vicious accent and that we have the natural'.[1]

Taking the Friar's advice, Coryate walked northwards up the valley of the Brembana. At first the ascent was gentle, 'but after I had passed some sixteen miles it was very laboursome and painfull to travell, as well in regard of the steepnesse, as of the extreme hard stones wherewith the greatest part of the way is pitched'. This difficult climb reduced his rate of progress to a mile an hour, but at last on the morning of the third day after leaving Bergamo, he reached the top of the Passo di San Marco, 5,500 feet high. A short distance from the summit he passed an inn, the Ca di San Marco; over the door an inscription in black letters upon a golden ground recorded the reopening and improvement of the road in 1594. The inscription was surmounted by a golden winged lion which stands there to this day. Here was the boundary between Venetia and the Grisons.

[1] For the subject of pronunciation of Latin in general, the Scaliger episode, and the quotation from Milton, see J. E. Sandys, *A History of Classical Scholarship*, Cambridge, 1908 edn., vol. II, pp. 233–4. Sandys quotes Coryate. For Lauder of Fountainhall see his *Journals 1665–1676*, ed. Donald Crawford, Scottish History Society, Edinburgh, 1900, p. 123. Fynes Moryson, surprisingly, says nothing about the pronunciation of Latin, but gives some unrepeatably obscene instances of misunderstandings resulting from Germans' faulty pronunciation of Italian: *Shakespeare's Europe*, pp. 322 and 417.

# CHAPTER VI

# The Grisons and Switzerland

T HE 'Gray Confederates', or Grisons, were a group of tiny, virtually independent republics which were not incorporated with Switzerland until 1803. The Valtellina into which Coryate now descended had been conquered by the Grisons nearly a century previously, but was to rebel and break away a dozen years after his visit. The valley was already famous for its wines, which Coryate noted were carried 'to all the principall and remotest places of the Grisons. None of those wines are carryed in Carts. Because the narrownesse of the waies is such that no carts can passe there: but al upon horses backs.'

The sharp rough stones which surfaced these narrow tracks were very painful to walk on. But it was pleasantly cool after the heat of the plain of Lombardy, and he had met a congenial companion at an inn the previous day. His new acquaintance was a Protestant and could speak good English, having lived for some years in Cambridgeshire in the service of Sir Horatio Palavicino.[1] The two travellers walked westwards from Morbegno along the Valtellina, obtaining a view of Lake Como and of the Forte Fuentez near Colico, the Spanish castle against which Coryate had been warned by the benevolent friar in Bergamo. They spent the night at a village by the side of the Lago di Mezzola, the little lake immediately to the north of Como.

During the night they were awakened by the sounds of thunder and torrents of rain, and in the morning found that the storm had flooded their road. They managed to get a boat to take them to the next village and thence continued on foot into Chiavenna. 'This towne ministred some occasion of comfort unto me because it was

[1] Born in the 1540's, died at Babraham, Cambridgeshire, 1600; Palavicino was Italian by birth, was granted Letters of Denization in 1585 and knighted two years later. For a full account of his life as financier, speculator, secret agent, and international intriguer, see Lawrence Stone, *An Elizabethan: Sir Horatio Palavicino*, Oxford, 1956.

the first Protestant town that I entred since I went out of Italy, yet not wholly Protestant. For some part of it embraceth Popery, and heareth daily masse ... This towne is rich, and inhabited with many wealthy merchants, also it hath great store of goodly vineyards growing about it.' It was the home-town and destination of his English-speaking friend, who treated him to a measure of excellent wine as a parting gift.

Coryate pressed on to Campodolcino, where he put up at an inn. The food in the Grisons was both good and very cheap. Although pickled beef appeared with great regularity, there were plenty of other dishes to choose from, served in wooden trenchers at least an inch thick 'and as large in compasse as a cheese of my country of Somersetshire that will cost a shilling'.

At this inn at Campodolcino 'a certaine Priest of this country cheered me with very comfortable wordes ... For he told mee that ... I travelled in as honest a country as any in all Christendome. For had I a thousand crownes about me, I might more securely travell with it in their country without company or weapon, then in any other nation whatsoever ... This his speech was afterward confirmed unto me in other places: which if it be true ... only this I say, that I never heard of such rare honesty before in all my life, in any people whatsoever before or since Christ.'

His route now lay over the Splügen Pass into Splügen itself—the first German-speaking town he had been in—thence along the valley of the Hinterrhein via Thusis to Chur, the capital of the Grisons, where he spent the afternoon and visited the cathedral. He left Chur at six o'clock the following morning, crossed the frontier into Switzerland at Ragaz, and having walked all day arrived at Wallenstadt at seven o'clock in the evening. Finding that he could get a boat to Zürich that very night, he embarked at three in the morning and arrived at Zürich just over twenty-four hours later.

In Zürich Coryate had the opportunity of meeting and talking to several of the exponents of that militant anti-Catholic hatred and extreme intolerance which had been inculcated by Zwingli in the previous century. It seems that he carried an introduction to the Protestant minister and controversialist Rudolph Hospinian (1547–1626), whose vast work *An History of the Errors of Popery* had appeared in successive parts between 1587 and 1602. Hospinian arranged for a young student, Mark Bueler, to act as Coryate's guide and together they visited all the chief churches of the city. He also met Henry Bullinger, 'a very vigilant preacher and a painefull labourer in the Lords Vineyard', who was a nephew of the famous reformer of the same name. Bullinger received Coryate at his home and showed him his library, including one of his most prized volumes—a treatise in praise of sodomy, handed down to him by his grandfather. Why a Protestant preacher should be proud to possess and exhibit such a work is explained by the fact that the reputed author was an Italian bishop; the book was therefore treasured as a monument of the abominable impurity of Popery.

An insight into the standards and ethics of the time is provided by Coryate's description of the punishments administered by the people of Zürich. Heresy and murder were of course capital offences, and so were incest, robbery, and arson, but there was a nice gradation in the method of execution. Only murderers suffered on the wheel; witches, sorcerers, and heretics were burnt and their ashes cast into the River Sihl; incestuous women were drowned but incestuous men shared the same fate as highway robbers, and were beheaded. The gallows were reserved for burglars and those who burnt houses. He visited the place of execution about a mile outside the city walls to the westward, 'a certaine greene place, made in the forme of a pit, neere unto the which there standeth a little Chappell, wherein some Clergieman doeth minister ghostly Counsell unto the offendour before he goeth to execution. In that Chappell I saw wheeles. If they should happen to tremble so much that they cannot stand upright (as sometimes offendours doe) they are punished in the Chappell.' There were two prisons in the city, one built into the city wall, to which petty criminals were committed, the other a tower surrounded by water reserved for capital offenders—and debtors.

Narrow intolerance and harsh justice did not, however, set the tone of the whole life of Zürich; the general atmosphere was one of peace and happy prosperity. 'Many ... bitter brunts ... this Citie hath often endured before the time of the confederation and since, having beene tossed to & fro from one Lord to another, as if shee had beene Dame Fortune's tennis ball. But at this day by the gracious indulgence of the heavenly powers, it enjoyeth great peace and a very halcedonian time with the rest of the Helveticall

Cities under that happy league of union, being subject neither to king nor kaysar. And if warres should happen, it hath so fortified it selfe in time of peace with store of munition and provision for warfare, that it is well able to defend it selfe against any forraine forces.'

This 'provision for warfare' was stored in the Armoury, which he was enabled to visit owing to the good offices of Gaspar Waser, the philologist and orientalist. Coryate was particularly proud to meet Waser, who was a man after his own heart, 'a great professor of eloquence, a singular linguist. For he spake seven languages, being very skilfull in the Hebrew and Greeke tongues, and a famous traveller. For besides Italy, Germany, and France, which he had travelled over, he had been also in England, Scotland, and Ireland, a man of so rare and excellent gifts, that he hath attained to that which the Grecians call ἐγκυκλοπαιδεία.[1] . . . This foresaid Waserus sent a scholer with me to the Tigurine [Zürich] Prefect, a noble man of the citie, . . . who used me very graciously, discoursed with me in Latin [and] sent a Mandato under his hand to the keeper of the armory to shew me the same.'

Apart from serving its primary purpose as a storehouse for modern weapons, the Armoury was a repository for ancient trophies and relics which included arrows, shields, and ensigns from Roman times, a standard won from the Burgundians, and William Tell's sword. The story of William Tell was at this time accepted unreservedly as historical fact in Switzerland; outside the Federation it was relatively little known, indeed the tale achieved world-wide fame only with the publication of Schiller's play in 1804. The account given by Coryate is based partly on what he was told in Switzerland and partly on the version of Sebastian Münster; it is of interest not only because it appears to be the earliest account in the English language, but also because of its peculiar charm as a piece of narrative writing.

'William Tell [was] an Helvetian of the towne of Swice who about some three hundred yeares since was the author of the Helveticall Confederation which hath been ever since retained in their popular government, by reason of a certaine notable exploit

---

[1] His knowledge was indeed encyclopaedian; apart from historical and philological works his books include a Hebrew Grammar, a mathematical treatise, and a study of Hebrew, Chaldean, and Syrian coins. He was born at Zürich in 1565, and died there in 1625.

that he atchieved ... When as the Germane Emperours being
Lords of the principall Cities of Helvetia constituted forraine
Prefects and rulers about three hundred yeares since as their
deputies over three townes, especially above the rest, namely
Sylvania, otherwise called Underwald, Urania, commonly called
Uri, and Swice, it hapned that the prefect of the towne of Swice
behaved himselfe very insolently, abusing his authority by
immoderate tyrannizing over the people. For amongst other
enormous outrages that he committed, this was one.[1] He commanded one of his servants to compell all travellers that passed
such a way, to doe reverence to his hat that was hanged upon a
staffe in the high way. The people unwilling to offend the Magistrate, did their obeysance unto the hat. But one amongst the
rest, even this foresaid William Tell, being a man of a stout
courage, refused to doe as the rest did. Whereupon he was
brought before the Magistrate, who being grievously incensed
against him for his contumacie injoyned him this pennance:
that he should shoote an arrow out of a cross-boe at an apple set
upon his sonnes head that was a little child, whom he caused to be
tied to a tree for the same purpose, so that if he fayled to strike
the apple, he must needs have shot through his sonne. This he
commanded him because this Tell was esteemed a cunning
archer: At the first he refused to doe it: But at last because he
saw there was an inevitable necessity imposed upon him, he
performed the matter greatly against his will, and that with most
happy successe. For God himself directing the arrow, he shot
him so cunningly, that he strooke off the apple from the childs
head without any hurt at all to the child. And whereas he had
another arrow besides that which he shot at his sonne, the Prefect
asked him what he meant to do with the arrow: he made him
this bould and resolute answere. If I had slaine my child with the
first, I would have shot thee through with the second. The
magistrate hearing that, commanded him to be apprehended, and
carried away in a barke. And when he was come betwixt the towne
of Urania [Altorf], and a certaine village called Brun [Brunnen],
having by good fortune escaped out of the boate [landing, according to tradition, on the shelf of rock known as Tell's Platte], he
ranne away with all possible expedition over the difficult places

---

[1] At this point Coryate begins to translate from Münster's *Cosmographia*, 1544.
See French edn., Paris, 1575, Bk. III, p. 1042.

12. The earliest known illustration of William Tell shooting the apple from his son's head. From a woodcut in Peterman Etterlin's *Kronica von der loblichen Eydtgnoschaft*, Basel, 1507.

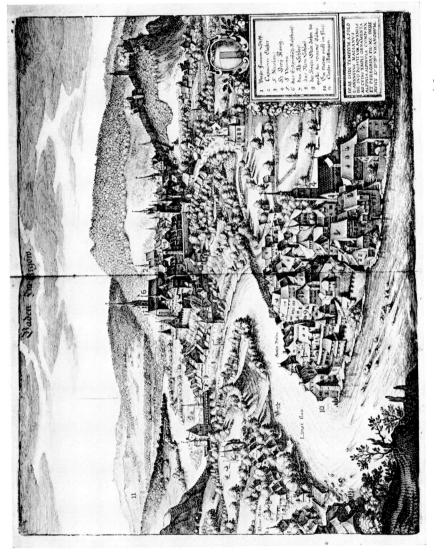

13. Baden, Switzerland. From Matthaeus Merian's *Neuue Archontologia Cosmica*, Frankfurt, 1638.

of the mountaines, where there was no common way, and so came to a place neere to the which he knew the tyrant would pass [traditionally the Hohle Gasse near Küssnacht], where he lay in ambush in a secret corner of the wood till he came that way, and then shot him through with his other arrow.[1] It hapned that this Tell did weare the foresaid sword about him when he atchieved these worthy actes, in regard whereof the Switzers have ever since that time hanged up the same in their Armoury for a most remarkable monument, though me thinks it had beene much better to have reserved the arrow with which he shot through the tyrant, then the sword that he wore then. This noble exploit was the first originall of the Helveticall confederation. For shortly after these matters were acted, those three foresaid townes of Underwald, Uri and Swice united themselves together in a league by a solemne forme of oath about the year 1316,[2] to the end to shake off the yoake of those forraine tyrants.'

Throughout the seventeenth and first half of the eighteenth centuries the story of William Tell was accepted almost without question as historical fact, thanks to Gilg Tschudi (1505–72), who assigned a date—18 November 1307—to Tell's feat of marksmanship, and wove the various and often conflicting versions of earlier chroniclers into a coherent though fanciful account by a combination of suppression, distortion and invention.[3] The truth of the legend was queried by Voltaire in 1754, and in 1760 it was openly attacked in an anonymous pamphlet by Freudenberger, a Bernese pastor. This attack was regarded as little short of treason; the Uri government ordered that the pamphlet should be publicly burnt and numerous proofs and documents were produced to bolster up the tottering idol whose very existence was now in doubt. One of these alleged proofs is a document stating that the chapel on Tell's Platte was built in pursuance of a resolution taken at a meeting held in 1388 at which 114 men were present who had been personally acquainted with

---

[1] Here Coryate ends his translation from Münster.

[2] Actually August 1291, though this was not established until 1760. Henry Naef, *Guillaume Tell et les Trois Suisses (Mythe et Réalité)*, Lausanne, 1942, p. 25.

[3] Tschudi's *Chronicon Helveticum* remained in manuscript until it was published in 1734, but his version of events was copied by his friend Josias Simler in *De Republica Helvetiorum*, 1575. Tschudi's version was also used, with enrichments and embellishments, but without alteration of the alleged salient facts, by Johannes von Müller in his *Geschichte der Schweizerischen Eidgenossenschaft*, 1786–1808.

Tell. This document seems to have been a deliberate and baseless forgery perpetrated about 1759, and the chapel itself probably did not exist before the beginning of the sixteenth century.[1] The entries in the parish registers designed to prove the existence of Tell have also been shown to be forgeries.[2] The person of Gessler the prefect has been demolished no less effectively, and it has been pointed out that the tale of the master shot occurs in the folk lore of many other countries. These devastating revelations by the scholars have neither discredited William Tell as a popular hero, nor put an end to the controversy. If Tell did not live in the fourteenth century he certainly lived thereafter, and not in Swiss hearts only, as a symbol of freedom, independence, and courage.

Coryate left Zürich on the afternoon of Saturday 27 August, and was accompanied for a couple of miles along his road by two of his new-found friends, one of them being the young student Mark Bueler, who seems to have become very attached to Coryate in the short time he had known him, and even shed tears on their parting. Some months after his return to England Coryate wrote to Bueler to thank him for all his kindness, to exhort him to learn Greek, and to ask him to persuade Waser, Hospinian, and Bullinger to answer his letters. Coryate inserted into the *Crudities* copies of his letters to all four, together with the replies which he received from Waser and Bueler. The young man's efforts to learn Greek as recommended by Coryate appear from his letter to have had only a limited success, and he seems to have had no success at all in persuading Hospinian and Bullinger to reply.

Having spent the night at a village short of Baden, he walked into the city early the following morning in search of the famous baths. He could find nobody who understood Latin to direct him and attempted to make himself understood in German by repeating 'Her ist das der raight stroze auf balnea?' The townsfolk were willing but perplexed. They all gave him directions, but if by chance they guessed what he wanted, he certainly did not understand their replies. He wandered on getting more and more lost until he reached the Monastery of Königsfelden near Brugg, where he found an obliging young Protestant scholar who

---

[1] This did not prevent the Swiss government in the middle of the nineteenth century from presenting a stone now incorporated in the Washington Monument inscribed: 'This block is from the original chapel built to William Tell in 1388 on Lake Lucerne, Switzerland, at the spot where he escaped from Gessler.'

[2] Naef, *op. cit.*, p. 98.

offered to walk back the five miles to the baths with him and mightily entertained him on the way with his friendly company and pleasant witticisms.

The hot sulphur springs at Baden are of great antiquity, and had become a much frequented resort as early as the fourteenth century, assisted by the fact that the city was for nearly three centuries the seat of the Swiss Confederates' Diet, and thus virtually the capital of Switzerland. There were in all some sixty baths, of which the two largest served the poorer people while the wealthy folk from Zürich, Basel, Berne, and Constance stayed at 'The Ox', 'The Bear', 'The Flower' (whose names have been retained by modern hotels), and other inns, each of which had its private bath. 'None are admitted to these baths in the Innes but the richer sort, and such as doe sojourne in the same. For many of the strangers are tabled there for a certain stinted price by the weeke. And some of the thriftier sort only pay for their lodging, and procure them provision from the Citie, For it is a place of great charge to them that pay for their weekly diet . . . Many of those people that lay [in the Inns] when I was there, were Gentlemen of great worth that repaired thither from the foresaid Cities partly for infirmities sake, and partly for meere pleasure and recreation. Most of the private bathes are but little, but very delicate and pleasant places, being divided asunder by certaine convenient partitions wherein are contrived divers windowes, to the end that those in the bathes may have recourse to each other, and mutually drinke together. For they reach out their drinking glasses one to another through the windowes.' He also saw people in the baths dining together off tables which floated on the surface of the water.

As usual Coryate managed to get into conversation, and was told by a learned man who was then bathing that the waters were particularly efficacious in curing 'the tertian and quartan ague, the itch, the cholicke, and the stone; and it hath one most rare vertue that I never heard of any bathes in all the world. For he told me that they are of admirable efficacie to cure the sterilitie of women, and make those that are barren, very fruitfull bearers of children. A matter verified and certainly confirmed by the experience of many women.' This may have been an oblique allusion by the learned invalid to the activities of some who came to the baths purely for pleasure and recreation. Baths often had a certain reputation, and there was good reason for our word 'stews' and the Italian 'bagnio' both having the same double meaning. Coryate wondered greatly to see married women bathing naked with men who were not their husbands, and 'not onely talking and familiarly discoursing . . . but also sporting after a very pleasant and merry manner . . . Here also I saw many passing faire yong Ladies and Gentlewomen naked in the bathes with their wooers and favorites in the same. For at this time of the yeare many wooers come thither to solace themselves with their beautifull mistresses.[1] Many of these yong Ladies had the haire of their head very curiously plaited in locks, & they wore certaine pretty garlands upon their heads made of fragrant and odoriferous flowers. A spectacle exceeding amorous.'

His young guide now offered to accompany him back to the Abbey of Königsfelden, and he spent the evening learning the history of this ancient foundation and copying inscriptions from the tombs. When at last he reached his inn at Brugg he was received by 'the kindest host that I had in my whole voyage out of England', though he does not particularize how the good man earned this tribute. So a day which started inauspiciously had ended well, and he congratulated himself on his good fortune in having been able to see so much in so short a time.

At six o'clock in the morning he walked on towards Rheinfelden, which he reached that evening. The following morning he walked into Basel. Here, as in Zürich, all males from ten years of age to a hundred wore codpieces and ruffs, but whereas the men of Zürich wore flat caps, both the men and women of Basel wore high brimless hats with a tapering flap turned up behind. He thought the women of Basel second only to English women for beauty, and admired their long plaits of hair braided with coloured ribbons.

Food at Swiss inns was appetizing, varied, and plentiful. Supper generally took one and a half to two hours—and it was not cheap, the average cost being the equivalent of fifteen to twenty pence per meal. After supper he slept soundly in comfortable beds, and soon became used to sleeping under a down coverlet instead of bedclothes.

In the inn at Basel he had the opportunity of observing the local

---

[1] Cf. Fynes Moryson, who visited Baden in 1592, 'many having no disease but that of love . . . come hither for remedy, and many times find it'. *Itinerary*, Vol. I, p. 55.

drinking habits and comparing them with those of his own country. Here one evening he witnessed a 'noble carowsing . . . where I saw the Germanes drink helter-skelter very sociably, exempting my selfe from their liquid impositions as well as I could. It is their custome whensoever they drink to another, to see their glasse filled up incontinent . . . and then they deliver it into the hand of him to whom they drinke, esteeming him a very curteous man that doth pledge the whole, according to the old verse:

Germanus mihi frater eris si pocula siccas.[1]

But on the contrary side, they deeme that man for a very rusticall and unsociable peasant, utterly unworthy of their company, that will not with reciprocal turnes mutually retaliate a health . . . Truly I have heard Germany much dispraised for drunkennesse before I saw it; but that vice reigneth no more there (that I could perceive) then in other countries. For I saw no man drunke in any place of Germany, though I was in many goodly Cities, and in much notable company. I would God the imputation of that vice could not be almost as truly cast upon mine owne nation as upon Germany. Besides I observed that they impose not such an inevitable necessity of drinking a whole health, especially those of the greater size, as many of our English gallants doe.'

Coryate spent much time in the Münster, which he regarded as the most beautiful Protestant church he had ever seen, saving only St. Paul's and Westminster Abbey. In saying this he was no doubt well aware that the design of the church itself and its slender towers owed nothing to Protestant inspiration, since it was completed long before the Reformation. He particularly admired the brightly coloured, blue, yellow, and red tiles on the roof, and from its tombs he copied a rich harvest of epitaphs, including that of Erasmus, all of which are set out at length in the *Crudities*.

In most of the university towns through which he passed Coryate either did not have the time or lacked the opportunity to see how teachers and students conducted themselves, and to compare continental methods with those which he had experienced at Oxford. At Basel, however, he was able to attend a lecture on Homer delivered by the Professor of Greek,[2] and he also went to

[1] German, thou shalt be my brother if thou drain'st the cups.

[2] Jakob Zwinger (1569–1610), physician and scholar; Professor of Greek at Basel since 1595. Author of medical and philological works.

the Divinity School to listen to a lecture by A. P. von Polansdorf,[1] a learned divine wearing a tall felt hat of the design peculiar to Basel which he kept on his head throughout the lecture. A few years previously Fynes Moryson had noted that the students at both Leyden and Wittenberg learnt little from private reading, but relied mainly on lectures dictated by the professor 'with a slowe and tretable voice, which they write out word by word, their many penns sounding like a great shower of rayne, and if the Professor utter anything so hastily that the Students cannot write it, they knocke upon the deskes till he repeate it more tretably'.[2] Much the same technique was used by von Polansdorf. 'For he did often repeat every principall sentence of note, a matter very avaylable for the hearers memory: not used by any publike professour of Oxford.'

Looking around among the sparse audience of students, Coryate noticed a venerable pastor, and on enquiring who this might be, he was told it was von Polansdorf's father-in-law, J. J. Grynaeus,[3] famous for his numerous theological works, some of which Coryate had read. Naturally he seized the opportunity as soon as the lecture was over of introducing himself to so distinguished a notability. 'I found him very affable, and full of learned discourse & singular variety of matter . . . facil and plausible in his delivery. He tooke great pleasure in discoursing of our English Universities, and of the learned men of England in former times . . . And also he highly commended Queene Elizabeth and our present King James.'

Early on the morning of the third day after his arrival in Basel, Coryate boarded a Rhine barque bound for Strasbourg. They sailed down with the current all that day and when night fell 'it was my chaunce to be about twenty miles on this side Strasbourg in my boate sub dio upon a wadde of straw, having for my coverled the cold open aire which did not a little punish me: yet I comforted my self with the recordation of the old verse,

Dulcia non meruit qui non gustavit amara,

that I did not deserve the sweet junkats of my little experience without some bitter pilles and hard brunts of adverse fortune'.

[1] Amandus Polanus von Polansdorf (1561–1610), born at Oppeln, Silesia; Doctor of Theology, Basel, 1590; Professor of the Old Testament, Basel, 1596; Rector of Basel University, 1609.

[2] Fynes Moryson, *Shakespeare's Europe*, pp. 308 and 374.

[3] Johann Jakob Grynaeus (1540–1617), Doctor of Theology, Tübingen, 1564; Professor of Theology, Basel, 1575; Antistes of Basel, 1586.

# CHAPTER VII

# *The Rhine*

STRASBOURG was a prosperous free city within the Holy Roman Empire with fine, clean, spacious streets bustling with people. Here Coryate concentrated his attention on two sights of special interest to visitors: the Cathedral tower and the famous clock inside the Cathedral. This 'Phoenix of al the clocks of Christendom' was built about 1571 and remained in use until 1789. Besides telling the time, it included an ingenious mechanism to determine the eclipses of the sun and moon, numerous moving figures, and a cock which crowed and flapped its wings at eleven in the morning and three in the afternoon 'yeelding as shrill and loud a voice as a naturall Cocke . . . It was my chance to heare him at the third houre in the afternoon.'[1] Examination of the clock was cut short by the sexton, who wished to lock up, but Coryate's description nevertheless covers several pages and is accompanied by an illustration. He had a special motive for going into so much detail. The clock was far in advance of anything to be seen in England and he hoped that his account might be read by some of the wealthy citizens of London who would thereby be encouraged to commission a similar clock for the adornment of St. Paul's.

He describes the Cathedral tower as one of the principal wonders of Christendom, which indeed it was, being for many years the highest building in Europe. Coryate gives the height as 574 feet; in fact it is 465 feet—still 61 feet higher than the spire of Salisbury Cathedral. Contrary to his usual practice, Coryate did not climb the tower, perhaps because he was forestalled by the sexton jingling his keys. He was thus deprived of a view across

[1] The cock, made of wrought iron with copper comb and beard, had been used in an even earlier clock built in 1354. An illustration and diagrams showing the mechanism for the articulation of the head, beak, and tongue, and for the flapping of the wings, appears in *A History of Technology*, Oxford, 1957, vol. III, p. 655. The present clock still includes parts of the clock which Coryate saw.

the plain of the Rhine to the Vosges in the west and the Black
Forest in the east.

It was towards the Black Forest that Coryate now made his way
in the late morning of 3 September. 'A little beyond the townes
end of Strasbourg I passed a wooden bridge made over the
Rhene.' At this time there was no bridge over the Rhine below
this one. It was 'a thousand four score and six paces long.
For I paced it, the longest bridge that ever I passed. But it is
nothing faire. For the boordes and plankes are verie rudely com-
pacted together. At one end thereof there is erected a little house,
where a certaine officer of the city dwelleth, that remayneth continually there at the receipt of custome to receive money of every
stranger that passeth that way for the maintenance of the bridge;
the common pay being something lesse then our English farthing.'

That evening he reached Lichtenau without incident, and set off
again early next morning, alone and on foot, towards Baden
Baden. He was now really in the Forest. 'I found the waies to be
so exceeding intricate, that after I had wandered almost three miles
about the wood alone by my selfe, at length to my great discon-
tent I returned to a village where I had beene about two houres
before. So that I was for the time in a kind of irremeable labyrinth,
not knowing how to extricate my selfe out of it.' He never mentions that he carried a map with him. If he did it would probably
have been too rudimentary and on too small a scale to help him
trace the route through this wild, thickly wooded country. It is
indeed surprising that he did not get lost more frequently. On this
occasion he was lucky enough to meet a peasant who was not
only able to understand that he wanted to go to Baden, but was
also able to set him on the right path.

Coryate was well aware of the risks he ran travelling alone and
weaponless, except for a staff and a knife, on this deserted road,
and became exceedingly alarmed on seeing two armed rogues in
ragged clothes advancing towards him. His thoughts turned to the
probability of having his throat cut or at least of being stripped.
'My clothes being but a thread-bare fustian case were so meane
(my cloake onely excepted) that the Boores could not have made
an ordinary supper with the money for which they should have
sold them.' But quilted into his jerkin was the gold which he
needed to complete his journey. Even if he escaped bodily harm,
the loss of his clothes would leave him penniless and friendless far

from home. Terror made him think quickly, and he hit upon 'such a politicke and subtle action as I never did in all my life. For a little before I mette them, I put off my hat very curteously unto them, holding it a pretty while in my hand, and very humbly (like a Mendicant Friar) begged some money of them in a language that they did poorly understand, even the Latin, expressing my minde unto them by such gestures and signes, that they well knew what I craved of them: and so by this begging insinuation I both preserved my selfe secure and free from the violence of the clownes, and withall obtained that of them which I neither wanted nor expected. For they gave me so much of their tinne money called fennies (as poore as they were) as paid halfe my supper that night at Baden, even foure pence halfe-peny.'

He arrived at Baden in the late afternoon and ate his supper at the 'Golden Lion', which like the inns at Swiss Baden, housed a number of baths. At the 'Golden Lion' there were no fewer than sixty-five, 'the space that is limited for each bath being square and very narrow, so that in one and the selfe same roome I observed four or five'. As he was not suffering from the asthma, moistness of the eyes, cramp, coldness of the stomach, the itch, dropsy, gout or any of the other complaints reputedly cured by these baths, he satisfied his curiosity merely by testing the heat of the water, putting his hand to one of the springs, 'which was so hot that I could hardly endure to handle the water, being of that force that it would scald my fingers very grievously if I had suffered it to runne upon them till I had but told twenty'.

From Baden he walked north-east towards Heidelberg. Although the country was well wooded, there were also broad stretches of cultivated land yielding grain and flax, cabbages, turnips, and radishes. Fruit trees were plentiful, particularly pears, which grew even in the hedgerows. The road was easy, the weather fine, and he made good progress through Ettlingen to Durlach, a handsome town with a fine palace where the Margrave of Baden sometimes held his Court. Here he had some difficulty in obtaining admittance. The gates were guarded by halberdiers, to whom he had to submit his papers for scrutiny by the Prefect of the Margrave's Court. This dignitary in due course received him courteously and affably enough, and gave him permission to spend the night in the town. Such precautions had nothing to do with the personal security of the Margrave since he was not then at Durlach, but at his Palace of Mühlburg, a few miles away.

The following morning Coryate obtained a distant view of Mühlburg across the expanse of country which was later to be occupied by the city of Karlsruhe. That day he walked only fourteen miles and spent the night at a solitary house. 'I departed from the foresaid solitary house the seventh day of September being Wednesday about sixe of the clocke in the morning, and came to the noble City of Heidelberg twelve miles beyond it about noone, being almost wet to the skinne with a vehement shower of raine.'

In Heidelberg, the capital of the Palatinate, Coryate enjoyed the hospitality of Jan Gruter, Librarian to the Elector and keeper of the Palatine Library. It seems probable that Coryate had obtained a letter of introduction to this illustrious classical scholar, but it may be that Gruter spontaneously befriended him on the strength of his being an Englishman who loved scholarship. Gruter himself had an English mother. His father had been Mayor of Antwerp, whence he had fled to England for political reasons, taking his wife and seven-year-old Jan with him. Young Gruter had studied at Cambridge and Leyden, and after some years in various academic appointments in Germany, had been appointed Professor of History at Heidelberg University. Finally in 1602 he became Librarian of the Bibliotheca Palatina and began to issue numerous commentaries on the Greek, and more particularly Latin, texts which abounded in the Library, and which attracted scholars from all over the Christian world. He was now in his late forties, still an indefatigable worker, standing always upright at his desk and studying far into the night. Despite his knowledge of English he seems to have conversed in Latin with his guest who observed that he was 'a very sweet and eloquent discourser. For he speaketh a most elegant and true Ciceronian phrase which is graced with a facill and expedite deliverie.'

Gruter found time to conduct Coryate personally to the Library, which was housed in two large rooms built over the roof of the Church of the Holy Ghost. But scarcely had they begun their inspection than there arrived two young Princes of Anhalt 'being ushered by their golden-chained Gentlemen. Whereupon I was constrained to withdraw my selfe speedily out of the Librarie, all the attendance being given unto the Princes: by which sinister accident I lost the opportunity of seeing those memorable antiquities and rarities which Mr. Gruterus intended to have communicated unto me, and so consequently I my selfe the same to my country.'

The omission of any detailed description of the Library's treasures did not greatly detract from the value of Coryate's description of Heidelberg from the point of view of future visitors. In 1622, after Heidelberg had been captured by Tilly, the whole Library was presented to the Pope and removed to Rome. Gruter's own private library went with it. Poor Gruter fled, but later returned and bought himself a little house in the country near Heidelberg, where he spent his declining years in gardening.

Coryate ardently desired to visit the Castle where the Elector Frederick IV held his Court. Gruter was dubious at first, pointing out that admittance to the Castle was a special favour which it was not even in his power to obtain. At length, however, he saw a way in which the matter might be contrived. Coryate had of course told Gruter about his recent adventures, no doubt at some length, and had proudly mentioned that he had made the acquaintance of Sir Henry Wotton, in Venice. Wotton had spent the winter of 1589–90 in Heidelberg studying German, and had become friendly with Georges Michael Lingelsheim, at one time the Elector's tutor, and now his adviser.[1] Gruter was aware that Lingelsheim knew Wotton and gave Coryate an introduction to him. 'Whereupon I repaired to his house, insinuating my selfe partly with a token from Master Gruterus, and partly by the meanes of Sir Henry Wotton's name, which was so acceptable unto him, that he entertained me after a very debonaire and courteous manner, and sent one of his men with mee to the Prefect of the Princes Court, who gave mee admittance into the Palace.'

The Castle was at this time approaching the zenith of its splendour, though some parts which still stand today, such as the Elizabeth Gate and Elizabeth Wing, were yet unbuilt. Two

---

[1] This friendship had its uses. Wotton was for a time one of the agents and secretaries employed by Robert Devereux, 2nd Earl of Essex. In a letter written in December 1594 giving an account of the acquaintances he had made abroad whom he found useful as political correspondents, Wotton says: 'In the Palsgrave his Court . . . one Lingelsheim, sometime schoolmaster of the Prince, now his chief favourite, a man of a notable style to deliver circumstances of state.' (L. P. Smith, *op. cit.*, vol. I, p. 300.)

years after Coryate's visit, in 1610, Frederick IV died and was succeeded by his fourteen-year-old son, Frederick V. It will be recollected that although Coryate was attached to the Court of Prince Henry, the household was in fact a joint one shared with his sister, Princess Elizabeth. It was this Princess who in 1613 was to marry the young Elector in London, and it was after her that the new gate and wing were to be named.

In the Otto-Heinrich Wing Coryate could see one of the finest examples of Renaissance architecture in Germany, but he preferred the magnificent façade of the Frederick Wing, which had been completed only the previous year. 'Truely for my owne part I was so exceedingly delighted with the sight of this rare frontispiece, that I must needes confesse I attribute more unto it, not out of any partiall humour or overweening phantasie, but according to the upright sinceritie of an unpartiall opinion, then to the Front of any Palace whatsoever I saw in France, Italy or Germanie.'

Accompanied by several gentlemen of the Court who had been instructed to show him round, he visited the cellars and was brought finally to the Great Tun standing by itself in 'a wonderfull vast roome'. This monstrous vessel exactly suited his passion for facts and measurements. He tells us that this particular Great Tun, which had been built in 1591, held between twenty-four and twenty-five thousand gallons.[1] It was built of 112 solid beams of wood twenty-seven feet long; the ends were sixteen feet high and the belly eighteen feet high. The cost of the labour, excluding materials, was £238, and the value of the wine which it held when full was £1,988. 8s. 0d. Later in Frankfurt he bought an illustration of the Great Tun, which was adapted to show Coryate himself standing atop with a wine glass in his hand—as indeed happened: 'For the gentleman of the Court accompanied me to the toppe together with one of the Cellerers, and exhilarated me with two sound draughts of Rhenish wine ... But ... I advise thee if thou dost happen to ascend to the toppe thereof to taste, that in any case thou dost drinke moderately, and not so much as the sociable Germans will persuade thee unto. For if thou shouldest chance to over-swill thy selfe with wine, peradventure such a giddinesse wil benumme thy braine, that thou wilt scarce finde the direct

[1] The Great Tun now to be seen in the Castle was built in 1751, and has a capacity of 49,000 gallons.

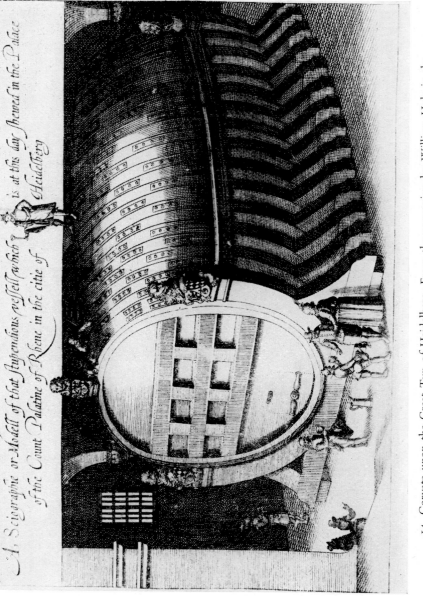

A Sciographie or Modell of that stupendous vessell which is at this day shewed in the Pallace of the Count Palatine of Rhene in the citie of Heidelberg

14. Coryate upon the Great Tun of Heidelberg. From the engraving by William Hole in the *Crudities*, 1611.

15. Ehrenbreitstein Castle, the confluence of the Moselle and the Rhine, and part of Coblenz. From G. Braun and F. Hogenberg, *Civitates Orbis Terrarum*, Bk. I, 1572(?)

way downe from the steep ladder without a very dangerous pre-
cipitation.'

From Heidelberg Coryate turned south-west and walked to
Speyer, the ancient residence and burial place of the German
Emperors. It is only twelve miles as the crow flies, but it took him
eight hours because he again became lost in the woods. Once
having reached the Rhine, he appears to have had no difficulty
in getting himself ferried across some three miles short of his
destination.

Speyer was rather larger than Heidelberg; 'the streets are many
and very faire as well for breadth as length; especially the great
streete that leadeth to the Cathedral Church, which is on both
sides five and thirty paces broade; for I paced it: and decked with
many sumptuous buildings that yeeld the farre fairer shew, because some of the principallest have their fronts very curiously
painted. Also that exquisite forme of building their houses . . .
by garnishing both the endes with battlements, which are by
little and little acuminated till they rise to a sharpe toppe, doth
especially adorne their buildings. Which fashion I observed in
Heidelberg also and in most Cities both of higher and lower
Germanie.'

Many of the towns and cities through which Coryate was now
passing were to suffer dreadful damage later in the century at the
hands of the French. Durlach, for example, was completely
destroyed in 1688, except for five houses; Heidelberg having
escaped serious damage in the Thirty Years War was devastated
in 1688, and again in 1693; Speyer was set on fire and almost
completely razed in 1689. During this attack the Cathedral was
desecrated and the tombs of the eight German Emperors so
carefully described by Coryate were ransacked.[1]

One might suppose that his description of Speyer would include some observations on the Imperial Supreme Court which
sat in the city and was notorious for the fact that its 'slowness and
formality passed that of any other legal body the world has yet

[1] The desecration of the imperial monuments was repeated in 1693 by order of
the French intendant Henz. By an extraordinary coincidence, exactly one hundred
years later the tombs of the French kings at St. Denis were despoiled under the
direction of a man named Hentz, a representative of the people, and the remains of
Louis XIV, the devastator of the Palatinate, were the first to suffer what appeared
to be a righteous retribution. See K. Baedeker, *The Rhine*, Coblenz and Leipzig,
1873, p. 185.

seen.'[1] However, Coryate frankly admits, in his Epistle to the Reader prefacing the *Crudities*, that he devoted little attention to the study of contemporary political institutions, firstly 'because I am a private man and no statist', and secondly because he lacked time. In the case of Speyer he specifically adduces the latter reason for not discussing 'their principall Magistrates' and 'their affaires in justice'.

Having spent two nights in Speyer he took the road down the Rhine valley towards Worms. Passing through Frankenthal he noticed with surprise that it consisted entirely of new buildings constructed within the last half century. He seems to have been ignorant of the reason, which was that the town had been founded by Dutch colonists expelled from their homeland by the Spaniards in 1554.

'There hapned unto me a certaine disaster about the middest of my journey betwixt Franckendall and Wormes, the like whereof I did not sustaine in my whole journey out of England.' In Italy he had been accustomed to pick grapes from the vineyards bordering the highway. In Germany he had already noticed and followed the example of many a poor traveller and pulled a few turnips and radishes from the fields. These, 'toothsome and pleasing to the palate', eaten with a slice of bread, provided a satisfying meal for the price of a farthing loaf, whereas to eat at an inn would have cost twenty times as much. So on this hot September afternoon he never thought twice about stepping off the road into a vineyard 'to the end to taste of their grapes wherewith I might something asswage my thirst: hoping that I might as freely have done it there, as I did often times before in many places of Lombardie without any controulement. There I pulled two little clusters of them, and so returned into my way againe travelling securely and jovially towards Wormes, whose lofty Towers I saw neere at hand. But there came a German Boore upon me (for so are the clownes of the country commonly called) with a halbert in his hand, & in a great fury pulled off very violently my hat from my head (as I have expressed in the frontispiece of my booke) looked very fiercely upon me with eyes sparkling fire in a

---

[1] James, Viscount Bryce, *The Holy Roman Empire*, London, 1928, p. 390, n. The *Kammergericht*, instituted in 1495, sat in Speyer until 1689. Its dilatoriness gave rise to the saying *Spirae lites spirant et non exspirant*: 'The lawsuits of Speyer respire but do not expire.'

manner, and with his Almanne wordes which I understood not, swaggered most insolently with me, holding up his halbert in that threatening manner at me, that I continually expected a blow, and was in deadly feare lest he would have made me a prey for the wormes before I should ever put my feete in the gallant City of Wormes.'

Coryate, who was not above average height and weight but certainly never lacked courage, realized that, armed only with a staff, he was no match for a violently irate and sturdy German wielding a halberd. So for some time he let the German speak his mind 'scarce opening my mouth once unto him, because I thought that as I did not understand him, so likewise on the other side he did not understand me. At length with my tongue I began to re-encounter him, tooke hart a grace, and so discharged a whole volley of Greeke and Latin shot upon him, supposing that it would bee an occasion to pacifie him somewhat if he did but onely thereby conceive that I had a little learning. But the implacable Clowne . . . was so farre from being mitigated with my strange Rhetoricke, that he was rather much the more exasperated against me. In the end after many bickerings had passed betwixt us, three or four good fellowes that came from Wormes, glaunced by, and inquired of me what the quarrell was.' Fortunately one of them could speak Latin and offered to act as mediator, but first he explained to Coryate that he 'had committed a penal trespasse in presuming to gather grapes in a vineyard without leave, affirming that the Germans are so exceeding sparing of their grapes, that they are wont to fine any of their owne countreymen that they catch in their vineyards without leave, either with purse or body; much more a stranger. Notwithstanding he promised to do his endevour to get my hat againe, because this should be warning for me, and for that he conceived that opinion of me that I was a good fellow. And so at last with much adoe this controversie was compounded betwixt the cullian and my selfe, my hat being restored unto me for a small price of redemption, which was twelve of their little coynes called fennies, which countervaile twenty pence of our English money. But I would counsel thee gentle reader whatsoever thou art that meanest to travell into Germany, to beware by my example of going into any of their vineyardes without leave.'

This incident took place within sight of Worms, which Coryate now entered, congratulating himself on his deliverance from an unpleasant situation. The city had greatly declined both in importance and population. In the twelfth century there had been 70,000 inhabitants,[1] but by this time they had dwindled to half this figure, and were soon to be further reduced by the effects of the Thirty Years War. Nevertheless the whole area was still very populous by the standards of the day; Coryate was told that within a radius of sixteen miles from Worms there were no fewer than 200 towns and villages. Around the city were numerous well-tended vineyards and much grain, particularly wheat, grown in broad rich fields. 'The situation of this famous city did as much delight me as of any city whatseover I saw in Germany. For it is situate in a most pleasant plaine that doth very plentifully yeeld great store of all manner of commodities serving as well for pleasure as profit.'

'The religion [of Worms] is mixed as that of Spira [Speyer]. For it is partly Protestant of the Lutheran religion and partly Papisticall. Unto the Papistes belongeth the Cathedrall Church as that of Spira, because the Bishop of this City is a Papist. But the Protestant faction is both the greater in numbers and the stronger in power. For almost all the better families of the City are Protestant.'

He paid a brief visit to the Cathedral but most of his time was spent in taking notes on the Bishop's Palace. It was in this Palace, which was utterly destroyed by the French in 1689, that the Diet of 1521 was held, at which Luther defended his doctrine before Charles V and six Electors. Coryate was denied entry but found plenty to interest him in the façade decorated with twelve Sibylline prophecies, 'a thing so notably memorable, that as I saw not the like before, and doe doubt whether I shall ever see the like againe hereafter in any place of Christendome in my future travels: so I hope it will be very pleasant to the learned reader to reade so rare a matter as I will now present unto him . . . These prophecies are written upon the front of the Bishops Wall . . . which hath been lately so beautifully repaired, that it is at this day the most sumptuous front of any Bishops Palace that ever I saw. Each of these prophecies hath the picture of the authour thereof made above it with his name annexed to the same, and a notation of the yeare is added to some of them but not to all, wherein they flourished before Christs incarnation.

[1] K. Baedeker, *op. cit.*, p. 226.

'The first is *Sibylla Delphica* under whom this is written. *Vixit ante adventum Christi* 1525. And againe under the same picture this prophecie is written in faire Roman letters. *Nascetur Propheta absque coitu ex Virgine, eum cognosces proprium Dominum tuum, ipse verus erit Dei filius.*'[1]

He spent the rest of the morning copying out the other eleven prophecies, all of which are faithfully set out in his book. That afternoon he walked to Oppenheim, spent the night there, and set out at six o'clock next morning on the road to Mainz.

'It was my hap in this journey betwixt Oppenheim and Mentz to have such a notable companion as I never had before in all my life. For he was both learned and unlearned. Learned because being but a wood-cleaver (for he told me that he was the Jesuits wood cleaver of Mentz) he was able to speake Latine. A matter as rare in one of that sordid facultie as to see a white Crowe or a blacke Swanne. Againe he was unlearned, because the Latin which he did speak was such incongruall and disjoynted stuffe.' This chance encounter on the road resulted in a new word being added to the English language. Coryate describes the woodcutter's mode of speech as 'antipriscianisticall', meaning ungrammatical, an adjective of his own manufacture which has justifiably failed to find a place in the Oxford English Dictionary.[2]

Perhaps it was at the suggestion of the ungrammatical woodcutter that Coryate visited the Jesuit College in Mainz where, somewhat to his surprise, he was kindly received despite his religion by the Principal who conducted him round the College Library. The Principal, whose name was Nicolas Serarius, was an authority on the local antiquities and showed Coryate a book which he had recently written about them.[3] On his particular recommendation Coryate visited the Eichelstein—literally the Acorn Stone—which is still a subject of interest to visitors. Coryate's version of its origin, which he no doubt acquired from

[1] The Delphic Sibyl. Lived 1525 B.C. 'A Prophet born of a Virgin, him dost thou know to be thine own Lord, the same shall be the true son of God.'

[2] Derived from Priscianus, the Roman grammarian. Coryate also seems to have coined 'Priscianist', which does appear in *O.E.D.*; he writes of a pilgrim whom he met at Lyons. 'I found him but a simple fellow, yet he had a little beggarly and course latin, so much as a Priscianist may have.' *Crudities*, vol. I, p. 211.

[3] *Mogunticarum rerum* . . . 1604. Nicolas Serarius (1555–1609) occupied the chairs of Theology and Holy Scripture at Würzburg and Mainz. See C. Sommervogel, *Bibliothèque de la Compagnie de Jésus*, Brussels and Paris, 1896, vol. XII, pp. 1134 and 1138. Coryate spells him 'Serrarius'.

Serarius, is that it was built by the Emperor Drusus to commemorate a victory over the Germans. The more usual tradition is that it was built in honour of Drusus in 9 B.C. by the IInd and XIVth Legions. It stands on the site of the Roman fort which, when Coryate visited it, was merely a hill on the south side of the city surmounted by a vineyard, but later reverted to its earlier role and became the citadel of Mainz. He was surprised to find that the monument bore no resemblance whatever to an acorn except that it had a rounded top. Serarius does not seem to have informed him that a few years previously some enthusiastic Christians had begun to demolish it because it was a pagan monument and had succeeded in reducing it from eighty feet to about half that height before their zeal had evaporated. Its name certainly has no connexion with acorns, but is probably a corruption of *aquila*, the Roman standard.

The city of Mainz was altogether rather a disappointment to him. He found the Cathedral very sumptuous, but inferior to others he had visited, notably Basel and Strasbourg. As the birthplace of Gutenberg, it provided him with the opportunity of writing a laboured homily on the virtues conferred on mankind by the invention of printing.

Hearing that Frankfurt Fair had started, he decided to make an expedition thither before continuing his journey down the Rhine. He accordingly embarked at Mainz on the morning of 13 September in a sailing boat which 'contained a strange miscellany of people . . . For in this barke there were some few of every principall nation of Christendome travelling towards Frankfurt Mart that began the day before.'

He landed from the boat at an unnamed town, probably Hoechst, and walked the last four miles into Frankfurt. 'There are two things which make this citie famous over all Europe. The one the election of the King of the Romanes, the other the two noble fayres kept heere twice a yeare, which are called the Martes of Franckford . . . As for the Fayre it is esteemed, and so indeed is the richest meeting of any place of Christendome, which continueth 14 daies together, and is kept in the moneth of March for the Spring, and in September for the Autumne.'

The fair was centred around the Römer, the splendid fifteenth-century town hall. 'The riches I observed at this Mart were most infinite, especially in one place called "Under Den Roemer", where the Goldsmithes kept their shoppes, which made the most glorious shew that ever I saw in my life, especially some of the Citie of Norimberg. This place is divided into divers other roomes that have a great many partitions assigned unto Mercers and such like artificers, for the exposing of their wares. The wealth that I sawe here was incredible, so great that it was unpossible for a man to conceive it in his minde that hath not first seene it with his bodily eies.'

Frankfurt was the traditional centre of the book trade in Europe. 'I went to the Bookesellers streete where I saw such infinite abundance of bookes, that I greatly admired it. For this street farre excelleth Paules Churchyard in London, Saint James streete in Paris, the Merceria of Venice, and all whatsoever else that I sawe in my travels. In so much that it seemeth to be a very epitome of all the principall Libraries of Europe. Neither is that streete famous for selling bookes onely, and that of all manner of artes and disciplines whatsoever, but also for printing of them. For this city hath so flourished within these fewe yeares in the art of printing, that it is not inferiour in that respect to any city in Christendome.'

Buying and selling went on throughout the city in private houses, and even within the precincts of the churches. Coryate says that he 'visited divers Cloysters full of wares and notable commodities, especially the Cloyster of Saint Bartholomewes Church; where amongst other things I saw a world of excellent pictures, inventions of singular curiosity, whereof most were religious, and such as intended to mortification . . . Every man selleth his ware in his owne house, except forreners and those that hire shoppes in the Burse [Exchange]. So that there is no common place either in the streetes or in any open yard or field . . . which maketh the Fayre seeme but little, though indeed it be very great.' This Bourse or Exchange was not a building like the Exchange in London, or the Rialto in Venice, but merely part of a street, thronged with wealthy merchants from all over Europe.

Frankfurt Fair was an important occasion socially as well as commercially. The German nobility came from far and near to see and buy; Coryate says that he saw 'some Pfaltzgraves' and many Earls. One of the latter was no German but his own 'thrice-honourable countryman' the young Earl of Essex whom, it will be recalled, he had just missed meeting in Lyons. Essex was now on his way home,[1] having been away for about two years, mainly travelling in France, though Coryate mentions that he had also visited Switzerland and some parts of High Germany. As he gives no further details about this encounter it seems likely that his reception, if it took place at all, was of a most perfunctory nature since he would certainly not have lost the opportunity of recording any flattering treatment received from his distant kinsman.

Another curious crossing of paths occurred at the Fair. Coryate was always ready to extol his fellow countrymen, but he must have found special pleasure in relating that 'the goodliest shew of ware that I sawe in all Franckford saving that of the Goldsmithes, was made by an Englishman one Thomas Stockfield a Dorsetshire man.' Stockfield had once been a servant of Coryate's father; he had gone abroad, a poor man, to seek his fortune, 'but after he had spent a few yeares at the Duke of Brunswicks Court hee so enriched himselfe of late, that his glittering shewe of ware in Franckford did farre excell all the Dutchmen, French, Italians or whomsoever else'.

Having spent two full days in Frankfurt, he travelled back to Mainz overland and there embarked on the morning of Saturday 17 September, to sail down the Rhine.

'All passengers which descend do pay but a small price for their passage; but . . . all that ascend doe strive very painfully against the streame. So that all their vessels are drawen by horses with great might and maine. For this cause all passengers that ascend into the higher parts of Germany doe pay much more for their carriage.' Although they were travelling downstream, progress was much slower than it might have been because the boat had to put in at numerous customs towns on the way. Thus it took them twelve hours to cover the thirty miles between Mainz and Boppard because they had to call at Bingen, Bacharach, Caub, and St. Goar. These customs posts 'belong to divers Princes Spirituall and Temporall, who receive a great yearlie revenue by them. All passengers whatsoever they are, noble or ignoble, must arrive in each of these places, and stay a while till the boateman hath paid custome for his passage. To the passenger it is no charge at all, but onely to the master of the boate. If any should

---

[1] The Governor of Flushing mentions his passage through that town in November 1608. See Stoye, *op. cit.*, p. 261.

dare in a resolute and wilfull humour to passe by any of these places, and not pay the stinted summe of money, the Publicans that sit at the receipt of custome will presently discharge (as I heard) a peece of Ordinance at them, and make them an example to all after-commers.'

At St. Goar there was more to be done than simply paying the customs dues. Coryate, as a newcomer, was eligible for initiation into the Society of Good Fellows, or the Fraternity of Boon Companions, as he calls it. The initiation was a mock solemnity of the kind which was dear to his heart, particularly since its origins were of indisputable antiquity. St. Goar takes its name from the saint who died and was buried there in 575. The chapel built over his grave became a place of pilgrimage, and a monastery was established close by. Charlemagne is said to have left the monks an annual income of twenty marks to be spent in the entertainment of strangers with Rhenish wine. The initiation ceremony seems to have grown from these beginnings, but during the Middle Ages it assumed commercial significance and became a kind of matriculation for strangers who wished to do business or enjoy the hospitality of the town. It still retained this character in the seventeenth century, for in 1627 the Landgraf George of Hesse reaffirmed all its ancient privileges, forbade the entertainment of all stranger merchants in the town, and prohibited them from trading unless they were admitted members of it.[1]

When a traveller entered St. Goar for the first time and claimed hospitality, he was taken to the toll house where a collar, at one time silver but in Coryate's day made of iron, was placed about his neck. He was then told that he must be baptized and was asked whether he would prefer this to be done with water or with wine. Coryate wisely chose wine. If he had chosen water he would have been soused with a bucket, but baptism by wine involved nothing more unpleasant than purchasing one's release from the collar 'with a competent measure of wine', which was forthwith poured down the throats of all those present. 'And at the drinking there is as much joviality and merriment as heart can conceive ... And so after much Mercuriall and Joviall conversation in

---

[1] The initiation ceremony seems to have died out sometime after the commencement of the steamboat traffic in 1827, but has been revived in the present century, and is still performed on three days in August each year. See J. Snowe, *The Rhine, Legends, Traditions, History*, London, 1839, vol. II, pp. 194-6, and an anonymous pamphlet *Der Hanse-Orden St. Goar*, St. Goarshausen, n.d.

this Towne of Saint Gewere, we returned again to our boate and
proceeded forward on our journey.'

At one period, probably subsequent to Coryate's visit, initiates
of St. Goar received the privilege of hunting on a neighbouring
sandbank in the Rhine, where of course there was no game, and
fishing on the summit of the Lorelei rock which lies immediately
to the south of the town. He does not mention the Lorelei by
name nor any of its legends, but says, 'Here I observed a swift
cataract ... Also I heard that there is a deep gulfe *rapidus vortex*
in this place, which with a most incessant greediness swalloweth
down the water ... which continuall drinking up of the water is
said to be the naturall cause of the great violence of the stream
... This place in the time of a raging tempest is so dangerous that
no boates dare passe that way.'

The numerous castles on this stretch of the Rhine were in
those days no mere ruins. A little beyond St. Goar Coryate remarked on the Castle of Rheinfels, 'very beautiful and stately
... the fayrest of all that I sawe that day'. He was even more
impressed when they arrived at Coblenz 'invironed with strong
walles, fayrly adorned with pretty little Turrets, that do yeeld
a very delicate shew' and saw 'on the other side of the river right
opposite to the City ... a very strong and impregnable Castell
called Hermenstein[1] situate upon a very eminent rocke'. Such was
the strategic importance of this fortress that its commandant
had to swear allegiance to the Emperor as well as to his Prince,
the Archbishop of Trier, and as Coryate writes, it was 'esteemed
the strongest and greatest Castell of all Germany beyond any
comparison'.

Having spent the night at Boppard, a further day's journey took
them another thirty miles to Oberwinter, stopping on the way to
pay customs dues to the Archbishop of Mainz at Lahnstein, the
Archbishop of Trier at Engers, and the Archbishop of Cologne at
Andernach and Linz. 'There is a very strange custome observed
amongst the Germanes as they passe in their boates betwixt
Mentz and Colen, and so likewise betwixt Colen and the lower
parts of the Netherlands. Every man whatsoever he be poore or
rich, shall labour hard when it commeth to his turne, except he

---

[1] Ehrenbreitstein. Coryate's name for it is probably a corruption of Hillinstein or
Helfenstein, a subsidiary castle added in the middle of the twelfth century on the
lower south projection of the rock on which the main castle stands.

doth by friendship or some small summe of money redeeme his labour. For their custome is that the passengers must exercise themselves with oares and rowing *alternis vicibus*, a couple together. So that the master of the boate (who me thinks in honestie ought either to doe it himselfe, or to procure some others to do it for him) never roweth but when his turne commeth. This exercise both for recreation and health sake I confess is very convenient for man. But to be tied unto it by way of a strict necessity when one payeth well for his passage, was a thing that did not a little distaste my humour.'

It seems that Coryate's turn came round on the stretch before Oberwinter, and that he elected to row and grumble rather than pay extra. They arrived at Oberwinter at six o'clock in the evening. 'In this place we solaced ourselves after our tedious labour of rowing as merily as we could.' Despite the fatigues of the day he sat up late with his companions, drinking wine and swapping stories. Perhaps he never went to bed at all that night for the boat sailed again at three in the morning. They called at Bonn, the last customs town before Cologne, and arrived at the great city at ten in the morning of Monday 19 September.

# CHAPTER VIII

# The Netherlands

I T is quite logical that Coryate should end his observations of High Germany with his arrival at Cologne and begin his account of the Netherlands with a description of that city. Commercially Cologne had for centuries looked down the Rhine rather than up it. Her merchants had disputed with Lübeck the supremacy in the Hanseatic League. The weights and measures of Cologne had been in use in almost every town of the Netherlands, as well as in the Rhineland and Westphalia where the domains of the Archbishop Elector lay. Politically the Electorate of Cologne had been embroiled for the last thirty years in the Dutch War of Independence against the Spaniards. It is probable that Cologne's possessions, particularly the strategic town of Rheinberg on the landward flank of the contending parties, would have made some degree of involvement inevitable. But the immediate reason why most of the Electorate had been reduced to a state of desolation was that the Archbishop Elector had fallen desperately in love.

Gebhard Truchsess, who succeeded to the Archbishopric in 1577, had become infatuated with the Countess Agnes von Mansfeld, and had been persuaded by her family that he must marry her. Truchsess had tried to solve the problem of how to wed the Countess and simultaneously retain his position, by becoming a Protestant and attempting to take the Electorate over with him to the reformed religion. This resulted in his deposition and the appointment of a Catholic Archbishop in his place. The Spaniards supported the Catholic claimant, while Truchsess was backed by the Dutch Republic and the English. In the ensuing War of Cologne the whole territory had been ravaged, plundered, and outraged by bands of freebooters enlisted in the rival causes of two Archbishops.

The War of Cologne had ended over twenty years previously with the defeat and withdrawal of Truchsess, but the northern territories of the Electorate continued to be marched over and fought for by Spaniards and Netherlanders; a general state of lawlessness prevailed. 'I have heard', wrote Coryate, 'that the free-booters doe make themselves so strong that ... Remagan ... some ten yeares since was miserably ransacked by ... so great a troope as consisted of almost three thousand persons. The towne itself they defaced not, but only took away their goods, to the utter impoverishment of the inhabitants ... I observed in a great many places, on both sides of the Rhene, more gallowes and wheeles betwixt Mentz and Colen, then ever I saw in so short a space in all my life, especially within few miles of Colen; by reason that the rusticall Corydones of the country which are commonly called the Boores and the free-booters ... do commit many notorious robberies neere the Rhene, who are such cruell and bloody horse leaches (the very Hyenae & Lycanthropi of Germany) that they seldome robbe any man but forthwith they cut his throat. And some of them doe afterward escape, by reason of the woodes neere at hand in which they shelter them selves free from danger. Yet others are sometimes taken, and most cruelly excarnificated [executed] upon these wheeles ... a doleful spectacle for any relenting Christian to beholde.' Coryate himself himself did not relent very far, for if he felt some compassion for the wretches on the wheels, he considered mere hanging on the gallows 'a punishment too good for these Cyclopicall Anthro-pophagi, these Canniball man-eaters'.

Despite all its troubles Cologne still retained many of the outward symbols of that wealth and grandeur of bygone days when it had been one of the most prosperous cities in Europe. The city walls 'distinguished with a great company of turrets' extended far along the bank of the Rhine and presented 'a passing beautiful shew unto them that approch towards the City upon the river'.

'The situation of Colen is very delectable. For it standeth in a pleasant and fruitfull plaine hard by the Rhene, which washeth the walls thereof ... The buildings of the City both publique and private are very faire, and many of their private houses I observed to be of a notable heigth, even foure stories high, whereof some are built altogether with stone, and some with timber.' Of the Rathaus Coryate remarks 'certainly the outward workmanship of it is a thing of such gorgeous magnificence and admirable state that I preferre it ... before any Senate house that ever I saw either in my owne country, or abroad: only the Praetorium of Padua excepted'. He particularly noticed the Renaissance portico, completed as recently as 1571, which was decorated with a relief depicting the exploit of Burgomaster Gryn. Coryate's version of the story, which he heard in Cologne and also read in Münster, is a further good example of his graphic narrative style: 'It hapned about the yeare of our Lord 1260 [actually 1262] that there was great dissention between the Archbishop of Colen and the City: at what time it chanced also that two of the Canons of the Cathedrall Church that favored the Bishops faction, had a certaine Lyons whelpe, which they fed and brought up for the honour of the Bishop. Now whereas the said Canons had a great spite and malice to the Consul of the city whose name was Hermannus Gryn, they invited him one day very kindly to dinner under colour of friendship, and when he came to their house, shewed him this young Lyon, whom they kept hungry without meate some two or three daies before, and so forced him unawares and fearing no such matter, to approach neerer to the Lyons denne then it was fitte for him. Presently after this the Canons conveighed themselves out of the roome, and having shut the dore waited without, still expecting when the Lyon would devoure the man. But the Consul being a man of a notable courage and stout spirit, when he sawe that he was by the treachery of these lewd Prelates brought to these extremes, either to be devoured by that mercilesse and fierce beast, or to fight manfully for his life, did put on a valiant resolution, verifying that speech of Virgil,

*Audentes fortuna juvat* [Fortune favours the brave]

clapped his cloake about his left hand which he boldly thrust into the Lyons mouth as he came gaping towards him, & with his right hand slue him, & so finally by this meanes escaped free from danger. Afterwards he sent Officers for the two Canons with commandement to apprehend them, and to see them incontinently hanged. Which was accordingly performed.'

It was no mere coincidence that the townsfolk had chosen the discomfiture of the Archbishop's adherents and the triumph of the Burgomaster as a fitting decoration for the Rathaus portico. Between the Archbishop, who was the temporal ruler of the widespread territories comprising the Electorate, and the City, which enjoyed the status of a Free City of the Empire, there was an age-long and perpetual feud. Internal dissension on politico-religious matters had contributed more than any other factor to Cologne's degeneracy.

This decline was reflected in her Cathedral. The foundation stone had been laid in the middle of the thirteenth century and for two hundred years the building had advanced. Then enthusiasm had subsided; the choir was completed, but of the two great towers which were to be five hundred feet high, one had been raised to about two hundred feet while the other remained a mere stub. When Coryate saw it no progress had been made for decades; it 'is a goodly building', he commented, 'but it is a great pitie that it is so imperfect. For it is but halfe ended.' It was to remain in much the same state, though becoming increasingly dilapidated, for the next two centuries and more.

Cologne was famous throughout Christendom for holy relics. Coryate saw them all; one of his first visits was to the Church of St. Ursula 'because shee was my countrywoman. For she was a Brittane borne.' He found the bones of the Saint reposing in an impressive stone sepulchre except for her head which was in a gold case above the high altar. The bones of the eleven thousand virgins martyred with her were distributed all over the Church lying 'in great heaps together. Under them are placed their skuls, all which are covered over with a slight kind of covering.' Even so there was not room for all and some were housed in the Church of the Maccabees 'in which they report the Bones of that holy mother of the Maccabees and her seven sonnes doe lye . . . Certainly this monument is very memorable, and worthy to be seene by a curious traveller, if a man were sure that those were the true bones of them. For truly for my owne part I will confesse, I love to see these kind of things as much as any man living, especially when I am perswaded that there is no delusion. But indeede there is so great uncertainty in these Papisticall reliques, that a man cannot certainly tell which are true, and which are false.' As the remains of the Seven Maccabean Brethren are also preserved at San Pietro in Vincoli in Rome, Coryate's comment in this context is particularly, though probably unwittingly, apt.

The most famous of all the relics in Cologne were those of the Three Wise Men, 'For what is he of any meane learning or understanding that hath not at some time or other in his life heard of the three Kings of Colen? Therefore because it is so remarkable a

monument, and so much visited by all strangers that come to the
Citie, I observed it after a more strict and curious manner then
every stranger doth. For I wrote out the whole history of them,
and have made as particular a description of the monument as I
could possibly doe. Therefore both the description of the sepulcher wherein the bones of the Kings lie, and the history I present
unto thee for a noveltie. For certainly I for mine owne part never
read it in print before I came thither.'

The Chapel which contained the reliquary is at the east end of
the Cathedral. Inside the Chapel there was a partition at which the
people knelt to make their prayers, or stood to gaze in at the
treasures. Access to the inner part of the Chapel was allowed only
between the hours of six and eight in the morning; here stood the
shrine which Coryate describes as being made of pure, bright,
shining brass raised some six feet from the ground. The shrine,
decorated with images in silver representing the Three Kings in
the act of presenting their gifts, was encrusted with precious
stones[1] 'whereof many are fully as big as my thumbe'.

All who could read Latin might study the history of the Magi
pasted on three tablets hung at the entrance to the Chapel. Coryate, an indefatigable and remarkably accurate collector of inscriptions, copied down every word. The history of the Magi thus
appears verbatim in the *Crudities*, together with Coryate's own
translation into English. There is a curious gap in the history since
nothing whatever is said about their activities during the whole
period of Christ's life after they had presented their gifts. But all
three enjoyed a protracted and vigorous old age:

'After Christes ascension they were more fully instructed by
St. Thomas the Apostle in the faith of Christ, and also baptized,
yea (which is more) they were ordained Pastors and Doctors, or
Bishops of the people amongst whome they lived, and brought a
great company of Gentiles to the worship of Christian religion;
and even as a plentifull harvest doth follow the first fruits: so the
faith of an innumerable multitude of people, as it were most
abundant corne, followed the Magi that were the first fruites of
the beleevers of the Gentiles . . .'

[1] Most of the precious stones disappeared at the end of the eighteenth century when
the reliquary was removed with the intention of ensuring its safety during the French
dominion of the city. At this time the Cathedral itself was turned into a hay store.

'After that in their old age they had departed out of this life, their bodies being brought first to Constantinople by the meanes of the Empresse Helena, then to Milan by Eustorgius, Bishop of that Citie, at last in the yeare after the incarnation of Christ 1164, being translated therhence to this city in the time of Reinolds Archbishop thereof . . . they were reposed in this place.'

The removal of the relics from Constantinople to Milan and their arrival in Cologne in 1164 are accepted as historical facts. Any doubts which Coryate himself may have had about the authenticity of the rest of the story appear to have been stifled by the wealth of biblical and other references adduced in its support. These other references range from Tertullian and Chrysostom to the Venerable Bede; all were faithfully copied down.

When at last he had finished his transcription one of the Canons of the Cathedral who had been watching him at work 'supposing that I was a stranger, and observing that I loved antiquities, invited me with a kinde of courteous and civill importunity to his house, though we never saw each other before, and entertained me with much variety of good cheare'. Since there can be little doubt that Coryate would frankly avow his faith, the Canon's kindness is another example of Christian charity transcending the bitterness of feeling between Catholics and Protestants. Such bitterness was particularly pronounced in Cologne where in that very year 1608 all Protestants had been deprived of their civic rights.

Religion was politics, and this of course held good in Britain just as much as it did on the Continent. Coryate saw exhibited for sale in Cologne 'the picture of our famous English Jesuite Henry Garnet . . . whose head was represented in that miraculous figure imprinted in a straw, as our English Papists have often reported. A matter that I perceive is very highly honoured by divers Papists beyond the seas.' Garnet, who was incidentally a fellow Wyke-hamist, though over twenty years senior to Coryate, had been tried on suspicion of being implicated in the Gunpowder Plot, and was executed in 1606. A devout young Catholic named Wilkinson, who was about to cross to the Continent to enter the Jesuit College at St. Omer, felt compelled to witness the execution with the intention of acquiring some relic of the martyr, and if possible of being hallowed by his blood. Garnet was, according to custom, first hanged, then beheaded, drawn, and quartered. When the quarters were thrown into the large basket filled with straw, an ear of corn spattered with blood dropped from the scaffold on to the young man, Wilkinson, below. He took it home and carefully preserved it.

Some days later when examining the straw he was astonished to see on one of the empty husks a minute likeness of Garnet. He showed this to the Catholics with whom he was lodging; tongues wagged, the story laid hold of people's imagination, and soon it was rumoured up and down the land that a miracle had been performed. The story continued to grow; the straw was said to have effected wondrous cures, and there were the most disquieting reports alleging that many hundreds of people had forsaken the Protestant faith and been converted to Catholicism by the mere sight of 'Garnet's Straw'. This was so embarrassing to the Government that the Archbishop of Canterbury was requested by the Privy Council to institute an enquiry which opened in November 1606. The straw itself had disappeared and was never produced at the enquiry, the main object of which seems to have been not to deny the existence of the miniature portrait, but to establish that divine power had not etched the traitor's head, and that it had in fact been contrived by human ingenuity. Artists were called as witnesses to testify that this was possible.

In the meantime prints[1] were made of the straw which showed two faces on the one husk, the face of Garnet, encircled in some cases with a martyr's crown, and the face of a cherub appearing in the midst of his beard. Thus depicted, 'Garnet's straw' became generally known throughout the Christian world. Sir Henry Wotton wrote from Venice in December 1607 to Sir Thomas Edmondes, the British Ambassador at Brussels, 'For your picture of Garnet and his straw received in your last . . . I do very much thank you', and nearly two years later Wotton writing to James I from Venice says: 'being in all event . . . even at the highest, consideration not above the value of Garnet's straw'.[2] Coryate's own verdict was sceptical as might be expected: 'I thinke the

---

[1] That reproduced here is from Henry Foley, *Records of the English Province of the Society of Jesus*, London, 1878, vol. IV, p. 133. At p. 199 Foley gives Wilkinson's own account. Another representation of the straw, in an upright position, is in the Public Record Office, S.P. 14. 216, Nʳ 218B.

[2] L. P. Smith, *op. cit.*, vol. I, p. 475.

truth of it is such that it may be well ranked amongst the merry tales of Poggius the Florentine.'[1]

Apart from being relatively quick and cheap, there was added safety in travelling by water. Coryate had already seen something, and heard more, of the deplorably lawless state existing in these territories around Cologne which were on the fringe of the war zone. He was now about to enter the main area of conflict where the official armistice appeared to be very near an end. From Cologne, therefore, he took ship once more and continued his journey down the Rhine. With him were five companions. One, Christopher Hagk, had come with him all the way from Mainz. He hailed from Königsberg, and was 'sonne and heire of the high Consul of the Citie. A sociable and pleasant Gentleman, and one that had beene a traveller for the space of a dozen years in the famousest regions of Christendome, as Germany, France, Italy, England, Denmark, Poland &c. He ministred great delight unto me with his elegant learning.' The other four were Englishmen: Peter Sage and James Tower of London, and William Tassell, a Cambridgeshire man, were all returning from Frankfurt Fair, while Richard Savage of Cheshire was on his way home from Munich, where he had been studying at the University. On the day of their departure from Cologne they made little progress and spent the night at a 'solitary house' eight miles beyond the city. They left at 3 a.m. the next morning and called at Düsseldorf, where Coryate had sufficient time to admire the exterior of the Ducal palace.

A little outside Düsseldorf he saw 'a certaine instrument that is very frequently used in these parts, called a crane, which serveth for the drawing up of vessels [containers] and such other things of very weighty burden, to the land from out of boates'. What Coryate saw was no doubt similar to the old Rhine crane which still exists a few miles up the river at Andernach. Indeed he must have seen that very crane four days previously since it was built in 1554, and remained in use until 1911. It is a sturdy circular, stone-built tower of pleasing proportions surmounted by a rotating turret from which projects the long slanting jib of the crane. Manpower, harnessed to a giant tread-wheel within the

---

[1] A reference to the best-known work of Poggio, later self-styled Bracciolini (1380–1459), *Liber Facetiarum*, a collection of humorous stories mainly against monks and secular clergy.

tower, raised and lowered the heavy weights—from Andernach they were mainly millstones for export to Holland—while another tread-wheel, similarly operated, swung the jib and its turret. Coryate justifies his mention of the machine near Düsseldorf by saying 'it was the most beautiful of that kinde that I saw in al Germanie', and if it was as fine as the crane at Andernach the adjective 'beautiful' is not inappropriate.

Between Duisburg and Rheinberg he makes the first mention of actual war damage: 'the lamentable tokens of the Belgicke Warres, three Churches very miserably battered and sacked, which was done by the souldiers of the Grave Maurice'. The War in the Netherlands had been going on since long before Coryate was born; it was forty years since the Duke of Alva had arrived to put down the revolt. All the leading figures of those days were dead. The present commander-in-chief of the Netherlands forces, Prince Maurice, the Stadholder, had been born in the year before Alva's arrival and the Marquis Spinola, the Genoese who commanded the Spanish forces, was two years younger than Maurice. It had ceased to be a shapeless civil war and had become a war along the frontiers of the United Provinces. Since 1606 all the territory bounded on the south by the Waal, on the east by the Yssel, and on the north and west by the sea, had become an impregnable Netherlands fortress.

Towards the end of 1606 the first peace feelers had been extended by Spain. The war was costing her 300,000 dollars a month and such sums were no longer forthcoming from her Treasury. Her soldiers were unpaid and mutinous. At home the almost imbecile Philip III was utterly in the power of the Duke of Lerma, whose first consideration was amassing wealth for himself. The whole Spanish administration was rotten. Although 70,000 men appeared on the pay-roll of the Army, there were only 30,000 in the field. The Dutch were also impoverished but they were by no means exhausted.

The first tentative approach by the Spanish intermediaries at the end of 1606 had resulted in the announcement of an armistice which was to run for eight months from May 1607 while commissioners conferred on the possibilities either of a peace or alternatively of a truce lasting for a period of years. The preliminary negotiations were so protracted that the armistice had to be extended and it was the end of January 1608 before Spinola

17. Garnet's Straw. From a 17th-century engraving.

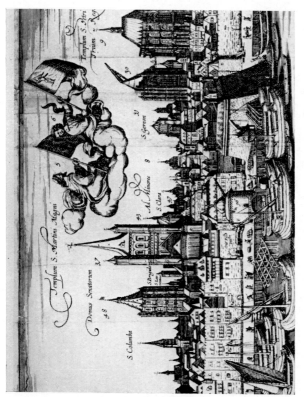

16. Cologne. Part of a view from the Rhine by Petrus Kaerius, Amsterdam, 1613, in the British Museum. The domed tower on the wharf is a crane of the type described on p. 101. The cathedral is in the right background.

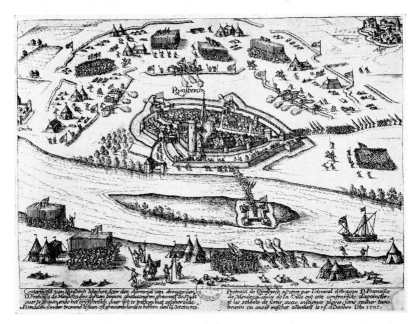

18. Rheinberg besieged by the Spanish forces, 14 October 1598. From a print published in 1605(?) in the British Museum, press mark 29740 (2).

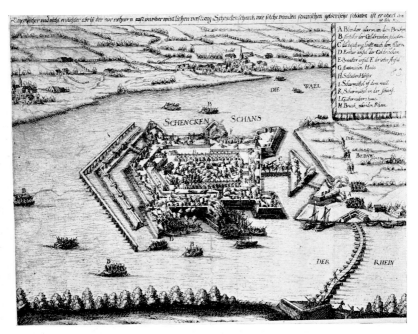

19. Schenkenschanz. The fortress being captured 28 July 1635. From an engraving in the British Museum, press mark Maps C.7. e.4. (61).

and the Spanish Commissioners arrived at The Hague. Talks continued for two months but by the end of March a deadlock had been reached. Prince Maurice, infuriated by what he regarded as prevarication on the part of the Spaniards, grudgingly agreed to renew the armistice during April and May.

During May, the month in which Coryate set out from England, there was fierce dissension between the Dutch war party led by Prince Maurice and the peace party led by Oldenbarnevelt. It looked as though the war party would have its way but at the eleventh hour Oldenbarnevelt managed to persuade Prince Maurice and his supporters to agree to a compromise. If the negotiations had still reached no definite result by 1 August 1608, they should forthwith be broken off and the war should be resumed. In fact 1 August came and went while the Dutch and Spanish delegations continued to wrangle. Eventually what appeared to be the decisive conference was held on 20 August and this ended in uproar. On 25 August the rupture was formally announced and the Spanish Commissioners were told that the war would continue unless the King of Spain acknowledged the absolute independence of the United Provinces before the end of September.

Coryate left Cologne on 21 September and thus arrived in the Netherlands at a most critical juncture. It looked as though the Armistice which had lasted for the past seventeen months had little more than a week to run, and both sides were girding themselves for battle.

Immediately upon their arrival in Rheinberg, which was occupied by a Spanish garrison, Coryate and his friends were left in no doubt that they had entered the war zone for, to their 'great terrour and amazement', they were all arrested. However, after two hours they were brought before the Governor of the town 'who was a Spanish Gentleman, a man that used us more graciously than we expected. For after a few termes of examination he gently dismissed us.'

Coryate was told that the sadly battered condition of the town was due to Prince Maurice and his soldiers. It is true that Maurice in person had twice besieged and taken the town. On the second occasion in 1601 he had exploded a mine which, besides doing immense damage to the fortifications, had blown one of the defenders almost unharmed into the Dutch camp and this man had given valuable intelligence which shortened the siege. But the most recent damage had been done when Spinola retook Rheinberg just two years prior to Coryate's visit. In any case the town had changed hands so many times in the previous twenty years that Coryate's informant must either have been a prejudiced party, or must have felt it prudent to place the blame for the devastation squarely on the enemies of the current possessors.

Rejoicing at their release by the Spanish Governor, Coryate and his friends sailed on past Wesel, where they saw many ships at anchor in the Lippe. Shortly afterwards they passed some deserted trenches and earthworks in an open field where the Dutch Army had taken up position. At about seven o'clock that evening they disembarked at Rees. Their troubles that day were not yet over for they found the gates of the town already locked and all their efforts to gain entry proved unavailing. The weather had deteriorated and they were cold and hungry, yet there seemed to be nothing for it but to go to one of the ships lying at the quay and 'take a hard lodging there all night upon the bare boordes. No sooner were we in the ship but I beganne to cheare my Companie as well as I could with consolatorie termes, and pronounced a few verses and fragments of verses out of Virgil, tending to an exhortation to patience in calamities, as:

*Quicquid erit, superanda omnis fortuna ferendo est'*[1]

Soon, however, they received more effective consolation than could be derived from Latin quotations. Their remonstrances at the gate had after all not been in vain; news of their plight had been brought to the burgomaster, who sent two soldiers with loaded muskets to examine them; 'and so after a few termes of examination they kindly conducted us to our inne, and that to our infinite comfort. For we were all most miserably weatherbeaten and very cold, especially I for mine own part who was almost ready to give up the ghost through cold. But when we came to our inne we were exceedingly refreshed with all things convenient for the comforting of distressed travellers.' All things, that is, except uninterrupted rest, for throughout the night at every hour the watch blew loudly upon a horn.

Next day the weather was so boisterous and the Rhine so rough

[1] Ænei. 5 [Coryate's note], line 710, Nautes speaking to Aeneas: 'whatever befall all fortune is to be o'ercome by bearing.'

that it was impossible to embark; Coryate spent the day in Rees admiring the brick houses with battlemented ends and pacing out the measurements of the market place—a favourite pastime. The following morning the weather had moderated and the boat was able to sail. They stopped for a few hours at Emmerich and arrived that afternoon at Nijmegen.

The Rhine followed a different course in those days. Rheinberg, for example, is now some distance from the river, and Schenkenschanz, now a country village, was an island at the point of bifurcation where the Rhine became the Waal and the Rhine. Furthermore, Schenkenschanz (Schenk's Fort) was not then a village but, as Coryate was told, one of the strongest fortresses in the whole of Europe. Its builder, Martin Schenk, came of an ancient and noble family of Gelderland. As a youth he had fought for William of Orange, but had then changed sides, purely for material gain, and in Parma's service had risen to high military command. After some years he transferred his allegiance once more and from 1585 until his death four years later, during an audacious midnight attack on Nijmegen, he was the terror of the Electorate of Cologne. He received an English knighthood for his prowess on the battlefield but he was the cruellest and most rapacious of those freebooters whom Coryate described as 'the very Hyenae and Lycanthropi of Germany'.

Schenk had made a contract with the States to defend Rheinberg and all the country round with his private army of 3,300 foot and 700 horse. In return he received 20,000 florins a month, the revenue from taxation on all vessels going up and down before Rheinberg and, most important of all, the 'brandschatz'. There is no exact translation of this term into English; it was in effect the indiscriminate blackmail of the unfortunate inhabitants, who were forced to pay cash in return for not having their houses burnt down, their property stolen, and their throats slit. Based on his island fortress, he ranged far up the Rhine beyond Cologne. He was never sober yet he never smiled; he could spend days and nights at a stretch in the saddle. His troops obeyed him like hounds and were treated like hounds; he gave and took no quarter and his men, if captured, paid their ransom with their heads. Although he had by this time been dead for nearly twenty years, it was not only by his fortress that he was remembered. As Coryate reported, the Electorate of Cologne was still subject to the savagery of marauders who had learnt their trade from Schenk.

Nijmegen had been taken for the Spaniards by Schenk when he had been one of Parma's Generals, and he had lost his life in trying to re-take it for the Republic. But where Schenk had failed Maurice succeeded two years later, and ever since it had been strongly held by Dutch forces. 'When I was in Nimmigen', says Coryate, 'there was a great garrison of soldiers planted there that consisted of three thousand men of armes, who did continually watch and ward for the defence of the City.' The garrison was divided into twenty companies, of which three were English. The triumph of the Republic had been to weld together into a splendid fighting machine an army composed not only of native Netherlanders but also English, Scots, Irish, Germans, and French. One of the reasons for their success was prompt weekly payment at extraordinarily high rates: private soldiers received two florins a week.[1] The English troops and most of their officers were professional soldiers of fortune, but some were young aristocrats campaigning for a season in order to study the art of war as part of their education. English mercenaries fought on the Spanish side as well; indeed both the opposing armies contained professional soldiers from almost every country in Europe.

Forty years of warfare had not impoverished Nijmegen, a busy commercial centre inhabited by many wealthy merchants, and the province of Gelderland, of which Nijmegen was the capital, gave Coryate the impression of being immensely rich and fertile. 'It is said that the whole Province is so plaine, that there is not as much as one hill of any note to be seene in it. Againe, all this plain is so exceedingly furnished with abundance of wood, that there are few vacant places unwooded. Besides it is esteemed so fertile a Territory that it bringeth forth all manner of commodities whatsoever, saving wine. For two thinges it is very memorable. For the admirable store of corne that it yeeldeth, and the goodly pastures and meadowes for fatting of Cattel. For the which it is so famous, that sometimes leane cattell are sent hither to grazing from the farthest confines of Denmarke. Also it is well watered with these three famous Rivers, the Rhene, the Maze and the Waal, and so populous that it containeth twenty two walled townes, and three hundred villages.' These statements, and some others concerning

[1] J. L. Motley, *The United Netherlands*, London, 1869, vol. IV, p. 623.

the Netherlands, are taken by Coryate from L. Guicciardini, *Descrittione di tutti i paesi bassi*, first published in 1567.[1]

Food and drink were plentiful and not particularly expensive, but the Netherlanders' eating and drinking habits were different from those which Coryate had met with in High Germany and from those to which he was used at home. 'One of their customes I much disliked, that they sit exceeding long at their meales, at the least an howre and halfe. And very seldome do they go to supper before seven of the clocke.' In England supper was usually served about five-thirty and was generally a shorter and simpler meal than dinner, which was eaten between eleven and twelve. 'It is their custome in the Innes to place some few peeces of browne bread hard by the guests trencher, and a little white loafe or two. In many places also at the beginning of dinner or supper they bring some martlemasse [salt] beef (which custome is used also in some places of the Grisons countrie as I have before mentioned), and a good pestle of bacon to the table, before they bring any other thing. This I observed at Colen, Rees, and other places: at the ende of the meal they alwaies bring butter . . . They usually drink beere & not Rhenish wine . . . For they have no wine in their country . . . whensoever one drinketh to another, he shaketh his fellow by the hand, and whensoever the men of the country come into an Inne to drinke, they use to take a tinnen tankard full of beere in their hands, and sit by it an howre together, yea sometimes two whole howres before they will let their tankards out of their hands.'

From Nijmegen he took ship once more and sailed down the Waal. All the way to Dordrecht he saw 'on both sides of the Waell . . . a great company of little castels or Forts not above an English mile distant asunder, which they call *Ridouts* wherein presidiarie soldiers doe lie for the defence of the country, fifty persons or thereabouts in each'. He was told that the object of these forts was to prevent marauders crossing the river into the States' territories by night, kidnapping some notable man, and holding him to ransom. In fact their primary purpose was much more important. The Waal had become the southern frontier of

---

[1] I am indebted to Dr. E. S. de Beer for pointing this out. It seems, incidentally, that Fynes Moryson used the same source, cf. *Itinerary*, vol. IV, p. 51: 'great Heards of Cattle brought thither [to Gelderland] out of Denmarke to be sold, and for great part fatted here.'

the Republic and Coryate was passing down the front line between the two armies. The river itself was patrolled by armed
vessels of the Republic.

Apart from the garrisoned forts there were few signs of the
war, though as he passed by Zaltbommel he 'saw a great bullet
strucke in the Tower of their Church, even about the toppe, which
was shot by the enemy in the yeare 1574, which figures (1574)
are subscribed in such great characters under the bullet, that a
man may very plainly discerne them afarre off'.[1] When he came
to Gorinchem, where he spent the night, he was charmed by its
mature and orderly peacefulness. 'The sweetnesse of the situation,
the elegancy of their buildings, the beauty of their streets, and
and all things whatsoever in this town, did wonderfully delight
me, in so much that as soone as I entred into one of the longer
streets, me thought I was suddenly arrived in the Thessalian
Tempe, or the Antiochian Daphne . . . And I observed some
of their streets to be passing beautifull, both for breadth and length.
And they are much graced by the fayre brick pavier. For every
streete is very delicately paved with bricke, which is composed
after that artificiall manner that a man may walke there presently
after an exceeding shower of raine, and never wet his shooes.
The buildings are all of brick, of a goodly heigth, and an excellent
uniformity in most of the streets, the toppes rising with battlements. I observed that these kinde of prety buildings are of a just
correspondency on both sides of the streets, which doe minister
notable beauty to the towne. Their market place is very spacious
and neatly paved with bricke like to the streets. At one side whereof there is a faire Stadt-house adorned with a beautifull turret,
from the toppe of which I heard it credibly reported by a Gentleman of good note, a man may plainly perceive in a faire day two
and twenty goodly walled townes, together with many faire
villages and Gentlemens Palaces in the county.'

Although there were a few signs of war damage, Coryate soon
saw the remains of a different kind of devastation, which had been
even more costly in human life and wealth and even more permanent in its effects. In April 1421 the sea had swept through

---

[1] This bullet was fired during an unsuccessful attack on the town by the Spanish
General Hierges on 20/21 August 1574. The bullet and date have been removed but
the church tower still exists. See F. A. J. Vermeulen, *De monumenten van geschiednis
en kunst in de provincie Gelderland . . .*, 's Gravenhage, 1932, p. 200.

what is now the Hollandsch Diep. The Maas, Waal, Linge, and Merwede, had all broken their banks; seventy-two market towns and villages had been inundated, and upwards of 100,000 people were drowned. The Saint Elizabeth flood, as it came to be called, created a great reed forest (Biesbosch) between Gorinchem and Dordrecht, and made Dordrecht itself into an island. Some of the inundated villages had been redeemed but Coryate was still able to see, nearly two hundred years later, 'the pitifull tokens' of this catastrophe. 'For I saw many Churches half drowned, all the upper part of the tower appearing very plainly above the water . . . Moreover I sawe a faire Castell drowned a little on this side Dort [Dordrecht], which in former times belonged to a noble man of the country. It was seated in a faire towne, which hapned to be so overwhelmed with water . . . that there remayneth not the least stone thereof to be seene, saving only a part of the foresaid Castell.'

The port of Dordrecht was still one of the richest towns in Holland and had long held the privilege of acting as an entrepôt between the rest of Holland and the outer world for wine, corn, timber, and other goods moving down the Rhine. 'For traffique I have heard that this towne doth more flourish then any other in Holland, saving famous Amsterdam. And the Merchants of the towne are said to be very wealthy. For heere is the principle Staple of Holland for all manner of Wines, especially the noble Rhenish Wine, from whence it is afterward transported into divers remote regions, as to England &c. But,' adds Coryate, 'the greatest part of it being first sophisticated in Dort with their &c. confections.'

Dordrecht's commercial eminence made it a cosmopolitan town; of its four churches two belonged to the citizens, one to the French, and one to the English. Ties with England were not solely of a commercial nature; Coryate notes that the garrison consisted of five companies, one of which was English.

The buildings, both sacred and civil, were all built of brick, and were 'garnished with those kind of pretie battlements that are so much used in the Batavian Cities'. He particularly admired the Mint, and carefully copied down the oracular Latin mottoes inscribed on its façade. Forty years of war lent them a peculiar irony: *Omnia pecuniâ effici possunt* was balanced by *Pecuniâ vincere speciosum non est*, and *Pecunia mater belli* by *Paci semper est consulendum*.[1] The other building which specially impressed him was 'the Doole'—Doelen, the old Dutch word for a shooting range, where the militia used to practice their marksmanship—'a very magnificent building, in which the Grave Maurice his Excellencie doth use to lie whensoever he is commorant in Dort'. Coryate adds, should it be thought odd that the commander-in-chief lodged in a shooting range, that Prince Maurice did on occasion put up at the Peacock Inn which had also been patronized by the opposing commander-in-chief, the Marquis Spinola. Dordrecht lay on the direct route to The Hague, where the peace negotiations were being held, and Spinola had made several journeys to and fro.

Coryate was still accompanied by William Tassell, the merchant from Cambridgeshire, and Richard Savage, the student from Munich. With them he embarked in a sailing ship about noon on Tuesday, 27 September. Leaving the island of Schouwen on their right hand, they sailed past Bergen-op-Zoom and anchored for the night in the vicinity of Terneuzen. On the way they saw a great multitude of peasants constructing a dike with earth and straw, labouring to prevent a recurrence of the appalling disasters to which this flat, low, sea-fringed land was subject. Here, too, they saw many more church towers sticking out of the water. Coryate took these to be further reminders of the flood in 1421 but they were now sailing over the Verdronken Land—the Drowned Land created in 1532 by a single flood in which three thousand people perished.

Although they left their anchorage off Terneuzen early in the morning it took them all day until six o'clock in the evening to beat up nine miles against the wind to Arnemuiden, where they disembarked and spent the night. Arnemuiden is now an inland township and all the surrounding land is under tillage, but it was then a great harbour. 'For there al the Ships that come from Dort do arrive, as in a safe station, & therehence many a great fleete doth often launch forth into the Ocean Sea.'

Next morning Coryate and his two companions walked to

---

[1] 'All things are capable of accomplishment with money'—'It is no fine thing to conquer with money'—'Money is the mother of war'—'Peace is always to be recommended.' By some curious misunderstanding of information supplied to him, Coryate states that both the Mint and the Doelen were built by the Earl of Leicester, which is quite untrue. His description of both buildings is enhanced by the fact that the Mint has been altered out of recognition and the Doelen was demolished in 1857.

Middelburg, which had specially close and ancient ties with England. Chaucer's Merchant 'Wold the sea was kept for anything
Betwix Middleburgh and Orewell', that is, he wanted the sea kept
open to trade between Holland and Suffolk. The course of trade
had long been to import raw cloth from England, dress and dye
it in the Netherlands, and then re-export it to England. Middelburg had grown and flourished with this traffic, but recently
the States General had deprived the town of its exclusive right
of deposit for the cloths imported from England. At the time of
Coryate's visit the trade had been still further upset by England's
prohibition of the export of undyed cloths, and by Dutch retaliatory legislation which imposed a ban on the import of English
cloth which had been dyed. Nevertheless the English merchants
resident in Middelburg maintained a fine house there, waiting for
the good times to come again.

Coryate gives no detailed description of the town but he did
visit 'the house of our English Merchants, which is a faire building having delicate gardens and walkes belonging to it' from which
it may be surmised that he had some business to transact with the
merchants. He might have arranged to draw cash from them, or
perhaps he had been advised to apply to them for a passage on a
ship leaving for England.

Whatever his business was, it was soon settled and he walked
on that afternoon to Flushing. 'The towne is not great: yet very
faire, and beautified with many stately buildings, that are made
all of bricke, according to the rest of the Zelandish and Holland-
ish cities. It is inhabited with many rich Merchants that have within these fewe yeares very much inriched themselves by the art of
navigation.' This was exactly true. Coryate estimated that there
were no less than two hundred ships in the harbour when he was
there. Trade had flourished and expanded under the Republic,
but in the Spanish provinces agriculture, commerce, and manu-
factures had all withered away. The result of the obedience of
Brabant and Flanders to Spanish rule had been their commercial
ruin. Antwerp, so recently the commercial centre of the world,
had sunk into listless impoverishment because the mouth of the
Scheldt was controlled by Flushing, and since 1585 Flushing had
been held by the English as a surety for the Republic's debt to
the English Crown.

The English garrison in Flushing provided him with enter-

tainment and spectacle during the couple of days he was there
waiting for a ship. A kindly reception by Sir Thomas Browne,
the military commander and deputy-governor, tickled his vanity
and his imagination was touched by a parade of troops at the
funeral of one of the English officers who was buried 'with a dol-
full beating of many drummes, and discharging of many volleys
of shot'.

Saturday 1 October had been set as the day on which the war was
to be resumed if the Spanish Commissioners could give no satisfactory answer to the States' demands. In fact the negotiations did
not utterly break down and eventually culminated in the truce
agreement the following year. But on that Saturday many of the
leaders on both sides felt that a resumption of hostilities was inevitable. If Coryate was aware of the crisis he makes no mention
of it. He merely records that he embarked about four o'clock
in the afternoon and 'enjoyed a very pleasant and prosperous gale
of winde all the way' to London. The favouring wind blew him
over the Channel and up the Thames into the heart of the City
so that he disembarked on Monday 3 October 1608 at the Custom
House, between the Tower of London and Billingsgate, just
forty-eight hours after leaving Flushing.

# CHAPTER IX

# *The* Crudities *and the* Crambe

CORYATE allowed himself a few days' recreation among his friends in London before completing the last stage to Odcombe. He says that these friends greeted him with open arms and sent him on his way to Somerset with a joyful heart.[1]

After an absence of several months from a well-loved home, the slightest change seems to be for the worse; even a new thatched roof is enough to cause offence to the eye which remembered only its previous state of comfortable decay. At his home-coming Coryate had to accustom himself to a more momentous alteration in circumstances. Only a few days previously, on 2 October, while he had been crossing the Channel, his mother had remarried. That the ceremony should have taken place so soon before his return suggests that mother and son were out of touch with each each other's plans, which is more than likely, or that his mother suspected that he would dislike the match. Nothing is known about the new husband except that his name was John Salmon, and he probably did not come from Odcombe.[2] There is no question of any permanent estrangement between mother and son; it is clear from his letters that he remained loving and dutiful, but he continued to address these letters to 'Mrs. Coryate', and added greetings to 'your husband' as an afterthought, so he may have felt more than the normal antipathy towards his stepfather. It seems probable that on her remarriage Coryate's mother removed to Yeovil; she was certainly living there a few years later. She had a long life, and towards the end of it, in 1642, she was living at Sherborne in Dorset. Her body was buried near that of her first husband in Odcombe Church on 3 April 1645.[3]

---

[1] Letter to Gaspar Waser, *Crudities*, vol. II, p. 119.

[2] Odcombe Parish Register (Bishop of Bath & Wells transcript).

[3] Coryate's Letter No. 6 from India is addressed to 'Mrs. Garthered Coriat at her house in the Town of Evill'. For her residence in Sherborne see *Aubrey's Brief Lives*, ed. Andrew Clark, Oxford, 1898, vol. I, p. 188. The date and place of her burial are given by Wood, *op. cit.*, vol. I, p. 335.

To this church on the hill where he had been baptized, where his father lay buried, and where his mother's new marriage had been solemnized, Coryate went to give thanks to God for his safe return. He took with him the clothes which he had worn on on his travels including the shoes which had carried him all the way to Venice and back, and obtained permission from the Rector to hang them up as a memorial in the church. While this may have been a gesture of genuine thanksgiving, its oddity was nicely calculated to attract notice and to evoke memories of William Kemp the comedian, who danced from London to Norwich and hung up his shoes in Norwich Town Hall. The parallel between Kemp the professional clown and Coryate the amateur buffoon is drawn in the verses which Sir John Strangwayes composed for the *Crudities*:

> 'Kemp yet doth live, and only lives for this
> Much famous, that he did dance the Morris
> From London unto Norwich. But thou much more
> Doest merit praise.'[1]

Coryate had an illustration of his empty clothes included in the title page of the *Crudities*, and Henry Peacham submitted a drawing of the shoes which was reproduced in the *Crudities* together with Peacham's verses. Several other contributors of verses to the *Crudities* mentioned the episode. Sir Henry Nevill of Abergavenny wrote:

> 'Unto thy shoes, thy shirt thy fustian case
> That hang at Odcombe, trophees of thy travels
> Joyne this fayre book of thine.'

Thomas Farnaby may have examined the illustrated title page[2] and noticed the animal life crawling on, and dropping from, the clothes:

> 'Which shirt, which shoes, with hat of mickle price,
> His fustian case, shelter for heards of lice . . .
> Hang Monuments of eviternall glory, at
> Odcombe, to th'honour of Thomas Coryate.'

[1] *Crudities*, vol. I, p. 34. Kemp, a member of Shakespeare's company of actors, was the original performer of the parts of Peter in *Romeo & Juliet*, and Dogberry in *Much Ado about Nothing*. He performed his dance in February 1599–1600, taking twenty-three days, of which nine were spent in actual dancing on the road, hence the title of his own account *Nine Daies Wonder Performed in a Dance from London to Norwich*, ed. Alexander Dyce, Camden Society, 1840.

[2] It is clear from other contributors' verses that the title page was printed and distributed some time before the *Crudities* was published.

Ben Jonson concentrated on the famous shoes, which remained hanging in the church until the beginning of the eighteenth century:[1]

'How well and how often his shoes too were mended,
That sacred to Odcombe are now there suspended,
I meane that one paire, wherewith he so hobled
From Venice to Flushing, were not they well cobled?'

Even Shakespeare may have made reference to this association of Coryate with his shoes since in *Measure for Measure* (Act IV, Sc. III) 'brave Master Shoe-tie the great traveller' is named among the occupants of the Duke's prison. But if this is indeed an allusion to Coryate it is doubtful whether Shakespeare himself was responsible for it since the play was produced in 1604, and 'Master Shoe-tie' must have been introduced as a topical note sometime between 1608 and 1623 when the text was printed for the first time.

If his mother removed to Yeovil, Coryate did not follow her there but established himself at Odcombe and immediately began to make a book out of his bundles of notes. To supplement these and his own recollections he borrowed freely from existing works. For Italy he made extensive use of F. Schott's *Itinerarium Italiae* though he does not make any specific acknowledgement: 'For seeing I made very short aboade in divers faire Italian Cities, as Cremona, Mantua etc . . . I held it expedient to borrow some few notes from a certaine Latin booke printed in Italie, rather then to write so briefly of the same, as the shortnesse of time would not otherwise permit me.'[2] His descriptions of Cremona and Mantua are in fact drawn largely from Schott. There are clear cases of translation or copying from this book elsewhere in his accounts of Venice and other Italian cities, not only of historical

---

[1] Odcombe folk talk to this day as though the shoes had only been taken down in recent times, but from a note in Philip Bliss's edition of *Wood's Athenae*, London, 1815, vol. II, p. 214, it appears that they were certainly no longer there in 1746, and he was told that they had been removed about 1702. Wood implies that only the shoes were ever exhibited. The evidence of the illustration on the title page of the *Crudities* is inconclusive, but Nevill's and Farnaby's verses, which were allowed to stand without any editorial correction by Coryate, indicate that originally all his travelling clothes formed the trophy. Ben Jonson's verses are among those prefacing the *Crambe*.

[2] *Crudities*, vol. I, p. 5.

anecdotes but also of architectural descriptions, classical quotations and some copies of inscriptions. In the chapters on Switzerland and Germany can be traced the same kind of borrowing from the *Cosmography* of Sebastian Münster, to whom he acknowledges his indebtedness.[1] For the section on the Netherlands it is clear that he had access to L. Guicciardini's *Descrittione di Tutti i Paesi Bassi*, probably in the original Italian version, which he would be able to understand adequately even though he could not then speak Italian.

Coryate set about his task in a methodical fashion, expanding his notes to a set pattern. The account of each city is prefaced whenever possible with the remarkably dull verses of Julius Caesar Scaliger (?1484–?1558), the Italian scholar, father of the more famous Joseph Justin Scaliger. Then follow a history of the city from the earliest times, and a general description based mainly on his own observations. Next he gives a detailed word-picture of the main buildings, including the history of each, with a liberal sprinkling of inscriptions. He sometimes adds short biographies of the city's most eminent inhabitants, and often mentions the chief battles fought in and around it. Institutions and forms of government are occasionally alluded to, but this aspect is generally skimped or omitted altogether. In pattern, therefore, the *Crudities* has much in common with a modern book, with the important difference that the whole work is strung upon the thread of his own experiences, and is enlivened by his personal prejudices and individual angle of vision.

It may have become apparent from the quotations already given that Coryate wrote in two quite different styles. His narrative prose is straightforward, vigorous, and rooted in medieval English. The *Crudities* was eventually published in the same year as the *Authorized Version* and one is continually reminded of similarities between the two in phrase and cadence.

His other style stems from study and admiration of classical models and from his training in rhetoric. In Elizabethan and Jacobean times it was considered acceptable to employ the figures of rhetoric in prose. Coryate differed from many of his contemporaries only in the degree to which he exaggerated rhetorical tricks and resorted to an extreme form of euphuism. All the characteristics of euphuism—excessive use of similes drawn from

---

[1] *Crudities*, vol. I, p. 5.

natural history, cross-alliteration, and various kinds of antithesis—
are to be found in the *Crudities*, and, in their extremest form, in
his orations, passages from which are quoted later in this chapter.
It seems that he developed this exaggerated style deliberately as a
personal badge, as a vehicle to show off his wit, and as a means of
self advertisement; sometimes it was intended to amuse, more
often to impress.

An important component of this rhetorical, euphuistic style is
the use of new words adapted from Latin and Greek. During
Coryate's life-time the English language was enormously expanded
with words introduced from the classical languages and from
Italian and French. His contemporaries never hesitated to coin
new words as they felt inclined, and Coryate was no exception.
'He is a great and bold Carpenter of words, or (to expresse him in
one like his owne) a Logodaedale', wrote Ben Jonson.[1] Of the
words which Coryate may claim to have introduced, 'antipriscianisticall', meaning ungrammatical, was still-born; 'lucifuga', a
creature shunning the light, seems to have suffered the same fate.
But 'umbrella', and 'hyperaspist', a defender or champion, have
received the honour of survival; so has 'refocillate', to revive or
refresh, a word which deserves to be better known. There are a
number of other new words which Coryate did not introduce but
which he helped to popularize, such as 'concinnate', 'charlatan', and
'tatterdemalian'. The fact remains, however, that his vocabulary
is limited, particularly as regards adjectives. 'Fair', 'curious',
'wondrous', 'infinite', and 'innumerable' are consistently over-
worked, and too often he falls back on a stock phrase: 'the fairest'
or 'the greatest' or 'the most wondrous . . . that ever I saw in my
life'.

He worked at his book throughout the winter of 1608–9, and
after five months' labour[2] produced a manuscript of some 200,000
words. Length in itself is not necessarily a defect, but the *Crudities*, it must be confessed, is frequently long-winded and often
lacks a sense of proportion. It is bulked out with all sorts of extra-
neous material, such as the exchange of correspondence with his
acquaintances in Switzerland, and his own translations of two
long Latin orations on travel by Hermann Kirchner, Professor of

[1] 'A Character of the Authour', *Crudities*, vol. I, p. 18.
[2] Ben Jonson's verses prefacing the *Crambe*: 'In five monthes he went it, in five
monthes he pend it.'

History and Poetry at Marburg University, the originals of which he must have picked up during his travels.[1]

If the book's faults are obvious, its virtues are manifold. The many quotations already given indicate the quality of the author's observations and the flavour of his prose. The scope, reliability, and, not least, the entertainment value of the *Crudities* gives it an assured place among the best in the literature of travel.

While writing his book Coryate was simultaneously engaged in a law-suit against Joseph Starre, the Yeovil linen-draper. It will be remembered that before leaving England Coryate had deposited £40 with Starre on condition that Starre should pay him 200 marks (£133. 6s. 8d.) if he returned safely from his travels, and fulfilled such other terms as may have been included in their contract, which was embodied in a bill of adventure and a bond drawn by Starre for 200 marks.

When he arrived home Coryate claimed to have carried out his side of the bargain and demanded his money. However, Starre was either unwilling or unable to pay, so Coryate sued him in the Common Law Courts. Starre was evidently advised that there was no effective defence under Common Law to an action on his bond for 200 marks. Coryate held the equivalent of what would today be Starre's post-dated cheque and now that it had fallen due for payment it was comparatively simple for Coryate to obtain judgement in his favour without having to prove the contract on which the drawing of the bond was based.

Faced with this position Starre tried to take advantage of the anomaly which then existed between the Common Law and the Court of Chancery. Common Law worked on a strict and narrow interpretation of rules and precedents, whereas Chancery had some regard for points of equity and took the scantiest notice of precedent. The conflict between the two jurisdictions was acute at about this time, and it was often possible to obtain redress in Chancery where the Common Law gave no relief. Starre therefore submitted a Bill to the Chancery Court asking for an order that the Common Law action started by Coryate should not be allowed

[1] Clare Howard, *English Travellers of the Renaissance*, London, 1914, p. 28, points out that nothing which appears to be the original of the *Oration in Praise of Travel* (*Crudities*, vol. I, p. 122) is given among forty-six works of Kirchner cited by J. G. Jöcher in *Gelehrten-Lexicon*, Leipzig, 1750–87. The *Oration in Praise of Travel in Germany* (*Crudities*, vol. II, p. 71) is listed by Jöcher as *Oratio de Germaniae perlustratione omnibus aliis peregrinationibus anteferenda*.

to proceed; he also asked that his bond for 200 marks should
be qualified or annulled, probably claiming that the obliga-
tions set out in the bill of adventure had not been properly
performed.

Part of Coryate's reply to Starre's Bill appears in the *Crambe*,
and this, together with a document discovered in the Chancery
Records,[1] provide the sources from which this reconstruction of
events has been evolved. Unfortunately Coryate regarded his
reply to the Bill not as an item of interesting autobiographical
material but as a piece of literary composition which was worthy of
preservation. He therefore deliberately omitted all that part of the
reply which discussed the original bargain, and we are left with
little more than the flowery phrases by which he hoped to impress
the Court: 'He [Starre] coacervateth and conglomerateth a meere
farrago of lyes. Also hee traduceth me about the smalnesse and
commonnesse of my Voyage, as having beene out of England but
five moneths. Can he justly call this a small and common Voyage,
to pass almost two thousand miles by land? to expose ones body
to such a world of iminent dangers both by Sea and Land as I did?
to passe those stupendious mountaines of the snowie Alpes? to
dispatch my journey with such a compendious celeritie? to performe it with such a dispendious disadvantage to my estate? &
after the consummation of my travels to be thus opposed by a
Vilipendious Linnen Draper? . . . These perils being considered
I hope your Lordship will say I have as hardly gotten my money
as poore laborious Brickmakers eight pence a day for making
Brick. Wherefore most humbly beseeching your good Lordship
upon the prostrate knees of my heart to have a Christian com-
miseration of my estate that have undergone such a multitude of
difficulties and calamities for the getting of this little wages (little
I may well call it in respect of my great travell), . . . which I
hope no man in the Christian world (except he be partiall) but
will say I have well deserved.'

The case was heard before the Master of the Rolls in May 1609.
How far the Chancery Court was swayed by Coryate's eloquence
is questionable, but it returned a verdict in his favour. It found no
reason in equity to interfere with the course which his Common
Law claim would have taken, and it made an Order that he should

[1] In the Public Record Office; a Chancery Order in the Entry Book of Decrees and
Orders, 1608–9 (C. 33/115), f. 1019.

be paid the amount of the bond and the costs he had incurred in suing upon it.

This apparently successful outcome was, however, no satisfaction to Coryate because Starre could not pay. At this juncture a new character appeared, called curiously enough Richard Rowe, but this Rowe was a real person and not the famous legal fiction of similar name. Rowe was Starre's guarantor, or if not a guarantor, then a person on to whom, for some reason unknown to us, the liability to meet the bond could be shifted and so that Coryate should have a chance of his money the two, Starre and Coryate, contrived 'by confederacye' to go against Rowe.

On 1 July 1609 Rowe sent Counsel into the Chancery Court to contest this attempted claim against him. Counsel advanced various arguments on Rowe's behalf, which are set out in the Chancery record. Here it is sufficient to say that Counsel's submissions found favour with the Court, which directed that the matter be referred to a Chancery Master for further consideration.

How long the case dragged on is not known, and the final outcome is a matter of conjecture. As no more documents appear in the Chancery records it is possible that a settlement was reached out of Court. If the £40 deposited with Starre was the only wager which Coryate made, then we can deduce that he got his 200 marks in the end, and we may also surmise how he spent it since his friend, Christopher Brooke, wrote some months later in the verses which he contributed to the *Crudities*:

> 'The Presse hath spent the three for one you got
> At your returne . . .'

meaning that the money which he won by betting on his safe homecoming had been spent in printing the *Crudities* at his own expense.

Starre, the cause of all the trouble, may have been forgiven, since in a letter which Coryate wrote to his mother from India in October 1616 he asked to be remembered to various people in Yeovil including 'Master Starre and his wife, with the rest of my good friends there', though he could of course be referring to a namesake.

It is very probable that Coryate was in London when his case was heard in May. He was certainly there in August since his letters to Waser and his other Swiss acquaintances announce the

fact though no address is given. It seems clear that he spent most
if not all the next three and a half years, from May 1609 until
October 1612, in and around London. He was already turning over
in his mind plans for further travels which would take him through
Germany and Italy, to the ancient cities of Greece, Constantinople, and the Holy Land, and his original intention was to defer
publication of the *Crudities* until after these further travels had
been completed. For the time being he was content to talk about
his experiences. 'The mere superscription of a letter from Zürich
sets him up like a top: Basil or Heidelberg makes him spinne',
wrote Ben Jonson. 'And at seeing the word Frankford or Venice,
though but on the title of a Booke, he is readie to breake doublet,
cracke elbowes, and overflowe the roome with his murmure . . .
All his Phrase is the same with his manners and haviour, such as
if they were studied to make Mourners merry . . . being not
only the Antidote to resist sadness, but the Preservative to keepe
you in mirth, a life and a day . . . And there is no man but to
enjoy his company, would neglect anything but businesse. It
is thought he lives more by letting out of ayre, then drawing in
(I meane in the fore parts, not the hinder) . . . He is alwaies
Tongue-Major of the company, and if ever perpetuall motion be
to be hoped for, it is from thence. He will aske, How you doe?
Where have you bene? How is it? If you have travelled? How
you like his booke? with, what newes? and be guilty of a thous-
and such curteous impertinencies in an houre, rather then want
the humanity of vexing you.'[1]

It is perhaps not surprising that most subsequent judgements
of Coryate have been based mainly on Ben Jonson's banter. Apart
from Jonson only one other contemporary, the Rev. Edward
Terry, left any assessment of his character: and Terry met Coryate
only a few weeks before Coryate died. Thomas Fuller's account
in *The Worthies of England—Somersetshire* gives the impression of
being founded on first-hand observation, which he certainly did
not possess since he was only four years old when Coryate left
England for the last time. It has been unfortunate for Coryate's
reputation that Fuller's description is one of his raciest and most
entertaining. The fact that some of Fuller's statements are of very
doubtful accuracy must give rise to doubts about the veracity of
his whole picture.

[1] 'A Character of the Authour', *Crudities*, vol. I, pp. 17–18.

Fuller says 'Prince Henry allowed him a pension, and kept him for his servant', but only one payment of £10 can be traced[1] and this was probably a present in return for the copy of the *Crudities* which Coryate presented to him. Ben Jonson is probably telling the truth when he says that Coryate served at Court 'in his owne Cloathes, and at his owne costs' and that 'he conditioned to have no office of charge or neerenesse cast upon him, as a Remora of [hindrance to] his future travaile'.

Coryate says that the decision to publish the *Crudities* before he set out once more on his travels was due to 'the importunity of some of my deare friends who prevailed with me for the divulging of the same: whereof one amongst the rest, namely that right worshipful Gentleman my most sincere and entire friend, M. Lionel Cranfield was the originall and principall animator of me'.

Cranfield, 'a very handsome young man, well spoken and of a ready wit',[2] was two years older than Coryate. In 1597, after a seven-year apprenticeship, he was admitted to the Mercers' Company. Two years afterwards he took the traditional first step to advancement by marrying his master's daughter. The sequel was atypical because later he had to support his father-in-law, but thanks to his great business acumen, he could soon well afford to do so. Besides trading as a Mercer, he became a member of the Levant Company and bought a one-eighth share in the lucrative farm of currants. In 1605 he purchased the Receivership of Crown Revenues in Somerset and Dorset. As the collecting centres were Bath, Yeovil, and Shaftesbury, it is possible that Coryate first met him in Somerset. By 1610 Cranfield already had a foot on the ladder of royal preferment up which he was to climb by way of the Customs, the Mastership of the Great Wardrobe, and the Court of Wards, to become Earl of Middlesex, and Treasurer twelve years later.

The other friend who particularly urged Coryate to publish his book was Laurence Whitaker, Secretary to Sir Edward Phelips of Montacute. Whitaker argued, says Coryate, 'that many sinister accidents might happen unto me betwixt the time of my next going out of England, and my arrivall againe in my Country;

[1] Peter Cunningham, *Extracts from the Accounts of the Revels at Court*, Shakespeare Society, 1842, pp. xvi–xviii.

[2] Godfrey Goodman, *Court of James I*, London, 1839, vol. I, p. 299. For Cranfield's life see R. H. Tawney, *Business & Politics under James I*, Cambridge, 1958.

and so consequently my friends and country might be deprived
of the fruits of my past travels, and of those to come: by these
and such like perswasions of my friends I was animated to publish
the Observations of my travels much sooner then I thought to
have done . . .'[1]

The decision to publish must have been taken some time in
1610. Coryate's next step was to obtain royal recognition and
approval for the book. He received an audience of Prince Henry,
'pronounced an oration unto him before a greate assemblie of
courtiers and withall presented unto him my Journall who soe
graciously accepted it that he hath promised to entertaine the
dedication thereof'.[2]

To illustrate his work Coryate engaged William Hole, who first
appears in 1607, when he executed numerous new maps for the
folio edition of Camden's *Britannia*. Between 1607 and his death,
which almost certainly took place in 1624, he was employed to
decorate more books by distinguished writers than any of his
contemporaries.[3] For the *Crudities* he drew the title page, Coryate
and the Courtesan, the Amphitheatre at Verona, and the portrait
of Frederick IV. All these are signed, and the engraving of the
amphitheatre is dated 1610. Mr. A. M. Hind considers that the
four other plates, the Clock at Strasbourg, the Great Tun at Heidelberg, the Crest of Prince Henry, and the Pembroke Dragon, are
probably also his work, though not signed.[4] In these plates there
are eleven likenesses of Coryate: a head and shoulders and eight
small drawings on the title page; a full-length portrait of Coryate
with the courtesan and a small figure standing on top of the Great
Tun.

None of Hole's engravings in the least corroborate Thomas
Fuller's description of Coryate's personal appearance: 'He carried
folly (which the charitable called merriment) in his very face.
The shape of his head had no promising form, being like a sugar

---

[1] *Crudities, The Epistle Dedicatorie*, vol. I, p. 5.

[2] Letter No. 1 to Sir Michael Hicks.

[3] Hole is also known as the earliest English engraver of music on copper plates;
in 1611 he dedicated to Princess Elizabeth *Parthenia or the Maydenhead of the first
musicke that ever was printed for the Virginalls*. Besides his work for George Chapman,
and for Michael Drayton's *Poly-Olbion*, he did a frontispiece for the *Muses' Sacrifice*,
1613, by John Davis of Hereford, the title page for the 1616 edition of Ben Jonson's
collected works, and a frontispiece for Sir John Hayward's *Sanctuarie of a troubled
Soule*, 1616.

[4] *Engraving in England*, Cambridge, 1955, vol. II, p. 328.

loaf inverted, with the little end before, as composed of fancy and memory, without any common sense.'[1] It is scarcely reasonable to accept Fuller's description, which was not founded on first-hand observation, in preference to Hole, who was an accomplished portraitist. It is true that his brilliant portrait of Prince Henry in *Poly-Olbion* is almost certainly not drawn from life, and may have been copied from Simon Passe, but of his portrait of George Chapman in the *Whole Works of Homer*, 1616, it has been said that it gives 'the air of being an excellent likeness . . . No better portrait of any of the great Elizabethan writers has come down to us.'[2] Coryate himself thought the head and shoulders portrait was a good likeness. There are no other portraits to form a basis for comparison—the woodcuts in the 1616 and 1618 pamphlets described below are small, rough caricatures—but the fact that all Hole's portraits of Coryate bear a close resemblance to each other suggests that they also bear a close resemblance to his subject.

If Coryate looked for a publisher he failed to find one, perhaps on account of the book's length, or simply because nobody had ever written a book quite like this before. It is possible, however, that he never made any attempt to interest a publisher, and was so confident of the book's success that he was prepared from the outset to print the *Crudities* at his own expense even though this meant laying out what was, to him, a large sum of money. Certainly the decision to be his own publisher does not seem to have been a despairing, last moment expedient, since John Donne, John Chapman, and William Austin, as well as Christopher Brooke, all allude to this unusual circumstance in their verses prefacing the *Crudities*.

Coryate invited a score or more of his eminent acquaintances to compose eulogistic verses. But word of what was afoot soon spread and with the encouragement of Prince Henry himself, the courtiers and wits set about composing mock panegyrics with gusto. It became the fashion to make fun of Coryate and his book. Some of the contributors had seen the manuscript, a few had even read it, but it is clear from most of the verses that the authors' knowledge of the *Crudities* was derived from the illustrated title

[1] *Worthies of England—Somersetshire*, ed. John Freeman, 1952, p. 502.
[2] Sir Sidney Colvin, *Early Engraving and Engravers in England*, London, 1905, pp. 90, 95, 96.

page, which was no doubt freely circulated together with copies of the verses which Ben Jonson and Laurence Whitaker wrote to explain the various incidents portrayed. During the ensuing weeks verses poured in, more than half of them unsolicited. There were verses in Greek and Latin, French, Italian and Spanish, Welsh, Macaronic, 'Antipodean', and 'Utopian'. There were verses set to music, verses shaped like an egg; a few were genuinely laudatory, but many were ironical to the point of offensiveness. Coryate became alarmed by both the tone and the number of contributions. 'At last when I saw the multitude of them to increase to so great a number, I resolved to put above a thousand [lines] of them into an Index expurgatorius, and to detain them from the presse. Whereupon the Prince Highnesse (who hath most graciously deigned to be the Hyperaspist[1] and Moecenas of my booke) understanding that I meant to suppresse so many, gave me a strict and expresse commandement to print all those verses which I had read to his Highnesse. Since then that inevitable necessity hath been imposed upon me, I have here communicated that copious rhapsodie of poems to the world that my learned friends have bountifully bestowed upon me: wherein many of them are disposed to glance at me with their free and merry jests, for which I desire thee (courteous Reader) to suspend thy censure of me till thou hast read over my whole booke.'[2]

Dr. Jessopp states that Ben Jonson undertook to edit this extraordinary collection of verses for the press.[3] I can find no corroboration for this and conclude that it was an assumption based on the fact that besides supplying explanations in rhyming couplets for the title page, Jonson wrote a Character of the Author and an Acrostic which appear immediately before, as it were prefacing the panegyric verses. Unlike most of Jonson's references to Coryate, his Acrostic is not uncomplimentary:

> T rie and trust Roger, was the word, but now
> H onest Tom Tell-Troth puts down Roger, How?
> O f travell he discourseth so at large,

[1] Coryate's note (*Crudities*, vol. I, p. 24) reads: 'A word that the author once used in an Oration to the Prince, metaphorically signifying . . . a Patron or Protector. Which word by a kind of conversion may be not improperly implied (as a certaine conceited [clever] Gentleman lately said) to the authour himselfe. Hyperaspist quasi hyperhorspist, that is, one upon whom never Asses pist, but Horses once pist on him, as when he lay upon straw at their heels in Bergomo . . .'

[2] *Crudities*, vol. I, pp. 20, 21.          [3] Article on Coryate in *D.N.B.*

M arry he sets it out at his own charge;
A nd therein (which is worth his valour too)
S hews he dares more than Paules Church-yard durst do.

C ome forth thou bonnie bouncing booke then, daughter
O f Tom of Odcombe that odde Joviall Author,
R ather his sonne I should have cal'd thee, why?
Y es thou wert borne out of his travelling thigh
A s well as from his braines, and claimest thereby
T o be his Bacchus as his Pallas: bee
E ver his thighes Male then, and his braines Shee.

All the evidence points to Coryate himself being responsible for the occasional editorial notes to the verses and for arranging the initial forty-eight contributors in a significant order of precedence.[1] The list is headed by Ἀποδημουντόφιλος (the friend of the sojourner abroad); this friend, who may have been Sir Edward Phelips, probably held the rank of knight at least, since the following twelve contributors are all knights, including Sir John Harrington (Ajax Harrington), Sir Lewis Lewknor, the King's Master of Ceremonies, and Sir Robert Phelips.

Then follows a group, fourteenth to twenty-sixth, which includes those for whom Coryate had a special regard, or with whom he was particularly intimate: John Donne, who supplied seventy-four lines of undeniably harsh comment, and a macaronic quatrain, Richard Martin, who had given Coryate the letter of introduction to Sir Henry Wotton, Laurence Whitaker, Hugh Holland, Christopher Brooke, John Hoskins, Lionel Cranfield, and Inigo Jones.

The next twenty-two names include some well-known figures such as Richard Corbet, Thomas Campion the writer of court masques, John Owen the epigrammatist, Michael Drayton the poet, and the mysterious Glareanus Vadianus, who is less concerned with Coryate and his book than with exhibiting his own knowledge of languages and medicine.

When all these had been set up in type still further verses arrived, eight new contributors including John Davis of Hereford and Henry Peacham, and still more verses by Glareanus Vadianus, whose flights of fancy with mock-learned footnotes help to leaven the lump of pedestrian rhymes, and laboured commentaries on

[1] For notes on the contributors see pp. 267–292 below.

episodes in the *Crudities*, which are characteristic of so many of the contributions. The joke of comparing Coryate with Ulysses wears very thin after several repetitions, but Glareanus strikes a fresh and deliciously nonsensical note:

> 'Tom's a* Bologna sawcidge lovely fat,
> Stuft with the flesh of a Westphalian sow,
> The shoing-horne of wine, that serveth pat
> To make the feeble strong, the strong to bow.

* A French Quelque chose farced with oilet holes, and tergiversations and the first blossoms of Candid Phlebotomie.'

Coryate rounded off all these contributions with thirty-four lines of macaronic verse composed by himself. Three other sets of verses on the *Crudities*, including more lines by Ben Jonson, arrived too late and were printed in the *Crambe*. Thus, excluding Coryate himself, fifty-nine contributions appear in print. Of these at least twenty-five appear in the *Dictionary of National Biography*. About a third have some known connexion with the Court, either as courtiers, or like Ben Jonson, Inigo Jones, and Thomas Campion, through being responsible for Court entertainments. At least eighteen are members of the Inns of Court, particularly Lincoln's Inn and the Middle Temple. There are numerous links with Oxford, Somerset, and the world of letters. At least eight were serving members of Parliament when the *Crudities* was published.

One further difficulty had to be surmounted. A censorship was exercised over all kinds of book production, and before a book could be printed it was necessary to obtain a licence. For books printed in London authority to licence seems at this time to have been delegated by the Crown to the Archbishop of Canterbury and the Bishop of London, who jointly appointed a panel of licensors.[1] Dr. Mocket, Chaplain to the Bishop of London, was a member of the panel and was acquainted with one of Coryate's Somersetshire neighbours, the Rev. John Seward of Yeovil. Coryate persuaded Seward to write to Mocket, enclosing a letter from Laurence Whitaker eulogizing the *Crudities*.[2] This roundabout approach was unsuccessful; no licence was forthcoming

---

[1] W. W. Greg, *Some Aspects and Problems of London Publishing between 1550 and 1650*, Oxford, 1956, pp. 51, 53.

[2] This eulogistic letter is printed in the *Crudities*, vol. I, p. 149.

from Mocket on the rather surprising pretext that the Bishop of London was able to licence only theological works.[1]

Coryate next applied directly to the Archbishop of Canterbury, Richard Bancroft, but to his dismay Bancroft died on 2 November 1610, before issuing the permit.

About this time Coryate attended a dinner party given by Arthur Ingram, a wealthy London merchant and close business associate of Lionel Cranfield. As a Member of Parliament and Comptroller of Customs for the port of London, Ingram was a man of some influence. One of the other guests at this party was Sir Michael Hicks, secretary to Lord Treasurer Salisbury. On the strength of this meeting Coryate decided to write to Hicks asking him to intercede with the Lord Treasurer to obtain the licence.

Coryate's letter to Hicks, dated 15 November, from his chamber in Bow Lane, is of special interest since it is the only extant example of his handwriting—and a remarkably handsome, clear hand it is. At Ingram's dinner party Coryate's wit had been directed rather pointedly at Hicks and the first part of the letter is an apology for this impertinence. He then relates how the book came to be written, why he had decided to publish it, and what unsuccessful steps he had already taken to obtain a licence. Finally he comes to the point and asks that 'you would vouchsafe to intercede for me unto my Lord Treasurer, that it would please his Lordship to give orders it may be printed in London with some expedition; the Prince not only approving yea applauding it together with all those selected flowers of gentilitie that flourish in his Princely Courte, but also earnestly expecting it especially since there is not as much as one line contained in my whole jornall that maketh against our State or any forraine Prince confederate with us, or against religion or good manners, my booke containing principally the most remarkable antiquities of those cities that I have described, yea and so many of them that I hope you will pardon me though I thinke that no man of our nation since the incarnation of Christe hath offered more for the time in the foresayd Countries . . .'

To be doubly sure of getting his licence without further delay Coryate made a direct petition to Prince Henry.[2] Either Hicks moved quickly, or the petition to the Prince bore fruit, since on

---

[1] Letter No. 1 to Sir Michael Hicks.

[2] 'A Petition made To The Prince shortly after the death of the Last Archbishop of Canterburie, concerning the Printing of the Booke of my Travels,' *Crambe*, Sig. A.

20. Autograph letter from Coryate to Sir Michael Hicks. The only known example of his handwriting and signature. The original letter is inserted into the back of Prince Henry's presentation copy of the *Crudities* in the British Museum.

## Incipit Laurentius Whitaker.

*(The enſuing verſes of theſe three Authors were made ſince my booke of Crudities came forth.)*

Courſe Muſicke plaid vpon the Odcombian Hoboy, to attend the ſecond courſe of *Coryats* Coleworts, and *dittied to the moſt melodious Comicall ayre, borne and* brought vp in the Seprentrionall ſuburbs, which the vulgar call, The Punks delight.

Aile bonnet iigging Feſtiuals, of Brittiſh land and others, your proudeſt Tuſcan Carniuals, and yee French Bals their brother: Dutch a *Pappigeay,* and b *Car-mas gay,* in ſeaſon after Eaſter, with Frow and Punke, All reeling drunke, both Boore and Burgomaſter.

Yee Churchales, and ye Morreſſes,
VVith Hobby-horſe aduancing,
Ye Round-games with fine *Sim* and *Sis,*
About the Maypole dancing;

1 A moſt ingenious ſport vſed in the low Countries by Citizēs, where in they vſe ſhooting with Crosbowes at a thing made like a Geay.
b A kind of drunkē Dutch faire held on Sundaies and holidaies in afternoones in Sommer time, both notes vnhappily omitted in the Authors text, which is their proper place.

Ye

21. *Coryat's Crambe.* Page Sig. b.2. Laurence Whitaker's encomiastic verses on the *Crudities* set to music. These verses arrived too late to be printed in the *Crudities.*

26 November the *Crudities* was entered in the Stationers' Register sponsored by two members of the Stationers' Company, Edward Blount and William Barrett.

It seems possible that the manuscript and plates had been delivered to the printers before the licence was received since before the end of March the book had been printed and bound. Printing in England was not good; it did not approach the degree of perfection already attained on the Continent, and in this case the printers' work fell far short of the author's exacting standards of accuracy. At the end of the book, before the List of Errata, Coryate added an interesting note, omitted from the editions of 1776 and 1905: 'I must tell thee (Courteous Reader) it grieveth me extremely to shut up my booke with an Index of so many faults as I now present unto thee, which it makes me in a manner blush for shame to behold. But impute it not I intreate thee to my ignorance: For I would have thee thinke I have that poore superficiall smattering in the Greeke & Latin tongues (which thou wilt perceive if thou shalt happen to reade over my whole booke) that it was not for want of learning that some grosse faults have passed, . . . the very remembrance whereof doth in a manner afflict me. Howbeit I wish there were no faults but of this kinde. But many errors have been committed also both in false pointing, and in false figuring of the leaves, and sometimes in the omitting not only of points which are very necessary for the perfiting of the sense, but also of certaine wordes, which being out of the text doe not a little maime the sense. Most of which ascribe I pray thee (candid Reader) to the negligence of the Corrector, and not to my unskilfulnesse. Therefore if it will please thee to affoord that favourable connivence unto these kind of errors that I doe earnestly crave of thee, I will ingage myselfe . . . to bestow that extraordinary care and industry in a most accurate and exactly true Edition of it the next time (if it shall happen to be reprinted before the beginning of my next travels, a thing not altogether unlikely) that I will be so bold to compare it for true orthographie and every thing else that ought to perfit the sense of a booke, with any booke whatsoever that hath beene printed in London these twenty yeares . . .'

It is characteristic of Coryate's self-confidence that he should be contemplating a second edition before ever the book appeared on the market. No second edition appeared, and the total number of copies printed is unknown. From about 1586 the Stationers' Company had ordered that no more than 1,250 copies of an ordinary book should be printed; if more were needed the type had to be distributed and set up afresh. But even Coryate could not have expected to sell anything like this number. Any book in English was of interest only to the literate few at home; for readers abroad he planned to make a Latin translation of both the *Crudities* and the book describing his future travels. At least forty copies of the *Crudities* are known to exist today, so it seems probable that several hundred were printed.

Coryate took special pains with several copies for members of the Royal Family which he determined to present in person. On Easter Monday, 26 March 1611, he was received by Prince Henry in the Privy Chamber at St. James's. The oration which he made on this occasion, and those he delivered when presenting copies to the other members of the Royal Family, are all preserved in the *Crambe*, and were composed in his most hyperbolical style, presumably with the intention of sustaining his reputation as a wit. In presenting the book to his patron the Prince, Coryate likens the *Crudities* to a new-laid egg, not doubting that his Highness will have the same effect as the sun, 'the great Phoebean Lampe, hath over a naturall egge-shel produced by a checkling Henne . . . I wish that by the auspicious obumbration of your Princely wings, this sencelesse Shell may prove a lively Birde . . . and so breede more Birds of the same feather that may in future time bee presented as novelties unto your heroycall protection. In the meane time receive into your indulgent hand (I most humbly beseech your Highnesse) this tender feathered Red-breast. Let his Cage be your Highnesse studie, his pearch your Princely hand . . .'

As Coryate points out in a footnote, the book was indeed a red-breast for it was bound in crimson velvet. The plates had been coloured and the errata carefully corrected in manuscript. This copy can be seen today in the British Museum, its glories still undimmed.

The King was at Theobalds, his favourite residence near Royston, formerly Lord Burghley's country house. Coryate next travelled thither, and on the morning of 2 April in the Presence Chamber he presented the book and made his oration. His Majesty may have been startled to hear himself described as 'the refulgent Carbuncle of Christendome'.

The proud author returned from Royston to London; he still had a number of presentations to make, not only to the other members of the Royal Family but also to several of the most prominent noblemen at court. As the books were bulky he decided to carry them in a box set upon a donkey's back, and he inscribed on the box in fair Roman capitals 'ASINUS PORTANS MYSTERIA'—the Ass carrying the Mysteries. This allusion to an illustration and some verses in Andrea Alciati's *Emblemata*[1] would be widely recognized and was a stroke of showmanship which Coryate no doubt hoped would loosen the purse strings of those to whom he was 'presenting' copies. It seems that he acquired the donkey only after his visit to Royston, but he certainly hoped that the incident would reach the King's ears since he says that he did it as a joke 'and to minister occasion of merriment to the King'.[2] Poor Coryate never suspected how the joke would shortly be turned against him.

He made no pretence that the copy which he presented a few days later to the Queen in the Privy Garden at Greenwich was for her enjoyment and edification. He told her that he was giving it to her in the hope that it might become 'irrefragably current through those kingdomes whereof your Majestie is justly stiled Queene; through that also where your Majestie first drew your vitall breath [Denmark], and all others where the name of Coryate the Traveller and Odcombe his natalitiall Parish shall be knowne to posteritie'.

On Sunday 7 April, Coryate and his donkey were at Lord Harington's house at Kew, where the fifteen-year-old Princess Elizabeth was staying. About noon he had the honour of deliver-

---

[1] *Emblemata*, Leyden, 1591, p. 23. Emblema VII. Henry Green, *Andrea Alciati and his Books of Emblems*, London, 1872, pp. 59–63, gives translations of this emblem into various languages, showing how well known it was, including the following from a manuscript of about 1600–10:

> A slow pas'd ass did Isis image beare
>   having hir shrine upon his crooked backe:
> And those to whom the goddesse did appeare,
>   did reverence hir, on knees by falling flat;
> The Asse suppos'd, this honor don to him
>   did then begin to puffe and swell with pride
> Till that the Carter whipping him gan sing,
>   Thou art no god, but god doth on thee ride.

[2] Henry Green, *op. cit.*, p. 160, states that James I was particularly fond of Alciati's works. The copy in the British Museum which Green states belonged to the King was in fact Prince Henry's. Lord Burghley's copy is also in the British Museum.

ing a copy into her 'Grace's lily white hands . . . in whose name, sexe and heroicall disposition me thinkes I see our great Queen Elizabeth revived and resuscitated unto life'. In case she should feel inclined actually to read the book, he added reassuringly, 'Let not my Title of Crudities (most Princely Lady) any thing dismay your Grace . . . Vouchsafe then I beseech your Grace to receive this . . . rough scabrous and unplaned work into your Grace's smooth hands, where I hope it will receive a secure protection against all the malignant bitings of virulent tongues. And so with all lowlinesse and submission of duetie, I most humbly kisse your Grace's foote.' Coryate realized that there were many who would follow the lead of those who had contributed mocking verses to the *Crudities*, or who for other reasons would traduce and sneer at his work. As we shall see, royal patronage did not protect him from his enemies, or make their attacks any less easy to bear.

From Kew he hastened to St. James's and on that same Sunday afternoon addressed the Duke of York as the 'Most glittering Chrysolite of our English Diademe in whose little yet most lovely Gracious, and elegant body doe budde most pregnant hopes like faire blossomes of great fortunes and greater vertues'. The young boy who was to become King Charles I seems to have enjoyed the flowing phrases of his extraordinary visitor, for the following month Coryate was again permitted to pronounce an oration before him to congratulate him upon his election and instalment as a Knight of the Garter.[1]

Apart from the Royal Family and prominent nobles of the Court there was at least one other recipient of a presentation copy of the *Crudities*. In 1598 Thomas Bodley had begun the formation of his Library, which had been opened in 1603. Here was a fitting repository for posterity. If Coryate did not think of the idea himself, it was put into his head by Christopher Brooke, who wrote in his eulogistic verses:

> 'And we ere long shall well perceive your wit,
> (Grave learned Bodley) by your placing it . . .'[2]

It seems that Bodley himself thought well of the book and esteemed its author. Hearing that Coryate was to visit Oxford, he went out of his way to honour both by writing a letter:

[1] *Crambe*, Sig. C4.          [2] *Crudities*, vol. I, p. 57.

'Sir
I Pray you let me intreat you, to send your Man to Mr. James, and to tell him from me, that Mr. CORYAT the famous Traveller will be at the Act, and sith he hath bestowed one of his Books on the Library, which is in the Custody of Mr. Thomas Allen, I would request him to send for it and to place it for the time in some such Place in the Library, as he may seem to have magnified the Author and the Book.'[1]

Coryate seems not to have been disappointed at the reception accorded to the *Crudities* and, perhaps with a view to capitalizing the notice taken of it, he announced almost immediately that he intended to publish a second book. This time there was no difficulty in obtaining permission to print. The book could by no stretch of the imagination be classed as a theological work but Dr. Mocket did not repeat the excuse which he made in the case of the *Crudities,* and it was licensed in his name and entered in the Stationers' Register on 7 June 1611. Despite the author's criticisms of the printing of the *Crudities* the same printer, William Stansby, took care of the printing of the second book. It was entitled CORYATS CRAMBE, OR HIS COLWORT TWISE SODDEN, *And Now served in with other Macaronicke dishes, as the second course to his Crudities.* The Latin word *crambe,* meaning cabbage, is evidently taken from the figurative use which Juvenal made of it in describing the distasteful repetitions of inept pupils of rhetoric:

occidit miseros crambe repetita magistros:—'served up again and again, the cabbage is the death of the unhappy masters'.[2]

'Colewort twice sodden' means cabbage cooked a second time, and was still current as a proverbial phrase meaning 'stale news'. The whole title was therefore nicely contrived to link it with the *Crudities* both in metaphor, and in self-depreciatory tone. It is not surprising that it should have been generally described as a sequel to the *Crudities.* This, though literally correct, gives a misleading idea of its contents. It is a slim volume of under fifty

---

[1] *Reliquiae Bodleianae,* London, 1703, p. 355. The addressee is unknown and the letter is undated, but must be either 1611 or 1612, more probably the former. At Oxford the Act took place in July. The graduates kept Acts, or discussed theses on Saturday and Monday; on the intervening Act Sunday two of the new Doctors of Divinity preached Act Sermons before the University. For the fate of this presentation copy of the *Crudities,* see p. 293 below.          [2] Satire VII, l.154.

pages. It opens with some further verses on the *Crudities*, including those of Ben Jonson, which arrived too late to be printed in that work. Next appear verses from Laurence Whitaker, Christopher Brooke, Antony Washborne, and William Rich specially composed for the *Crambe*.[1] These are the 'other Macaronicke dishes' referred to in the title.

The verses are followed by the text of Coryate's petition to Prince Henry enlisting his assistance in producing a licence for the *Crudities*; the texts of the orations made to members of the Royal Family when they were presented with copies of the *Crudities*; the oration made to the Duke of York in May 1611 congratulating him on his instalment into the Order of the Garter; part of Coryate's answer to Joseph Starre's Chancery Bill, and the description of the Church Ales at Yeovil and Odcombe in 1606.

This little book was on the point of publication when there suddenly appeared upon the market another slim volume entitled *The Odcombian Banquet Dished foorth by Thomas the Coriat, and served in by a number of Noble Wits in prayse of his Crudities and Crambe too*. This was a pirated reprint of the 'Panegyricke Verses'[2] and some of the other preliminary matter prefacing the *Crudities*, with two cruel additions. Immediately below the title there was printed in bold capitals:

ASINUS
PORTANS
MYSTERIA

On the last page appeared an anonymous announcement:
'Know (gentle Reader) that the booke, in prayse whereof all these preceding verses were written, is purposely omitted for thine, and thy purses good: partly for the greatness of the volume . . . and partly for that one,

Whose learning judgment, wit and braine,
Are weight with Toms iust to a graine.

Having read the booke with an intent to epitomize it, could he but have melted out of the whole lumpe so much matter worthy the reading, as wold have filled foure pages: but finding his labour

---

[1] For notes on these contributors see p. 269 *et seq*. below.

[2] The only omissions are the music prefixed to John Hoskins' verses, and the Greek verses by Thomas Farnaby.

# CERTAINE ORATIONS
## PRONOVNCED BY THE AV-
### THOR OF THE CRVDITIES, TO
THE KING, QVEENE, PRINCE, LADY
ELIZABETH, AND THE DVKE OF
Yorke, at the deliuerie of his Booke
to each of them.

This Oration following was pronounced to the Prince in
the Priuie Chamber at S. *Iames* vpon Easter Munday
laſt, betweene ſixe and ſeuen of the Clocke in the afternoone.

Oſt ſcintillant Phoſ-
phorus *of our Brit-
iſh* Trinacria, *Euen
as the* Chriſtalline
*deaw, that is exhaled
vp into the ayre out of
the cauernes & ſpun-
gie pores of the ſucculent Earth, doeth by his*

A 2     *diſtillation*

* This was the
ancient name
of *Sicily*, ſo cal-
led, *Quaſi
τρία ακρα,
viz. ἐχων,*
that is, hauing
three promon-
tories, namely
*Pelorus, Pachy-
nus,* and *Lily-
bæum.* As for
our Brittiſh I-
land, I there-

---

22. *Coryat's Crambe.* Page Sig. A.2.

EMBLEMATA.
Non tibi, sed religioni.
EMBLEMA VII.

ISIDIS effigiem taratus gestabat asellus,
Pando verenda dorso habens mysteria.
Obuius ergo Deam quisquis reuerenter adorat,
Piasque genibus concipit flexis preces.
Ast asinus tantum praestari credit honorem
Sibi, & intumescit, admodum superbiens:
Donec eum flagris compescens, dixit agaso,
Non es Deus tu, aselle, sed Deum vehis.

B 4                    Quâ

24. The ass carrying the mysteries. From the Leyden, 1591. edition of Andreas Alciati's *Emblemata*.

THE
ODCOMBIAN
BANQVET:
Dished foorth
BY
THOMAS the CORIAT,
AND
Served in by a number of Noble Wits
in prayse of his
CRVDITIES and CRAMBE too.

ASINVS
PORTANS
MYSTERIA

Imprinted for Thomas Thorp.
1611.

23. Title page of *The Odcombian Banquet*, 1611. *Reproduced by courtesy of Messrs. Maggs Bros. Ltd.*

lost, and his hope therein fallen short, is resolved to defer it, til the Author of the Crudities have finished his second travels; which may perhaps afford something either worthy thy reading, or supply thy need in such cases of extremitie, as nature and custome ofttimes inforce men unto.'

Naturally Coryate was furious. That part of his book which had made it the talk of the Court and of literary London, and which was calculated handsomely to increase its sales was now available to the public at a fraction of the cost of the whole work. This, however, was an aspect which he did not publicly refer to. What galled him even more were the added insults of the misuse of his donkey's motto and the denigration of the main body of his work. He was able to vent some of his wrath in an *addendum* which was written just in time to be included at the end of the *Crambe* before it was published:

'At the conclusion and upshot of this Booke, let mee a little advertise thee (gentle Reader) of a Booke lately Printed in hugger-mugger, intituled The Odcombian Banquet. And I am the rather induced to make mention of it because it doth not a little concerne my credit to cleere myself of two very scandalous imputations laide upon me by that virulent and rancorous pessant, some base lurking pedanticall tenebricious Lucifuga[1] that set forth the booke. Whereof the first is the Motto in the first leafe of the booke. ASINUS PORTANS MYSTERIA.' Coryate gives the original source of the Motto and relates how he had written it on his donkey's book box. The perpetrator of the *Odcombian Banquet*, however, by placing it on the title page had 'most sinisterly and malignantly applied it (as all the Readers doe interprete it) to myselfe' and had 'thereby very perversely wrested it from that allusion which I intended'.

Turning to the pirate's insulting announcement 'that he could not melt out of the whole lumpe of my Booke so much matter worthy the reading as would fill foure pages, I will boldly affirme for the better justification of my Observations, and by way of opposition against the malicious censure of that hypercriticall Momus, that of the six hundred fiftie and four pages (for indeede so many are in the booke) he shall find at the least five hundred worthy the reading'. It is a remarkably frank admission for an

---

[1] cf. lucifugous, lucifugal, shunning the light. The noun seems to be Coryate's invention.

author to make a few months after his book has been published that nearly a quarter of it is not worth reading, though this verdict would be endorsed by most modern readers.

According to its title the *Odcombian Banquet* purports to be 'in prayse of his *Crudities* and *Crambe* too', yet the *Odcombian Banquet* appeared before the *Crambe*. The explanation would seem to be that the forthcoming publication of the *Crambe* was known by public advertisement—it was customary to fix copies of the title page at recognized posts throughout the town—or through its circulation in manuscript, which was also a common practice and one which we know Coryate had adopted in the case of the *Crudities*. An alternative solution is that the *Crambe* was already in circulation before the *Odcombian Banquet* appeared, and that Coryate's protest was added only to the unsold copies. This theory, although supported by the fact that Sig. G4 of the *Crambe* is a blank, and the protest starts on sheet H, seems very unlikely since no copy of the *Crambe* lacking sheet H has been found.[1]

Various speculations have been made about the identity of the pirate. It is inconceivable that Ben Jonson was responsible; though he made fun of Coryate he had played a prominent and good-humoured part in the prefatory matter to the *Crudities* and Coryate continued to regard him as a friend to the end of his life. John Taylor, the Water Poet, about whom more will be heard shortly, has also been suggested on the grounds that the pirate's style is similar in tone to the abusive ridicule which Taylor heaped on Coryate's head later. My own view is that the publisher of the *Odcombian Banquet*, Thomas Thorpe, was the culprit and that he was probably in league with another member of the Stationers' Company, Edward Blount. These two, Blount and Thorpe, were friends and both had a reputation as procurers of 'neglected copy'. In 1598 Blount, then still a stationer's assistant, picked up Marlowe's unfinished and unpublished *Hero and Leander* and got it printed. Two years later Thorpe acquired a 'private' copy of Marlowe's unpublished translation of the first book of Lucan. As owner of the manuscript Thorpe chose his patron and supplied the dedicatory epistle. This patron, on whose good offices Thorpe relied to get his treasure trove printed, was none other than his friend Edward Blount.

[1] Prof. W. A. Jackson, *The Carl H. Pforzheimer Library*, New York, 1940, vol. I, p. 218.

Between 1600 and 1624 Thorpe was associated with the publication of twenty-nine volumes, but in almost every case he confined himself to procuring and trading in the 'copy'. This he occasionally purchased from the author but more often, as in the case of his best-known coup, the first edition of Shakespeare's sonnets, he picked up a private transcript of a work which was circulating and was not under the author's protection.[1]

It will be recollected that Edward Blount was one of those in whose name the *Crudities* had been entered in the Stationers' Register. He was thus ideally placed to intimate to Thorpe that an opportunity existed to take advantage of a loophole in the law, or at any rate in the practice, of the time. If the *Crudities* had been published by a member of the Stationers' Company that body might have used its powers to search for, seize, and burn the *Odcombian Banquet,* and to imprison or fine the guilty. On the other hand they might have taken no steps at all. Complaints that a work had been published without the knowledge or consent of the author or his representatives were frequent, and instances in which action was taken are rare. But since Coryate had published his book himself and since he as an individual had no standing with the Stationers' Company, the pirates were able to issue and sell the *Odcombian Banquet* with impunity—and no doubt with some financial advantage.

[1] Sir Sidney Lee's introduction to *Shakespeare's Sonnets, Clarendon Press facsimile of the first edn.,* 1609, Oxford, 1905, pp. 29–31. For a more flattering view of Thorpe see Leona Rostenberg's article on him in *The Papers of the Bibliographical Society of America,* vol. 54, pp. 16–27, New York, 1960.

# CHAPTER X

## *Friends and Enemies*

---

IT has already been suggested that the order in which Coryate arranged the verse contributions to the *Crudities* is significant, and that those which appear immediately after the verses composed by the titled courtiers include contributions from his more intimate friends.

John Donne, fifteenth in the order, is followed by Richard Martin, Laurence Whitaker, Hugh Holland, Robert Richmond, Walter Quin, Christopher Brooke, John Hoskins, John Pawlet, Lionel Cranfield, John Sutclin, and Inigo Jones. To these must be added Ben Jonson, Sir Robert Phelips (eighth, among the knights), and his father Sir Edward, who may occupy first place under the pseudonym Ἀποδημουντόφιλος.

The evidence justifying the conclusion that this group includes many of Coryate's close acquaintances comes not from the verses but from other sources, of which Coryate's five letters from India are the most important. The original letters have disappeared and only printed versions[1] survive; it is clear from these that the manuscript texts have in some cases been severely edited, but fortunately the writer's numerous requests to be commended to his friends have not been excised. Every member of the group named above with the exception of Richmond, Quin, Pawlet, Cranfield, and Sutclin, is greeted at least once in these letters. Richmond remains unidentified; Quin was Prince Henry's music master; Pawlet a near neighbour in Somerset and probably one of the Gentlemen of the Privy Chamber Extraordinary in Prince Henry's household; Cranfield has already been introduced, and Sutclin, or Suckling, was Cranfield's brother-in-law, a distinguished civil servant and, incidentally, father of the poet.

Of the five letters from India one is addressed to Sir Edward Phelips, one to Laurence Whitaker, Sir Edward's Secretary, one

---

[1] For details see Bibliographical Notes, below.

to the High Seneschall of the Mermaid Club, and two to his mother. There can be little doubt that Sir Edward and his son Sir Robert had been originally responsible for introducing Coryate to Prince Henry's household and to London society. Both had been closely connected with the Court for some years; eventually, in 1610, Sir Edward was appointed Chancellor to Prince Henry and in the following year he became Master of the Rolls. At his country house at Wanstead and his town house in Chancery Lane he seems to have been the centre of a circle of younger men, mainly members of the Inns of Court—the 'third University'. Besides asking to be remembered to Sir Edward's wife, Sir Robert and his wife, Coryate greets Christopher Brooke, John Hoskins, Richard Martin, William Hakewill, 'and the rest of the worthy gentlemen frequenting your honourable table that favour vertue and the sacred muses'. Brooke and Hakewill were both members of Lincoln's Inn while all the others were members of the Middle Temple.

Brooke contributed verses to both the *Crudities* and the *Crambe* and was an intimate friend of Hoskins and Martin. He had been John Donne's 'chamber-fellow' at Lincoln's Inn and in 1601 witnessed Donne's secret marriage with the daughter of Sir George Moore. The ceremony was performed by Christopher's brother Samuel, and the bride's infuriated father had contrived to commit Donne and the two Brookes to prison.

The cruelty of Donne's verses in the *Crudities*[1] did not sour Coryate's admiration for him; writing from India he asks to be remembered to 'Master John Donne, the Author of two most elegant Latine Bookes, *Pseudo-martyr* [which is not in Latin] and *Ignatii Conclave*: of his abode either in the Strand, or else-where in London, I thinke you shall be easily informed by the meanes of my friend, Master L[aurence] W[hitaker].'

Donne was friendly with Hugh Holland, now best known as the author of the sonnet prefixed to the First Folio of Shakespeare, who supplied verses for the *Crambe* as well as the *Crudities*, and whom Coryate greets in his letter from India to Laurence Whitaker. Brooke, Hoskins, and Martin were also close friends of Holland.

Martin, it will be remembered, had provided Coryate with a letter of introduction to Sir Henry Wotton, and it may have been to Martin that Coryate owed his introduction to Lionel Cranfield

---

[1] For a discussion of these verses and a particularly neat translation of Donne's macaronic quatrain see *Notes & Queries*, 3rd Series, vol. VII, p. 145.

since the two were business associates, and Martin acted as legal adviser to several of Cranfield's syndicates. The part which Cranfield played, with Whitaker, in urging forward the publication of the *Crudities* has already been alluded to; in addition Cranfield acted for a period as Coryate's banker. Banking and money-lending were a side-line in which Cranfield had been interested since about 1605. His known transactions[1] with Coryate are as follows:

|  |  | *Cr.* | *Dr.* |
|---|---|---|---|
| 1611 March 27 |  |  | 4 |
| Apr. 16 | 4 |  |  |
| Apr. 28 | 30 |  |  |
| May 30 |  |  | 6 |
| June 30 | 8 |  |  |
| July 4 | 12 |  |  |
| Dec. 24 | 126 |  |  |
| Dec. 28 |  |  | 26 |
| Jan. 13 |  |  | 5 |
| Jan. 14 |  |  | 4 |
| Jan. 15 |  |  | 11 |
| Jan. 18 |  |  | 6 |
| Jan. 20 |  |  | 20 |
| Feb. 19 |  |  | 11 |
| 1612 Apr. 11 | 'Paid Mr. Coriat in full' |  | 37 |
|  |  | 126 | 120 |

No record of the original deposit has been discovered and it will be noted that the final withdrawal does not result in an exact balance. Clearly, therefore, some entries are missing and it would be unwise to read too much into what is nevertheless a recognizable pattern conforming with Coryate's known activities at this period. It looks as though Coryate deposited with Cranfield at some date prior to 27 March 1611 about £80 which might repre-

[1] Extracted from 'The Private Ledger of Lionel Cranfield, 1603–1611', pp. 245–69 (which includes the entry for 1612) to be found among the unpublished Cranfield Papers kept by the Historical Manuscripts Commission, also from Cranfield's Cash Book, *Sackville Papers, Vol. I, Cranfield Papers*, Hist. Mss. Comm., Series 80, London, 1940, pp. 254, 255, 349, 350.

sent his winnings from Joseph Starre and possibly other similar wagers, less what he required to finance the printing of the *Crudities* and to meet day-to-day expenses. He drew £4 on 27 March 1611 before setting out for Royston to present the *Crudities* to King James. During April he deposited £34, probably the proceeds from 'presentations' and from sales to the public. During June and July he banked a further £20 which might represent earnings from the *Crambe* and the *Crudities*. Thus on 24 December, when Cranfield drew up a list of his debts, Coryate was £126 in credit. Thenceforward no further sums are deposited and the frequency and size of the amounts withdrawn suggest either that he was paying off debts or that he was laying out his money in new directions.

He may have transferred his account to John Williams, the King's Goldsmith, who is twice greeted in the letters from India. Williams hailed from Caernarvonshire and lived in Cheapside. He was about five years older than Coryate and may have been related to him on his mother's side, but he is certainly not the Uncle Williams to whom Coryate also refers in his letters, and from whom he had 'expectations'. 'Pray remember my commendations with all respect to Mr. Williams the goldsmith and his wife and to Benjamin Johnson and to reade this letter to them both', he wrote to Laurence Whitaker. The link between Williams and Jonson may have been simply that Coryate expected them both to be interested in his travels. Certainly the account which he sent to Whitaker would have revealed to Jonson a side of Coryate's character—the toughness, audacity, and perseverance of the pioneer traveller—which Jonson does not recognize in any of several allusions to him. At home Coryate deliberately played the fool in order to attract attention and Jonson took him at face value. Though most of his references to Coryate are contemptuous, they are not, like his attacks on Inigo Jones, malicious. In one of these attacks Jonson brings in Coryate and hints at an intimacy between the two:

'That scarse the Towne designeth any feast
    To which thou'rt not a weeke bespoke a guest;
That still th'art made the suppers flagge, the drum,
    The very call, to make all others come:
Thinks't thou, MIME, this is great? . . .

Or (mounted on a stoole) thy face doth hit
  On some new gesture, that's imputed wit?
O, runne not proud of this. Yet take thy due
  Thou dost out-zany COKELEY, POD; nay, GUE:
And thine owne CORIAT too. But (would'st thou see)
  Men love thee not for this: They laugh at thee.'[1]

Jonson could use Coryate as a stick with which to beat Jones, because Coryate expected to be laughed at—if it was for the right reasons and provided the laughing was done by his social equals or superiors—whereas Jones took himself very seriously as Britain's leading producer of masques and Surveyor of the Works to the Heir to the Throne.

Some interesting corroborative evidence of the circle in which Coryate moved is provided by a comic Latin poem about a Convivium Philosophicum which was to be held at the Mitre Tavern in London on 2 September of an unspecified year, probably 1611.[2] The expected guests, in the order in which the poem mentions them, are:

| | |
|---|---|
| Christoferus Torrens | Christopher Brooke |
| Johannes Factus | John Donne |
| Gruicampus | Lionel Cranfield |
| Arthurus | Arthur Ingram |
| Robertus Equorum Amicus | Sir Robert Phelips |
| Nevile Henricus | Sir Henry Nevill |
| Cuniculus Quercianus | Richard Connock |
| Janus Caligula | John Hoskins |
| Richardus Guasta Stannum | Richard Martin |
| Henricus Bonum-Annum | Sir Henry Goodier |
| Johannes Occidens | John West |
| Hugo Inferior-Germanus | Hugh Holland |
| Ignatius Architectus | Inigo Jones |
| Coriatus | Thomas Coryate |

[1] Epigram No. CXXIX *To 'Mime'*, i.e. Inigo Jones. Cokeley, and perhaps Gue too, were professional jesters, while Pod is spoken of in *Bartholomew Fair*, Act V, Sc. I, l.8, as Leatherhead's 'master'. Leatherhead is himself a caricature of Inigo Jones and in Act III, Sc. 4, Trash says of him 'But put him a top o' the Table [i.e. in the jester's place] where his place is, and he'll doe you forty fine things. Hee has not been sent for, and sought out for nothing, at your great city-suppers, to put downe Coriat and Cokeley.' Other allusions to Coryate occur in *Bartholomew Fair*, Act III, Sc. V, l.231, *The Masque of Love Restored*, l.85–86, and *The Under-Wood*, Poem No. XIII, l.128.

[2] The authorship, and various texts of this poem are discussed in the Bibliographical Note, p. 302 below.

Of these all but West, Ingram, and Connock had contributed verses to the *Crudities*, and all but these, Cranfield, Nevill, and Goodier, are greeted in Coryate's letters from India. There were various strands of mutual interest linking the group together. The most important was the Court with which all had close connexions. Membership of the Inns of Court was also common to eight of them, Connock, Goodier, and West belonging, like Martin, Hoskins, and Phelips, to the Middle Temple, while Brooke and Donne were members of Lincoln's Inn. It may also be noted that eight were active members of the Parliament of 1604–10.

The poem, of which there is a contemporary translation, gives no specific indication of why the Convivium was held:

| | |
|---|---|
| Quilibet si sit contentus | Whosoever is contented |
| Ut statutus stet conventus | That a number be convented |
|   Sicut nos promisimus; |   Enough but not too many; |
| Signum *Mitrae* erit locus, | The *Miter* is the place decreed, |
| Erit cibus, erit jocus | For witty jests and cleanly feed |
|   Optimatatissimus. |   The betterest of any. |

Having introduced all but one of the expected guests the poem continues:

| | |
|---|---|
| Sed jocus, nisi invitatus | But yet the number is not ri(gh)ted; |
| | |
| Veniet illuc *Coriatus* | If *Coriate* be not invited, |
|   Erit imperfectus. |   The feast will want a tiller. |
| | |
| Nam facete super illum, | For wittily on him, they say, |
| Sicut malleus in anvillum, | As hammers on an anvil play, |
|   Unusquisque ludet. |   Each man his feast may breake |
| Coriatus cum potavit, | When Coriate is fudled well |
| Lingua regnum peragrabit | His tongue begins to talke pelmel |
|   Nec illum quicquam pudet. |   He shameth nought to speake |

and so on for another eleven stanzas ending with:

| | |
|---|---|
| Unusquisque sic facessit, | Thus every man is busy still |
| Cor nullius conquiescit, | Each one practising his skill |
|   Nemo habet satis |   None hath enough to gayne. |
| Solus Coriatus sapit, | But Coriate liveth by his witts |
| Nihil perdit quicquid capit, | He looseth nothinge that he getts |
|   Nec stultescit gratis. |   Nor playes the fool in vayne. |

Coryate is certainly the central figure in the poem and the inference is that he was the cause of the Convivium being summoned. It has been suggested that this was a farewell party given for him before he set sail for Constantinople in October 1612, but there are strong arguments against this.[1] Whatever the pretext, this Latin poem is of considerable interest since it is the earliest evidence of any tavern meeting of the kind popularly considered to have been held at the Mermaid Tavern.

The idea that Shakespeare and many of the other leading poets, dramatists, and wits of the time were members of a club which met at the Mermaid Tavern is so widely accepted that it comes as something of a shock to discover that there is no contemporary evidence whatever of Shakespeare attending regular meetings at the Mermaid or any other London tavern, and that the membership of most of the other literary giants popularly supposed to be included in the circle is distinctly not proven.

How, then, can the legend be accounted for? The story starts with Aubrey who, writing sixty or seventy years after the events he describes, has a gossipy note that Sir Francis Stuart was 'one of the Club at the Mermayd in Fryday Street with Sir Walter Ralegh &c. of that Sodalitie; Heroes & Witts of that time. Ben Jonson dedicates *The Silent Woman* to him.'[2] This Francis Stuart, brother of James, 3rd Earl of Moray, appears to have come to England only after James's accession: he matriculated at Oxford at the age of fifteen in 1604, by which time Sir Walter Ralegh was imprisoned in the Tower, where he remained until 1616. While it is unlikely, to say the least, that the haughty Ralegh should have organized tavern meetings at any time, it is impossible that Stuart could have belonged to any such Club with Ralegh.

Nevertheless, Aubrey's statement was copied down uncritically by Anthony à Wood and incorporated almost word for word in his *Athenae Oxonienses* where it was found by William Gifford (1756–1826), Ben Jonson's editor. Gifford had also read Fuller's *Worthies*, 1662: 'Many were the wit combats betwixt him [Shakespeare] and Ben Jonson: which two I behold like a Spanish great Gallion and an English man of war: Master Jonson (like the

---

[1] As I. A. Shapiro points out, *Modern Language Review*, 1950, p .7, n, Donne was one of those expected but he had been abroad since November 1611. Furthermore there are separate references to the Lord Treasurer and the Earl of Northampton which imply that the Earl of Salisbury was still alive. He died in May 1612.

[2] MS. Aubrey 8, f. 91.

former) was built far higher in learning: solid, but slow in his performances. Shakespeare, with the English man of war, lesser in bulk, but lighter in sailing, could turn with all tides, tack about, and take advantage of all winds, by the quickness of his wit and invention.' Fuller was of course 'beholding' in his mind's eye only: he was eight years old when Shakespeare died, and he says nothing whatever about where these wit combats took place. Even supposing they did take place at the Mermaid, this does not mean that Shakespeare or Ben Jonson were members of the Mermaid Club.

Out of these meagre threads Gifford wove a splendid little tapestry, so deceptively vivid that it has gained the widest acceptance: 'Sir Walter Ralegh . . . had instituted a meeting of beaux esprits at the Mermaid, a celebrated tavern in Friday-street. Of this Club, which combined more talent and genius, perhaps, than ever met before or since, our author was a member; and here, for many years, he regularly repaired with Shakespeare, Beaumont, Fletcher, Selden, Cotton, Carew, Martin, Donne, and many others, whose names, even at this distant period, call up a mingled feeling of reverence and respect. Here in the full flow and confidence of friendship, the lively and interesting 'wit-combats' took place between Shakespeare and our author: and hither in probable allusion to them, Beaumont fondly lets his thoughts wander, in his letter to Jonson, from the country.'

Beaumont's verse letter was probably written as late as 1613:

> 'What things have we seen,
> Done at the Mermaid! heard words that have been
> So nimble, and so full of subtle flame,
> As if that every one from whence they came
> Had meant to put his whole wit in a gest,
> And had resolv'd to live a fool, the rest
> Of his dull life; then when there had been thrown
> Wit able enough to justify the Town
> For three days past, with that might warrant be
> For the whole City to talk foolishly
> Till that were cancell'd, and when that was gone
> We left an air behind us, which alone,
> Was able to make the two next companies
> Right witty: though but downright fools, more wise.'

These lines certainly indicate that Jonson and Beaumont had been present with other wits at gatherings at the Mermaid but these could have been quite unconnected with the Mermaid Club which may just as well have been one of the 'two next companies' referred to by Beaumont.

The plain but surprising fact is that Coryate's letter from India to the High Seneschall of the Mermaid Club provides the only definite proof that such a Club existed. Although Coryate tells us several details about its constitution and activities, the question of membership remains extremely open. It can, however, be stated with certainty that Gifford's assertion that the members included Shakespeare, Fletcher, Selden, and Carew is an invention uncorroborated by any contemporary evidence.

Having unpicked Gifford's spurious embroideries, what remains of the truth? According to Coryate the Club met on the first Friday of every month, at the sign of the Mermaid in Bread Street in London. Jonson confirms that the Mermaid was in Bread Street,[1] but Aubrey, it will be remembered, says it was in Friday Street. Its tokens, of which one is preserved at Stratford-on-Avon, are inscribed 'Ye Mermaid Tavern, Cheapside'. The probable explanation is that it did indeed stand in Bread Street but had passage entrances from Cheapside and Friday Street.[2]

Coryate calls the members 'the right Worshipfull Fraternitie of Sirenaicall Gentelmen', or simply 'Sirenaics'—a term due to the confusion of the mermaid with the Siren. Possibly there was also a playful allusion to the Cyrenaic philosophers who held that pleasure was the chief aim in life.

The letter from India is addressed to the High Seneschall, not to a named individual, implying that at the time of writing, 1615, he did not know who held the office. We know that it was held for a limited period since Coryate refers to Laurence Whitaker as 'the quondam Seneschall'. Purchas states that the messenger who brought the letter from India handed it to him which suggests that Purchas may have presided in 1616. As will be seen from the discussion on membership below, this is not an altogether impossible supposition.

Guests seem to have been welcome, indeed the chief object of

---

[1] Epigram No. CXXXIII.

[2] H. B. Wheatley, *London past and present*, London, 1891, vol. II, p. 527. The Mermaid was destroyed in the Great Fire.

Coryate's letter is to introduce its bearer, the Rev. Peter Rogers, and to 'intreat your generosities to entertaine him friendly for my sake to exhilarate him with the purest quintessence of the Spanish, French and Rhenish grape which the Mermaid yeeldeth'.

We know that the Club was meeting in 1612 because, before Coryate left for Constantinople, the members provided him with a passport: 'that incomparable elegant safe-conduct, which, a little before my departure from England, your Fraternity with a general suffrage gave me for the security of my future peregrination, concinnated by the pleasant wit of that inimitable artizan of sweet elegancy, the moytie of my heart, and the quondam Seneschall of the noblest Society M[aster] L. W[hitaker]'. One can visualize the kind of document which was composed and presented and can scarcely be surprised at Coryate writing to Whitaker that the 'most elegant and incomparable safe-conduct that they have graciously bestowed upon me I have left in Aleppo, not having made any use of it as yet, neither shall I in all my peregrination of Asia'.

In a postcript to his letter to the High Seneschall Coryate writes, 'Pray remember the recommendations of my dutiful respect to all those whose names I have here expressed, being the lovers of vertue, and literature . . .' The people listed appear in the following order:

Lady Mary Verney and her daughter Lady Ursula Verney
Sir Robert Cotton, the antiquary
Rev. William Ford, who had been Chaplain at Constantinople
George Speake, of the Middle Temple, whose home was near Odcombe
John Donne
Richard Martin
Christopher Brooke
John Hoskins
George Gerrard, one of Donne's intimate friends
William Hakewill
Ben Jonson
John Bond, chief Secretary to Lord Chancellor Ellesmere
Dr. Mocket, who licensed the *Crambe* and became Warden of All Souls
Samuel Purchas and his assistant Master Cooke

Inigo Jones
John Williams, the King's Goldsmith
Hugh Holland
Robert Bing, whose identity is doubtful
William Stansby, who printed the *Crudities* and the *Crambe*.
All the Stationers in St. Paul's Churchyard, but especially
John Norton, Simon Waterson, Matthew Lownes, Edward
Blount, and William Barrett.

In a further postscript Coryate asks to be remembered to the
Bishop of Bath and Wells, Dr. Montague.

Fuller details of these twenty-six people are shown in the
Biographical Notes below. It is significant that the list includes
six of those who both occur in the group of contributors to the
*Crudities* and also were expected at the Mitre Convivium—Donne,
Martin, Brooke, Hoskins, Inigo Jones, and Holland, while
Ben Jonson also appears. Whitaker's name does not occur as he
received a separate letter which he was expected to read to the
members. In that letter Coryate asks to be commended to 'M[aster]
Protoplast and all the Sirenaicall gentlemen'. From this it seems
clear that 'Protoplast' was a member. Taking protoplast to mean
'the first created of the human race', i.e. Adam, this might possibly
be the nickname of Thomas Adams,[1] one of the booksellers of St.
Paul's Churchyard. If one recognizes the fact that there is no contemporary evidence to show that the Mermaid Club was an exclusive group of poets, playwrights, and wits, then it becomes easier
to accept that a prominent and reputable bookseller like Adams
may have been a member, and that Purchas, Hakluyt's successor,
could have held the presidency. It is, however, stretching the point
too far to suppose that all the Stationers in St. Paul's Churchyard
could have been members, and the fact that Coryate's list is headed
by the two ladies seems to prove conclusively that it is not a list
of Sirenaics.

Coryate wrote two letters to the Club, the first from Aleppo in
1614, which has disappeared, the second from India, which has
survived, though not in the original manuscript. Maybe that first
letter, or some other evidence, will one day appear. Meanwhile it
is high time that students of the period should purge their minds
of Gifford's romancing.

[1] See Biographical Note, p. 287 below.

26. Lionel Cranfield. From the full-length portrait attributed to Daniel Mytens which hangs in the Leicester Gallery at Knole. *Reproduced by courtesy of Major-General Lord Sackville.*

25. Sir Edward Phelips. From the painting by an unknown artist, owned by David Phelips, Esq., which hangs at Montacute House. The mace indicates that the portrait was painted after he was elected Speaker of the House of Commons in 1604. *Reproduced by courtesy of the owner.*

28. John Donne. From the painting by an unknown artist in the National Portrait Gallery. *Reproduced by courtesy of the Trustees of the Marquess of Lothian.*

27. John Taylor, the Water Poet. From the painting by an unknown artist in Watermen's Hall. *Reproduced by courtesy of the Court of the Company of Watermen and Lightermen of the River Thames.*

Coryate now became involved in a prolonged altercation which caused much public amusement. The trouble started in 1612 with the publication of a pamphlet entitled *The Sculler's Travels . . . or Gallimawfry of Sonnets, Satyres . . . and a quarterne of new catched epigrams, catched the last fishing tide*. This seems to have been the first published work of John Taylor who assumed the title of 'the water Poet' by reason of his calling which was that of a Thames waterman. Many of the epigrams are rumbustiously bawdy; some are positively obscene and the work must have raised many a ribald chuckle in the City and on Thames side. The lines addressed 'To Tom Coriat' are not indecent but they are certainly not complimentary:

> What matters for the place I first came from
> I am no Duncecomb, Coxecomb, Odcomb Tom
> Nor am I like a wool-pack, cramm'd with Greek,
> Venus in Venice minded to goe seeke;
> And at my backe returne to write a Volume,
> In memory of my wits Gargantua Colume.
> The choysest wits would never so adore me;
> Nor like so many Lackies run before me,
> But honest Tom, I envy not thy state,
> There's nothing in thee worthy of my hate;
> Yet I confesse thou hast an excellent wit:
> But that an idle Braine doth harbour it.
> Foole thou it at the Court, I on the Thames,
> So farewell Odcomb Tom, God blesse King James.

Coryate, as we have seen, persistently went out of his way to make a fool of himself in order to satisfy his desire for self-advertisement. But it was one thing for the wits and gallants to flatter him with their notice by laughing at his antics and quite another to be publicly called a dunce by an upstart waterman.

In fact, although Taylor was at this time quite unknown in literary circles, he was not a complete nonentity. He was born of humble parents in Gloucestershire. Having shown that he had no aptitude for Latin grammar he was removed from Gloucester Grammar School and apprenticed to a London waterman. While still a youth he served in the Navy. He was present at the siege of Cadiz in 1596, took part in the Azores expedition the following year, and by 1603, according to his own account, had made

sixteen voyages in the Queen's ships.[1] Having suffered some injury
to his leg he retired, or was discharged, and became a Thames
waterman. He soon acquired access to some dispenser of favours
and was appointed collector of the ancient perquisite of wine
which the lieutenant of the Tower exacted from every ship bringing wine into the Thames—two black leathern bottles each
containing three gallons, a proportion of which found its way
down Taylor's thirsty gullet. It was certainly a mark of favour,
and an indication of his ability, that he was appointed in 1613 to
arrange the details of the water pageant on the Thames at the
marriage of Princess Elizabeth.

His facility for writing remained dormant until 1612 when
*The Sculler* appeared. From then on a stream of rollicking verse
and lusty prose bubbled from him and during the remainder of
his long life nearly one hundred and sixty separate works, none
larger than a pamphlet, came from his pen.

Autobiographical details are one of the main ingredients of
many of Taylor's productions, and it is entirely from such details
that the story of his quarrels with Coryate emerges. In all
Coryate's surviving writings there is no mention whatever of
Taylor, and the lack of any corroboration of Taylor's evidence
suggests the possibility that he invented the retaliatory measures
taken by Coryate simply so that he could carry the ding-dong
battle of insults into further rounds. However, apart from other
considerations, this theory does not fit in with what we know of
Coryate's touchiness whenever he felt his self-esteem to be
wounded.

It may therefore be assumed that Taylor was reporting what
actually occurred when he wrote:

> A Pamphlet printed was *The Sculler* nam'd
> Wherein Sir *Thomas* much my writing blam'd;
> Because an Epigram therein was written,
> In which he said he was nipt gald and bitten.
> He frets, he fumes, he rages, and exclaimes,
> And vowes to rouze[2] me from the River Thames.
> Well, I to make him some amends for that
> Did write a Booke was cald, *Laugh and be fat*.[3]

[1] John Taylor, *Pennyles Pilgrimage*.
[2] Probably 'rouse' in its nautical sense, 'to haul with force'. *O.E.D.*
[3] John Taylor, *The Eighth Wonder of the World*.

In *Laugh and be fat* Taylor adopts an air of truculent innocence:

> Now Monsieur *Coriat*, let them laugh that wins
> For I assure you now the game begins
> 'Tis wondrous strange how your opinions vary,
> From judgement, sence, or reason so contrary;
> That with infamous rash timerity,
> You raile at me with such severity;
> The broad-fac'd Jests that other men put on you,
> You take for favours well bestow'd upon you.
> Yet no man's lines but mine you take in snuffe.

Taylor goes on to analyse the epigram in *The Sculler* and to argue with some wit and ingenuity that each remark would be taken by any sensible man as being innocuous:

> The cause, I heare, your fury flameth from,
> I said, I was no dunce-combe, coxcombe *Tom*:
> What's that to you (good Sir) that you should fume,
> Or rage or chafe, or thinke I durst presume
> To speake, or write, that you are such a one?
> I onely said, that I my selfe was none . . .
> I further said, I envied not your state,
> For you had nothing worthy of my hate
> In love, your innonence I truly pitty,
> Your plentious want of wit seemes wondrous wittie.
> Your virtue cannot breed my hatefull lothing,
> For what an asse were I to hate just nothing?

The alternative title of *Laugh and be fat* is *A Commentary upon the Odcombian Banquet* and a large part is taken up by a rather tedious and insipid discussion in verse, sometimes in the form of comment and sometimes paraphrase, of the eulogistic poems prefacing the *Crudities*, which of course were pirated to form the content of *The Odcombian Banquet*, a name which stank in Coryate's nostrils.

As a parting thrust Taylor concludes with a parody of Coryate's oratorical style: 'Contaminous, pestiferous, preposterous, stygmaticall, slavonious, slubberdegullions; since not the externall unvalued trappings, caparisons, or accoutrements, that I weare as outward ornaments or invellopings of the more internall beauty of the mind that is incaged within them; . . . since not the sword of *Ajax*, nor the words of *Ulisses*; since no meanes, nor project, neither of force nor policy, could stay the rugged robustious rage that your innated hereditary incivility or inhumanity hath made you to inflict on me; I vow and sweare, by the burning beard of scorching *Sol*, and by the bloudy cut-throat cuttleaxe of swaggering *Mars*, and by the dimple in faire *Venus* chin, and by the armed cornuted front of sweating *Vulcan*, that I will execute on you such confounding vengeance, that your offsprings offspring, to the 39th generation shall ban with execrations as bitter as Coloquintida[1] the day, houre, and bald-pated Time of this your audacious insolency.'

Far from making amends, as Taylor professed was his intention, *Laugh and be fat* roused Coryate to such a pitch of fury that he petitioned the King with the request that Taylor should be punished for abusing him in writing, to which James replied, according to Taylor, that when the Lords of his Honourable Privy Council had leisure and nothing else to do, then they should hear and determine the differences between Master Coryate the scholar and John Taylor the sculler.[2]

Hearing what was afoot Taylor himself submitted a petition in verse to the King, subsequently published in *Wit & Mirth*, which likened Coryate and himself for no particularly appropriate reason to the two women who brought their dispute over a child to King Solomon:

> The King, whose wisdom through the world did ring,
> Did heare the cause of two offending harlots
> So I beseech the (Great) great Britaine's King
> To do the like for two contending varlots.
> A brace of knaves, your Majesty implores
> To heare their suites as Solomon heard whores.

It seems unlikely that the King paid any more attention to Taylor's ludicrous petition than he did to Coryate's solemn one, or that the Privy Council found sufficient leisure to give the squabble their consideration, but by some means Coryate achieved a measure of redress. Taylor says that in *Laugh and be fat* Coryate felt himself

---

[1] The colocynth or bitter cucumber, cf. *Othello*, Act. I, Sc. 3, l. 355, 'The food that **to** him now is as luscious as locusts, shall be to him shortly as bitter as coloquintida.'

[2] John Taylor, *Wit & Mirth*.

> wrong'd ten times more
> And made him madder than he was before.
> Then did he storme, and chafe and sweare and ban,
> And to superior powers amaine he ran
> Where he obtain'd *Laugh and be fat's* confusion,
> Who all were burnt, and made a hot conclusion.[1]

The burning of books was a common occurrence at this time. It was, however, a penalty normally invoked solely for political purposes in order to prevent the circulation of anything which might encourage civil dissension. As politics and religion were so bound up in each other this meant that the most usual reason for a book being condemned to be burnt was that it brought into question the unity and authority of the Established Church. There is, however, nothing in *Laugh and be fat* which could cause it to be convicted on political, theological, or even moral grounds, the three heads under which the censorship theoretically took action.

A possible solution lies in the fact that there is no entry of *Laugh and be fat* in the Stationers' Company Register before 1613. By this time Coryate was abroad and was scarcely in a position to make his displeasure felt or to take action with the authorities from remote Constantinople. It seems possible that *Laugh and be fat* first appeared some time before October 1612, when Coryate sailed; that, having failed in his petition to the King, he cast about for some other means of revenge and, discovering that the pamphlet had not been licensed, appealed to the Wardens of the Stationers' Company, who on these grounds invoked their powers to search, seize, and burn, though they appear to have stopped short of fining or imprisoning Taylor which they were also empowered to do.

It was inevitably a Pyrrhic victory for Coryate. News of the seizure and burning would spread almost as quickly as the flames which devoured the pamphlet, and would simply serve to excite interest in its contents. Furthermore, there was nothing to prevent Taylor from obtaining a licence and re-issuing the work, which is exactly what he did in 1613.

An indication of the success achieved by *Laugh and be fat* is that Taylor followed it up immediately with two further satires,

[1] *The Eighth Wonder of the World.*

published in May and August 1613. The first was entitled *Od-comb's Complaint, A Sad, Joyful, Lamentable, Delightful, Merry-go-sorry Elegie or Funeral Poem upon the supposed Death of the famous Cosmographicall Surveior and Historiographicall Relator Mr. Thomas Coriat*:

> O for a rope of Onions from Saint *Omer's*,
> And for the muse of golden tongued *Homer's*
> That I might write and weep, and weep and write,
> *Odcombian Coriat's* timelesse last good-night.
>         .       .       .       .       .       .
> Hee was the Imp, whilst he on earth surviv'd,
> From whom this west-worlds pastimes were deriv'd,
> He was in City, Country, Field and Court,
> The Well of dry brained Jests, the Pump of sport.
> He was the treasure house of wrinckled laughter,
> Where melancholly moods are put to slaughter:
> And in a word, he was a man 'mongst many,
> That never yet was paralleld by any:
> Who now like him in spite of wind and weather
> Will weare one shiftlesse shirt five months together?
> Who now to do his native country grace,
> Will for a Trophee execute his case?
> Who now will take the height of every *Gallowes*?
> Or who'll describe the height of every *Alehouse*?
> Whether his *Host* were bigge, or short, or tall,
> And whether he did knock e're he did call?
> The colour of his *Host* and *Hostesse* haire?
> What he bought cheap, and what he paid for deare?
> For Veale or Mutton what he paid a joynt?
> Where he sat down? and where he loos'd a poynt?[1]
> Each Tower, each Turret, and each lofty steeple,
> Who now (like him) will tel the vulgar people?
> Who now will set aworke so many writers,
> As he hath done in spite of his back biters,
> With Panegericks, Anagrams, Acrosticks,
> T'emblazon him the chiefe among fantasticks?
> Alas, not one, not one alive doth live,
> That to the world can such contentment give . . .

[1] Tagged lace for attaching the hose to the doublet, or for fastening instead of buttons. *O.E.D.*

There follows a fantastic account of Coryate's imaginary drowning on the voyage to Constantinople with a silly description of fish feeding on his body and becoming accomplished Grecian Latinists. The hotch potch ends with some verses *In praise of Mr. Thomas, the Deceased, fashioned of divers Stuffs, As Mockado, Fustian, Stand-further-off, and Motly* which are remarkable because they show that Taylor was an accomplished nonsense-poet:

The nine-fold Bugbeares of the Caspian lake,
Sate whistling Ebon hornpipes to their Ducks,
*Madgehowlet* straight for joy her Girdle brake,
And rugged Satyrs frisk'd like *Stagges* and *Buckes*.
The untam'd tumbling fifteene footed Goat,
With promulgation of the Lesbian shores,
Confronted *Hydra* in a sculler Boat,
At which the mighty mountaine *Taurus* rores,
Meane time great *Sultan Soliman* was borne
And *Atlas* blew his rustick rumbling horne.

Taylor wrote for gain, and it would seem that *Odcomb's Complaint* gave its author a good profit since three months later he brought Coryate back to life again in *The Eighth Wonder of the World, or Coriat's Escape from his supposed drowning*. By this time news had reached London of the mock-knighthood conferred on Coryate among the ruins of 'Troy'.[1] Taylor does not lose the opportunity of using this spurious title and accompanies it by an unkind dig:

Here there was double dub'd a doughty knight,
Rise up Sir Thomas, worship'd may'st thou be
Of people all (that are as wise as thee).

By this time Coryate was too far away, and perhaps too absorbed in other matters, to retaliate. As we shall see, he certainly read some of these later squibs in Constantinople, and he may have derived some consolation from the fact that, even if the context was generally unflattering, his name was being persistently brought to his countrymen's notice. Taylor was not the only writer to make use of Coryate's fame and reputation. A passage in Thomas Tomkis's *Albumazar* (Act I, Sc. 3), acted before King

[1] See p. 169.

James and the Court in the Hall of Trinity College, Cambridge, on 7 March 1614 suggests that, despite eighteen months' absence, Coryate and his doings were still the subject of court gossip:

*Ronca:* 'Look you there, what now?'
*Pandolfo* (looking through a magic telescope with which he has already espied the Court at Cambridge): 'Who? I see Dover Pier, a man now landing
    'Attended by two porters that seem to groan
    'Under the burden of two loads of paper.'
*Ronca:* 'That's Coriatus Persicus and 's observations
    Of Asia and Afric.'[1]

Apart from a few lines of verse in *The Nipping and Snipping of Abuses*, 1614, Taylor left his victim in peace for some time. Then in 1617 he published an account in prose of a journey to Hamburg. This pamphlet entitled *Three weekes, three daies and three hours Observations* is indicative of a slight mellowing in Taylor's attitude and also of continuing public interest in Coryate. It is not a parody of the *Crudities*, but has sufficient similarities in style and treatment for the resemblance to be recognized even without the dedication 'to the absent Odcombian Knight Errant Sir Thomas Coriat. Great Brittaines Error, and the Worlds Mirror . . . the Cosmographical, Geographical describer, Geometrical measurer; Historiographical Caligraphical Relater and Writer . . . the Od-combian Deambulator, Perambulator, Ambler, Trotter, or un-tired Traveller . . . Knight of Troy, and one of the dearest dar-lings to the blind Goddess Fortune.'

Having paid Coryate a belated compliment by using the *Crudities* as a pattern, the next year Taylor carried the process one stage farther by somehow getting hold of the last letter which Coryate wrote to his mother,[2] which he published under the title of *Master Thomas Coriat to his Friends in England sends Greeting* with two hundred verses by himself. Taylor goes out of his way to emphasize that the letter really is Coryate's work and not a leg-pull. The fact remains that the whole attraction of the pamphlet, as Taylor well knew, lay in the letter and not in his verses, and that he was nevertheless prepared to use Coryate's work for his

[1] There are also allusions to Coryate in *Pathomachia*, (Act I, Sc. 4 and Act IV, Sc. 4), probably acted first in 1616 or 1617, printed 1630. For other allusions in later plays, see pp. 295–6 below.     [2] Letter No. 6.

own gain. It is by no means certain that he obtained Coryate's mother's permission to use the letter since an article of such rarity would probably be copied and passed from hand to hand. It is, however, possible that he was allowed to use it in return for a promise that in his accompanying verses he would make some amends for the insults which he had showered on Coryate in the past. The verses are in the main a dull commentary on the text of the letter, but they are undeniably complimentary in tone. If he did pirate the letter he seems to have suffered no remorse, for he included both the verses and the complete letter in the folio edition of his works published in 1630.

When the letter and verses appeared in pamphlet form in 1618 Coryate was already dead, and when the news eventually reached England, Taylor paid him an apparently sincere tribute in some lines forming part of *Praise of Hempseed*, 1620:

> O famous Coriat, hadst thou come againe
> Thou wouldst have told us newes, direct & plaine, . . .
> Of cranes, and pigmies, lizzards, buzzards, owles,
> Of swine with hornes, of thousand beasts and foules . . .
> But farewell Thomas, never to returne
> Rest thou in peace within thy forraigne Urne,
> Hempseed[1] did beare thee o'er the raging fome
> And O I wish that it had brought thee home,
> For if thou hadst come back, as I did hope,
> Thy fellow had not beene beneath the Cope.
> But we must loose that which we cannot save.
> And freely leave thee whom we cannot have.

[1] Sails made from the product of hempseed.

# CHAPTER XI

# *Zante, Chios, and the Trojan Plain*

BEFORE the publication of the *Crudities* Coryate had already decided to make a journey to Constantinople, the cities of ancient Greece, and the Holy Land—all within the dominions of the Ottoman Emperor, the Grand Signor. Historians agree that the power of Turkey reached its zenith in the third quarter of the sixteenth century, and by this time was already in decline. But, though individual Christian travellers might hopefully note signs of decadence, the general view which the world took in 1612 was quite different. Turkey was still the strongest of all the Powers both by land and sea, and it still seemed possible that she might overwhelm and enslave the whole of Christendom. Even in England, detached from the mainland of Europe and far removed from the frantic efforts to stem and contain Turkey's landward advance, the dread was real and potent: 'O Almighty and Everlasting God, our Heavenly Father, we thy disobedient and rebellious children, now by thy just judgement sore afflicted, and in great danger to be oppressed, by thine and our sworn and most deadly enemies the Turks . . .' Thus began a prayer introduced into the English liturgy in 1565, and repeated for many years thereafter.[1] Englishmen might pray for deliverance, but nevertheless they were only too pleased to do business with these enemies of God, and English merchants, with royal encouragement, were rivalling the French and competing with the Venetians in the rich trade with the Levant. While England received her share of the contempt with which Turks regarded all foreigners, and in particular those preoccupied with commerce, the events of Queen Elizabeth's reign had created a measure of mutual esteem on both sides. Moryson tells how the Grand Signor, on being shown England on the map, wondered why the King of Spain did not 'dig it with mattocks and cast it into the sea',[2] and marvelled that

[1] Parker Soc., vol. XXVII, p. 522.
[2] Fynes Moryson, *Shakespeare's Europe*, ed. Charles Hughes, London, 1903, p. 31.

so small a country ruled by a woman should have prevailed against two of his own arch-enemies, the Pope and the King of Spain.

England's contact with Turkey was through sea-borne commerce and it was by sea that Coryate elected to reach Constantinople. He did not have far to look for assistance in procuring a passage and obtaining letters of introduction to the English Ambassador at Constantinople, and the merchants whom he was likely to encounter on his journey, since Lionel Cranfield, his friend, admirer, and banker, and Richard Martin, who had introduced him to Sir Henry Wotton in Venice, were both influential members of the Levant Company.[1]

He had begun and ended his European travels at Odcombe, and it is not difficult to believe that he started this second much more ambitious and dangerous journey from the same point and that, as Wood states, he made a farewell oration at the village cross. The text of this oration has not survived, but no doubt he told his countrymen that wherever his travels should take him the memory of his beloved birth-place would sustain and refresh him, and that one day, God willing, he would return to tell of the wonders he had seen.

From Odcombe he may have travelled to London and joined the ship there, or he may have embarked at a port in the West Country. The ship was probably owned by the Levant Company or chartered by it. Such vessels varied from 120 to 350 tons burden and carried crews of thirty to seventy men; they flew the royal arms of England with a red cross on white, and all were heavily armed.[2]

Coryate set forth on 20 October 1612.[3] His own account of the voyage has disappeared and only an echo of his maritime adventures has reached us in some verses published in pamphlet form with four of his letters from India.[4] It seems that his ship met with adverse weather from the outset and she may have been

[1] It does not seem to have been previously noted that the names of both appear as members in the Charter granted to the Company in 1605. A transcript of the Charter itself appears in M. Epstein, *The Early History of the Levant Company*, London, 1908, p. 153.

[2] M. Epstein, *op. cit.*, pp. 225–6, and A. C. Wood, *History of the Levant Company*, Oxford, 1935, p. 21.

[3] Purchas gives the date but does not state whether this was when Coryate left home, when he embarked, or when the ship sailed.

[4] *Thomas Coriate Traveller for the English wits: Greeting*, London, 1616. The pamphlet includes ninety-six lines of verse signed R. R., possibly Robert Richmond, q.v., p. 138, or Robert Rugge, q.v., p. 169.

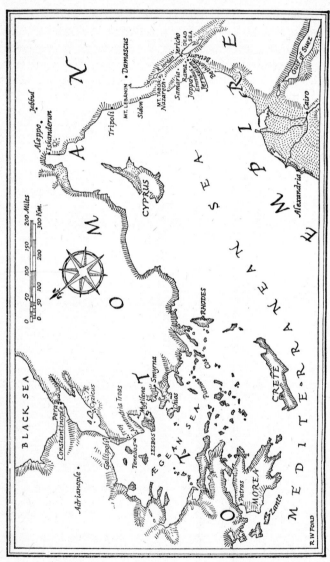

Map 2. The Levant.

further delayed by calls at Lisbon or Cadiz. At all events she was
still only on the threshold of the Mediterranean on Christmas Day
when she was hit by an easterly gale which forced her to shelter
off Gibraltar. Having ridden out the storm it seems that the ship
had a brush with the corsairs since the writer of the verses says
that on Coryate's return

> Of Drums, Guns, Trumpets he will tell
> Of haling Ships, of Pyrats fell.

Any voyage to Constantinople was a hazardous undertaking.
The Channel and Bay of Biscay were the hunting grounds of the
pirates based on Dunkirk; in the Mediterranean ships of every
nationality were prey to the corsairs of the Barbary Coast. The
three states of Algiers, Tripoli, and Tunis, though nominally
subject to the Sultan at Constantinople, were in fact independent
military republics living by piracy and by ransoming their enslaved prisoners. In the twelve years from 1607 to 1619 over
twelve thousand Christian prisoners of all nationalities were
brought into Algiers alone.[1] Of these some turned renegade and
themselves became pirates, a few were fortunate enough to be
ransomed, but the great majority lived out the rest of their days
in miserable slavery.

Coryate may not have been aware that he was making the voyage through the Mediterranean at the most dangerous time of
the year. From May to October the Turkish navy was at sea with
a fleet of sixty galleys 'to annoye the enemy, suppresse Pirats,
collect tribute and reforme disorders in the Maritime townes'.[2]
But during the winter months the galleys were laid up, and pirates,
both Christian and Mohammedan, plundered, slew, and enslaved
throughout the Mediterranean, having to reckon only with the
defences of their prey. Although the Levant Company's ships
were armed and normally sailed in convoy, no less than 466
English vessels were captured between 1609 and 1616.[3] The
so-called Christian pirates were quite as ferocious as the Moors;
it was men like the notorious Englishman, Ward, his courtly
recruit Sir Francis Verney, and the formidable Dutchman, Simon
Dansker, who taught the Barbary corsairs much of their know-

[1] J. B. Gramaye, *Diarium rerum Argelae gestarum ab anno 1619*, Düsseldorf, 1623.
In 1619 Gramaye was himself one of the 20,000 Christian slaves then living in Algiers.
[2] George Sandys, *A Relation of a Journey*, London, 1615, p. 40 (1652 edn.).
[3] A. C. Wood, *op. cit.*, p. 60.

ledge of ship construction and their skill in sea fighting.[1] If Coryate's ship had been worsted in an encounter with one of these he could have expected no less ugly a fate than at the hands of a Mohammedan. But the attack, if it took place, was repelled; the little ship continued her voyage in more favourable weather, and on 13 January 1613 Coryate landed safely on the Venetian island of Zante.

In these early days of the Levant Company's trading, the main commodity for which so many ships and English lives were risked was currants, and most of the currants came from Zante. Coryate, now permitted by his editor Purchas to take up the narrative, says the island was famous 'over most of Europe, Asia and Africa for three principall commodities . . . Wine, Oile, and Currans'. Lithgow, who visited Zante about this time, comments that sixty years previously nobody had heard of the island and that the inhabitants would have remained 'a base beggarly people . . . if it were not for some liquorish lips here in England of late, who forsooth can hardly digest bread, pasties, broth, and bag-puddings, without these currants'.[2] As there was practically no market in Zante for English goods, ships usually made a brief call here outward bound for stores and fresh water and returned to load currants on their homeward voyage.

After three months of ship-board life shared on uncomfortably close terms with sailors whom he regarded as 'leaden-pated fools', Coryate set about making the most of his brief stay. He made the acquaintance of some of the English merchants resident on the island and discussed with them the cause of the frequent earthquakes for which Zante was then, as now, notorious. 'The Earthquakes', he says, 'are so frequent with them that sometimes they feele ten of them in a moneth. At the time of my being in the same there was a little feeling of an Earthquake, which was perceived for some five or six dayes together . . . It often falleth out to bee so violent, that people fearing least the houses would falle downe then have been driven out of doores, even out of their naked beds, men in their shirts, women in their smockes, carrying their clothes with them, that they have hastily caught up, and have at leisure put them on afterward.'

---

[1] Samuel C. Chew, *The Crescent & the Rose*, New York, O.U.P., 1937, pp. 340–62, gives an interesting account of piracy in the Mediterranean at this period.

[2] William Lithgow, *Travels*, Edinburgh, 1760 edn., p. 65.

Because of the earthquakes the inhabitants lived in low, flat-roofed houses with wooden lattice instead of glass in their windows, 'which Lattice leaves in the Summer time they doe commonly take of[f], and then, seeing they are Greekes, and merrie Greekes too, they may be very properly said to keepe open houses'. Coryate always had an eye for a pretty face and he was particularly struck by the gentlewomen of Zante who, attired in their silks and damasks and attended by a page on foot who was generally a slave, rode about the town on donkeys. But more remarkable and perhaps even shocking was the fact that they rode astride, a custom 'which I never read or heard of amongst any other women'.[1]

With his usual thoroughness he took an inventory of the churches, and found that there were forty-three in all, 'only they are so little that a faire Towne Church of England will make very neere half a score of them'; of these thirty-nine in the town were Greek while the Venetian overlords had three churches in the citadel and one, St. Mary's, in the town. In the court of St. Mary's he was shown an ancient and neglected grave without any inscription or monument which nevertheless 'cannot but strike a kinde of veneration into any man that hath any sparke of learning', for it was thought to be the tomb of Cicero and his wife Terentia, discovered in the middle of the previous century when the church was being built. The Venetians had removed the inscribed commemorative stone from the grave and carried it to Venice. Coryate recalls with indignation that he had seen this stone fixed to the courtyard wall of a private house.[2] Now, contemplating the unmarked tombs, Coryate reflects, 'I could not but condole the misfortune of that famous and incomparable Orator from the inexhausted Fountaine of whose incomparable Learning so many excellent Orators have drawne liquor of Rhetoricall invention.' Privately, at any rate, Coryate placed himself among the ranks of the excellent orators.

Whether Coryate continued his voyage in the ship which

---

[1] Dr. E. S. de Beer tells me that in Italy courtesans and others frequently travelled in men's clothes and rode astride. Coryate was evidently unaware of this practice which is noticed by Fynes Moryson, *Itinerary*, vol. IV, p. 222.

[2] *Crudities*, vol. I, p. 320. In O. Dapper's, *Naukeurige Beschryving van Morea*, 1688, p. 150, there is an illustration of the tombstone and also the burial urn. The tombstone and inscriptions are considered to be spurious, see *Corpus Inscriptionum Latinarum*, Berlin, vol. III, 1873, Pt. 1, p. 5.

brought him from England or in another vessel is not known. We next find him in the Turkish-ruled island of Chios. Early in the reign of Henry VII English vessels were already calling here to obtain cargoes of sweet Malmsey wines, and in 1513 Henry VIII appointed an Italian to be consul there.[1] For some years after 1570, when the Turks took Chios from the Genoese, there was a hiatus in trading relations but these had been resumed and increased since the inauguration of the Levant Company who themselves maintained a consul there.[2]

On his arrival, Coryate introduced himself or was introduced to some of the resident English merchants, three of whom arranged to accompany him on an expedition to the monastery of Nea Mona. The party rode on donkeys over the steep, rough, mountain tracks and climbed to the monastery which had already stood on its hill for six hundred years, and still stands there now. They were taken by some of the monks into the ancient round chapel, where Coryate's eye was immediately attracted by an enormous candle, 'the goodliest waxe candle that ever I saw in my life, some eight foote high fastned to a wall, and so bigge as my middle for I measured it with my girdle'. He tried to speak to the monks in Greek with disappointing results 'for I could not finde as much as one learned man of the whole two hundred . . . they can onely read in their own Manuscript Greeke Bookes, but can neither understand nor speake any learned Greeke but the moderne'.

Coryate's companions were anxious to reach home before dark, so they rode back in the late afternoon through numberless plots of cotton. This, says Coryate, the islanders wove into dimity and scammato cloth which the Levant merchants' ships carried home to Britain. But already the same ships were carrying raw cotton wool, and in a very few years Smyrna, Cyprus, and Syria would be supplying quantities of the raw product to feed the newly founded spinning and weaving industry in Lancashire.[3] The whole island was very rich and fertile. According to Coryate's estimate it was able comfortably to support 80,000 inhabitants which is about one-fifth larger than the present population. Even more important to its prosperity than cotton were the plantations of *Pistachia*

[1] A. C. Wood, *op. cit.*, p. 2.
[2] It does not appear to have been previously noted that at this time one consul covered both Chios and Smyrna. Levant Co. Papers, S.P. 105/147, f. 133.
[3] A. C. Wood, *op. cit.*, p. 74.

*lentiscus*, the little evergreen shrub yielding gum mastic which in duty alone, so Coryate says, gave the Sultan of Turkey an annual revenue of 20,000 sequins.

About the middle of February, and the day after this excursion to the monastery, he sailed for Constantinople in the English ship *Samaritan*. On 22 February they anchored off the coast of the Troad, and Coryate with fourteen other Englishmen and a drago-man went ashore, all armed to the teeth against possible assault by the inhabitants, to explore what they took to be the ruins of Homer's Troy. So accurate are Coryate's observations that it is possible to say with certainty that they were in fact among the ruins of Alexandria Troas which lie on the coast within sight of the Island of Tenedos, about fourteen miles south-west of the real Troy. Alexandria Troas was originally named Antigoneia after its founder Antigonus, who assumed the title of King in 306 B.C. Lysimachus enlarged it and changed its name in honour of Alexander the Great. Its favourable position for securing the trade of the northern Aegean caused it to become one of the great cities of the Graeco-Roman world, and some time before 12 B.C. the Emperor Augustus made it a Roman Colony—Colonia Augusta Troadensium.

If it should be wondered why Coryate uncritically accepts the ruins of Alexandria Troas as being those of Troy, it must be re-membered that the ancient geographers, in particular Strabo with whose work he was acquainted, are by no means specific, and Pierre Belon, whose book[1] he had also carefully studied, positively identifies these ruins as Troy. Furthermore, the local guides had become aware of what was expected of them and would un-hesitatingly point out the tombs of Hector, Ajax, Achilles, Troi-lus, Hecuba, and other worthies[2] to travellers, whose knowledge of classical history and enthusiasm for Homer and Virgil made them anxious to believe what they were told, whereas the less educated might prove less gullible. It was only gradually during the latter part of the seventeenth century that the identification of Alexandria Troas with Troy was abandoned,[3] and it was of course

[1] *Les observations de plusieurs singularitez . . . en Grèce, Asie, Indee, . . .* Paris, 1553. Coryate probably used the Latin translation by C. de Lécluse, Antwerp, 1589, which was republished in the collected works of de Lécluse, Antwerp, 1605.

[2] Lithgow, *op. cit.*, p. 117.

[3] T. J. B. Spencer, *Robert Wood & the Problem of Troy in the Eighteenth Century.* Journal of the Warburg & Courtauld Institutes, vol. XX, 1-2, 1957, p. 84.

not until the nineteenth century that Schliemann finally solved the riddle.

Coryate was by no means the only Englishman of his day to visit the Troad. John Sanderson went there in 1592, but gives no details whatever. Thomas Dallam, sent out by Queen Elizabeth in 1599 with a pair of organs as a present for the Sultan, visited 'Troy' and 'thence I broughte a peece of whyte marble piller, the which I broke with my own handes, having a good hamer, which my mate Harvie did carrie a shore for the same purpose, and I brought this peece of marble to London'.[1] William Lithgow gives a brief and superficial account in his *Travels.* George Sandys landed at Sigeum and surveyed the plain, but dared not venture far from the coast, and does not give any close or accurate description of the few ruins which he did see. Fynes Moryson sailed past, but has very little to say about the Troad in particular or indeed of the Hellenic world in general. In marked contrast to all these, Coryate's description, even in Purchas's abbreviated version, runs to over 4,500 words, most of which is vivid and detailed personal observation. He is the first Englishman to reveal a lively interest in the antiquities of the Troad.[2]

Several Turks who approached Coryate and his armed companions when they landed regarded them with curiosity but without hostility, and explained that they were offering their services, for suitable remuneration, as guides. So, having struck a bargain with them, Coryate was able to forget his weapons and prepare the writing materials and measuring instruments which he had brought with him.

Near their landing place, which was a short distance from the old harbour, he saw 'foure or five goodly Marble Sepulchers of a great length, one of which I measured, and found it to be nine of my feete long. These Tombes consist of one intire Marble stone, even of white Marble; upon every corner of one whereof are foure round knobs, made in the forme of little pillowes, and the middle part riseth with a sharpe line, like unto the sharpe part of a Costlet or breast plate; likewise there was another of white Marble, on the left side whereof the whole proportion of two hands (which I

[1] *Diary* in *Early Voyages and Travels in the Levant*, ed. J. T. Bent, Hakluyt Society, 1893, pp. 49-50.

[2] Warner G. Rice, *Early English Travelers to Greece & the Levant*, University of Michigan Publications, Language and Literature, vol. X, University of Michigan Press, 1933, p. 236.

29. A fight with Barbary Corsairs. From the painting by Cornelis Vroom, dated 1615, in the National Maritime Museum, Greenwich. One of the corsair galleys is sinking, dragging down the Christian slaves, still chained to the benches.

30. Alexandria Troas. An early 19th-century view of some of the ruins engraved by R. Wallis after W. H. Bartlett.

*Radio Times Hulton Picture Library*

conjecture to have bin the hands of some great Lady) were so
curiously expressed, that it is impossible for Praxiteles or any
other that was the most excellent carver in the World to surpasse
it. I finde Petrus Bellonius[1] his observations of these Sepulchers
to be very true; for that which hee writeth of them is very certaine, that they are excavated, that is, made hollow in the inside,
in the forme of a Chest, & that the corners doe remaine whole and
entire . . . It grieved me to the heart that I could not learne either
by inscriptions, or any other meanes, whose Monuments these
were; for it is vaine to be induced by conjectures, to say they were
these or these mens; onely I hope no man will taxe me of a rash
opinion, if I beleeve one of them might be the Monument of King
Ilus, the enlarger of the Citie of Troy; for I remember that Homer
saith in his eleventh *Iliad*, that Ilus was buried in the open, as this
was; and that another of them might be the Monument of King
Priamus, it is not altogether unlikely, for Virgil writeth in his
second *Aeneid* that King Priamus, after the late fatall destruction
of the Citie, was slaine by Pyrrhus the Sonne of Achilles, neere the
Trojan shoare; for thus saith he—*jacet ingens littore truncus*. Now
though mercilesse Achilles persecuted the dead carkase of Hector
with that barbarous crueltie, as to dragge him starke naked at a
Carte taile, three times about the wals of the Citie; yet it is likely
they would so much honour the old silver haired King Priamus
(especially since they had now fully satisfied their furie, both by
burning of the Citie and massacring of all the most Noble
Citizens, and with the rest their last King) as to cover his body
with some royall monument beseeming his regall state: pardon
me (gentle reader) for this my conjecture. I affirme nothing cer-
tainely, onely I gesse, as another industrious traveller would doe,
that hath or shall observe the same things that I have done, that
one of those goodly Monuments might be the Sepulcher of King
Priamus.'

From the place where these tombs lay Coryate and his companions walked to the ruins of the ancient port. They never suspected that they were standing near the scene of events which had
affected their lives far more deeply than anything which occurred
at Troy. Somewhere in the city on the hill above them the vision
of the man from Macedonia had appeared to St. Paul, and it was
from this harbour that St. Paul had sailed to carry the Gospel from

---

[1] i.e. Pierre Belon, see p. 165, Note 1.

Asia into Europe.[1] But Coryate was busy speculating on more
ancient happenings. 'As you walke up from this mould [haven]
towards the Citie, you see the stately Pallace of the King before
you, standing in a direct line opposite to your face; by the consideration of which I did the better confirme that beliefe in my
selfe, that the Pallace, which I will shortly speake of, might be the
place of the Kings royall residence: for it was a very delicate
passage for the King, either in a Chariot or a Horse backe from
this mould through a stately faire streete, to his owne Pallace,
distant but a little mile from the water: . . . a great part of the
ground betwixt the mould and the Pallace is beset with certaine
Trees of divers kindes, as Mulberry trees, Firre trees, boxe trees,
Olive trees, Live Oake trees, Almond trees, whereof some wee
saw beare blossomes when wee were there; also it beareth Broome
of a great height, and such as yealdeth a prettie kinde of sent . . .
We approached neere to the foot of the Pallace . . . The whole
Frontispice consisted of a most beautiful white stone, cut square
like our Azure stones[2] in England, the fairest for the breadth,
length, and thicknesse that ever I saw; though now through
Antiquitie of time the beautiful grace of the stone is somewhat
diminished. The whole front of the Pallace saving a little at the
top consisteth of such square stones. Every stone hath in the
middle part of the front thereof a certaine little hole, which to
what end it served I know not. This front for a piece of plaine
stone Worke doth yeald the fairest shew that ever I saw in any
Palace in my life. And though I thinke it is as ancient as the Citie
of Troy, yet to strangers that saile upon the Channell neere at
hand it presenteth such a faire white shew, that the first time I
looked upon it without the helpe of an Opticke Glasse,[3] I thought
it had beene some new Building raised within these few yeeres.

The front is beautified with three Arches, whereof that in the . . .
middle . . . is some fortie Geometricall foote broad, and sixe and

[1] *Acts*, ch. xvi, 8–11. It was here also, at Alexandria Troas, that St. Paul raised
Eutychus from the dead, *Acts*, ch. xx, 7–12.

[2] The usual meaning, lapis lazuli, is clearly inappropriate here. John Bullokar,
*An English Expositor*, 1616, speaks of 'Lazule stone, a blewish greene stone of the
kinde of marble'. *O.E.D.*

[3] Coryate implies that he owned or borrowed an 'optic glass'. This would almost
certainly be a single magnifying lens. Telescopes were being made in London by the
end of 1609, but were known as 'perspectives', 'cylinders', or 'Dutch trunks'. 'Tele-
scopio' was first used by Galileo in 1611 and 'Telescopium' by Kepler in 1613.
See *O.E.D.* and H.C. King, *The History of the Telescope*, London, 1955, p. 33.

thirtie foot high, but from the very top of the Frontispice from the ground, I take to bee eightie foot high, for I tooke the Altitude and Latitude of it by a Mathematicall Instrument.'[1]

The ruins were very much more imposing and complete than they are today. There was little contemporary interest in archae-ology—none at all on the part of the Turks, but there was and continued to be a very pronounced interest in putting fine, dis-used building stone to practical use. Coryate remarks that 'divers of these Trojane ruines have been transferred to many of the neighbour countries to serve for their publike and private build-ings . . . Yea the Turkes from some part or other of the Trojane Territories doe daily carry away stones in their Gallies.' Some of the finest marble pillars seen by Coryate were removed by Muhammad IV (1649–87) to adorn the mosque Yeni Valideh Jami' in Constantinople. Visitors helped in the work of destruc-tion; Coryate himself emulated Dallam, the organ-builder. He saw on what he took to be Priam's palace 'white marble very exquisitively carved with curious Borders and Workes expressed therein . . . from the which I brake of[f] certaine stones to carrie with mee into my Countrie'.

'It happened that when wee had thoroughly satiated our eyes, with contemplation of these ancient ruines, the Chiefetaine of the Company, a sworne Brother of mine, Master Robert Rugge, ob-serving that I had taken paines for some few houres in searching out the most notable Antiquities of this the worthiest part of Troy to yeeld mee some kinde of guerdon or remuneration for my paines, in a merrie humour drew his Sword out of his Scab-berd, and ascending to one of these great stones that lye in the open part of this middle Gate Knighted mee, that kneeled upon another stone on my right knee, by the name of the first English Knight of Troy, and at the knighting of mee, pronounced those wittie verses *ex tempore*:

> Coryate no more, but now a Knight of Troy,
> Odcombe no more, but henceforth England's Joy.
> Brave Brute of our best English wits commended;
> True Trojane from Aeneas race descended.
> Rise top of wit, the honour of our Nation,
> And to old Ilium make a new Oration.

[1] This may have been either a quadrant or a Jacob's staff, borrowed perhaps from the *Samaritan*.

'Two poore Turkes that stood not a little way from us when hee drew his naked Sword, thought verily hee meant to have cut off my head for some notorious villany that I had perpetrated. Those Verses I answered *ex tempore*, also our Musketteeres discharged two volleyes of shot for joy of my Knighthood.

> Loe heere with prostrate knee I doe embrace
> The gallant title of a Trojane Knight.
> In Priams Court which time shall ne're deface;
> A grace unknowne to any Brittish Wight.
> This noble Knighthood shall Fame's Trumpe resound,
> To Odcombes honour maugre Envie fell,
> O're famous Albion throughout that Iland round
> Till that my mournfull friends shall ring my knell.'

Naturally Rugge's invitation to make an oration was not refused and Coryate, mounting a high stone, harangued his applauding countrymen to the further astonishment of the Turkish onlookers. Having congratulated himself and them on their good fortune in being able to visit what was, after Jerusalem, the most famous city in the world, he reminded them that other famous visitors included Alexander the Great and the Emperors Hadrian and Septimus Severus. He exhorted them to look well at the stately ruins, then 'cast your eyes againe upon some other parts, where you may behold greene wheate growing amidst the old fragments of stones, and then remember the notable speech of the Poet Ovid:

*Jam seges est ubi Troja fuit*[1]

These famous words would strike a chord in the heart of his English audience, for they had come to form part of a popular English ballad, *The Wandering Prince of Troy*, with the refrain:

> Waste lie those walls that were so good
> And corne now grows where Troy Town stood.[2]

Coryate ended his oration on a moral note, with a sharp dig at fast living in London Town. Although the Trojan Horse was the

---

[1] *Heroides*, i, 53.
[2] Cited by T. J. B. Spencer, *op. cit.* The ballad was entered in the Stationers' Register in 1603, and may be older. The earliest surviving text is dated about 1620; it is reprinted in *The Roxburghe Ballads*, ed. W. Chappell and J. W. Ebsworth, 1866–99, vol. VI, p. 547.

immediate cause of the fall of Troy, the underlying reason for the collapse was, he said, the moral rottenness of its inhabitants: 'You may also observe as in a cleere Looking-glasse one of the worst pregnant examples of Luxurie, that ever was in the World in these confused heapes of stones, that lie before your eyes. For Adulterie was the principall cause of the ruines of this Citie, which is well knowne to all those that have a superficial skill in Historie, by the remembrance whereof I will now take occasion to wish one charitable wish to the Metropolitane Citie of mine owne Countrie, and with the same as with an Epilogue conclude my speech, that as Luxurie destroyed this Citie of old Troy, to which most ardent petitions upon my prostrate knee, I beseech the great Jehovah, which is the rewarder of Chastitie, and severe punisher of Incontinence to avert the punishment from our new Troy, (for indeed, London was in former times called Troyno-vante[1]) which I thinke is as much polluted and contaminated with extravagant lusts, as ever was this old Troy.'

On the way back to the shore a curious incident took place. Coryate and one of his companions, Francis Flyer,[2] saw a plough-man at his work, and marched towards him. One can imagine the consternation of the ploughman at the purposeful approach of two fully armed foreigners and his bewildered relief when he had comprehended and agreed to their demand, which was simply that they might each, one after the other, drive the plough a little way 'that if wee live to be Old men we may say in our old age, we had once holden the Plough in the Trojane Territorie'.

Coryate was so delighted with his visit that he said he would have willingly foregone five hundred pounds to make it, a sum which is probably greater than he ever possessed. Furthermore he considered that such a visit was worth a special journey from England. 'Therefore let me advise all my Country-men that meane to travell into the world for observation to see this famous place in their Travels, as being farre the most worthiest of all the ruined places in the world that are not Inhabited.'

'But', interposes the infuriating Purchas, 'me thinks I heare some Trojan complaine of another tedious ten yeeres siege: I will

---

[1] Cf. William Dunbar (1465?–1530?), *London*, l.9, 'Thou lusty Troynovaunt'.

[2] Sworn a member of the Levant Company at a General Court held on 1 October 1612 (S.P. 105/147, ff. 24–25). It therefore seems likely that he came from England at the same time as Coryate.

therefore abruptly breake off the rest,' and this he does. We therefore know nothing of his voyage through the Dardanelles and across the Sea of Marmora to Constantinople.

We can, however, surmise that the *Samaritan* was becalmed in the Sea of Marmora off the Erdek Peninsula, and that Coryate went ashore there to investigate the ruins of Cyzicus, the once powerful Milesian colony, with whose existence and history his classical reading would have made him acquainted. Certain it is that he visited Cyzicus, and as he does not appear to have done so on the return voyage from Constantinople, he must either have made a special expedition during his stay in Constantinople or landed from the *Samaritan*.

Here, prying among the debris, he found a white marble head which he carried away with him, and of which he was immensely proud. In one of his letters from India he asks to be remembered to the famous antiquary, Sir Robert Cotton. 'Pray tell him that I have a very curious white Marble head of an ancient Heros or Gyant-like Champion found out very casually by my diligent pervestigation among the ruins of . . . Cyzicus.' Cotton would no doubt have been interested in this information, but could scarcely have been pleased by a sting in the tail of the message, since Coryate claimed that this head would make all Cotton's 'best Antiquities whatseover veile bonnet'.

CHAPTER XII

# *Constantinople*

---

SINCE representatives of the Levant Company were to be Coryate's mentors and associates for the next two years it will be as well, at this point, to give a few details about the Company's constitution and *modus operandi*.

Although England's direct participation in the Levant trade was a recent development, those who could afford the high prices, imposed by scarcity and inflated by the intervention of innumerable middlemen, had for generations been able to enjoy the exotic luxuries of the Levant and the Orient. In the fourteenth and fifteenth centuries eastern goods had reached England via Venice in a fleet of merchant galleys dispatched annually from about 1317. This trade fell away in the first half of the sixteenth century and for a period Antwerp superseded Venice as the great depot for eastern merchandise. But Antwerp was soon eclipsed, first by commercial quarrels in the 1560's, and then by the revolt in the Netherlands. Not until 1580 was the first treaty signed between England and Turkey, giving the English trading rights similar to those accorded to the French nearly half a century earlier. In that year Queen Elizabeth laid the foundation of the Levant Company by granting the monopoly of the Levant trade to twelve merchants. Two years later Henry Harborne, the merchant who had carried out most of the negotiations for the treaty in Constantinople, was appointed by royal commission 'our true and undoubted orator, messenger, deputie and agent'— not, be it noted 'ambassador', though that is what he was. Furthermore, the Queen insisted that the merchants should pay for all Harborne's expenses, and for the indispensable flow of presents to the Sultan and his Court, though she graciously allowed these costly gifts to be offered in her name.

From the outset the Ambassador played a difficult and ambiguous role. The sovereign approved the appointment, but the

Ambassador was chosen and paid by the Levant Company. The Turks disdained all foreign infidels, and they particularly despised those engaged in commerce, yet the man who was the accredited representative of the Crown was at the same time the head of the English merchant community in the Levant.

When James I granted a new Charter to the Company in 1605 this system remained unchanged. Not only the Ambassador but his Secretary or deputy at Constantinople, the Consuls, Chaplains, and Physicians at Constantinople and Aleppo, and the Consuls at the various other trading centres, were all appointed and maintained by the Levant Company. The Company taxed itself for all its necessary expenses and levied duty, or consulage, on the merchandise in which its members were dealing; it was the Consul's prime function to collect and remit these monies. King James's Charter continued almost unchanged for the remainder of the Company's existence; not until 1803 did the British Government assume the responsibility for appointing and paying the Ambassador, his Secretaries, and some of the Consuls. The rest of the Consuls remained a charge on the Levant Company until it ceased to exist by voluntarily surrendering its Charter in 1825.

In Coryate's day the most important English export to the Levant was cloth. In this trade the English merchants were in competition with the long-established but waning power of the Venetians. While imitating the Venetians in colour—mainly purple and crimson—the English were able to offer good-quality cloth at a cheaper price than their competitors with the result that between 1600 and 1620 cloth exports increased by one-third.[1] A large proportion of the best-quality cloth went to Constantinople for sale to members of the Sultan's Court, or to merchants who forwarded it by caravan to the Persian market. As trimmings and linings for the elaborate Turkish costumes the Levant Company's ships brought English furs: very large quantities of black cony skins and also the skins of squirrels, martens, and polecats.[2] Cornish tin was an important export; Sandys says it was the most profitable of all 'here [i.e. in Constantinople] exceedingly used and exceedingly wasted; for they tinne the insides of their vessels, and monethly renew it'.[3] In addition to basic English products such as lead, pewter, and wrought iron, the Company had already

[1] A. C. Wood, *op. cit.*
[2] Epstein, *op. cit.*, pp. 18 and 232–8.
[3] Sandys, *op. cit.*, p. 67.

started to ship re-exported East India merchandise, in particular pepper. The return cargoes were currants, spices, drugs, silk, grograin made of silk and mohair, chamblette—a stuff mixed with camel hair—galls for making ink, carpets, oils, and wines. The Company's ships even carried caviare, on which the consulage was 8*d.* per ton![1]

Coryate arrive in Constantinople towards the end of March 1613, and his first action on landing was to present himself and make an oration before the Ambassador, Mr. Paul Pindar. Pindar was getting on for fifty years old, but his portrait painted in Constantinople about the time of Coryate's visit is of a man who might have been some years younger. He lived to be well over eighty, so his youthful appearance may not have been due to artistic flattery. It seems unlikely that even an early seventeenth-century portraitist would have endowed him with such surprised, protuberant eyes, and such a very large, questing nose if he had been bent on humouring his subject rather than striving to record the truth.

Pindar had started life as an apprentice to an Italian merchant settled in England, who employed him as his agent in Venice. After fifteen years in Venice he removed to Turkey, and before the turn of the century was appointed Secretary to the Ambassador. This post, which involved acting as the Ambassador's deputy, he filled with some distinction. One of the Levant Company merchants described him in those days as 'a sensible, wise gentellmanlike man and one that hear hath much creadited our nation'.[2] In 1606 he was appointed Consul at Aleppo, where he remained for four or five years. He then came home and in the autumn of 1611 was in London, 'a person of growing importance and very dear to Lord Salisbury with whom he had long interviews'.[3] These talks seem to have redounded to Pindar's advantage for in November that year he was appointed Ambassador.

Although the collection of Arabic and Persian manuscripts

---

[1] Epstein, *op. cit.*, p. 237. It seems probable that the caviare came from North Sea sturgeons. 'In the mouth of the River Elbe neere Hamburg . . . they catch so many Salmons and Sturgens, as they transporte great quantity thereof to forrayne parts, and feede theire servants so plentifully with them, as they abhorr that meate, and condition with their masters how many tymes in the weeke they should feede therewith.' Fynes Moryson, *Shakespeare's England*, p. 357.

[2] John Sanderson, *Travels*, ed. Sir William Foster, London, 1931, p. 186.

[3] *Cal. S. P. Venetian*, 1610–13, p. 202.

which he presented to the Bodleian Library is an indication that he had some intellectual interests, his main preoccupation, apart from protecting and furthering the interests of the Company and his country, was the amassing of an enormous private fortune. He seems to have managed to go on accumulating wealth despite the fact that as Ambassador he was forbidden to engage in trade. On his return to England in 1620 he was knighted, and in his later years he lent large sums to the Exchequer, presented £19,000 towards the repair of St. Paul's Cathedral, and, on the outbreak of the Civil War, sent generous help to the King.

It is possible that Coryate had met Pindar in London, and probable that he carried letters of introduction to him from Cranfield or some of Cranfield's fellow businessmen. Since the publication of his two books Coryate was no longer a nonentity, and Pindar may well have felt it expedient as well as amusing to have him as a guest in his house. The visitor's arrival and activities were of sufficient interest for Pindar to write to Sir Dudley Carleton, the Ambassador in Venice, who had succeeded Wotton: 'Heare is with me that famous travailer of Odcombe Sir Thomas Coryate whoe lying at Temidos [Tenedos] wynde bound some few daies had tyme, and tooke the opportunitie to view the Antient Ruynes of Troye where some of the Companie knighted him in the name of Kinge Priam, under the gate of his Royall Pallace which he sayeth, is yet to be perceaved, by manie notes which he hath observed, as more at large shalbe made knowen in his books he myndeth to putt forthe at his retorne into England.'[1]

This letter, which is dated 14 April 1613, goes on to outline Coryate's plans for the future. From Constantinople he intended to travel to Jerusalem and Cairo, and then return to Venice. 'In the meantyme he hath verie often solicited me to mancione hym to your Lordship: to the which he hath letters of Recommendacons from your Lordships hon: good ffreindes.' At this date, therefore, Coryate seems to have had no intention of journeying to India.

Carleton replied from Venice in September: 'to assure your Lordship that I have no quarrel to your famous Coriat I can give you no better proof then these rimes which goe herewith and were newly sent me out of England. And yf the newes of his great hazards and fortunes were not wellcome unto me, my friends

[1] *S.P.* 97/7, f. 32–33.

32. Rev. Samuel Purchas. From the title page of his *Pilgrimes*, 1625.

31. Paul Pindar.

33. Turkish Punishments. 'Stakeinge, gaunchinge, drubbing or beating on the feete' from the eye-witness drawing by Peter Mundy who visited Constantinople in 1620.

would not so often charge me as they doe with the postage of such pamflets.'[1] Evidently he was kept supplied with John Taylor's squibs as they were published, and it is interesting to note that although Carleton found them amusing to read, neither he nor Pindar seems to have regarded Taylor's target as a mere buffoon.

It was usual for the few English visitors to Constantinople to be the personal guests of the Ambassador. Moryson, Lithgow, and Sandys were all guests of Pindar's predecessors, and Sandys stayed for nearly four months. It seems probable that Coryate lived in Pindar's house for the duration of his stay, though this eventually extended to more than ten months, by the end of which time the Ambassador might excusably have been anxious to see him on his way. There is, however, no hint of strained relations. Coryate seems to have received nothing but kindness and consideration from Pindar, and he was frequently included in the Ambassador's suite on state occasions.

Only the Ambassador of the Holy Roman Emperor resided within the walls of Constantinople, but this was the reverse of a privilege since the object was to facilitate a narrow watch on his movements and activities. All the other Ambassadors lived on the far side of the Golden Horn in Pera. Pera was the Greek name, Galata the official Turkish name, but as it was the foreign part of the town it was popularly known by Turks as 'the pig quarter' —*dumus* (hog) being the usual appellation of all Franks or Western Christians.

The British Ambassador's house was on 'the top of the hill within a large field and pleasant gardens compassed with a wall'.[2] Besides the Ambassador and his servants there were about twenty English factors and their servants resident in Pera,[3] for whose spiritual and physical health the Levant Company maintained a chaplain and a physician. It was mainly a bachelor community. There was probably not one English female in the whole city at this time—unless she was a slave. Usually only the Ambassador had his wife with him, and Pindar was unmarried. The authorities at home discouraged marriage because women and children could be nothing but a nuisance and a danger. Although Franks

---

[1] *S. P. Venetian* 99/13, Pt. III, f. 220.
[2] Fynes Moryson, *Itinerary*, vol. II, p. 92.
[3] A. C. Wood, *op. cit.*, p. 240.

were forbidden to touch a Turkish woman on pain of death, and the English were cut off from most other Franks by the difference in religion, it did not follow that the English were entirely deprived of female companionship. As Sandys put it, speaking of Franks in general: 'They live freely and plentifully: and many will not lie alone where women are so easily come by. For besides the [slave] markets, it is a use not prohibited but onely by our religion, to purchase for their concubines the beautiful daughters of the Grecians, wherewith the adjoyning Islands are plentifully stored.'[1]

During his long stay Coryate must have assembled an enormous quantity of notes. He carried these with him as far as Aleppo and sent them home before starting thence on his long trek to India in September 1614. By that time he had been away from home for just under two years. These notes came into Purchas's possession after he had published three of Coryate's letters from India in his *Pilgrimes*, Part I, Book IV, Chapter 17, but in time to be included in Part II, Book 10, Chapter 12. Purchas, however, compressed Coryate's notes into a mere fifty pages. His reasons for doing so are fairly clear. Coryate's material had to be trimmed to fit in with the general pattern of the *Pilgrimes*, which already included a number of contemporary accounts of similar travels. Judging what Purchas has left us against the pattern of the *Crudities*, it is apparent that he must have cut out a vast amount of historical detail, most of the descriptions of buildings, and reports of many incidents and customs which had already been covered by other writers. What remains is therefore nothing like a complete picture of the Turkish dominions as Coryate saw them. But we are given the distillation of his exceptional powers of observation, and the account is of particular value since it concentrates mainly on incidents which are either totally ignored, or dealt with less fully by other writers.

It is clear that Coryate's original notes took the form of a diary, and most of the entries preserved by Purchas are preceded by a date. The earliest to deal with life in Constantinople reads: 'The first of Aprill being Thursday, and the day immediately before Good-friday I with divers of my Countrimen went about midnight to the Monastery of the Franciscan Friers, where within a little after I came thither, I observed a very rigorous and austere

---

[1] Sandys, *op. cit.*, p. 67.

kind of Discipline, whereof indeed I had often heard before that time, but never saw till then. Just about the point of Midnight, a little after Masse was begun, certaine fellowes prostrating themselves in the middle of the Quire of the Church, directly before the high Altar, whipped themselves very cruelly, and continued in the mercilesse punishment of themselves at the least an houre and a halfe . . . their faces were covered with Canvasse vayles so that no man could perceive any of them, & all the middle part of their back was naked which they lashed with certaine Napkins at the end whereof were . . . inclosed certaine little sharp peeces of Iron, made like the straight part of the rowell of a Spurre, which at the very first blow . . . did easily draw blood. They kept a certaine order in laying on their blowes, now on the right shoulder, & after over the left, in the space of a quarter of an houre, I saw one of them that dealt somewhat roughly with himselfe by redoubling his blowes a little faster then the rest, did fetch of[f] all the skin from the middle part of his backe, which was a very dolefull and tragicall Spectacle, and when hee had very bitterly whipped himselfe, there came a certaine fellow with a Cloth in his hand steeped in Vinegar with which he wiped away the blood that it should not rankle [fester].'

These flagellants were not penitent sinners but galley slaves acting as proxies for rich Christians—among them the French Ambassador—who were to pay the price of the slaves' liberty. This form of penance appears to have been an annual spectacle, for Sanderson mentions that he saw it, though he does not describe it. It was not peculiar to Constantinople: Montaigne witnessed a procession of five hundred flagellants in Rome, many of whom were galley slaves acting as deputies in order to acquire their freedom. Purchas remarks in a marginal comment 'these hypocrites which doe Penance by others, must go to Heaven by proxie too'.

Four days later Coryate accompanied the Ambassador on an official visit to the Admiral in Chief of the Turkish Navy—the 'Captain Bashaw' as Coryate calls him. Nothing is known of this first introduction to the Ottoman Court, but a curious incident occurred when they were on their way back from the Palace. Pindar espied a Turk fishing under the wall of the Seraglio, whom he recognized as Rama, the Sultan's soothsayer. Rama was prepared, for a suitable consideration, to practise his art on a foreigner, and Pindar persuaded Coryate without much difficulty to have his fortune told. 'Unto him my Lord sent me with Master Edward Connock his Secretary and one of his Druggemen, to the end he should tell me my Fortune, whereupon he delivered unto me two Dice, and willed me to cast them upon a certaine smooth greene stone that lay before him, which when I had done, hee wrote with his Pen certaine Turkish Characters upon the same stone, by virtue whereof he Prognosicated my Fortune and presaged to this effect, as the Druggeman interpreted his speech, viz. That I was a man desirous to Travell into remote Regions, that according to my desire I should travell farre, and should be in danger for my Religion sake, and should also escape that danger, after that I should come to a great Citie (perhaps he meant London) where many would flocke about me to hear me Discourse of those things that I had seene and done in my Travels.' A man does not become the Royal Fortune-teller unless he is exceptionally good at telling his clients what they want to hear. When Mr. Connock had given the fellow money he added for good measure that Coryate would write a book of his travels and publish it to the benefit of his countrymen and many thousands besides. These predictions were of course a reasonably accurate summary of the past. As regards the future, Coryate had less than four years of life ahead of him, and was to die with his travels uncompleted and his book unwritten.

Fires in the city were frequent; Coryate records that there were three serious ones in under five weeks. Some were accidental, but in other cases 'it doth happen that Janizaries doe of purpose set Houses on fire, even to the great endangering of the Citie for prey and spoyle sake, especially the houses of Jewes. For which cause the Jewes within these few yeares, have both made their Houses stronger then they were wont to be, and also have made Vaults under their houses, into the which they may conveigh their Goods whensoever there chanceth any sodaine Fire.'

On 20 April about midnight a great fire began, which would have done much damage, but for the prompt and vigorous intervention of the 'Captain Bashaw', who had every reason to be energetic 'least if there should have beene any great hurt done, perhaps he might have lost his Head after the kings returne to the Citie'.

The 'Captain Bashaw' was on this occasion assisted by the

'Bustan' [Bostanji-Bashi], an important functionary who combined the offices of Chief Gardener with that of Sultan's Helmsman and Lord High Executioner. He brought two thousand men with him from the Seraglio, and their combined efforts soon had the fire under control after about fifty houses had been destroyed. While the fire was being fought the 'Captain Bashaw' himself killed with his mace a Janissary whom he saw rifling a house. 'It is the Custome that whensoever any Fire riseth in the Citie, to Hang up him in whose House it beginneth, as now a Cooke in whose house it began was Hanged presently after the Fire ceased.'

Hanging was a merciful fate by Ottoman standards, and was a sentence passed only as a favour on those condemned to death. Brothers of the reigning Sultan and other great personages were strangled with a bow-string; military officers convicted of stealing were shot from the mouth of a cannon, while adulterous women were thrown into the sea tied in a sack. But the commonest form of execution seen by all visitors and described by most of them was ganching [Italian: gancio, a hook]. The condemned 'were stripped into their linnen breches, with thier hands and feete bound all four together at their backs, and so drawne up with a rope by a pullie uppon the gallowes and lett faule uppon a great iron hooke fastened to a lower crosse barr of the gallowes, most comonlie lightinge uppon thier flancke and so through thier thye. Ther they hange, sometim[e]s talkinge a day or two together. But yf they be gaunched throughe the belly, and backe then ar they dead in two or three howers. Thus they use thier common theeves at Constantinople.'[1]

Towards the end of April the capital prepared to receive its monarch, who had been away in Adrianople since December. Achmet I had succeeded to the throne ten years previously at the age of fourteen in inauspicious circumstances. His father, Mohammed III, had murdered nineteen of his brothers on his accession, and after this display of energy had relapsed into a life of debauchery. His eldest son, Mahmoud, was a man of character and determination who might have curbed the power of the Janissaries, and mitigated the corruption of the governing class which, in the half century since the death of Solyman the Magnificent, had been insidiously sapping the gigantic strength of the Empire.

[1] Sanderson, *op. cit.*, p. 87.

But the Sultan became suspicious of his eldest son and jealous of his ability, so he had him dispatched with a bow-string, and stifled remonstrance by killing the young man's mother and all his closest friends. A few weeks later a Dervish prophesied to the Sultan that in fifty-five days' time a great calamity would befall him. On the fifty-fifth day Mohammed III died and his eldest surviving son, Achmet, found himself elevated to supreme power.[1]

Achmet I spent most of his time with the women. He had neither the inclination nor the ability to take an active part in the affairs of state, which he left to his Grand Vizier. Corruption and injustice led to general impoverishment, which in turn led to frequent revolt and violent oppression. But although historians have demonstrated that the Ottoman Empire was already in decline, this was not apparent to her enemies at the time. In any case none of them was strong enough to do her serious injury. War with Persia continued fitfully, and generally to Turkey's disadvantage, but the Persian armies were unable to penetrate the Empire's vitals. Cossack fleets raided the southern coasts of the Black Sea, and in 1614 they laid waste the rich port of Sinope, but such attacks were pinpricks. On her northern frontiers Poland, though hostile, was torn with internal dissension, while the Holy Roman Emperor had concluded peace with Turkey in 1606, and was shortly to have all his energies absorbed by the Thirty Years War. Venice and Spain, two traditional enemies of the Porte, were themselves in a state of decline. France and England were friendly towards the Turks, though they eyed each other's actions in the Levant with suspicion.

The underlying weakness of the Ottoman Empire was not reflected in the outward shows of pomp and power surrounding the person of the Sultan, and elaborate plans were made for his triumphal entry into Constantinople with a retinue fifteen thousand strong. Preparations had originally been made on the assumption that the Sultan would reach the city on 1 May, but everything had to be re-arranged when he decided to arrive three days earlier. Then all was put in confusion once more when it became known that he would encamp three miles outside Constantinople on the evening of 27 April, and make his entry the following morning.

The Ambassador and his entourage, of whom Coryate was one,

---

[1] J. von Hammer-Purgstall, *Geschichte des Osmanischen Reiches*, 1883 edn., vol. IV, p. 343.

started out at 5 a.m. to take up their positions by the Adrianople
Gate on the route of the procession. But when they arrived they
found that the Sultan had persisted in being perverse and had
forestalled everybody by riding in before dawn, together with his
Sultana and children and all their attendants.[1] Even without the
imperial family and a large part of the Court the procession must
have taken several hours to pass by. The religious, administrative,
and domestic orders, as well as the military, all had their place,
and the innumerable contingents presented to Coryate's quick eye
a strange variety of sights, some grotesque, and one or two distinctly comic. But the general effect was one of awe-inspiring
might and splendour. 'The pompe of it was so gallant that I never
saw the like in my life, neither doe I thinke that the like hath beene
used amongst any Princes of the world saving these Musulmen,
since the time of the Romane Emperours.'

The march was headed by the Governor of Constantinople and
Galata with an escort of cavalry and musketeers. 'Next followed
French Souldiers, a company of fugitive Rogues, that to get a
large pay fled to Constantinople to be entertained by the Grand
Signior, of whom the greatest part of them doth receive halfe a
Dollar [about three shillings] a day for their pay.' This of course
was an enormously high wage for a common soldier. These
Frenchmen had originally been part of the Christian garrison of
the Hungarian town of Papa, where they had become exasperated
at receiving no pay at all. In 1600 some two thousand of them had
attempted to fight their way through to the Turkish camp fifty
miles away in return for a promise that the Sultan would make good
their arrears. Five or six hundred got through, and the survivors
remained as a fighting force in the Sultan's service for twenty
years, renowned for their bravery in battle and for their savagery
to any Christians who fell into their hands.[2] The fortunes of war
and the passage of time had much reduced their numbers but, as
Coryate relates, they could still muster a hundred musketeers led
by their Colonel and some twenty mounted officers.

After the French renegades came a naval contingent 'carrying a
Gallie with a man in, a verie strange and ridiculous conceit, for
indeed everie one laughed heartily at it'. Next came 'squibsters'
[? artillerymen] and these were followed by a great multitude of

---

[1] *Levant Company Papers*, S.P. 101/94, f. 147.
[2] J. von Hammer-Purgstall, *op. cit.*, vol. IV, pp. 293-4.

the Sultan's slaves, Ajem Oghlan, or 'Gemiglandes' as Coryate calls them, young men compulsorily recruited from the children of the Sultan's Christian subjects who were made Mohammedans and trained for various duties; many were in due time enrolled as Janissaries.

At length the Sultan's empty coach appeared, covered with cloth of gold, and attended by a single outlandish warrior in a dress of fur and feathers. This was a Deli, one of the 'Corps of Madcaps' who, fortified with religious zeal and relying on their fantastic uniform of skins and plumage to strike fear into the enemy, offered themselves for any particularly hazardous enterprise. It was said that not one had ever shown his back to the foe, whatever the odds.

Next came a company of mounted 'chauses', two hundred of them attended by six hundred servants on foot. The Chiaus, a personal messenger of the Sultan, was not unknown in England; indeed his title had recently been incorporated in our language in the form of the verb 'to chouse' as the result of an incident which had cost the Levant Company a lot of money and caused considerable merriment in London.

Among the duties of a Chiaus was that of accompanying notable foreign travellers when traversing the Ottoman dominions to protect them from exaction by the provincial authorities. In 1605 a Chiaus named Mustafa had left Constantinople in the suite of the returning French Ambassador. Before his departure Mustafa had contrived to procure from the Sultan letters to the Kings of France and England, on presentation of which he hoped to receive from each monarch a generous reward. Although the British Ambassador had sent due warning of Mustafa's status and intentions, King James's ministers felt that he should be handsomely treated—particularly when they heard that he had been received by the King of France. Eventually in July 1607 Mustafa arrived in London, announcing himself as an ambassador from the Sultan, though he did not venture to assume any higher style than Chiaus, to which he was entitled. The King, however, was at this time absent on progress so the audience was postponed until September. Meantime, according to custom, the burden of providing him and his twelve servants with board and lodging was laid upon the Levant Company, as the body chiefly concerned in maintaining amicable relations with Turkey. This cost the Com-

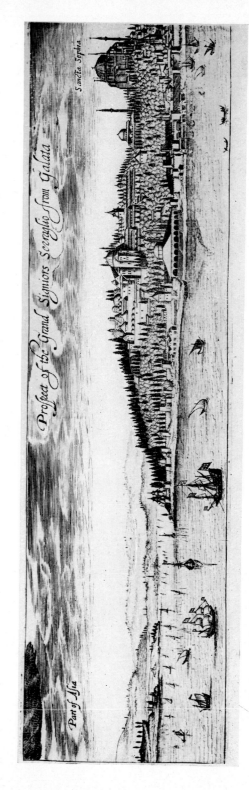

Part of Asia

S.ancta Sophia

Prospect of the Grand Signiors Seraglio from Galata

34. Prospect of the Grand Signior's Seraglio from Galata. From an engraving by Francis Delaram in George Sandys, *Relation of a Journey*, 1615.

Se Ianiſſaire allant à la guerre.

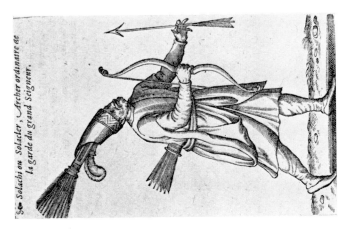

Se Solachi ou Solacler, Archer ordinaire de
la garde du grand Seigneur.

Se Delly, qui ſignifie fol hardy.

35–37. Turkish Troops. Deli, Solak, Janissary. From Nicolas de Nicolay, *Les Navigations*, 1576.

pany £5 a day until in November 1608 they gave him a sea passage back to Constantinople. The discovery that a man of no particular importance in his own country had been solemnly entertained for some months at great cost in the exalted rank of ambassador titillated the English public's sense of humour, and to play the Chiaus (or, in shortened form, to 'chouse') seems to have become a popular synonym for imposture. Ben Jonson, in *The Alchemist* (1610), thrice uses 'Chiause' in this sense.[1]

To return to the procession: after the 'chauses' seven state coaches preceded the main body of escorting troops, which consisted of four thousand Janissaries armed with muskets. These were followed by yet more Janissaries on horseback, with pennons fluttering from their lances, and a further detachment of veterans whose valour in battle had earned them the distinction of wearing ostrich plumes in their caps.

The religious orders were represented by 'certaine Turkish Saints with verie long haire', there were also Dervishes on foot, the green turbaned kinsmen of Mohammed on horseback and the Mufti himself. Eight or nine of the principal Viziers of the realm with their attendants were followed by 'squeaking Musicke both Vocall and Instrumentall'. Animals traditionally formed part of the procession. There was a black elephant, then 'nine goodly Horses of the Kings led by Chiauses verie richly adorned', each with a shield of beaten gold encrusted with jewels hanging from the saddle, and 'the Kings Greyhounds . . . clothed with coverings of Cloth of Gold: of these there were at the least one hundred'. There were two large groups of Ladies on horseback, each escorted by numerous attendants.

Far back down the line of march came the sacred religious standard 'a Streamer of greene Taffata, wherein was an Arabian Inscription in very great Letters', and near to it the secular standard 'that is the taile of the horse fastened upon the toppe of a long staffe', the emblem which struck terror into countless hearts.

Finally, behind the standards, marched a magnificent company of archers wearing plumed silver headdresses and attired in fine linen shirts which reached to the calf. Their long sleeves were richly embroidered and each carried an arrow fitted to his bowstring, ready to shoot down any attacker. These were the Solaks,

[1] Sir William Foster, *Travels of John Sanderson*, Hakluyt Society, 1931, pp. xxxiii–xxxv.

veteran Janissaries who normally marched on foot beside the Sultan. But that day their imperial master was already safe in his Seraglio, so the procession inevitably ended in anti-climax.

Apart from state ceremonials of this kind when the Turks no doubt thought it good for foreigners to see and marvel at the Ottoman glory, their relations with the Franks were severely restricted to the minimum required to conform with their peculiar brand of courtesy, and for the transaction of official business.

The Turks were notorious for their haughty and often offensive arrogance towards foreigners and particularly towards Christians. No doubt Coryate had a specific instance in mind when he wrote: 'The pride of the Turkish Visiers or Bashawes is so great, that when a Christian Ambassador doth either bring them or send them a present of great worth they have not the honestie as to thanke him.'

The obvious barrier of language Coryate set himself to over-come by learning Turkish, and perhaps his adaptability and per-tinacity enabled him to break down some of the other obstacles to acquiring knowledge, but the fact remained that the differences in almost every detail of social life, and the incompatibility of the Christian and Muslim points of view, rigidly maintained on both sides, made any form of familiarity extremely difficult.

It was not necessary for a Christian intentionally to insult a Turk to bring dire consequences on his head. Going about the streets in European dress was enough to invite attack. In self-protection all the Frankish merchants wore Turkish dress in public, and no doubt Coryate did the same. Some of the factors even sported long mustachios as the natives did. It was said that many of the English and Dutch factors were indistinguishable from real Turks, but that the French, despite their robes, could always be recognized by their manner.

Judging by his behaviour in Europe and subsequently in India, Coryate would have found it difficult to refrain from religious altercation, but it must have been impressed upon him from the outset that 'the Turkes will not suffer three things to be medled withall by a Christian or Jew, his Religion, his Women, his Slave'. And there were plenty of cautionary sights and tales to remind him that as a Christian he was little better than an animal, and that his presence in the Sultan's dominions rested only upon a contemptuous sufferance. Any Friday he might visit the slave

market and see Christian men and women sold for sums ranging
from about £25 for a comely virgin to a few shillings for an
elderly man or woman. He saw Greek debtors with chains about
their necks fastened at the other end to their Turkish keepers'
middles, being led about the streets to beg until they had paid;
and he had heard what befell one of the servants of Sir Thomas
Glover, the Ambassador preceding Pindar. When the Sultan had
occasion to leave his capital, it was held to be a bad omen if he
should meet a Christian on the way. This servant had the misfortune to be found in the Sultan's path, for which crime he was
seized 'and had so many blowes on his buttockes (his breeches
betwixt) that he died thereof within a few daies after'.

Yet in contrast to so much revolting cruelty 'the true Musul-
man will scarce kill a louse, if he find him in his apparell, but
throwes him away, affirming, that it is contrary to the rules of
charitie to kill him, or any thing else that hath life in it, except
those things that they kill for their sustenance. And as for Birds
that they see inclosed in a Cage, they will buy them for some
money of the owner, and after let them flie out of the cage, for
they thinke that there is injurie done to them to debar them of
their libertie.'

One of Coryate's interests, which sets him apart from contemporary English travellers, is his careful observation in the sphere
of natural history. 'I observed in Constantinople in the moneth of
May certaine Butter-flies as great as Reare-mise [bats] with foure
wings, each whereof distinguished with a round spot made cir-
cularly, consisting of two colours Purple and Blacke, and two
hornes in their head made in the forme of branches of a tree;
they spawne thirtie or fortie Spawnes in a night.' He remarks on
the prevalence of locusts, especially in June and July, when they
are brought in by an east wind and fall so thick 'that a man cannot
passe in the streets of Constantinople or Galata, but hee shall
everie where tread upon them'. Summer brought another insect
pest, 'those kind of Flies that troubled me in Italy, did in the
night time as much infect mee in Constantinople ... I meane
the Cimices, after that being once taken and bruised upon the
naile of a man, doth cover the whole naile with bloud and stinke.'
He was so intrigued by the fireflies which he observed every
evening that he caught one and having 'opened his bellie, I found
a certaine bright and glistering sparke of fire in his taile ... These

kinde of Flies doe much use to flie abroad in the Summer time in Constantinople, onely in the evening, which a stranger that never saw them before, would take to be true flakes of fire.'

One day a servant of the Levant Company's Consul shot a pelican and presented it to the Ambassador. Coryate was intensely interested and gives a detailed description of the bird. 'The Turkes say that when Mecca was building, these [pelicans] to helpe forward the worke brought stones in their bills that served for the building of the Walles of the Citie', and his informant proved the plausibility of the legend by taking a dog and thrusting it into the pelican's pouch.

This dog was probably a pet kept by one of the English. To a Turk all dogs were unclean, and he would on no account allow one into his house, though he might demonstrate his charity by buying bread for the large numbers of masterless curs which roamed the streets. Charity bread was not their only source of sustenance since it was not uncommon for a death sentence to include the final indignity of leaving the corpse in some public place to be devoured.

In that summer of 1613 plague was more than usually prevalent and the authorities decided that the dogs were primarily responsible for spreading it and should be banished. The idea found favour in the eyes of the Sultan, and he also approved the method proposed for putting the scheme into operation, which had the customary advantage of discriminating against the Christian and Jewish population. It was therefore decreed that by a certain date, on pain of a fine of four sequins, every Christian and Jew should deliver to the authorities a dog which would thereafter be shipped away in special boats 'not much unlike our lighters in London'. The original intention was to land the dogs well away from the city and there kill them but 'the Muftie who is the Turkish oracle would not give his consent to that, affirming that it would be a very uncharitable action', so no doubt they were left in some deserted spot to die of hunger instead.

Within a week Constantinople was cleared of dogs. Twenty thousand had been transported, but they were still numerous Christians and Jews who had not fulfilled their obligation. The problem was solved by men of Galata with a sharp eye for business who bought up all the dogs they could find and shipped them over to Constantinople, where they were sold at enhanced prices;

'Mungrels and Curres that before strayed up and downe the Citie being now worth twenty or thirty Aspers.'[1] Without dogs to kill the rats and scavenge the streets the risks of infection must have greatly increased.

During the whole of his stay in Constantinople Coryate enjoyed his usual vigorous health except for three days when he was afflicted with an ague. In this brief illness he was glad to be attended by the Levant Company's physician, who cured him by a little letting of blood. He had seen the Turkish surgeon's methods, which were altogether more drastic. 'The Turkes, as they shave publickely in the streets, likewise they let bloud often-times in the streets, but so indiscreetly that they suffer sometimes a man to bleed at the least two or three pounds of bloud, to the extreme weakening of their bodies: Whereas few of our men suffer their Patient to bleed above halfe a pound.'

In addition to learning Turkish he was also taking lessons in Italian, which was at this period the chief medium of communication between Europeans in the Levant. Indeed in its debased form, the 'lingua franca' or 'franco piccolo', it was the tongue in which commerce was conducted all along the shores of the Mediterranean. His teacher was the Rev. William Ford, a gentle and charming man then in his middle fifties, who had been the Levant Company's Chaplain in Constantinople for several years past. Coryate conceived a warm regard for him, and later, writing home from India, asked to be remembered 'to that courteous, sweet and elegant-natured and nurtured Gentleman'.

One Saturday in August Coryate and Ford were invited by William Pearch, one of the Levant Company Merchants whom Coryate calls 'my courteous friend', to visit the house of a Jew for an unusual purpose. The Jew himself was unusual, at any rate

[1] As the export of English coin was forbidden by law there was no direct exchange between English money and other currencies in the Levant. It is therefore extremely difficult to fix relative values, which in any case were subject to fluctuation. The asper (akcheh), a silver coin, was the chief unit of Turkish currency used in dealings between Turks and foreigners, but for actual payments in gold the Venetian sequin (zecchino), because of its constant weight and purity, was preferred to the approximately equivalent Turkish gold sultānī. The term 'dollar' appears to have covered the sultānī as well as the Hungarian gold dollar, the Italian scudo, and the Spanish ducat, which were all of about the same weight and value. Between the sultānī and the asper the ratio value seems to have fluctuated at least between 120 and 160 owing to periodical debasements of the asper by the admixture of brass. In the Levant Company Court Minutes for 10 November 1613 (*S.P.* 105/147, ff. 132–3) the dollar is valued at six shillings.

in the matter of his birthplace. His name was Amis, and he had
been born in Crutched Friars in London, where he had spent the
first thirty years of his life. 'To this man's house . . . wee came . . .
about nine of the clocke in the morning to see a matter, which in
my former travells I wished to have seene, especially in Venice,
but never till then had the opportunitie to attaine unto, namely,
a circumcision. It was done in a private house, according to the
custome of the Jewes resident in Constantinople, and not in a
Synagogue as it is with the Jewes in other Countries. This foresaid Amis, for the love hee bore to our English Nation, . . . as
also for his good will sake, which hee bore to my foresaid friend
Master William Pearch, received us with very courteous entertainment, presenting unto us at a Table in a fine little roome
where he placed us, divers delicate dishes and fruits with a cup of
most excellent Wine, often welcomming us with many heartie and
wel-wishing speeches. While wee were at breakfast, divers Jewes
came into the roome, and sung certaine Hebrew Songs, after which
the child was brought to his father, who sate downe in a chaire,
and placed the child being now eight days old in his lap. The
whole Company being desirous that wee Christians should observe
their ceremonies, called us to approach neere to the child. And
when wee came, a certaine other Jew drawing forth a little Instrument made not unlike those smal cissers that our Ladies & Gentlemen doe much use, did with the same cut off the Prepuce or fore-
skinne of the child, and after a very strange manner unused (I
beleeve) of the ancient Hebrewes, did put his mouth to the childs
yard, and sucked up the bloud. All his Privities (before hee came
into the roome) were besprinkled with a kind of powder, which
after the Circumciser had done his businesse, was blowed away by
him, and another powder cast on immediately; . . . the same also
after his worke was done, tooke a little strong Wine that was held
in a Goblet by a fellow that stood neere him, and powred it into the
childs mouth to comfort him in the middest of his paines, Who cried
out very bitterly. The paine being for the time very bitter indeed,
though it will be (as they told me) cured in the space of foure and
twentie houres. But those of any riper yeeres that are circumcised
(as it too often commeth to passe, that Christians which turne
Turkes) as at fortie or fiftie yeeres of age doe suffer great paine for
the space of a moneth; the Prepuce that was cut off was carried to
the Mother, who keepeth it very preciously as a thing of worth.'

A few weeks later he witnessed the less intimate scenes of the corresponding Mohammedan ceremony when three of the Vizier's sons were circumcised with traditional festivity. In the early part of the day the three boys, gorgeously dressed and mounted on handsome palfreys, paraded through the town. They were preceded by slaves, and escorted by horse guards riding two and two; flute players provided music which Coryate found 'very ridiculous and squeaking'. There was a great feast in the Vizier's palace, and when darkness fell 'their Father the Visier made notable shewes upon the water before the Grand Signior with fire-workes. For there were sixteene Boates that served for the same purpose, wherein prettie Castles were contrived, the people in which skirmished together at the least an houre, spending such abundance of Powder in their fire-workes, that I never saw the like before, sending up divers of their flashes in the Aire, as high as the highest Steeple in Constantinople ... Amongst the rest of these fire-workes I observed some made upon the very shoare itselfe with singular cunning resembling the shape of Cypresstrees; a very pleasing and delectable object to behold.'

In the autumn the festivals held by the various religious sects followed one on top of another. On the same day that the Vizier's sons were circumcised the Jews began their Feast of Tabernacles, which lasted nine days, and before this was over the Christians began their Vintage Celebration, which lasted six. The vineyards, starting on the outskirts of Pera, stretched out on both sides of the Bosphorus towards the Black Sea. 'In each of these days you might have seene the greatest part of the way betweixt the farther end of Pera, and the Vineyards full of Horses that went to and fro from morning to night, to carrie away into the Towne the Grapes in certaine deepe wooden pots ... likewise the owners of the Vineyards with their Families going and comming.' In pavilions set up among the vines 'was much solace amongst the Christians for this time with food cheere, Musicke, &c.' During the harvest strangers were allowed into the vineyards and were permitted to eat as many grapes as they liked. At any other time anyone 'apprehended stealing Grapes in a Vineyard by any Janizaries, and carried to the Subbashaw of Galata, perhaps he might have twentie or fortie blowes upon the feet. Besides an Imposition of a thousand Aspers ... for exercise sake I holpe the poore Greekes both to gather their Grapes & to stampe some

of their wine. For in certaine Buts & other lesser Vessels they
bruised many of their Grapes in the Vineyards themselves, and
afterward in their private houses finished the making of their
Wine. Their vines grow not as in France & Germany, being
underpropped, with little stalkes, but rather as little small shrubs
which grow so stiffe, that they need not any stakes to support
them.'

Among the capitulations granted to Queen Elizabeth by the
Sultan in 1601 was a provision that any member of the English
community 'where he dwelleth may buy grapes and make wyne
in their houses and non to interrupt or molest them'. Many of the
vineyards were owned by Turks, who were forbidden by their
religion to drink wine. The prohibition was sometimes discreetly
disregarded, and at vintage time some relaxation was officially
permitted, since must did not count as wine. But if any Mohammedan was found drunk during Ramadan he was killed by having
boiling lead poured into his mouth and ears, as happened to one
wretch while Coryate was in Constantinople.

Ramadan began that year on Monday 4 October, and at night
all the mosques—seven hundred and seventy of them, according to
Coryate's estimate—were hung with lamps. He had seen this
wonderful sight in April at the festival of the birth of Mohammed,
'but it happened that their Lampes were hanged out much later
this night than I have observed at other times. For before, they
used to hang them out about the closing of the Evening, even
about Sun-set. But this night they did not before midnight, which
came to passe by reason that they could not see the Moone, notwithstanding the Grand Signior being advertised by his expert
Astronomers, about ten of the clocke at night, that it was very
likely the Moone was risen, though being darkened by clouds it
did not shine, commanded that there should be an expresse order
given forthwith that they should hang forth their Lampes; whereupon within the space of two houres, the Steeples belonging to
all the Moskies in Constantinople and Galata shined suddenly
with Lampes, a shew indeed very glorious and refulgent, some of
their Steeples having only one row of Lampes, which contained
some fiftie particulars; some three rows, which make a very
beautiful shew.'

Purchas must have cut out most of Coryate's comments on
food and drink, which are a feature of his accounts of foreign

lands, but he does tell us that a brace of pheasants cost 60 Aspers, and that partridges could be bought for 20 Aspers a pair. Cheese, 'not pressed as our Cheese is, but in crumbles is verie leane and drie, but fierie salt'. During his frequent passages across the Golden Horn between Pera and Constantinople he often noticed great swollen buffalo skins being towed across to Constantinople by small boats. On reaching the shore eight men were required to lift the skin and its contents out of the water. He discovered that these skins were full of butter 'the most filthy and unsavorie that is made in any other part of the world', and that this butter came into the capital from as far afield as Moldavia, one of the northernmost dependent states within the Ottoman Empire.

Beyond Moldavia lay Poland, whose vast territories stretched from the Baltic to within 150 miles of Moscow, and 100 of the Black Sea. As the representative of the largest monarchy in Christendom, the Polish Ambassador was a man of some importance in Constantinople, and at the beginning of October, the British Ambassador, accompanied by his retinue and most of the English residents of Pera, paid him an official visit to congratulate him on his safe arrival at the Porte. Listening with attention to the Pole's speech of thanks, which was made in Latin, Coryate had the satisfaction of detecting a deviation from acceptable style, which he doubtless expounded fully to Pindar and his staff, as well as noting it in his diary.

Coryate loved meeting important people, but, except perhaps in the case of royalty, he was no respecter of rank for rank's sake. Shortly before leaving Constantinople he arranged through a Greek acquaintance to have an audience of Timotheus the Patriarch of Constantinople. 'When we came to the doore of his Conclave wee did put off our shooes, and leaving them without the doore went in to him; and sate upon our tailes crosse-legged as the Turkes doe upon certaine Carpets, without either Chaire, Stoole or Forme to sit on, he himself sate in the like manner, clad in a black broad cloth Gowne that was furred, and a blacke habit of say over his head.' We do not know what subjects were discussed, but Coryate's verdict is terse and uncompromising: 'He is a man unlearned and verie unworthy of the place.'

Coryate probably stayed longer in Constantinople than he had originally intended. It may be that he found so much to interest him that it took him the best part of a year to complete his investigations. Perhaps he felt it desirable to spend time in improving his knowledge of Turkish and Italian before venturing farther afield. He was still bent on visiting Jerusalem, and though he never took much account of physical dangers and difficulties, he may have paid heed to the sound advice that travelling was both easier and less expensive towards Eastertide when the concourse of pilgrims was greatest. All we know for certain is that in the middle of January 1614 the English vessel *Great Defence* was preparing to sail from Constantinople to Iskanderun and Coryate decided to take passage in her.

# CHAPTER XIII

# Pilgrimage to the Holy Land

---

THE *Great Defence* created something of a stir at Constantinople when she arrived in the latter half of December. She had made the passage from Chios to Constantinople, a distance of over 250 nautical miles by the shortest sea route, in only forty-two hours, including the obligatory call at Gallipoli for Customs clearance. The *Samaritan*, in which Coryate had made the same voyage, took six weeks. Nobody could foretell within weeks when a ship might reach her destination, but it was the Levant Company's usual practice at this time to lay down in advance the rotation of the ports of call and the number of days to be spent in each. The length of time spent in port, dictated mainly by the unpredictability of land traffic movements, needed to be exceedingly generous in relation to the size of the ships and the consequent smallness of the cargoes to be discharged and loaded. The *Great Defence*, for example, spent nearly a month in Constantinople, so Coryate had ample notice to make his farewells and complete his preparations for departure.

Winter had set in when he sailed on 21 January 1613 'in as tempestuous and extreame a season as ever I travelled in my life, either by Land or water, for the snow which fell incessantly for the space of almost two dayes and two nights, bred such a rigid cold that some of us were even benummed. Besides, the contrarie winds so crossed our passage, that we found it a very fastidious [disagreeable] and tedious voyage. Notwithstanding the adverse windes when we came within three or foure miles of Gallipoli, by tacking about and turning to windward . . . with some kind of difficultie we entred into the Port. After we were come in, a certaine Jew that was in our Ship perceiving that wee sailed so bravely against the winds, told me that the Englishmen by reason of their dexteritie in sailing, might bee not unproperly called the fishes of the Sea.' They stayed three days at Gallipoli, 'partly for the dispatch of our businesse with the Turkish Magistrates of the Towne, and partly by a thicke mist upon the Sea, during which wee could not securely goe forward for feare of falling into shallow parts of the Sea'.

On 14 February they landed at Mytilene; 'it is very mountainous and rough . . . The people flocked about us, many of them women, the ugliest sluts that ever I saw, saving the Armenian trulls of Constantinople.' They touched at Chios on the 18th and perhaps Coryate took the opportunity of visiting the friends he had made there almost exactly twelve months previously.

From Chios[1] the Master of the *Great Defence* got a chance to show off his ship's paces. Favourable winds carried them within sight of Patmos and Cos, from the Aegean into the Mediterranean, and so eastwards to Iskanderun, where Coryate landed on 24 February.

Everything about Iskanderun belied its importance as the port of Aleppo. Coryate says it consisted of 'about fortie houses, the poorest Cotages that ever I saw, being but a few boards weakly compact and covered with Reeds'. There was no proper harbour; the Levant Company ships lay for as long as fifty days on end, waiting for cargo in the open anchorage, where they were subjected to the ever-present risk of sea-borne attack by pirates and of deadly fever wafted from the mainland. Another traveller who was there in 1617 described it as 'surrounded by high hills hindringe the approach of the Sunne Beames untill nine or ten a Clocke in the morning, lyeinge in a great Marsh full of boggs, foggs and Froggs'.[2] Coryate confirms that it was 'infamous for the infectious aire caused by foggie clouds after Sun-set, and till nine in the morning hovering about the mountaines, and letting fall an unwholesome dew . . .; which cause many to leave their carkasses there to be devoured of the Jackals, which scrape them out of their graves. I saw one somewhat like a Mastive Dog but somewhat lesse, his taile as long as of a Foxe.' Iskanderun was

---

[1] Terry (who has been copied by other writers) states that Coryate sailed from Smyrna to Alexandria, went up the Nile to Cairo and back, then took ship for Joppa and so reached Jerusalem. This, however, is quite inconsistent with Coryate's own account. Terry's memory may have played him false, as it did in other instances, or he may simply have got confused between what Coryate had done and what Coryate told him he intended to do on the return journey, which he never lived to make.

[2] *The Travels of Peter Mundy*, ed. Sir Richard Carnac Temple, Hakluyt Society, 1905, vol. I, p. 19.

known as 'the bane of Franks',[1] yet the merchants living comfortably in Aleppo preferred it to Tripoli, a hundred and fifty miles farther south, which offered an anchorage protected by Turkish artillery and a healthier climate. Iskanderun was only three to four days from Aleppo, whereas the journey to Tripoli took twice as long, which doubled the chances of loss by robbery while goods were at risk on their way to or from the ship.

In London, however, the Levant Company had taken note that the chance of survival of their Factor Marine at Iskanderun was not more than twenty to one,[2] and, two months before Coryate's arrival, had resolved to write to Pindar in Constantinople stating 'that for as much as the trade of Aleppo hath proved very chargeable to the Company and dangerous to their servants many of whom have dyed at Scanderone through the infeccion of the Ague, that therefore the Company have a purpose to recall home their Consull of Aleppo and lessen their trade to that port praying his lordship to write his opinion largely of that matter'.[3] There was something more to this enquiry than a concern for the health of the Company's servants. Apart from the high rate of mortality at Iskanderun, the dangers of robbery ashore, piracy at sea, and the unpredictable demands of the Turkish provincial authorities, the Levant Company were becoming alarmed at the revolution which was taking place as a result of the opening up of the sea route to the East. Oriental goods, instead of being carried via Aleppo, were arriving in the ships of the newly-founded East India Company, and were even being re-exported from England to the Levant. But the fears of the Levant Company turned out to be exaggerated. The Consul at Aleppo was never recalled; ships continued to call at Iskanderun, and fever continued to take toll of their crews, and of the unfortunate young men appointed to look after the Company's interests ashore. In later years Aleppo's prime position as a trading centre was usurped by Constantinople, but at this time it was still, as Coryate says, 'the principall emporium of the Orient world'. Thither rode Coryate from Iskanderun, taking the best part of four days over the journey. The road was bad and it was imperative to make the journey in company because of the danger from robbers.

---

[1] William Biddulph, *The Travels of Certain Englishmen* . . ., Harleian Collection of Voyages, vol. I, p. 785.     [2] Fynes Moryson, *Itinerary*, vol. II, p. 61.

[3] *Levant Company Papers*, S.P. 105/147, f. 134.

After a tedious sea voyage and the disagreeable first impression created by Iskanderun, Aleppo provided a heart-warming contrast, with pleasant air, fertile gardens and orchards, and an animated population of many races. Besides Turks, Greeks, Armenians, and Jews there were merchants from Venice, France, Britain, and the Netherlands. A sign of its cosmopolitanism was that Christians were allowed to ride horses there, an unusual privilege in the Grand Signor's dominions. At least a dozen English merchants were resident in Aleppo, headed by their Consul, Bartholomew Haggett, whom Coryate found to be a very congenial host. They were predisposed to like each other because they both hailed from Somerset. Haggett came from Wells, and was therefore familiar with some of the country scenes so dear to Coryate's heart. In addition to providing pleasant company and generous hospitality, Haggett himself found the time to act as Coryate's guide to Aleppo and its neighbourhood, with which his residence of over three years in the city made him well acquainted.

One day the two of them rode out to view the saltpans in the Valley of Salt near Jebbul, about twenty miles south-east of Aleppo. For such a journey an armed escort was essential, and on this occasion it probably consisted of one or more of the Janissaries whom the Turkish authorities placed at the permanent disposal of each Christian consul. These Janissaries were well worth the cost of their pay and their keep, indeed they were indispensable, and so great was their prestige that the presence of even one was a reasonable, though not absolute, safeguard against molestation. The travellers passed through several Bedouin encampments and Coryate had his first experience of a mirage: 'Wee seemed to see a Towne standing like an Iland in water, and when wee came thither found no waters, but a kind of shrub like wild withered Time, which covering the Mountaine made with the white sprigs a shew of water afarre off.

'The Poole where the Salt is made is twenty miles long, and two broad, exceedingly frequented with plentie and varietie of Fowle. The water continueth all the yeere saving July, August, September, at which time it is quite dried up, beginning to wast (or to change into Salt) in July: and then is there nothing but a hard massie Salt, which appeareth like hard Ice digged thence with mattocks, heaped [in] hillocks, and carried to Giabbul a village on Camels and Asses, and there customed ... It yields 20,000 dollars yeerly to the Grand Signior.' He adds that the salt itself is 'as fine and excellent as any in the world'.

The salt-pans were an object of interest to travellers partly because they were a curiosity in their own right and partly because as Coryate tells us, the site was confidently identified with 2 Samuel, chapter VIII, verse 13 : 'And David gat him a name when he returned from smiting of the Syrians in the valley of salt, being eighteen thousand men.' At some undetermined date those British who visited the valley became eligible for admission to a select Order whose Grand Master seems to have been the British Consul at Aleppo. The candidate was initiated by receiving into his mouth a lump of salt presented to him on the point of a rusty blade, facetiously asserted to be King David's own sword. The ceremony was accompanied by other foolery and much good cheer, and one is tempted to wonder whether Coryate, who had already become the first Knight of Troy, may not also have inaugurated the Knights of the Valley of Salt; the Order was certainly in existence some seventy years after his visit.[1]

It has already been suggested that Coryate timed his departure from Constantinople in order to join one of the pilgrim caravans which assembled in Aleppo and arrived in Jerusalem by Easter. From Coryate's point of view this was both the most reliable and the cheapest of the three alternative routes to the Holy City, the other two being from Cairo across the Sinai Desert, and by sea to Joppa. Until about 1585 the sea route to Joppa had been the one most used by European pilgrims, and every year pilgrim galleys, each with a complement of from one hundred to four hundred souls, had left Venice on or after Ascension Day. But the dangers of the journey and the unpredictable exactions of the Turkish authorities had brought this custom to an end. Expense played an important part in reducing the number of Western Christians to a trickle. Fynes Moryson and his brother Henry, starting from England and travelling in no great style, spent the enormous sum of £500. The cost would have been even greater if Henry had not died near Aleppo on the return

---

[1] Henry Teonge, *Diary*, ed. G. E. Manwaring, 1927, pp. 153-5. Teonge, a naval chaplain, was initiated on 16 May 1676, in Aleppo. Because his ship was on the point of sailing from Iskanderun he received a special dispensation absolving him from visiting the saltpans, but not from eating his mouthful of salt.

journey. In 1612 at Eastertide, there were only nineteen Franks, or Western Christians, in Jerusalem. Most of these, naturally, were Catholics who, in return for the hazards and the expense, had the consolation of knowing that they would earn remission of sins by their visit and their devotions. Though Protestants were denied this source of encouragement, they still had the powerful incentive of curiosity to see with their own eyes the places where events had taken place which determined their whole mental and spiritual attitude to the past, the present, and the eternal future. 'I had no thought to expiate any least sinne of mine,' says the Protestant Moryson, in enumerating his reasons for going to Jerusalem, 'much lesse did I hope to merit any grace from God; but when I had once begun to visite forraigne parts, I was so stirred up by emulation and curiosity, as I did never behold any without a kind of sweet envy, who in this kind had dared more than my selfe.'[1] It must have been with sentiments very similar to these that Coryate planned his own pilgrimage.

He set out on foot from Aleppo on 15 March 1614 with a caravan consisting mainly of Armenian pilgrims. These had the honour of being led by their Bishop, who carried a crosier of hazel-wood and wore a resplendent white and blue turban. The caravan may also have included Turkish merchants on their way to Damascus and Cairo. It was certainly escorted by Turkish troops. One caravan which travelled from Aleppo to Jerusalem exactly two years previously comprised 900 Armenian pilgrims, men and women, 600 Turkish merchants, 100 soldiers, 6 Janissaries, and 3 chiauses.[2] Coryate was accompanied by one other Englishman, Henry Allard of Kent, and it is probable that they were the only Franks in the caravan.

They took ten days to cover the two hundred miles to Damascus. The first half of the journey was relatively easy. The road was good and at night there were *khans* to lodge in, large rectangular buildings usually of hewn stone, some of them capable of holding a thousand travellers, as well as their beasts and belongings. Inside was a great court used for stabling, and at intervals round the walls were chimneys for the cooking fires. The travellers slept either with the animals or in a raised gallery which ran round the outer wall. In some *khans* this gallery was elaborated into a series of separate cell-like rooms. Lodging was free, and in some,

[1] Fynes Moryson, *Itinerary*, vol. II, p. 1.          [2] Lithgow, *op. cit.*, p. 194.

known as *imaret*, food and fodder were free too, provided by the
Sultan or by rich Turks as an act of charity to all travellers rich and
poor, irrespective of race or creed.

The second hundred miles was more arduous. The road became
difficult and dangerous, drinking water was difficult to procure,
and there were no more *khans* until they arrived in Damascus.
Here, however, a large *imaret* dispensed free food and fodder
twice a day,[1] and some of the less robust pilgrims were glad to do
little but rest for the four days during the which caravan remained
there. Not so Coryate, who set about seeing the sights with his
customary zest.

Mohammed, it is said, once viewed Damascus and on seeing its
delightful situation and stately prospect refused to enter the city
lest he should be tempted to blunt his desire for the heavenly
paradise by remaining there for the rest of his days. Coryate
apparently knew the story, and in this one respect found himself
in agreement with the opinion of the Prophet. Damascus, he
declares, seemed to possess all things conspiring to an earthly
paradise; sumptuous buildings, pure water running in a thousand
conduits through shaded streets, fruits innumerable and delicious,
victuals so cheap that he and his companions seeking some varia-
tion from the free diet of bread and porridge provided at the
*imaret* were able to dine well at a cook house in the city for three
farthings a man.

He spent New Year's Day 1614 relishing the delights of the city
and began his diary entry for the following day 'The 26 [March]
in Damascus I saw Roses——' At this point Purchas breaks off
the narrative with the excuse that 'wee have travelled with so many
Travellers to Damascus and thence to Jerusalem, and observed so
much on those parts, that I dare not to obtrude Master Coryats
prolixitie on the patientest Reader. He was indeed a curious
viewer of so much as his bodily eyes could comprehend, to which
he added (not so faithfull intelligence of) his inquisitive eares; for
mysteries of State and Religion hee would be a safe traveller and
free from suspicion.'

Purchas confesses that he himself found much pleasure in
walking with Coryate, but it was a pleasure which he decided to
deny to posterity, and all we know of the tour of Palestine, and
Coryate's return to Aleppo, are a few of the main events sum-

[1] *Ibid.*, pp. 196-7.

marized by Purchas, facts given by Coryate himself in his letters from India, and some details which he recounted to the Rev. Edward Terry, who many years later included them in his book.[1] Nevertheless it is possible to piece together a connected narrative from the fragments.

From Damascus onwards holy sites became increasingly frequent. Just outside the city was the spot where the conversion of St. Paul took place, and here it was customary for all pilgrims to fall upon their knees for prayers. They crossed the Jordan by Jacob's Bridge, so called because nearby Jacob had wrestled with the Angel, and halted near the foot of Mount Tabor, so that the more energetic pilgrims could make the ascent on foot to the scene of Christ's Transfiguration. Coryate was one of those who scrambled to the summit up the pathless slope, which was so steep that it was necessary to work one's way up by holding on to the long grass and scrub which covered the mountain side. Some of those who reached the top hoped to see the remains of the three tabernacles built for Christ, Moses, and Elias,[2] but the only visible building was an uninhabited tumbledown cottage.

At Mount Tabor the route turned westwards to Nazareth. Here the Virgin Mary's house still stood, though evidently in need of frequent reconstruction, since the pilgrims in one caravan alone are alleged to have carried away 5,000 pounds weight of its stones as souvenirs.[3] No Catholics were guilty of this pilferage because they all knew that the Virgin's real house had been spirited away to Loreto; the building of chief interest to them was the church erected on the site where the house had been, containing two porphyry columns on the places occupied by the Archangel and the Virgin at the moment of the Annunciation.

The escort of troops provided a vanguard and rearguard on the march, and sentries at night, but the presence of armed guards was no guarantee of unmolested passage. Every contemporary account relates encounters with Arabs. In some cases these were not the professional robbers they were taken for by the terrified pilgrims, but the keepers of the roads demanding several times more than they were entitled to receive. At other times events left no room

[1] *A Voyage to East India*, London, 1655. The part dealing with Coryate is reprinted in the 1776 edition of the *Crudities*, vol. III.

[2] *St. Matthew*, ch. xvii, 4; William Biddulph, *op. cit.*, p. 815.

[3] Lithgow, *op. cit.*, p. 207.

for doubt; while a caravan was toiling through a defile two or three pilgrims would pitch over into the dust while others staggered screaming from the column, transfixed by arrows shot from the surrounding hills. Dead and wounded were alike forsaken, and the escorting troops belaboured those who attempted to tarry and succour the stricken. How far the escorts and attackers were in league remained an open question, but they certainly shared common views on the status of infidels, and on their usefulness as a source of gain.

The march continued through the city of Samaria, past the well where Christ asked water of the woman of Samaria. 'We were exceeding thirsty and drank thereof liberally & freely. The water thereof goeth down very pleasantly like unto milk,' remarked one English pilgrim.[1]

At length they reached Rama. This was the meeting point of the roads from the north via Damascus, and from the seaport of Joppa to the west. Here, Philip the Good, Duke of Burgundy, had built a monastery on the site of the house of Nicodemus; all the monks had gone now, but Sion House remained a lodging for pilgrims, though little better than a stable. At Rama dwelt the official Christian guide to Jerusalem, into whose charge you had no choice but to commit yourself. If anyone tried to evade his control and charges, the dragoman could send word to the Arabs who would see to it that the pilgrim paid dearly for his impudence.

When at last, after all their tribulations, the pilgrims came within sight of Jerusalem it is little wonder that they burst into song, and many grown men wept for joy. Coryate entered the Holy City on 12 April; at the gate his name was registered in a book by a Turkish official, and he was called upon to pay an admission fee. According to Terry, Coryate told him that he had to pay the equivalent of five shillings, but more than twice that sum appears to have been usual. When these formalities had been completed the resident representative of the pilgrims' sect took charge of him. None of the Protestant rulers contributed to the upkeep of any foundation at Jerusalem, so if he was a Protestant he came with all the other Franks to the Roman Catholic monastery of San Salvatore. Coryate's knowledge of the experiences of previous visitors must have given him a fairly clear idea of what to expect. In particular, he probably obtained useful information

[1] William Biddulph, *op. cit.*, p. 817.

from his friend Hugh Holland, who had stayed at the monastery in June 1607.

There seem to have been very few Frank pilgrims in Jerusalem for the Easter celebrations in 1615. The original register of pilgrims kept by the monastery has not survived, but in a transcript made in 1633 the only arrivals during April are recorded as follows:

'16 Apr.　R[everendissimus] D[ominus] Petrus Goudier Sac[erdos]
　　　　　Joannes Ramsei Anglus
　　　　　Alessander Auchtmoutie Scotus
　7 Apr.　Thomas Coriato
　　　　　Henricus Ellard de Parochia Biddenden in Comit[atu]
　　　　　Chansie.'[1]

The Englishman and the Scotsman were probably Catholics. Some of the few Protestant travellers who visited Jerusalem about this time went to extraordinary lengths to conceal their religion for fear of reprisals from their Catholic hosts, and most make some complaint or jibe against them. Dark hints were even dropped that the friars had recently been responsible for the death by poisoning of five Englishmen,[2] and Lithgow records the disgust of the head of the monastery, the Father Guardian, when he learnt that in carrying out the ritual of humility and service he had inadvertently washed a Protestant's feet.[3] Though Catholic intolerance in Europe lent some weight to Protestant apprehensions, little reliance can be placed on such reports since Protestants themselves pushed their prejudice to such lengths that most of them either coupled Catholics with Muslims in their abhorrence, or else conceded certain virtues to the Mohammedans in order to emphasize the iniquities of Rome. Coryate was certainly

---

[1] *Cantium* is the usual Latin form of Kent. This transcript, covering the years 1561–1632, forms part of P. B. Zimolong's *Navis Peregrinorum*, Cologne, 1938. The date, 7 April, against Coryate and Allard, is five days before their arrival, according to Purchas. The transcription from the original register may be faulty: the register normally runs in strict datal order but it will be noted that the immediately *prior* entry is dated 16 April. The lack of indication of Coryate's provenance is also unusual. None of these other April visitors appears to have published an account of his visit, see R. Röhricht, *Bibliotheca geographica Palestinae*, 1890.

[2] Sandys, *op. cit.*, p. 145, and Henry Timberlake, *A true and strange discourse*, London, 1603 [or 1616?]. Reprinted in Harleian Miscellany, vol. I, see p. 335 (1744 edn.).

[3] Lithgow, *op. cit.*, p. 224.

not free from Protestant bigotry, but at least he was prepared to recognize and acknowledge true charity wherever he found it. It seems most unlikely that he would have deigned to indulge in subterfuges to disguise his faith; it also appears that he was not penalized for his frankness and that he received nothing but kindness and benevolence from the Franciscan friars.

Some of the friars were at the Gate to meet him and his companion Allard, and conduct them straight to the monastery. Here they were courteously received by the Father Guardian, who washed their feet according to custom. They were then served with a good meal and afterwards the friars went in procession round their cloister, giving thanks to God for having brought the two Englishmen safely to the Holy City.

On the following day they began to visit the Holy Places. The first thing that struck Coryate about Jerusalem was its emptiness. Of all the cities he had visited, only in Padua were so few people to be seen in the streets. He estimated the total population to be scarcely 10,000 people. Three-quarters of the inhabitants were Christians who dwelt there for devotion. Most of the remainder were Turks who lived there for the income derived from the Christians. So virulent was the Christian feeling against the murderers of The Saviour that a Jew scarcely dared to show his face within the walls.

The number of places in and about Jerusalem visited and venerated by pilgrims increased amazingly during the Middle Ages, and this growth may be traced in the narratives of successive pilgrims from the tenth century to Coryate's day. Purchas notes that Coryate visited all the Holy Places observed by four other English travellers[1] whose accounts he included in his *Pilgrimes*, and these make a formidable list. The guide spoke in Italian so Coryate had a better chance of understanding what he was being shown than some of his countrymen. Almost every incident of the New Testament history was exactly localized; where Christ composed the Lord's Prayer, and where the Apostles composed the Creed—

[1] Sandys, Sanderson, Timberlake or Timberley, and Biddulph. George Sandys went abroad in 1610 and published *Relation of a Journey* in 1615; John Sanderson visited Jerusalem in 1601; Henry Timberlake was there the following year, and in 1603 published *A True & Strange Discourse of the Travels of two English Pilgrims*, while the Rev. William Biddulph, who had been Chaplain at Aleppo, was in Jerusalem concurrently with Timberlake, and published anonymously in 1609 *The Travels of certaine Englishmen into Africa, Asia . . .*

even the stone on which the cock stood to crow at St. Peter's downfall. There were besides, the houses of Annas, Caiaphas, Dives, Veronica, Mary Magdalen and Pilate, the school which Our Lady attended and the fountain where she used to wash her baby clothes. Old Testament incidents were not forgotten; there was the orchard where Bathsheba bathed, and the terrace from which David beheld her, but the tombs of David and Solomon were now surmounted by a mosque, and no Christian was allowed to enter.

But the interest of all Christians of every Church or sect naturally centred on the Holy Sepulchre. From a different point of view this was also the chief interest of the Turks who exacted heavy entrance fees, the profits from which were farmed out for 80,000 Sultānīs a year.[1] A Western Christian paid a fee of nine sequins (about fifty-four shillings) which probably entitled him to more than one visit. Christians who were subject to the Turk paid a reduced amount, but only if the visitor was a member of a religious order could he gain admittance without charge.

Coryate made three separate visits to the Church of the Holy Sepulchre, the first being on the eve of Palm Sunday which fell that year, in accordance with the Julian calendar, on 17 April. He and his party from the monastery of San Salvatore came each equipped with a pillow and a sleeping carpet; the monastery cook with a supply of victuals came too, for it was the custom to spend at least twenty-four hours in the Temple. At the doorway there were several strings attached to bells in the living quarters inside the church, where some 350 Christian men and women lived in permanent devotion, receiving their food through a hole in the door. The door itself was only opened on special occasions, and was guarded by a Turkish keeper who exacted his private fee from all visitors.

Having seen the Holy Places, Coryate went to repose himself in the upper gallery of the church, where he was awakened by the confused cries of a multitude of men, women, and children. Looking down into the church he saw a world of lamps being carried before and behind eleven Greek Orthodox banners of silk and cloth of gold, and he realized that the people were crying 'Kyrie eleison'. During the ensuing day he witnessed five separate processions organized respectively by the Armenians, Maronites,

[1] Sandys, *op. cit.*, p. 125.

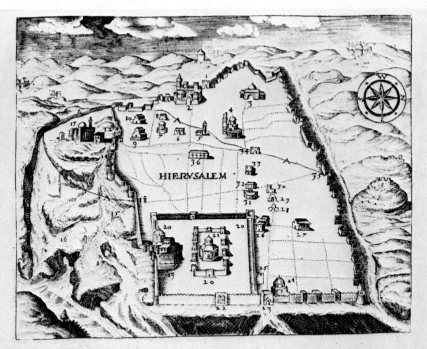

1. The gate of Ioppa.
2. The Castle of the Pisans.
3. The Monastery of the Franciscans.
4. The Temple of the Sepulcher.
5. A Mosque, once a collegiat Church where stood the house of Zebedeus.
6. The iron gate.
7. The Church of S. Marke where his house stood.
8. A Chappell where once stood the house of S. Thomas.
9. The Church of S. Iames.
10. The Church of the Angels, where once stood the pallace of Annas the High Priest.
11. The Port of Dauid.
12. The Church of S. Saniour, where stood the pallace of Caiphas.
13. A Mosque, once a goodly Temple there standing, where stood the Cœnaculam.
14. Where the Iewes would haue taken away the body of the Blessed Virgin.
15. Where Peter wept.
16. The fountaine Siloe.
17. The fountaine of the Blessed Virgin.

18. Port sterquiline.
19. The Church of the Purification of the Blessed Virgin, now conuerted into a Mosque.
20. The court of Solomons Temple.
21. A Mosque, where stood the Temple of Solomon.
22. The Golden gate.
23. The gate of S. Steuen.
24. The Church of Anna, now a Mosque.
25. The Poole Bethesda.
26. Where the pallace of Pilate stood.
27. Where stood, as they say, the pallace of Herod.
28. Pila's arch.
29. The Church of the Blessed Virgins swouning.
30. Where they met Simon of Cyrene.
31. Where the rich Glutton dwelt.
32. Where the Pharisie dwelt.
33. Where Veronica dwels.
34. The gate of Iustice.
35. Port Ephraim.
36. The Bazar.
A. The circuite of part of the old City.

38. Jerusalem. From George Sandys, *Relation of a Journey*, 1615. The original view was drawn by Giovanni Zuallardo and used to illustrate his book *Il Devotissimo Viaggio di Gerusalemme Fatto . . . 1586*, Rome, 1587.

A. Mount Oliuet.
B. Bethfage.
C. The Fountaine of the Apoftles.
D. Where the houfe of Martha ftood.
E. The ftone whereon Chrift fate.
F. Where the houfe of Marie ftood.

G. The fepulcher of Lazarus.
H. The houfe of Lazarus.
I. The houfe of Simon the leper.
K. The valley of the curfed figtree.
L. The way to Ierufalem.
M. Quarantania.

about

39. Bethany and the surrounding countryside. From George Sandys, *Relation of a Journey*, 1615. The original view was drawn by Giovanni Zuallardo and used to illustrate his book *Il Devotissimo Viaggio di Gerusalemme Fatto . . . 1586*, Rome, 1587.

Jacobites, Copts, and Abyssinians. Comparing the splendours of one with another he came to the conclusion that the Armenians made the bravest show of all. 'Their Patriarch weare a cape of cloth of Gold, a Miter of like cloth on his head beautified with many rich stones, with a Crucifix in his hand beset with Diamonds, Rubies, Amethists, Saphires, and other Stones of great worth; his Priests also sumptuously attired, wearing embroidered Caps of Velvet and sattin with Crosses on the tops. Some carried Olive boughes in their hands, with burning Waxe Candles therein, and one a branche of Palme-tree. Some of the priests went before the Patriarch backward perfuming him. Some carried Drums on their shoulders, which others behinde did strike upon. The Cophties [Copts] and Abassines had also certaine clappers of Brasse & Wood, which made strange Musicke. They continued four houres in their circumgiration about the sepulchre, with vociferations such as did amaze the beholders.'

Outside, other Palm Sunday ceremonies were being enacted. In the afternoon the Father Guardian set out for Bethphage, and returned riding on an ass, the people shouting 'Hosanna' and strewing the way with boughs and garments. In 1612 the six thousand oriental Christians who took part made too much noise for the liking of the Turkish soldiers at the city gate, who forthwith pulled the Father Guardian off the ass's back and beat him, his attendant friars, and all the Frank pilgrims till they were bruised and bloody.[1]

On Good Friday Coryate returned to the Church of the Holy Sepulchre and remained there until Easter Day, during which time ceremonies were constantly conducted by the various Churches, reaching a climax with the descent of the Holy Fire from heaven into the Holy Sepulchre. Roman Catholics and Protestants alike expressed disbelief in this annual marvel as openly as the Turks, who nevertheless came in great numbers to watch. For most of the other Churches it was the supreme crisis. Coryate describes how by eleven o'clock on the Saturday morning the church was filled with 2,000 Christians, half of them Armenians. The door of the Sepulchre itself having been locked and bolted, 'they walke round about till five of the clocke in the afternoone without intermission, most of them carrying a bundle of white wax candle in their right hands, bound about with the holy thred

[1] Lithgow, *op. cit.*, p. 232.

or garters which have touched holy places, about forty in a bundle lifted over their heads, invocating the holy Ghost, the Greeks crying Kyrie Eleison, the rest in Arabian, with such stentorean outcries, for that sixe houres procession, thinking therewith to pierce the Heavens, as hath not elsewhere been heard. About three quarters of an hour after foure, the door [of the Sepulchre] was unlocked, and the Patriarchs of the Greekes and Armenians went in, with an Abassine. This last entreth into the grotta, and there in hugger-mugger contriveth his businesse, and having beene there a quarter of an houre, cometh forth with his bundle of lights lighted, and leaping furiously forth is caught by the zealous people ravished with joy at this appearance, the Priest is in danger of stifling whiles each strives to light his candle first.'

The cumulative effect of all that Coryate saw in this the most sacred of all Christian places of worship must have aroused in him an extraordinary mixture of feelings: religious awe interfused with fascinated amazement at so many utterly outlandish sights and sounds, and horrified revulsion when he discovered that the holy precincts were defiled with excrement, 'and that not for want of necessarie places, which there were publicke and common, but through meere beastlinesse in superlative degree'.

Having exhausted the sights in Jerusalem, it was possible to make various day excursions from the city. Coryate and Allard made such a journey to Bethlehem through fields set about with fig and olive trees, and past that very field where the Angels appeared to the shepherds who watched their flocks by night. The village of Bethlehem consisted of only a few poor cottages, inhabited mainly by Greeks and Armenians who earned a living by acting as guides and selling models of the Stable or Grotto. Over the spot where Christ was born stood the splendid Church of the Nativity. The Grotto itself was enclosed in a sumptuous chapel with two separate entrances, one for Christians, the other for the many Mohammedan pilgrims who also came to worship there.

Outside the village visitors were taken to see the cave where Our Lady was hidden while Herod sought the Baby's life. Here the Virgin's miraculously abundant milk spilt upon the ground, turning the earth snowy white and endowing it with the property of giving milk to those mothers who lack it. Its miraculous properties are mentioned by many writers; Lithgow brought home a pound of it which he presented to Queen Anne, and to this day visitors to Bethlehem may purchase small packets of the sandy soil.[1]

Coryate also visited Bethany to see the house of Martha and Mary Magdalene and Lazarus's tomb, exquisitely fashioned in alabaster, enclosed in a little chapel. Yet another excursion took him to Emmaus passing the house of Simeon and the spot where David slew Goliath, returning by a different road to see Samuel's house and the Valley of Gibeon where the sun stood still at Joshua's command.

But the longest and most dangerous expedition was to the River Jordan. This took place only once a year about Easter time because only then was there a sufficient concourse of pilgrims to pay for the large escort of Turkish troops required as protection against the Arabs. Coryate set out from Jerusalem on 28 April. It was more than a day's journey, so the night was spent in the open. One Scottish pilgrim who made this journey on foot two years before Coryate, says that sometimes he was up to his middle in sand and 'true it is, in all my travels, I was never so sore fatigued, nor more fearfully indangered than that night'.[2] Despite a guard of sixty horse and forty foot the Arabs attacked after nightfall, sending down a shower of arrows from the hills and wounding some of the escort who succeeded in driving them out of range after a sharp skirmish. Lithgow states that of the poorer pilgrims who could not afford a mount many died either from exhaustion or from fear, and this is confirmed by the Italian Della Valle, who was there in 1616.

It was usual to start again before daybreak and reach the banks of the Jordan at dawn. Here a fantastic scene took place, excitement among the medley of nationalities reached fever pitch as they neared the place where Christ was baptized. Men, women, and children stripped themselves naked and douched themselves in the chilly water which would wash away their sins. Some drank, some were baptized by friends, some dipped their clothes as well as their bodies. Coryate records that he stepped from the bank and sank up to his middle in mud.

Apart from natural souvenirs, such as Jordan water and tamarisk wands cut from the river bank, which were greatly prized in Christian countries, there was a busy trade in manufactured sacred keepsakes. Coryate particularly mentions garters and girdles.

[1] Samuel C. Chew, *op. cit.*, p. 92.　　　　[2] Lithgow, *op. cit.*, p. 239.

These could be purchased, richly wrought in silk, inscribed in golden letters 'Santo Sepulchro' and 'Jerusalem'. The girdles were made exactly the length of the Holy Sepulchre, and had acquired virtue by being placed therein. The monastery of San Salvatore issued its own souvenirs: a certificate which recited all the memorable things the pilgrim had seen, sealed with the Father Guardian's great seal, and a special supplementary certificate if he had bathed in Jordan water.[1]

The Father Guardian was also empowered to create Knights of the Holy Sepulchre. Coryate probably witnessed the ceremony which took place in the Church of the Holy Sepulchre on Easter Day but, quite apart from the substantial fee of thirty sequins, he would not have accepted the honour since it involved taking a vow to pray for the Pope and swearing enmity to all Protestants. Nevertheless, some Protestants found it within their conscience to have a gilded spur fitted to their right heel and to be dubbed with the sword of Godfrey de Bouillon who lay in his tomb a few paces away.

Coryate took away with him mementos of a different kind. He had the Jerusalem cross—four small crosses, one in each quarter of a larger cross, representing the five wounds suffered by Christ—tattooed upon his left wrist, and upon his right wrist a single cross with the words *Via, Veritas, Vita*. He was very proud of these devices and later in India showed them to Terry, and described to him how they had been 'made by sharp needles bound together, that pierced only the skin, and then a black powder put into the places so pierced, which became presently indelible characters to continue with him so long as his flesh should be covered with skin; and they were done upon his arms so artificially as if they had been drawn by some accurate Pencil upon parchment'. The more timorous Moryson declined to be tattooed lest the marks should betray his religion during his travels through Mohammedan territory. But Coryate knew no such scruples and Terry

[1] Fynes Moryson, *Itinerary*, vol. II, p. 37, 'Moreover they gave to each of us freely and unasked . . . a testimony under the seale of the Monastery that we had beene at Jerusalem, and for better credit, they expressed therein some markable signes of our faces and bodies.' Lithgow had to pay three sequins for his certificate, and gives an illustration of the great seal, *op. cit.*, facing p. 269. This illustration also shows the two devices, one being the Jerusalem cross, with which Lithgow was tattooed. Henry Timberlake seems to have received his supplementary certificate even though he never went near the Jordan.

relates that he 'would pride himself very much in the beholding of those characters, and seeing them would often speak those words of St. Paul written to the Galatians, Gal. 6. 17. (though far besides the Apostle's meaning) "I bear in my body the marks of the Lord Jesus".'

According to Terry, Coryate and Allard never returned to Jerusalem after the Jordan expedition but, having viewed the murky surface of the Dead Sea, and seen the ruins of Jericho, struck north to Mount Lebanon, the home of the Maronites. Though Terry's testimony as regards itinerary is not entirely reliable, it seems probable that this is what they did. Many Maronites would be returning from the pilgrimage, and could thus afford them company. It is likely that they would if possible choose a different route for their return journey, and in any case the Maronites' mountain territory was worth seeing. They were a simple upright industrious people who, at the price of extortionate tributes, kept all Turks out of their homeland. In contrast to the barrenness of Canaan, that land once flowing with milk and honey from which God's blessing had been withdrawn, the Maronites had created a thriving countryside in their hilly fastness by hard work and Christian discipline. The country abounded in corn, oil, cotton, silk, honey, wax, and excellent wines made from grapes the size of prunes; their sheep were fat and their partridges as big as hens. Then there were the cedars, a score of more still surviving from the time of Solomon which, because of their antiquity, the Maronites regarded as Saints.[1]

From Mount Lebanon the two friends walked on to Aleppo where they parted company.[2] Allard embarked for England, taking with him letters from Coryate, none of which has survived. Coryate stayed on in Aleppo and it seems that by this time he had taken the fateful decision to turn his back on home and march towards the East.

[1] See the account of Jerome Dandini, sent as Papal Nuncio to the Maronites in 1596, published as *Missione Apostolica al Patriarcha e Maroniti del Monte Libano*, Cesena, 1656, of which a translation, excluding the narration of his visit to Jerusalem, is included in *Harleian Voyages*, London, 1745, vol., I. p. 831 *et seq.*

[2] According to Terry, Coryate and Allard descended from Mount Lebanon to Sidon, where they took ship for Iskanderun. This, however, cannot be reconciled with Coryate's specific statement in Letter No. 2 that he walked all the way from Jerusalem to Ajmer.

# CHAPTER XIV

# *The Great Walk from Aleppo to Ajmer*

---

O N his return to Aleppo in May 1614, Coryate's first task was to complete writing up the notes of his travels in the Holy Land; he left these at Aleppo and they eventually found their way home to Samuel Purchas. Next he began making plans for the journey to India.

His friends in Constantinople and Aleppo were probably able to give him little first-hand information about the vast territories which lay between him and the dominions of the Great Mogul, since few Englishmen, or indeed Europeans of any nationality, had ventured far along the caravan routes. The prime sources of Coryate's knowledge were the Old Testament and the ancient Greek geographer Strabo. He may have read Arrian and Plutarch; at all events he knew the story of Alexander's eastern campaigns.

About Tamerlaine (1336–1405) he knew enough to tell the Great Mogul, when eventually he obtained the opportunity of addressing him, that his ancestor's 'fame, by reason of his warres and victories, is published over the whole world'. Coryate added: 'perhaps he is not altogether so famous in his own country of Tartaria as in England.' That suggestion was not entirely fanciful; when Marlowe wrote *Tamburlaine the Great*, first published in 1590, there were some forty authors in whose writings he could have found some account of Timur's career.[1] These histories included works in Greek, Latin, Italian, and English—the languages known to Coryate—but none of them afforded much guidance to an intending traveller.

A few accounts of Persia by sixteenth-century European travel-

---

[1] See *Tamburlaine the Great*, ed. U. M. Ellis-Fermor, London, 1930, p. 34, and pp. 305–8, where a full bibliography is given.

lers had been published, such as those of the Venetian Ambassador, Ambrosio Contarini, and the Venetian jeweller, Balbi, but there is no evidence that Coryate had read them.[1] He could have gleaned some scraps from Hakluyt's collection of papers concerning the exploits and experiences of the Muscovy Company merchants who had penetrated down the Volga and across the Caspian into northern Persia during the second half of the sixteenth century.[2] More recently two Englishmen had written accounts which, despite their brevity, were of some practical value to the traveller. In 1611 the Rev. John Cartwright had published *The Preacher's Travels* about his journeyings in Persia; if Coryate had not read this little book he must certainly have heard of the astonishing achievements of John Mildenhall, whom Cartwright accompanied during the first part of his travels.

These two strangely assorted Englishmen, the intrepid, ambitious merchant, and the inquisitive, venturesome parson, had left Aleppo in July 1600. After many months Mildenhall parted company with Cartwright and travelled via Yezd, Kerman, and Kandahar to Agra, where he arrived in 1603 and presented himself at the Court of the Great Mogul to crave privileges of trade on behalf of himself and his fellow countrymen. Three years later he returned to Aleppo by much the same route. Some time prior to April 1611 Mildenhall started on a second expedition to the East carrying with him goods belonging to a number of English merchants for sale in Persia. He is said to have betrayed his trust and to have fled with the merchandise, intending to sell it in India. Two Englishmen sent in pursuit overtook him and forced him to return with them to Ispahan where he surrendered the disputed property. Then one of his erstwhile pursuers, Richard Steel, who appears later in Coryate's life story, joined fortune with him and

---

[1] A. Contarini, *Il Viaggio dell'Ambrosio Contarini, ambasciatore della signoria di Venetia al Uxan-Cassan, ré di Persia* . . . Venice, 1543. Gasparo Balbi went to Aleppo in 1579, thence to Babylonia. He embarked at Ormus for Diu and so reached Goa. After visiting Pegu he returned home in 1588. His book *Viaggio dell'Indie Orientali* . . . was published in Venice in 1590. Other accounts include C. Zeno, *Commentarj del viaggio in Persia* . . . Venice, 1558; Bredenbach, *Liber de Armeniorum ritibus, moribus et erroribus*, Basel, 1577, and A. Manutio, *Scriptores rerum Persicarum*, a small collection of travels which had appeared in Italian in 1543 and 1545.

[2] *The Principal Navigations* . . . 1598–1600. See in particular, vol. III, pp. 15–38, for Anthony Jenkinson's famous exploits, and pp. 136–66 for Geoffrey Ducket's less well known but vivid account of life in Persia, from which Cartwright borrowed in *The Preacher's Travels*.

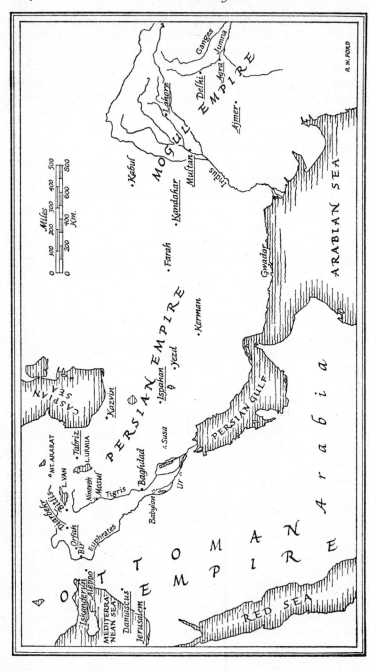

Map 3.  The great walk from Aleppo to Ajmer.
Underlined place-names are those known to have been on Coryate's route.

accompanied him to India, where Mildenhall fell ill and died at Ajmer in April 1614.[1] Mildenhall holds the distinction not only of being the first Englishman ever to reach India by the overland route, but of having accomplished the journey twice. Apart from Mildenhall, and the one or two, including Steel, who travelled with him,[2] there is no record of any other Englishman travelling overland before Coryate.

Mildenhall was also the first Englishman to complete the overland journey in the reverse direction from India to Aleppo, a feat which was repeated by two of his countrymen a few years later in curious circumstances. Paul Pindar may have told Coryate how, one day in December 1610, when he was Consul at Aleppo, two ragged and exhausted travellers had arrived there, destitute except for the camels which carried them. Their names were Robert Coverte and Richard Martin, members of the crew of the East India Company's *Ascension*. Fourteen months previously their ship had been wrecked off Surat and, finding no certain opportunity of reaching home again by sea, they had, in a matter of fact way, travelled overland via Agra, Kandahar, Ispahan, and Baghdad. Pindar fed and housed them during their stay in Aleppo, and provided them with funds for the voyage home. Coverte gratefully acknowledged Pindar's generosity in *A true and almost incredible report* . . ., his brief account of their wanderings, which Coryate could have read, since it was published in 1612.

From such written sources as were available to him, from conversations with Franks, and probably also with eastern merchants encountered at Aleppo, he must have built up some sort of picture of the distances involved, the extremes of heat and cold which he would have to endure, and all the other hardships and dangers which he was bound to encounter. The more he knew, the more insanely daring does his plan appear. His decision to *walk* to India may have been partly due to lack of money, but the chief reason was undoubtedly his thirst for fame and his determination to establish beyond argument that the Odcom-

---

[1] Mildenhall's body was taken to Agra and there buried in the Roman Catholic cemetery. His tomb is the oldest English monument in India. See Sir William Foster, *Early Travels in India*, pp. 48–59. There is a photograph of the tomb facing p. 50.

[2] Cartwright mentions John Parrot who went out to Persia as a member of the Sherley brothers' entourage, 'who afterwards died in Lahore, being in Mr. Mildenhal's company'. *The Preacher's Travels* in Harleian Collection of Voyages, vol. I, p. 738.

bian Legstretcher was the greatest walker the world had ever seen.

In September 1611 he set out from Aleppo with a caravan bound for Ispahan, the Persian capital. His foretaste of caravan life in Syria and Palestine had been mainly in the company of inexperienced pilgrims, many of whom had never been more than a few days away from their homes before. Now he was with professionals: merchants, camel drivers, and muleteers who spent a large part of their lives traversing these wild expanses.

Much depended on the skill of the caravan commander. He alone decided the route, the time of starting, and the duration of the day's march. At river crossings and the major townships there were tolls to pay, assessed either on the number of beasts or on the value of the goods they carried. As Coryate had no camel, and nothing but his personal belongings, he was free from these exactions. At many towns there was a halt of days, sometimes even weeks, for rest, for trade, or to satisfy the whim of the local governor. On the march the caravan travelled sometimes for twelve or even fifteen hours a day; where there was vegetation the camels were allowed to browse as they went, which reduced the pace to a mile an hour. In extreme heat, such as could be met with in Mesopotamia during September, men and beasts lay low during the day and travelled during the hours of darkness.

After four days they arrived at the Euphrates which they probably crossed at Bir, the modern Birejk. Four days more brought them to Orfah, the ancient Edessa of Seleucus, which Coryate calls 'a very delicate and pleasant cittie'. There are several local traditions linking Orfah with Abraham; one that he died there, one that he stayed there on his way from Ur to Canaan, and yet another that he was born there, which explains why Coryate confused Orfah with Ur, and, encouraged by the remarkable state of preservation of the many Biblical remains which he had already seen, spent some time in an unsuccessful search for the house where that faithful servant of God was born.

After a halt of four days the caravan pushed on to the fortress city of Diarbekr whose massive, black, basalt walls can be seen from far away across the surrounding plain. Caravans did not enter the city, but encamped beneath the walls near the banks of the Tigris. Merchandise carried thus far by camels was shifted on to mules which were able to climb the steep, narrow, mountain tracks ahead. Perhaps while this process of reorganization was going on, and the city officials were collecting the tolls, Coryate climbed up to the city to explore.

Here at Diarbekr calamity befell him for a Spahi (horse-guard) robbed him of almost all his money. He was not left quite penniless 'by reason of certaine clandestine corners' where he had hidden some gold and silver pieces, but shortly afterwards this small store was further depleted by some trickery. The place and circumstances are obscure, and we only know that 'certaine lewd Christians of the Armenian nation *cousened*' him of ten shillings. In his already straitened circumstances this was a doubly bitter blow; ten shillings represented four months victuals in lands where he was often able to eat adequately for a penny a day. No wonder that months afterwards he remembered these two setbacks with indignation when writing home from India.

The rainy season had not yet begun, so the Tigris was easily fordable. Coryate waded over from Mesopotamia into Armenia, and found that the water reached no higher than the calf of his leg. The route through Armenia is uncertain, but it probably lay upwards into the mountains, through Bitlis, and along the shores of Lake Van, over 5,000 feet above sea-level, where a mule could work its way along the narrow rocky shelf of road only by brushing and shouldering its burden against the cliff face. Far away to the north-east could be seen the peak of Ararat[1] capped with eternal snow. Snow might now at any time descend on the caravan, making the difficult mountain tracks even more treacherous for man and beast.

Physical discomfort mattered little to Coryate. In his letters he makes no mention of the cold, but neither does he speak of the scorching heat of Mesopotamia, the comfortless nights on hard ground, the rough fare, the dust, the flies and the vermin. The desolation of the countryside did impress him: 'A great part of the Turks land is extreme barren and sterill as I have observed in

[1] Terry says that Coryate saw 'or else our traveller was made to believe that he saw the very mountain of Ararat whereon the Ark of Noah rested after the flood', which is quite consistent with the evidence from Coryate's letters about the route he followed between Aleppo and Kandahar. The route according to Terry was via Nineveh (Mosul), Baghdad (which he confuses with Babylon—a common error at that time), Ispahan, Shushan (Susa), and thence to Kandahar, which cannot be reconciled with the statement that he saw Ararat, or with Coryate's own evidence. It seems that once again Terry confused what Coryate had done with what he planned to do on his return journey.

my peregrination thereof, particularly in Syria, Mesopotamia and Armenia; many large portions thereof being so wonderfull fruitlesse that it beareth no good thing at all, or if any thing there "infelix lolium et steriles dominantur avenae".[1]

Apart from the customs dues levied at each major township, there were the random and arbitrary demands of the bands of Kurdish tribesmen, who prowled like wolves along the caravan routes ready to cut off straggling men and beasts, or rode down in force armed with bows and scimitars to demand safe-conduct money. Then the caravan commander had to decide whether to brush them aside, relying on the escort's firearms—weapons which the Kurds did not yet know how to use—or to bargain with them and buy them off with a fraction of what they asked for. In either case there was the risk of an ambush later on. Cartwright calls them 'a thievish lot, as infamous as the Arabs', and records that his caravan was waylaid by them no less than five times.

Encounters with savage hordes of roving tribesmen were particularly likely in the great band of territory disputed between Turkey and Persia, through which they were now passing. In the centre of this vast war-wasted area, which stretched from the Caucasus in the north to within about a hundred miles of the Persian Gulf, lay Tabriz. This had been the proud first capital of the Safavid dynasty of Persian Shahs, but in 1585 the Turks had besieged and taken the city and descended with fire and sword on all the surrounding territory. Shah Abbas had succeeded in retaking Tabriz in 1603, but the place was still in ruins. Coryate spent six days here 'among the dolefull testimonies of the Turkish devastations, more wofull ruines of a city saving that of Troy and Cyzicum . . . never did mine eyes beholde'.[2]

From Tabriz it was at least ten days'[3] journey to Kazvin, three days through snow-covered mountains and then across the plain which has the reputation of being the coldest district in all Persia. But in Kazvin they were well clear of the war zone. Here was a meeting point of trade routes from east, north, and west. In its bazaars Persian silks and rugs were exchanged for Indian jewels and spices, sables and martens out of Muscovy, red and purple

[1] Letter No. 2. The quotation is from Virgil, *Georgics*, Bk. I, l. 154: 'the luckless darnel and barren oats hold sway'.  [2] Letter No. 2.
[3] 'Two days' given in the printed texts of Coryate's letters is a manifest impossibility. The two places are 250 miles apart. Cartwright took ten days.

cloth from Venice, English broadcloth, kersies, and tin. Kazvin, set in a large, fertile plain and surrounded by vineyards and corn-fields, was equal in grandeur to any other city of the Persian Empire, Ispahan excepted.

Travelling between Kazvin and Ispahan was relatively easy and so safe that caravans split up into smaller groups which could lodge every night in a Persian village, or in fine stone caravan-serais, built on the same pattern as the Turkish *khans*. Improve-ment of the roads, erection of many caravanserais, and the ruthless repression of robbery, were not the least of the outstanding achievements of the great Shah Abbas who had already occupied the Persian throne for more than twenty-five years and had res-tored his country's fortunes as much by the wisdom and vigour of his internal administration as by resounding military successes against his encroaching neighbours.

As a symbol of Persia's reborn power and of his own magni-ficence he had founded a new capital at Ispahan graced with palaces and mosques, courts, gardens, and pavilions, some com-pleted, some still being constructed by the best craftsmen from all over Persia. Coryate entered this superb and exciting city twenty-three days after leaving Kazvin, with high hopes of obtaining an audience of the Shah himself, and of obtaining a handsome present from him which would alleviate his financial difficulties. But in this design he was disappointed, since he found that the Shah was away in Georgia 'ransacking the poor Christians there with great hostility, with fire and sword'.

Sir Thomas Herbert, who visited Ispahan fourteen years after Coryate, estimated the population at about 200,000, including many merchants from both East and West: English, Dutch, Portuguese, Poles, Muscovites, Indians, Arabs, Armenians, Georgians, Turks, and Jews, all drawn thither by the magnetic power of gain.[1] Coryate may have found one or two of his country-men there as early as 1614. All we know is that he spent two months in Ispahan and left in someone's care the notes which he had accumulated since leaving Aleppo, already too voluminous to be carried farther.

Coryate departed from Ispahan in February 1615. Kandahar, the nearest outpost of the Mogul Empire was still well over eight

---

[1] Thomas Herbert, *Travels in Persia*, 1628. He gives a detailed description of Is-pahan as he saw it in April 1628, pp. 116–40.

hundred miles away. He may, like Mildenhall, have travelled via
Yezd and Kerman, but from Yezd he could have taken a more
northerly route through Farah.[1] We know that he travelled with
an enormous caravan consisting of 2,000 camels, 1,500 horses,
over 1,000 mules, 800 asses, and 6,000 people.

No caravanserai could contain so vast a concourse and it was
often necessary to camp in open country remote from any protecting township. Then the beasts would be tethered in a great
square facing inwards. Within, the travellers set up their tents and
cooked their supper over camel-dung fires—rice, lentils, herbs, and
dates, occasionally gobbets of camel-flesh roasted on a skewer,
washed down with water which was generally tepid and often
brackish. Beyond the square was an outer line of fires beside which
crouched the watch, and outside the fires ranged the patrol. The
caravan was an entity like a town or a ship at sea, never wholly
asleep. If Coryate sat late writing up his notes by the flickering
firelight he could hear the thin warbling of a Persian song from
the watch fires, camels grumbling, and horses snorting, until at
last he rolled himself in his blanket to sleep, and be awakened by
the drummer sounding the signal to prepare for another day's
march.

Somewhere near the frontier between India and Persia they met
a caravan travelling in the opposite direction. But this caravan was
different from all the others, for towering above the loaded camels
there marched two fine elephants. Naturally he lost no time in
inspecting the animals at close quarters, and making enquiries
about their owner. He elicited that they belonged to an Englishman who was travelling in great state with his wife to the Court of
Shah Abbas. With his curiosity redoubled Coryate sought and
obtained an interview. The Englishman turned out to be the
famous adventurer 'Sir' Robert Sherley who, to Coryate's immense
delight, produced from his luggage both his books 'neatly kept'.

That the author should be confronted with his *Crudities* and
*Crambe* in the wilds of central Asia would appear to be a coincidence of fantastic improbability, and to give an explanation of this
peculiar conjunction of circumstances it is necessary to touch on
the extraordinary career of Robert Sherley. Some sixteen years
previously Robert and his elder brother Anthony had entered the

---

[1] Coverte in 1610 and Richard Steel in 1615 both passed through Farah on their
way from Kandahar to Ispahan.

40. Ispahan. From A. U. Pope, *A Survey of Persian Art*, Oxford, 1938. The grand square which formed the heart of Shah Abbas's new city.

41–42. Robert Sherley in Persian dress and his Circassian wife Teresia. From their portraits by Van Dyck at Petworth House. *Reproduced by courtesy of John Wyndham, Esq., and the National Trust.*

service of Shah Abbas. Anthony had stayed only a few months before departing again for Europe as the Shah's ambassador, never to return.[1] Robert had remained in Persia for over nine years. It is said, on slender evidence, that he played an important part in reforming the Persian army and equipping it for the first time with artillery. He certainly fought with distinction in the Shah's campaigns against the Turks.

While in Persia Robert had married a noble Circassian lady of Christian faith, and in 1608 he departed with her for Europe on an embassy from the Shah to the Christian rulers of Europe. His mission was mainly to promote commercial relations, but also to invite European aid for a war against the Turks. The embassy had started auspiciously; the Emperor Rudolf II had knighted him in Prague: the Pope had received him, dressed as always in Persian robes with a golden crucifix in his turban, and had not only created him Count of the Sacred Palace of the Lateran, but endowed him with the power of legitimatizing bastards. Incidentally he never possessed any English title, and the disservices which he performed to his native land might well have been regarded as treason, and could have earned recognition of quite another kind. Before coming to England he spent more than a year in Madrid carrying on unfruitful commerical negotiations with Philip III, King of Spain and Portugal. Nevertheless James I received him graciously at Hampton Court in the autumn of 1611, and in November Queen Anne consented to become godmother, and the Prince of Wales godfather, to his only son, who was accordingly christened Henry. Sherley had thus been at Court just at the time when the *Crudities* and *Crambe* were being read and talked about. It is therefore not so surprising that he should have possessed copies.

Despite Sherley's apparent social success at the English Court, his commercial and political proposals were coldly received. The

---

[1] In 1600 *A True Report of Sir Anthony Sherleys Journey* had been published anonymously and suppressed. It was suppressed again the succeeding year, probably because it was mainly pirated from the work of one of the Sherleys' English followers, William Parry, who published a *New and Large Discourse* in 1601. The sensational exploits of Anthony, Robert and the eldest brother Thomas, who became a pirate, were brought to the attention of the British public, and possibly to Coryate, in a highly coloured pamphlet by Anthony Nixon, *The Three English Brothers*, which appeared in 1607. The first serious account is E. P. Shirley's *The Sherley Brothers*, Roxburghe Club, 1848. See also Boies Penrose, *The Sherleian Odyssey*, Taunton, 1938, and Sir E. Denison Ross, *Sir Anthony Sherley & his Persian Adventure*, London, 1933, which includes the narratives of Parry and two others in the Sherleys' suite.

Levant Company merchants feared that any close relations between Britain and Persia would enrage the Turk and jeopardize their lucrative trade with the Ottoman Empire. Sir Thomas Roe, shortly to become the first British Ambassador at the Court of the Great Mogul, and to be closely connected with the closing episodes of Coryate's life, was present at the negotiations and formed an unfavourable opinion of Sherley's character and of his plans. Later in India, when Sherley's machinations were causing Roe concern, he recalled this first meeting and added of Sherley himself 'as he is dishonest, so is he subtile'.[1]

Sherley lingered on in England until January 1613 when he set sail in an East Indiaman to return to Persia by sea. Arrived at Gwadar on the Persian coast, he was about to disembark when he discovered a plot on his life and decided to sail on to India. Here the Portuguese tried to blow up his lodgings and several of his party met violent ends. With considerable justification Sherley complained to the Great Mogul, who with his usual interest in foreigners, invitied him to recuperate from his misfortunes at Court. Sherley had remained with the Great Mogul for some months and was now at last on his way back to his Persian master, bringing the two elephants and eight antelopes as presents, but little else to show for his seven years' absence.

Coryate says that Sherley and his long-suffering and remarkably hardy wife were 'so gallantly furnished with all necessaries for their travailes, that it was a great comfort unto me to see them in such a flourishing estate'. These generous feelings on the part of the penurious pedestrian were not entirely altruistic: he saw some of the costly presents given to them by the Great Mogul which raised his hopes of receiving royal bounty in due course himself. Furthermore, it seemed likely that such an important and affluent personage as Sherley would be munificent in the grand manner to a fellow countryman in straitened circumstances. 'Both he and his lady used me with singular respect,' he says, 'and they seemed to exult for joy to see mee,' but all he extracted from Sherley was a promise that he would show his books to the Shah, and urge him to bestow a princely reward on the author when he returned through Persia. Lady Sherley, however, demonstrated her regard in more practical fashion by giving him the equivalent of forty shillings in Persian money to help him on his road.

---

[1] *Embassy of Sir Thomas Roe*, p. xlvii, n.

At the frontier the Persian officials were diligent in enforcing the Shah's laws. Merchants entering the country were dealt with leniently, but those on their way to India were questioned and searched. Neither slaves nor horses might be exported and it was forbidden to take gold or silver out of the country on pain of death. Some travellers were stripped naked, but if Coryate was searched his 'clandestine corners' kept the secret of his little horde.

So at last he reached Kandahar. During the later stages of the journey from Ispahan it was usual for the great caravans to break up into smaller parties since large groups could not find enough water and fodder in these desert regions. At Kandahar these small bodies re-grouped themselves into large caravans for the passage through the mountains of Afghanistan where the Pathans lay in wait. This process of reorganization took two or three weeks during which the people of Kandahar administered to all the bodily needs of desert-weary travellers at grossly inflated prices.

The journey through the mountains down into the valley of the Indus seems to have been uneventful except that somewhere on the way Coryate first encountered Richard Steel. Steel, it will be remembered, had accompanied Mildenhall to India by the overland route in the previous year. He was now on his way back to England via Ispahan, carrying a letter from the Great Mogul to King James, and also letters from the East India merchants to the Company in London. It seems unlikely that Coryate would let slip this unexpected opportunity of sending a letter home, but no such letter survived. When he reached home Steel certainly reported that he had met Coryate and there is a sequel to the story which will be related later.[1]

Two days after crossing the Indus, 'the famous river Indus' Coryate calls it, 'which is as broade againe as our Thames at London', he arrived at Multan. According to Steel all caravans were compelled by the Governor to stay eight, ten, or even twelve days at Multan, so that the city, and no doubt the Governor, might benefit from supplying the travellers' wants. While he was there Coryate met a Mohammedan Indian who could speak Italian. Many years previously this man, having been captured by Floren-

[1] Steel left Multan on 27 May 1615, and arrived at Kandahar on 7 July. The account of his journey from Ajmer to Ispahan is in Purchas, vol. IV, p. 266, and several details from it have been incorporated in this account of Coryate's journey in the reverse direction.

tines while travelling in a galley between Constantinople and Alexandria, had been carried off as a slave to Leghorn. By the time that he regained his liberty he had learnt his captors' language. The conversation turned to religion and the man had the temerity to call Coryate an infidel. All the time he had been in Turkey and Persia Coryate had had to endure such insults in silence, but now he decided to take advantage of the tolerance practised in the Great Mogul's dominions and launched forth into an extempore oration, giving vent to his pent-up hatred of the Mohammedan faith in the most violent terms.

'What thy Mahomet was, from whom thou dost derive thy religion, assure thy selfe I know better than any one of the Mahometans amongst many millions; yea, all the particular circumstances of his life and death, his nation, his parentage, his driving camels through Egipt, Siria, and Palestina, the marriage of his mistris by whose death he raised himselfe from a very base and contemtible estate to great honor and riches, his manner of cozening the sottish people of Arabia, partly by a tame pigeon that did fly to his eare for meat, and partly by a tame bull that hee fed by hand every day, with the rest of his actions both in peace and warre, I know as well as if I had lived in his time, or had been one of his neighbours in Mecca. The truth whereof if thou didst know aswell, I am perswaded thou wouldest spit in the face of thy Alcaron [Koran] and trample it under thy feete, and bury it under a jaxe [privy], a booke of that strange and weake matter that I my selfe (as meanely as thou dost see me attired now) have already written two better bookes (God be thanked), and will hereafter this (by Gods gratious permission) write another better and truer.'

This would seem to be trying his listener's patience to a fool-hardy extent, particularly since the Indian who alone could understand what Coryate was saying, translated the parts he could remember—which were no doubt the most insulting—to the crowd of a hundred who had by this time assembled. But they let him speak on; Mohammed, he asserted, was so dull of wit that he was not able to write the Koran himself, but was largely helped by the renegade monk Sergius, and that whereas Christian prayers are heard and answered, Mohammedan prayers 'what with your vain repeti[ti]ons and divers other prophane fooleries . . . doe even stinke before God, and are of no more force then the cry of thy camell when thou doest lade or unlade him'.

Coryate was very proud of this piece of invective which he afterwards wrote down in English and sent in a letter to his mother. 'If I had spoken thus much in Turky or Persia against Mahomet,' he told her, 'they would have rosted me upon a spitt; but in the Mogols dominions a Christian may speake much more freely than hee can in any other Mahometan country in the world.'

His outburst is not only indicative of the climate of religious toleration in Mogul India, it is also a testimony of Christian ignorance and blind prejudice. Out of his own mouth he refutes his claim to expert knowledge of the Muslim faith by repeating some of the best-known legends and slanders which Mohammed's opponents had elaborated and spread abroad. It would indeed be surprising if his standpoint were more enlightened, since no impartial source of information was available to a Christian. It seems certain that Coryate had never read the Koran, though a Latin translation (including arguments and diatribes against Mohammedanism) had appeared about 1543.[1] Probably Coryate's chief source of information was Münster's *Cosmography*, which includes the story of the dove—or pigeon as Coryate calls it—a fable quite unknown to Moslems. The tale of how Mohammed tricked a wealthy widow into marriage was another fabrication which gained wide acceptance in Christendom, perhaps because it was not beyond the range of ordinary Christian experience, while the legend of Sergius the renegade monk was very much alive in Elizabethan England.

The caravan moved on from Multan to Lahore, which seems to have been its goal. It had taken a little over four months to travel from Ispahan. Coryate was much impressed with Lahore: 'a goodly city . . . one of the largest cities of the whole universe, for it containeth at the least XVI miles in compasse and exceedeth Constantinople itself in greatnesse.' But his desire to reach his final destination prevented him from lingering. He turned south, in company with other travellers, following the fine straight road connecting Lahore with Agra. Throughout its length of about 440 miles it was bordered on either side with shady evergreen trees and ran through a rich, well cultivated plain—'such a deli-

---

[1] *Machumetis Sarracenorum Principis Vita et Doctrina omnis*, by Theodorus Bibliander or Buchmann. For a detailed study of Europeans' knowledge of, and attitude towards, the Muslim faith at this time, see Samuel C. Chew, *The Crescent & the Rose*, New York, 1937, pp. 387–451.

cate and eeven tract of ground as I never saw before . . . the most
incomparable shew of that kinde that ever my eies survaied'.
Later Coryate described this road, the 'Long Walk', to Sir Thomas
Roe who had it incorporated, trees and all, in the famous map of
India which he compiled in collaboration with William Baffin,
the navigator.[1] All along the way were villages and towns and
about every ten miles there was a fine caravanserai where travellers could find rest and refreshment. At one point he was tempted
to make a deviation in order to investigate an intriguing report
that some ten miles to the east lay a mountainous area where
polyandry was practised—as it still is in some Himalayan districts—but he wisely decided to keep to the great road where
travelling by day was safe. Robbers were abroad even on the
'Long Walk' during the hours of darkness, so all travelling had
to be done under a searing June sun. But at least the going was
easy beneath the shade of the trees, and Coryate and his companions were able to cover a little over twenty miles a day.

In Delhi, then largely in ruins, he stopped long enough to
view what he described to Edward Terry, Roe's chaplain, as being
'a very great pillar of marble, with a Greek inscription upon it
which Time hath almost quite worn out'[2] erected, as he conjec-
tured, by Alexander the Great to commemorate his victory over
King Porus in 326 B.C. This pillar evidently made a particularly
deep impression on Coryate—he mentions it and its supposed
purpose again in his letter to Laurence Whitaker. No doubt what
he actually saw was one of the famous Asoka pillars. He was
wrong about the language of the inscription—but the Prakrit
characters, effaced by time, could be mistaken for Greek, and as
regards the pillar's age he was not far out. In Coryate's time no one
had even heard of King Asoka, whose achievements have since
been revealed by the labours of European scholars. Yet prior to
Akbar he was the greatest and most enlightened ruler India ever
knew. He ruled from *c.* 272 to 232 B.C. over an empire which was
even vaster than Akbar's, embracing most of Central and Northern India, Kashmir and Nepal.

[1] See illustration. The original is in the British Museum, ref. K.115(22). It is the
earliest British attempt to map the Mogul territories. For an interesting account of
the circumstances of its production, the information it contains, and the extent to
which it guided (and misguided) later cartographers, see Sir William Foster, *The
Embassy of Sir Thomas Roe*, Hakluyt Society, 1899, vol. II, pp. 542–6.
[2] Terry, *Voyage to East India*, 1655, p. 81.

This mighty pillar is all that Coryate mentions of Delhi, and we know from his timetable that he could only have made a brief halt here on his journey southwards, but it seems more than likely that he paid a second visit later since Terry tells us that he 'took special notice of this place'.[1]

On reaching Agra a brief survey was enough to convince him that it was in every way much inferior to Lahore. These were the two principal cities of the Mogul Empire, and Agra was nominally the capital, but some two years previously the Emperor had decided to establish himself and his enormous court in the little town of Ajmer, a further ten days' march to the south-east.

So Coryate completed the final stage of his great walk and arrived safely in Ajmer in the middle of July 1615. He had accomplished a feat which no European had even attempted since Alexander's Macedonian infantry reached the Ganges two thousand years before. Whereas they had the discipline and resources of an unconquerable corps, and the inspiration of a great leader, Coryate's had been a solitary achievement, with none to trust in but his Maker and with only his faith and determination to sustain him through all those months of hardship.

Not the least remarkable fact about his journey was that during his ten months' travel from Aleppo to Ajmer he spent only fifty shillings 'yet fared reasonably well everie daie; victuals being so cheape in some countries where I travelled, that I often times lived competentlie for a pennie sterling a day'.

As he measured his European journey from his physical home at Odcombe, so he measured this, his greatest journey, from his spiritual home, Jerusalem. But he was too modest in his calculations; he estimated that between Jerusalem and Ajmer he had walked 2,700 miles, whereas he must in fact have covered at least 3,300 miles 'all which way I traversed afoot, but with divers paire of shooes, having beene such a propateticke ... that is, a walker forward on foote, as I doubt whether you ever heard of the like in your life'.

[1] *Ibid.*, p. 81.

# CHAPTER XV

# The Court of the Great Mogul

THE first Englishman known to have set foot in India was another Wykehamist, the Jesuit Father Thomas Stevens, who sailed from Lisbon in 1579, and reached the Portuguese settlement of Goa the same year, remaining there till his death forty years later. If one excepts Stevens, Coryate was the first Englishman to enter India with no thought of trade. His prime object was to collect material for the book which he intended to write about his observations and experiences. There is little doubt that if that book had been written, the knowledge of local languages which he acquired, and the journeys which he undertook during his two and a half years' stay, allied with his capacity for detailed and accurate study, would have made it a more illuminating account than any that exist of the Mogul Empire under the Emperor Jahangir. As it is, even the notes which he must have been carrying with him at the time of his death disappeared without trace and all that we are left with are five truncated letters, a few notes given to Purchas by Sir Thomas Roe, and some details and anecdotes preserved by Terry. From these morsels, so full of zest and savour, it is possible to gain some conception of the feast which has been denied us.

At Ajmer Coryate was greeted with open arms by the little group of East India Company's servants. There were ten of them in all, headed by William Edwards 'an honest man that useth me with verie loving respect'. As yet there was no ambassador, but Edwards, who had arrived from England nine months previously, had been authorized to represent himself as 'a messenger' sent expressly by King James. Coryate lived in the merchants' house and at their expense during the whole of his long stay in Ajmer 'not spending one little peece of money, either for diet, washing or any other thing'.

Although the East India Company had been established in 1600 it was only just under eight years prior to Coryate's arrival that the first ship to display the English flag on the coast of India had arrived off Surat. Until 1604 England was at war with the United Kingdoms of Spain and Portugal, and mainly for this reason the East India Company's First and Second Voyages did not visit India, where the Portuguese were known to be in strong force, but went farther afield to Java, Sumatra, and the Far East.

The Portuguese had been in India longer than the Moguls. They were the only European nation with any territorial possessions, these being centred at Goa, which was the seat of the Portuguese Viceroy. Their control of the neighbouring seas was tacitly accepted by Jahangir as it had been by his father Akbar. Naturally, the arrival of the British was strongly resented, and the Portuguese did everything in their power to persuade the Emperor to deny them trading facilities.

The Portuguese endeavours to speed the departure of their new competitors, through setting the authorities and the Indian merchants against them by a policy of systematic denigration and threats, were almost successful. In February 1612 the British sailed away from Surat and it seemed that any prospect of obtaining permission to trade with India had gone for ever. But a new expedition was already on its way out from England and in September 1612 Captain Best with the *Dragon* and *Hosiander* anchored off Surat. This goaded the Portuguese into the use of physical force, which proved their undoing. They attacked with a fleet of four galleons and a swarm of frigates only to be driven off with heavy loss. Two further engagements took place ending with the complete defeat of the Portuguese squadron. Meanwhile news had arrived at Surat that the British ships, which had left Surat at the beginning of the year and joined up in the Red Sea with a fresh fleet from England, had intercepted a number of Indian vessels trading to Mokha and Aden, forced them to exchange their goods for English commodities and, furthermore, compelled those vessels belonging to Surat and the neighbouring port of Diu to pay a heavy ransom as a penalty for the exclusion of the English.

These actions had a great effect in India. Best's victory showed that the British were quite as powerful at sea as the Portuguese, and the interference with the valuable Red Sea trade made it

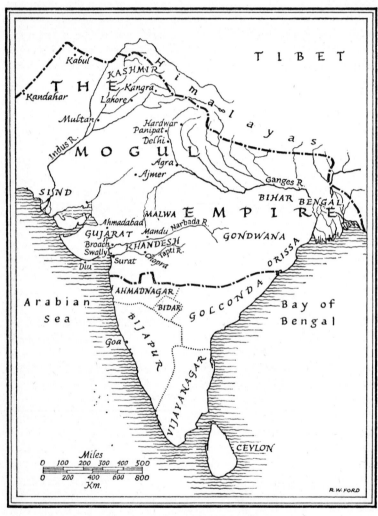

Map 4. India in 1615.
Only place-names relevant to the narrative have been included.

apparent that it might be more dangerous to ignore the claims of the British than to listen to the menaces of the Portuguese. Henceforth Surat was opened to the East India Company's trade.

But this more propitious turn of events by no means meant the end of the struggle. The Portuguese had powerful friends at Court, including the Jesuits, whose chief acted as their official representative, and who had religious as well as political reasons for not wanting to see the British firmly established. For many years to come the East India Company had to contend with obstruction and misrepresentation. A concession secured by the Company after weeks of negotiation and judicious present giving might nevertheless be withdrawn peremptorily when the Portuguese got to hear of it and intervened with promises, threats, and counterbribes. These difficulties, though he was a witness of them and their effects, were of little concern to Coryate who, with constitution and energy unimpared by his strenuous journeyings, set about observing the strange sights afforded by the small town of Ajmer, swollen to several times its normal size by the Emperor's Court.

Jahangir, the sole surviving son of Akbar, was forty-six years old,[1] and in the eleventh year of his reign. His mother was a Hindu Rajput Princess; on his father's side he had Turkish, Mongol, and Persian blood in his veins, and was eighth in descent from Tamerlaine; through his great-great-grandmother, the mother of Babur, he was descended from Genghis Khan. The Empire over which Jahangir ruled was still ten years short of its centenary. Babur, its founder, had been King of the little state of Farghana, five hundred miles north of Kabul. He captured Kabul, descended into India, and in 1525 at the battle of Panipat defeated the Afghan dynasty which had ruled at Delhi during the preceding three-quarters of a century. Babur's son, Humayun, was driven from his throne by the Afghan ruler of Bengal and Bihar, but recovered his kingdom in 1555 only to die the following year, leaving his son, Akbar, then sixteen, in precarious control of a territory which is today represented by parts of the Punjab and the United Provinces of Agra and Oudh. Akbar's aim was to rule from sea to sea, and at his death in 1605 he had largely achieved that ambition. The Empire which Jahangir inherited covered the

[1] Coryate says he was fifty-three, an error possibly attributable to the difficulty of translating lunar into Roman years.

whole of Northern India. On its southern frontiers lay the Mohammedan kingdoms of Ahmadnagar in the west and Golconda in the east, while the rest of the peninsula, except for the Mohammedan kingdom of Bijapur, was still ruled by petty Hindu princes.

Coryate describes Jahangir's personal appearance in one of the best existing word pictures of him (and, incidentally, by using himself as a comparison, Coryate gives us a clue to his own physique): 'Hee is of complexion neither white nor blacke but of a middle betwixt them; I know not how to expresse it with a more expressive and significant epitheton then olive; an olive colour his face presenteth. Hee is of a seemelie composition of bodie, of a stature little unequall (as I guesse, not without grounds of probabilitie) to mine, but much more corpulent than my selfe.'[1]

Jahangir scarcely merited his name, which means 'World-Grasper' or 'Conqueror of the World'. He inherited none of his father's military skill nor his administrative ability, but shared Akbar's love of hunting and other sports, his personal concern for the dispensing of justice, and his considerate bearing towards strangers. He had a weakness for strong liquor which he fought against more successfully than his two younger brothers who both died of *delirium tremens* at an early age. His weak-mindedness was particularly apparent in his complete submission to the will of his wife Nur Mahal, and of his favourite son Sultan Khurram, who afterwards succeeded him as Shah Jahan.

The Moguls were not remarkable for family unity. Jahangir rebelled against Akbar, was defeated and pardoned. History repeated itself when Jahangir's eldest son Khusrau rebelled against his father. Coryate tells how Khusrau's forces were defeated at the battle of Lahore, and Khusrau was taken by Jahangir along the road leading into the city to see two thousand of his principal supporters impaled on stakes or hanging from flesh hooks. Jahangir asked his son how he liked the spectacle. Khusrau replied that he was sorry to see so much cruelty and injustice on the part of his father in executing those who had done nothing but their duty; it was he himself, the author of the rebellion, who should have been punished.

Khusrau was not executed but ever afterwards Jahangir kept

[1] Letter No. 2.

him under close surveillance. Coryate relates that the Emperor, about to depart on a four months' hunting expedition, resolved 'to build a towre and immure him within it, without gate, doore or window except some small holes to let in ayre, higher then he could come unto; putting in all sorts of provision whatsoever, both fire, clothes etc., with some servants to abide with him for that time'. Khusrau had but one wife, to whom he was devoted. She was equally devoted to him, and while these preparations were going forward she came and threw herself at the Emperor's feet and begged leave to be shut up with her husband. 'The king much perswading to enjoy her libertie, she utterly refused any other comfort then to be the companion of her husbands miseries amongst which this was the greatest, that if any of these that were immured (being in number fiftie) should have dyed in the kings absence, there was no means to burie them, for that no man was admitted to come near the towre.'

Khusrau did not inherit his monogamous mode of life from Jahangir, who in Coryate's words 'keepeth a thousand women for his own body'. Coryate describes how the stock of concubines was renewed at an annual spring fair when all the tradesmen's wives, accompanied by their prettiest daughters, entered the Palace with merchandize for sale to the Emperor's women. 'Observe that whatsoever is brought in of virill shape, as instance in reddishes, so great is the jealousie and so frequent the wickednesse of this people, that they are cut and jagged for feare of converting the same to some unnaturall abuse.' While the women chose trinkets and delicacies the Emperor looked over the tradesman's daughters: 'by this meanes he attaines to the sight of all the prettie wenches of the towne. At such a kinde of faire he got his beloved Nor-mahal.'[1]

Another important event which took place in Ajmer shortly after Coryate's arrival was the Emperor's birthday when he was ceremonially weighed, and though Coryate did not manage to see the ceremony itself, he tells Laurence Whitaker that he saw the golden scales in one side of which the Emperor sat while the other was loaded with gold which was afterwards distributed to the poor. We know that in 1616 the Emperor weighed 12 stone

[1] This statement is confirmed by contemporary chronicles, see Beni Prasad, *History of Jahangir*, Allahabad, 1930, p. 176. The fairs are described by Peter Mundy, *Travels*, vol. II, p. 238.

5 lb.[1]—in terms of gold a mere grain in the harvest which Jahangir garnered from his subjects. Coryate puts his annual revenue at £12 millions, which is a substantial under-estimate; William Hawkins, writing a few years earlier, put it at £56¼ millions, which has been accepted as accurate by modern research.[2] Either figure would appear astronomical to an Englishman whose country's annual revenue at that time was well under half a million pounds.

Jahangir's expenditure was in proportion to his income. Coryate estimates that it cost not less than £10,000 per day simply to feed the 30,000 Imperial elephants and lions and other beasts. This is perhaps an over-estimate. Hawkins put his total daily household expenses at about this figure.[3]

One of Coryate's ambitions was to ride upon an elephant, and when he wrote to his old friend Laurence Whitaker at Michaelmas 1615 he was able to announce with pride that he had done so, and that it was his intention 'to have my picture expressed in my next booke sitting upon an elephant'. When this and other letters were printed in London the following year the publishers realized his wish by inserting an illustration on the title page, and for good measure repeated it twice more in the pamphlet. The picture of the elephant is rather more accurate than the portrayal of Coryate who is shown in English costume whereas he always dressed in native style.

Elephants were symbols of power and wealth in the Mogul Empire, and not only symbols since they were used in war, for sport, and as royal presents. The traditional Mogul battle tactics were to manoeuvre and strike with cavalry; the supporting infantry forces were drawn up in rear of the cavalry and the elephants in rear of the infantry. Here they could strike awe into the enemy, but might, with luck, never be engaged. Everyone knew that if hurt they tended to do more damage to friend than foe.

Coryate himself witnessed and described their role in sport:

---

[1] Foster, *Embassy*, p. 412, n. The weighing ceremony was an old Hindu custom adopted by Akbar. The Emperor was weighed twice each year, once on his solar birthday against twelve articles including gold, quicksilver, silk, perfumes, grain, and salt, once on his lunar birthday against eight commodities ranging from silver and tin to cloth and vegetables. For description of the ceremony see Jahangir's Memoirs, *Tuzuk-i-Jahangiri*, trans. Alexander Rogers, ed. Henry Beveridge, London, 1909, pp. 77 and 333. Roe and Terry also describe it.

[2] Foster, *Early Travels in India*, p. 99.          [3] *Ibid*, p. 104.

'Twice every week elephants fight before him [the Emperor], the bravest spectacle in the worlde. Many of them are thirteene foot and a halfe high; and they seeme to justle together like two little mountaines, and were they not parted in the middest of their fighting by certaine fire-workes, they would exceedingly gore and cruentate one another by their murdering teeth.'

He also had the opportunity to observe the use made of elephants as regal gifts when, about the middle of August 1615, an embassy arrived in Ajmer from the King of Bijapur. 'Since my arrivall heere, there was sente unto this King one of the richest presents that I have heard to be sent to any prince in al my life time. It consisteth of divers parcels; one beeing elephants, whereof there were 31, and of those two so gloriously adorned as I never saw the like, nor shal see the like again while I live. For they wore foure chaines about their bodies all of beaten gold; two chains about their legges of the same; furniture for their buttocks of pure gold; two lyons upon their heads of the like gold; the ornaments of each amounting to the value of almost eight thousand pound sterling; and the whole present was worth a hundred thousand pounds sterling.'

Another embassy, bearing presents of considerably less value, was at this time sailing towards the Indian coast. The little fleet bringing Sir Thomas Roe from England arrived off Surat on 18 September 1615. Rogers, the East India Company's chaplain at Ajmer, was to sail for home with this fleet, and to him Coryate entrusted a number of letters. That addressed to the High Seneschal of the Mermaid Club had as its particular object the commending of Rogers to the members' hospitality. 'Mr Rogers who in divers loving offices hath bene so kind unto me that I intreat your generosities to entertain him friendly for my sake.' Coryate added a postcript to his long letter to Laurence Whitaker:

'There happened betwixt the day of the writing of this letter and the day of the sealing of it up, a memorable occurent not to bee omitted. We received newes at this court . . . [on] . . . the eight of October, of the arrivall of foure goodly English ships at the haven of Surat in India, and in the same of a very generous and worthy English knight, a deare friend of mine, Sir Thomas Rowe, to come to the court with some mature expedition, as an ambassadour from the Right Worshipfull Company of London Merchants that Trade for India. He cometh with letters from our King and certaine selected presents of good worth from the Company; amongst the rest a gallant caroch [coach], of 150 pounds price. Also there came with him 15 servants, al Englishmen. Forty daies hence at the farthest, we expect (θεοῦ διδόντος) [God granting it] his arrival at this court. This newes doth refocillate[1] (I will use my old phrase so well knowne to you) my spirits; for I hope he will use me graciously, for old acquaintance sake.'

His previous acquaintance with Roe was a happy stroke of luck. Roe was a year or two younger than Coryate. Soon after leaving Oxford he had been appointed an Esquire of the Body to Queen Elizabeth. After the Queen's death he continued at Court, and in 1605 was knighted by James I. The young courtier formed close friendships with Prince Henry and his sister; the former had been Roe's patron in a voyage of discovery to Guiana which he undertook in 1610; the latter, when she became Electress Palatine and titular Queen of Bohemia, kept up a long and intimate correspondence with 'Honest Tom', as she called him.[2]

It therefore seems probable that Roe and Coryate had met at Court, and one may guess that the difference in their social positions was bridged by their mutual friendships with John Donne and Ben Jonson. As early as 1603 Donne was addressing Roe as 'Dear Tom', and their intimacy lasted until death.[3] Ben Jonson was a close friend of Roe and his two brothers, Sir John and William. In Jonson's *Epigrams* there are seven poems addressed to them; three to the eldest, Sir John, who died of the plague in Jonson's arms; two to Sir Thomas and two to William. Sir Thomas is almost certainly the author of eulogistic verses on Jonson's *Sejanus* and *Volpone*. Those on the latter, signed 'T.R.' and addressed 'To my friend Mr. Jonson' pleasantly convey Roe's dignified modesty:

> Jonson, to tell the world what I to thee
> Am, tis *Friend*. Not to praise, nor usher forth
> Thee or thy worke, as if it needed mee
> Send I these ri'mes to adde ought to thy worth: . . .[4]

[1] See pp. 34, 117 above.
[2] See *The Letters of Elizabeth, Queen of Bohemia*, ed. L. M. Baker, London, 1953.
[3] Sir Edmund Gosse, *Life & Letters of John Donne*, vol. I, p. 121.
[4] These verses are quoted in Ben Jonson, *Works*, ed. Herford and Simpson, vol. XI, p. 319. The Epigrams addressed to Sir Thomas Roe are Nos. XCVIII and XCIX.

Roe was a man to inspire admiration as well as affection. Recurring ill-health failed to sap his iron resolution; for himself he sought nothing but the honour of carrying out his duties to the utmost of his ability. The fact that the East India Company were compelled to follow the precedent set in the Levant Company, whereby the ambassador was officially appointed and paid by the Company, was just as much a handicap in India as it was in Turkey. But Roe's bearing and behaviour did much to overcome the stigma of being connected with commerce. He was a skilful diplomat, courageous and utterly regardless of consequences where the honour of his King and nation were concerned. His Indian diary and correspondence reveal a character epitomizing all that was best in the long line of those who built up the British dominion in India.

Roe did not leave Surat for Ajmer until the end of October. The English had constant difficulties in landing their merchandise. Not only goods for sale, but the very presents for the Emperor and his court were held, sampled, and even appropriated outright by the rapacious local officials. Roe's experiences were no happier than those of his predecessors, and eventually he had to leave without most of the presents. Once on the way, though ill and weak, he soon demonstrated his mettle. Ten days' arduous travelling brought him and his suite to Chopra. 'Here, having pitched my tents without the Towne according to my Custome, the kings officers came and tould me that there were 200 theeves in the hills and I could not lye without great danger, perswading me to pitch within the Towne. I answered I was not afrayd: if they Came I would leave some of them on the ground for them in the Morning, and that now I would not stirr. They replyed they could not answere it to the Mogull if any thing happened unto me; but if I would stay without, they desired a dischardge in writting that they had warned mee. I tould them I was resolved not to moove, but if the dainger were soe important I required a better guard to watch with mee; which was granted, and the Governor with the other officers came out with 30 horse and 20 shott and watched all Night. In the Morning they brought me to their precinctes, to whom I gave a small present and reward to the Souldiers.'[1]

Meanwhile preparations were being made by the English merchants at Ajmer to receive their Ambassador. Coryate, on the

[1] Foster, *Embassy*, vol. I, p. 88.

strength of his acquaintance with Roe, was permitted to accompany the deputation which went out to meet him a stage from Ajmer. Roe recorded in his diary for 22 December 1615: 'At noone Master Edwardes the Agent met me accompanied with the famous unwearied Tho. Coryatt (who on foote had passed most of Europe and Asya and was Now arrived in India, beeing but the beginning of his purposed travells) and some other Christians residents in Adsmere. I lodged in the feilds, Master Edwardes having sett up his tents and provided for me.' Coryate could not let such an occasion pass without making an oration, and sure enough Peyton in his Journal[1] records that Coryate welcomed Roe with one which was both eloquent and long.

Coryate's knowledge that Roe had been appointed by the East India Company is evidence that no concealment was practised concerning the main purpose of his mission. But the Portuguese and their agents were quick to take advantage of the Emperor's contempt for trade, and made the most of the fact that Roe was acting on behalf of a handful of English merchants. Admittedly he came with letters and presents from King James himself, but the English monarch was of little account to the Great Mogul, to whom only the Shah of Persia and the Grand Turk could even pretend to equality with himself. In Jahangir's Memoirs[2] the Persian embassies are fully reported, but Roe is never once mentioned.

The matter of presents was extremely important and as yet not completely understood by the Company at home. What was very rare and valuable in England, such as Chinese porcelain, was often commonplace in India. The presents had to be worthy of the station of the Great Mogul, but novelty was quite as important as intrinsic worth. The Company were on the right tack when they shipped out some English mastiffs. During the voyage one gave a premature demonstration of its impetuous courage by jumping overboard after some porpoises, but two arrived safely. On the way to the court one broke loose, and immediately fell upon a full-grown elephant, fastening upon its trunk and hanging on while the trumpeting beast whisked it to and fro in the air. Eventually it was flung clear and survived unharmed. This story pleased Jahangir very much when the dogs were presented to him; he allowed each four attendants, two to carry them in palanquins and

[1] Brit. Mus. Addl. Ms. 19276.
[2] *Tuzuk-i-Jahangiri*, trans. Alexander Rogers, ed. Henry Beveridge, London, 1909.

two to fan the flies off them. He even had a pair of silver tongs made so that when he pleased he might feed the dogs with his own hand.[1]

Robert Coverte, the shipwrecked seaman already referred to, scored a complete success when he gave Jahangir a little golden whistle set with sparks of rubies. The Emperor was delighted with it and whistled away for nearly an hour.[2] The 1612 fleet brought as the East India Company's chief presents two musicians and their instruments—the virginals and the cornet. The virginals made no impression, 'whereupon the unfortunate player dyed with conceiptt', but the cornet created an immense sensation. Jahangir himself attempted to blow it and immediately ordered his work-men to make six more, which turned out to be failures. One of the Emperor's chief musicians was put under the instruction of the English cornet player and managed to perform tolerably well after five weeks, but his exertions brought on a fatal illness. So the Englishman was left the only cornet player in the Mogul Empire, though a very discontented one, for Jahangir, while often making him play, rewarded him with a mere fifty rupees.[3]

The coachman who brought out the coach referred to by Coryate fared better, being granted a pension of $1\frac{1}{2}$ rupees a day,[4] but did not long survive to enjoy it. The coach itself was only a limited success. The design pleased the Emperor well enough, but the finish and decoration fell far short of his standards. The coach was taken to pieces completely and two copies were made. The crimson Chinese velvet upholstery of the original coach was ripped out, and all three were furnished with cloth of gold.

The Emperor did not have the same high standards in the matter of housing, at any rate where his courtiers were concerned. Roe, writing to Lord Carew, described Ajmer as 'a base old Citie, wherein is no house but of mudde, not so great as a Cottage on Hownslo-heath; only himselfe [the Emperor] hath one of stone. His lords live in Tents . . .'[5] Roe himself had taken up residence in the East India Company's house in which Coryate was already living—a sorry affair of bamboo, mud and straw, to which Roe added a dozen rooms of the same material to accommodate the new influx.

[1] Terry, *op. cit.*, 1777 edn., pp. 140–1.       [2] Robert Coverte, *op. cit.*, p. 58.
[3] Foster, *Early Travels in India*, pp. 189–90.   [4] Foster, *Embassy*, vol. II, p. 323, n.
[5] Roe to Lord Carew, 17 January 1616, quoted in *Embassy*, vol. I, p. 113.

The ill-health which had overtaken Roe on his journey from the coast still persisted. 'Since my arrival in this Country', he wrote to the Earl of Southampton, 'I have had but one Month of health and that mingled with many relapses, and am now your poor servant scarce a Crowes dinner.' In another letter[1] he mentions the welcome distraction from his troubles provided by conversations with his guest 'whom the fates have sent hither to ease mee, and now lives in my house. He came heither afoote: hath past by Constantinople, Jerusalem, Bethlem, Damascus, and (breefely) thorowgh all the Turkes territory: seene every Post and Pillar: observed every Tombe ... His notes are already to great for Portage: some left at Aleppo, some at Hispan—enough to make any stationer an alderman that shall but serve the Printer with Paper. And his exercise here or recreation is making or repeating orations, Principally of my Lady Hartford.'

The inference is inescapable that Coryate was composing and declaiming these orations as other love-lorn admirers might recite sonnets or sing lyrics to the object of their affections. Roe's letter is the only evidence that Coryate had a passion for this or any other lady, but we do know that Lady Hertford was a famous and haughty beauty capable of inspiring desperate emotions. She was Frances, daughter of the first Viscount Howard of Bindon. Her first husband, a wealthy London wine-merchant, died when she was still in her twenties, and eighteen months later, in 1601, she had married the ageing Earl of Hertford, whereupon Sir George Rodney, a rival for her hand, wrote her a farewell love song with his blood and ran upon his sword. In 1602, and again in 1608, Hertford had been Lord Lieutenant of Somerset and Wiltshire, which suggests that Coryate might have met or at least seen her while he was at home. Whatever Coryate's feelings for her may have been, it is unlikely that she could have regarded him with anything other than distant amusement. She was very conscious of her noble ancestry—though Hertford used to temper her arrogance by tapping her cheek and saying 'Frank! Frank! how long is it since you married the vintner?'[2]

There was another oration on which Coryate was working—an oration to the Great Mogul himself. For this purpose he had to learn Persian, and simultaneously he was carrying on his studies

[1] Roe to Lord Pembroke, 14 February 1615–16, quoted in *Embassy*, vol. I, p. 104, n.
[2] *The Complete Peerage*, London, 1926, vol. VI, p. 506.

44. Frances, Countess of Hertford. From the engraving by Francis Delaram. (Ashmolean Museum.)

43. Coryate riding on an elephant. Title page of the pamphlet, published in 1616, composed of four of Coryate's letters from India.

45. The Emperor Jahangir weighing his son Prince Khurram (afterwards Shah Jehan) against gold. Mogul School: about 1615. From a painting in the British Museum.

of Turkish and Arabic. With these three languages he could pass through all the territories lying between the Mogul Empire and Christendom. 'At this time I have many irons in the fire; for I learne the Persian, Turkish and Arabian tongues, having already gotten the Italian (I thank God). I have been at the Mogul's court three moneths already, and am to tarry heere (by Gods holy permission) five moneths longer, till I have gotten the foresaide three tongues, and then depart herehence to the Ganges, and after that directly to the Persian court.'[1]

That had been his plan at Michaelmas 1615, but such a programme turned out to be too much even for his industry and scholarship. He eventually spent fourteen months at Ajmer, 'which though I confesse it were a too long time to remaine in one and the selfe same place, yet for two principall causes it was very requisite for me to remaine there some reasonable time: first to learne the languages of those countries through which I am to passe betwixt the bounds of the territories of this prince and Christendome, matters as availeable to me as mony in my purse, as being the cheifest or rather onely meane to get the mony if I should happen to be destitute, a matter very incidentall to a poore footman pilgrim as my selfe, in these heathen and Mahometan countries through which I travell; secondly, that by the helpe of one of those languages (I meane the Persian) I might both procure unto my selfe access unto the King, and be able to expresse my minde unto him'.[2]

Although Coryate himself does not mention the fact, we know from Terry that he was picking up Hindustani, the language of the common people: 'he having got a great mastery likewise in the Indostan or more vulgar language, there was a woman, a laundress belonging to my Lord Embassadors house, who had such a freedome and liberty of speech that she would sometimes scould, brawl and rail from the sunrising to sun-set. One day he undertook her in her own language, and by eight of the clock in the morning so silenced her that she had not one word more to speak'.[3]

No doubt the laundress came to some back yard to do her daily work since the Ambassador banned all women from the house. This rule had to be relaxed one night in May when the Emperor's officers came to the house at midnight with a woman slave, who

---

[1] Letter No. 2.    [2] Letter No. 6.    [3] Terry, *op. cit.*, 1777 edn., p. 67.

had been dismissed for some offence from the Queen's service, and whom the Emperor had decided to give to the Ambassador as a mark of favour. The officers were informed that the Ambassador was abed but insisted on presenting the woman to him in his bedroom. The embarrassed Roe lodged her for the night in his dining-room, and the next day quartered her in the house of one of his married Indian servants until he could tactfully obtain the Emperor's permission to dispose of his unwanted gift.[1]

Roe imposed the highest standards of propriety on his household and himself set an example of sober yet stately living. He insisted on furnishing his dining-room with table and chairs in the British fashion, and on eating off plate. The food was both plentiful and good. Coryate, who had had to put up with the roughest and cheapest fare during his long journey, could now fortify himself with excellent wheaten bread, butter, and cheese; buffaloes provided both meat and milk. There was mutton and poultry—a whole sheep cost only a shilling, and eight hens could be bought for the same price. Partridges were three a penny and hares a penny each. There were geese, ducks, pigeons, quails and peacocks, venison, and fish in great variety. The Ambassador's household revelled in melons, pomegranates, lemons, oranges, dates, figs, grapes, bananas, mangoes, and even pineapples introduced into India from America by the Portuguese, and tasting, as Terry put it, like 'strawberries, claret-wine, rose water and sugar well tempered together'.

That nobody seems to have been aware of the disease-carrying properties of some fruits and that the usual drink was water, must account for much of the illness, particularly dysentery, which carried off so many. The Ambassador's chaplain and his English cook both died in the summer of 1616. Life was never either secure or uneventful. The flimsy walls of the house kept out neither wind, nor dust, nor rain. The houses all around were built of the same combustible materials, and every night there was a fire somewhere in the town which quickly spread with the breeze, and was fed by the piles of grass, hay, corn, and wood which people kept at their doors. Since the Ambassador's house served also as the East India Company's factory, its destruction would have been disastrous. There had already been three serious alarms when fire had spread to 'within a quoyts Cast' of the house. Then on 9 May

[1] Foster, *Embassy*, vol. I, pp. 174–6.

the whole household was brought out of bed by yet another conflagration which was soon raging on three sides of them. In one house nearby fourteen women and some men perished. The Ambassador, Coryate, and the merchants, stood at the door fearing for their lives no less than for their belongings—Coryate must have been particularly concerned about his sheaves of notes. At the last moment the wind changed and they were saved. Roe and the merchants decided that such risks to life and property were intolerable. In one day Roe had the wholy flimsy structure pulled down and in a further ten days it had been replaced by a house of brick and loam with seven good rooms.

But three months later the new house was nearly overwhelmed by a fresh peril. It was built on the edge of a watercourse, which after even normal rain became a torrent impassable by man or beast. On the night of 19 August there was exceptionally heavy rain, which continued on the 20th. Suddenly an alarm was given that the water had broken through the stone dam of a reservoir and was likely to sweep away that whole quarter of the town. Prince Khurram forsook his house with all his women; then the Ambassador's nearest neighbour and his family moved off with his elephants and camels to seek safety in the hills. Night came; the Ambassador characteristically decided to stand firm and guard the merchandise as long as possible, but horses were kept saddled and waiting at the door, while the assembled household stayed up watching and listening to the waters lapping round the walls of the house. At last word came that the Emperor had ordered a sluice to be cut, which effectively diverted the floods. In the morning it was discovered that the water had so breached and undermined the walls of the house that there was danger of its collapsing. 'All was soe moyled with dust and water that I could scarce lye drye or safe, soe that I must be at new chardge in reparations,' remarked Roe ruefully. 'Thus were wee every way afflicted —fires, smokes, floodes, stormes, heate, dust, flyes, and no temperate or quiett seasons.'[1]

One day in the middle of July some of the Emperor's men came to an open space near the Ambassador's house and dug a deep narrow pit. Soon guards arrived bringing a young gentlewoman from Queen Nur Mahal's household. She was lowered into the pit up to her armpits, and her feet bound fast to a stake at the

[1] Foster, *Embassy*, vol. I, pp. 246–8.

bottom. Then the earth was replaced and rammed hard, leaving her bare head and arms exposed to the violence of the sun. She had been caught kissing a eunuch in the Emperor's house. The eunuch had been condemned to the elephants—a common form of execution which could be either a speedy trampling to death or else, at the direction of the elephant's keeper, a slow torture in which the elephant broke the malefactor's joints one by one as men were broken on the wheel. But the girl was to be pardoned if she survived three days and two nights in the pit without food or drink. For hours on end the Ambassador's household had to listen to her piteous moans as she cried over and over again, 'Ah my head! my head!' until at last after a day and a half she died.[1]

Tuesday in each week was the day of blood, when Jahangir administered justice and afterwards witnessed execution being done. A few weeks after the incident described above the Emperor sentenced to death a band of a hundred thieves. The leader and thirteen of his fellows were led in chains to the street by the Ambassador's house. Here the leader of the band was torn to pieces by twelve ravening dogs. Then his accomplices had their hands bound to their feet and their necks cut with a sword 'but not quite off, and so left naked, bloody and stincking to every mans vew and incomodytie'.[2] The remainder of the band were similarly executed in other quarters of the town.

There is no doubt that Jahangir was cruel—his own memoirs prove that—but he was also capable of a benevolence and toleration which in Coryate's view put Christian (or at any rate Roman Catholic) ideals of charity to shame. He was particularly impressed by the observance of a ceremony which took place in Ajmer at the shrine of Kwāja Muinuddin Chishti. The Emperor and his women processed on foot to the tomb near which Jahangir and Nur Mahal with their own hands kindled a fire under an 'immense and Heidelbergian aequipollent[3] brasse-pot, and made kitcherie [khichri, whence Kedgeree] for five thousand poore, taking out the first platter with his owne hands and serving one; Normahal the second; and so his ladies all the rest. Cracke me this nut, all ye Papall charitie vaunters.' This ceremony is still observed during the Urs Mela festival at Ajmer, when a gigantic mixture of

---

[1] *Ibid.*, p. 215, and Terry, *op. cit.*, 1655 edn., p. 407.
[2] Foster, *Embassy*, vol. I, pp. 227–8.
[3] Equal in capacity to the Great Tun of Heidelberg, see p. 82 above.

rice and spices is cooked in a cauldron at the expense of some rich devotee and distributed to the poor.

It was to this shrine that Akbar had walked on pilgrimage from Agra to give thanks for Jahangir's birth. The influence of this titanic figure was still very much alive and his aura shone with pervasive brightness. One of Coryate's rough notes records that Akbar was gifted with magical powers which enabled him to cut off his favourite wife's head and make her whole again, but this should not be taken as proof that Coryate believed the tale. Another note relates Akbar's devotion to his mother; he 'never denyed her any thing but this, that shee demanded of him, that our Bible might be hanged about an asses necke and beaten about the town of Agra, for that the Portugals, having taken . . . the Alcoran . . . tyed it about the necke of a dogge and beat the same dogge about the towne of Ormuz. But hee denyed her request, saying that, if it were ill in the Portugals to doe so to the Alcoran, being it became not a King to requite ill with ill, for that the contempt of any religion was the contempt of God, and he would not be revenged upon an innocent booke.'

Akbar had enforced religious toleration as a deliberate act of policy, realizing that diversity of religious beliefs was the chief obstacle to his ambition of creating a politically united India. But he had moral as well as political motives. At heart Akbar was a mystic and, in his search for eternal truth, he explored all the faiths known to him and found good in all.

He built a House of Worship and invited members of the sects of Islam, Sunnis, Shias, and Sufis as well as Hindus, Jains, Parsees, Zoroastrians, Jews, and Christians, to debate their faiths. The Christians were Jesuits whom he summoned from Goa; he allowed them freedom to build churches, to teach and convert, and even handed over one of his younger sons to their instruction. He himself had many long discussions with them, which often lasted half the night, and for a time it seemed that he might be converted. But he found that the Jesuits were quite as intolerant as the Muslims, in whose faith he had been born. While revering the person of Christ and delighting in the Gospels, he could not bring himself to accept either the doctrine of the Trinity or the Virgin Birth. Furthermore he flatly refused to contemplate dispensing with all but one of this three hundred wives.

The solution which he evolved was magnanimous but doomed

to failure. At a General Council in 1582 he promulgated the Divine Faith, an attempt to unify all religions 'in such fashion' as he said 'that they should be both "one" and "all", with the great advantage of not losing what is good in one religion, while gaining whatever is better in another. In that way honour would be rendered to God, peace would be given to the peoples and security to the Empire.'[1]

Jahangir, though brought up in the new faith, did nothing to promote it, either out of indifference or because he realized that the whole conception was a failure, and that the religion designed to unite all pleased none. He did, however, continue his father's policy of toleration; Coryate, discussing the Emperor's attitude to religion, says 'hee himself being of none but of his own making, therefore suffers all religions in his kingdom . . . It is saide that he is uncircumcised, wherein he differeth from all the Mahometan princes that ever were in the world. Hee speaketh very reverently of our Saviour, calling him in the Indian tongue *Isazaret Eesa* [*Hazarat Isa*] that is, the Great Prophet Jesus; and all Christians, especiallie us English, he useth so benevolently as no Mahometan prince the like.'[2]

Though Jahangir continued to enforce toleration throughout his far-flung territories, he had little sympathy with religious turn-coats. Coryate illustrates the point with two stories: 'An Armenian, desirous to turn Moore procured a noble-man to bring him to the king; whom the king asked why hee turned Moore: whether for preferment? Hee answered: No. Some few monethes after, craving some courtesie of the King, he denyed it him, saying that hee had done him the greatest favour that could bee, to let him save his soule: but for his bodie, hee himself should provide as well as he could.'

The second story concerns a Muslim converted to Christianity. One day Jahangir was discussing religious matters with an Armenian, a Christian by birth, and asked if he knew of a single man who had been converted by the Jesuits out of conviction and not for gain—the Jesuits used to give converts the equivalent of 3*d.* a day. The Armenian replied that he had a servant who had been born a Muslim but had genuinely and unshakeably embraced the Christian faith. The Emperor sent for this servant and asked him why he had become a Christian. The servant gave 'certaine

---

[1] Laurence Binyon, *Akbar*, London, 1932, p. 130.　　　　[2] Letter No. 2.

feeble, implicite, Jesuiticall reasons' (Coryate could not resist a dig at the Jesuits). 'Whereupon the king practised by faire speeches and large promises to withdraw him to the folly of Mahomet, offering him pensions, meanes, and command of horse, telling him hee had now but foure rupias a moneth wages, which was a poore reward for quitting his praepuced faith; but if hee would recant, hee would heape upon him many dignities; the fellow answering . . . that hee was a Christian in his heart, and would not alter it. This way not taking effect, the King turned to threatnings and menacings of tortures and whippings; but the proselyte man-fully resolving to suffer any thing, answered hee was readie to endure the kings pleasure. Upon this resolution, when all men expected present and severe castigation, the King changed his tune, highly commending his constancie and honestie, bidding him goe and returne to his master, and to serve him faithfully and truely; giving him a rupia a day pension for his integritie.'

About two months later the Emperor went hunting wild pigs, which he was accustomed to distribute to Rajputs and Christians —Roe received more than one. On his return he sent for the Ar-menian, but as he was not at home the convert, now the Armenian's principal servant, came to know the Emperor's pleasure and was ordered to take a pig back to his master. The servant started to carry the pig home but was so hooted at by Mohammedans on the way that he threw the Emperor's present into a ditch and never told his master what had happened.

A few days later Jahangir asked the Armenian whether the pig had been good eating and the whole story came out, the servant confessing that he had been mocked for touching the pig and in his shame had thrown it away. Then the Emperor cried, 'Now I see thou art neither good Christian nor good Mahumetan, but a dissembling knave with both. While I found thee sincere, I gave thee a pension; which now I take from thee, and for thy dissimu-lation doe command thee to have a hundred stripes . . .' And the Emperor bade all men take heed by this example that while he gave liberty to all religions, he expected men to stick to the one which they chose and professed.

It seems, however, that Jahangir was prepared to ordain that exceptions should be made to liberty of conscience when his own interests were at stake. He had his deceased younger brother's sons converted to Christianity, and the Jesuits rejoiced at what they took to be an indication of Jahangir's own true sympathies. In fact it seems that Jahangir intended, by depriving his nephews of the allegiance of the Muslim population, to nullify a prophecy that his own sons would be disinherited and that the Empire would pass to his nephews. These young converts reverted to Islam as soon as they were able, but the prophecy was not fulfilled.

Jahangir took a special interest in holy men, fakirs, and pilgrims. Coryate relates 'often when hee awakes in the night [he] cals for certaine poore and old men, making them sit by him, with many questions and familiar speeches passing the time; and at their departure cloathes them and gives them bountifull almes often, whatsoever they demand, telling the money into their hands'. It is probable that this note is based on information from Roe, who himself had witnessed just such a scene. One evening when he visited the Emperor he was astounded to see a poor, dirty, ragged old wretch *sitting* at Jahangir's feet—even the Emperor's sons were compelled to stand in his presence. The beggar presented Jahangir with a cake of coarse grain, all burnt and covered with ashes, which to Roe's disgust the Emperor accepted most willingly and ate. Then the Emperor sent for a hundred rupees (about 2*s*. each) and poured them into the beggar's lap, and those which spilt over he picked up for him. When the Emperor's supper arrived he gave the beggar half of all that he himself ate. Finally he rose, took the old man up in his arms, embraced him, 'which no cleanly body durst have done', called him father, and thus departed.

The Emperor's readiness to receive ragged fakirs set the pattern for Coryate's plan to realize his long-cherished ambition of making an oration before him. Coryate felt that he had by this time sufficiently mastered the Persian language to be able not only to address the Emperor but also to understand what Jahangir might say to him. Moreover, it was becoming imperative to replenish his purse since, although he had been living gratis at the expense of the East India Company all these months, his incidental disbursements for language tuition, writing materials, and the like had reduced his funds to a few shillings. Coryate decided that his chances of being heard and receiving a generous bounty were better if he presented himself in his usual native garb as the poor pilgrim he was, than if he appeared in borrowed English plumes. He strongly suspected that the Ambassador would disapprove, so he kept his plan secret except for telling one special, private, and nameless friend.

Jahangir followed a regular routine, showing himself to his people three times each day, once at sunrise, once at midday, and once a little before sunset. At these times anyone with a petition might be heard. So one day Coryate presented himself at the Palace, obtained entry into the courtyard, and joined the crowd who waited and watched the window, shaded by a sumptuous embroidered canopy supported by silver pilasters, at which the Emperor would appear. When the proud, sallow, mustachioed face at length looked down from the window the hundred nobles who stood beneath made their obeisance, sweeping their rich robes in the dust, touching the ground with the back of the right hand, then rising and bringing the palm up to the crown of the head.

How long Coryate had to wait on tenterhooks, rehearsing his words, we do not know, but at last he was called forward beneath the window and having made his obeisance, was ordered to address the Emperor, which he did in these terms: 'Lord Protector of the World, all haile to you. I am a poore traveller and world-seer, which am come hither from a farre country, namely England, which auncient historians thought to have been scituated in the farthest bounds of the West, and which is the queene of all the ilands in the world. The cause of my comming hither is for foure respects. First, to see the blessed face of Your Majesty, whose wonderfull fame hath resounded over all Europe and the Mahometan countries; when I heard of the fame of Your Majesty, I hastened hither with speed, and travelled very cherefully to see your glorious court. Secondly, to see Your Majesties elephants, which kind of beasts I have not seen in any other country. Thirdly, to see your famous river Ganges, which is the captaine of all the river[s] of the world. The fourth is this: to intreat Your Majesty that you would vouchsafe to grant mee your gracious passe that I may travell into the country of Tartaria to the city of Samarcand, to visit the blessed sepulcher of the Lord of the Corners,[1] whose

---

[1] In letter No. 6, to his Mother, Coryate gives his original Persian text and the English translation repeated here. He explains in parentheses that Lord of the Corners 'is a title that is given to Tamberlaine in this country in that Persian language, and whereas they call him the Lord of the Corners, by that they meane that he was lord of the corners of the World, that is, the highest and supreme monarch of the universe'. Foster, *Early Travels in India*, p. 265, n, points out that although *Sāhib Qirān*,

fame, by reason of his warres and victories is published over the whole world: perhaps he is not altogether so famous in his own country of Tartaria as in England . . . These foure causes moved me to come out of my native country thus farre, having travelled a foote through Turky and Persia. So farre have I traced the world into this country that my pilgrimage hath accomplished three thousand miles; wherein I have sustained much labour and toile, the like whereof no mortall man in this world did ever performe, to see the blessed face of Your Majesty since the first day that you were inaugurated in your glorious monarchall throne.'

Jahangir appears to have had no difficulty in understanding Coryate's Persian for on completion of the speech he told him that, as no great amity existed between himself and the Tartar princes, no letters from him would facilitate Coryate's journey to Samarkand. Furthermore that the Tartars would certainly kill any Christian they could lay hands on, and he therefore strongly advised him to give up all thought of such an enterprise. The Emperor then closed the interview by throwing down into a sheet suspended by its corners near to the ground a hundred silver rupees, worth about ten pounds sterling.

Coryate was elated at having achieved his ambition of addressing the Great Mogul, but seems to have been disappointed at the smallness of the present. It will be noted that he received the same amount of money as the old beggar seen by Roe; Terry, recounting the incident, asserts that Jahangir looked upon Coryate as a dervish, votary, or pilgrim 'for so he called him, and such as bear that name in that country seem not much to care for money; and that was the reason ( I conceive) that he gave him not a more plentifull reward'.

News of this exploit soon reached the ears of the Ambassador, who, as Coryate had anticipated, was extremely displeased. Roe pointed out that it was unbecoming for an Englishman to present himself like a beggar craving money before the Emperor and that

the actual words used, are indeed a title largely used by Tamerlaine, Coryate was wrong as to their meaning, which is really 'Lord of the (auspicious) Conjunction', alluding to the grand conjunction of the planets at the time of Tamerlaine's birth. Foster suggests that Coryate confused *qirān* with *karān* ('boundary' or 'limit'). Terry, *op. cit.*, 1777 edn., p. 66, gives what purports to be a summary of this oration, which bears no resemblance to Coryate's text, but which may be what Terry remembered of the speech that Coryate had composed and intended to deliver before the Shah of Persia.

such behaviour would redound to the discredit of the nation. Coryate did not deny that it had been his object to obtain money 'since never had I more need of money in all my life then at that time; for in truth I had but twenty shillings sterling left in my purse', but he would not admit that there was anything ignominious about receiving the Emperor's bounty. Coryate claims to have had the best of the argument; 'I answered our Ambassador,' he says, 'in that stout and resolute manner that he was contented to cease nibling at me.'

# CHAPTER XVI

# Exploring India; The Last Walk

C ORYATE's audience with Jahangir must have taken place about August 1616, by which time he had been in Ajmer for over a year. He was now anxious to resume his wanderings. In any case other circumstances compelled a move. The Emperor had announced his intention of making a progress southwards. It was the Ambassador's duty to accompany the Emperor wherever he might go, but since the march was likely to be an arduous one only Roe's immediate attendants were to be taken, while the East India Company's factory at Ajmer was to be dissolved when the Court departed.

At the beginning of September, before finally leaving Ajmer, Coryate made an expedition to the salt-pans on the Sambhar Lake about forty miles to the north-east. By walking the distance in two days he was able to prove to himself that he had not become soft with relatively luxurious living in Ajmer. However, his main motive in making the journey may not have been either to test his physical fitness or even to study the saltworks. The office of collector of the salt revenues was held by an Armenian Christian, one Mirza Zulkarnain,[1] who had a reputation for noble generosity, 'to whom by means of my Persian tongue I was so welcome that hee entertained me with very civill and courteous complement, and at my departure gave mee very bountifully twenty peeces of such kind of mony as the king had done before, countervailing 40 shillings sterling'.

On his return to Ajmer he found everything at sixes and sevens as preparations went forward for the removal of the Court. Two of the English merchants were about to leave for Agra and Coryate took the opportunity of accompanying them. They

[1] See Father Hosten's article on him in *Memoirs of the Asiatic Society of Bengal*, vol. V, No. 4, p. 122. Hosten proves that it was one of Zulkarnain's father's servants about whom Coryate told the story of the pig (see pp. 246–7 above).

left Ajmer on 12 September 1616, and arrived in Agra ten days later.

Shortly after his arrival a terrible plague broke out in the city, which raged for three months, and at its height carried off a thousand people a day. At the end of October he wrote at some length to his mother—the last of his extant letters. It was perhaps natural that he should not mention the plague, but he showed his total lack of concern, which was certainly not shared by the English merchants with whom he was living, by telling her that he intended to stay on in Agra for about six weeks longer in order to take advantage of an excellent opportunity which would then offer to travel to the Ganges for the annual Hindu bathing festival. 'After I have seen this shew, I wil with all expedition repaire to the city of Lahore, twenty daies journey from this, and so into Persia, by the helpe of my blessed Christ . . . I have not had the opportunity to see the King of Persia as yet . . . but I have resolved to goe to him when I come next into his territories, and to search him out wheresoever I can find him in his kingdome; for, seeing I can discourse with him in his Persian tongue, I doubt not but that, going unto him in the forme of a pilgrime, he will not onely entertaine me with good words, but also bestow some worthy reward upon me, beseeming his dignity and person; for which cause I am provided before hand with an excellent thing, written in the Persian tongue, that I meane to present unto him. And thus I hope to get benevolences of worthy persons to maintaine me in a competent maner in my whole pilgrimage till I come into England; which I hold to be as laudable and a more secure course then if I did continually carry store of mony about mee . . .

'Our Ambassador gave mee a peece of gold of this Kings coine worth foure and twenty shillings, which I will save (if it be possible) till my arrivall in England. So that I have received for benevolences since I came into this country twenty markes sterling saving two shillings eight pence[1]; and by the way upon the confines of Persia a little before I came into this country three and thirty shillings foure pence in Persian mony of my Lady Sherly.[2] At this present I have in the city of Agra, where hence I wrote this

[1] The mark was worth 13s. 4d; Coryate's total income in India had thus been £13. 4s., made up of £10 from the Emperor, £2 from Mirza Zulkarnain, and a gold mohur given him by the generous Roe on the eve of his departure from Ajmer, which Coryate values at 24s.

[2] Coryate previously estimated the gift at 40s. (see p. 222).

letter, about twelve pounds sterling, which, according to my maner of living uppon the way at two-pence sterling a day (for with that proportion I can live pretty well, such is the cheapnes of all eatable things in Asia, drinkable things costing nothing, for seldome doe I drinke in my pilgrimage any other liquor then pure water), will mainetaine mee very competently three yeeres in my travell with meate, drinke and clothes. Of these gratuities which have been given me, willingly would I send you some part as a demonstration of the filiall love and affection which every child bred in civility and humility ought to performe to his loving and good mother; but the distance of space betwixt this place and England, the hazard of mens lives in so long a journey, and also the infidelity of many men, who though they live to come home, are unwilling to render an account of the things they have received, doe not a little discourage me to send any precious token unto you; but if I live to come one day to Constantinople againe (for thither doe I resolve to goe once more, by the grace of Christ, and therehence to take my passage by land into Christendome over renouned Greece), I will make choice of some substantial and faithfull countriman, by whom I will send some pretty token as an expression of my dutiful and obedient respect unto you . . .

'But what the countryes are that I meane to see betwixt this and Christendome, and how long time I will spend in each country, I am unwilling to advertise you of at this present, desiring rather to signify that unto you after I have performed my designe then before. Howbeit, in few words I will tell you of certaine cities of great renown in former times, but now partly ruined, that I resolve (by God's help) to see in Asia, where I now am, namely, ancient Babilon and Nymrod's Tower, some few miles from Ninive, and . . . Caire in Egypt, heretofore Memphis, upon the famous river Nilus . . . But in none of these or any other cities of note do I determin to linger as I have done in other places, as in Constantinople, and Azmere in this Easterne India; onely some few daies will I tarry in a principall city of fame, to observe every principal matter there, and so be gone . . .

'I pray you, mother, expect no more letters from me after this till my arrivall in Christendom; because I have resolved to write no more while I am in the Mahometans countries, thinking that it will be a farre greater comfort, both to you and to all my friends whatsoever, to heare newes that I have accomplished my travelles in Mahometisme, then that I am comming up and down, to and fro in the same, without any certainty of an issue thereof. Therefore, I pray, have patience for a time. About two years and a halfe hence I hope to finish these Mahometan travelles, and then either from the citie of Raguzi [Ragusa] in Sclavonia, which is a Christian citie and the first we enter into Christendome from those parts of Turky by land nere unto the same, or from famous Venice, I will very dutifully remember you againe with lines full of filiall piety and officious respect.'

The letter ends with a long list of friends to whom he wished to be remembered; not, seeing that he was writing to his mother, the wits and celebrities in London, but the neighbours and good humble folk of Odcombe and Yeovil. 'I pray you remember my duty to Master Hancoke, that reverend and apostolicall good old man, and his wife, if they are yet living; to their sonnes Thomas and John, and their wives . . . the poore Widow Darby, old Master Dyer, and his sonne John, Master Ewins, old and young with their wives . . . I had almost forgotten your husband: to him also, to Ned Barber and his wife, to William Jenings . . .' Most of them cannot now be identified, but included on the list are Master Gollop, who had succeeded Coryate's father as rector of Odcombe; the Rev. John Seward of Yeovil, to whom Laurence Whitaker addressed a letter in praise of the *Crudities* printed in the introduction to the book; 'all the Knights', by which he may have meant Sir Edward and Sir Robert Phelips, and Master Starre of Yeovil, probably none other than the 'vilipendious linendraper', his 'craftie adversarie' of the lawsuit now transformed by justice, Christian charity, or simply the passage of time into one of 'my good friends'.

'And so finally I commit you and all them to the blessed protection of Almighty God.
Your dutifull, loving, and obedient sonne, now a
desolate pilgrim in the world.
Thomas Coriat.[1]

This letter gives a clear idea of Coryate's future plans; first he would fulfil his ambition of visiting the Ganges, then immediately return to Lahore, and thence make his way back through Persia.

[1] This is the spelling used in the printed version of the letter. In the only extant original autograph (see Pl. 20) the spelling is Coryate.

We know from Terry[1] that he visited Hardwar to see the bathing festival held on the first day of the Hindu sidereal year, which in 1617 would fall about the end of March. Terry also tells us that he visited the great fortress of Kangra or Nagarkot in the north-east of the Punjab, and the famous temple of Mata Devi at Bhawan, a suburb of Kangra. Coryate described the shrine to Terry as 'a chappel most richly set forth both seeled and paved with plate of pure silver most curiously imbossed over head in several figures, which they keep exceeding bright by often rubbing and burnishing it. In this place they keepe an idoll, which they call Matta, visited yeerly by many thousands of the Indians, who out of devotion cut off part of their tongues to make a sacrifice to it, which (they say) grow out againe as before; but in this', adds Terry, 'I shall leave my Reader to a belief as much suspensive as is my own in this particular.'[2]

Either Coryate himself or one of his friends sent home a description of what he saw, which probably became embellished by repetition. This account came to the King himself and the Archbishop of Canterbury, George Abbot. In February 1619 the Archbishop wrote to Roe[3]: 'I heard the kinge our master much blame his [Coryate's] judgment for some thinge, which as it seemeth was written hither out of his Memoires. And that was that in one place I cannot tell where, hee should say that hee saw men have their eies pulled out and their tongues cutt of and other thinges of like nature, and yet before an idole they should speedily be restored againe. His Majesty saith that this cannot be done by the power of Sathan, and hee is sure it is not by the finger of God. It was then in Thomas *deceptio visus*.'

However, an anecdote collected by Coryate which had likewise come to the Archbishop's ears created a more favourable impression: 'A great Raja, a Gentile, a notorious atheist and contemner of all deitie (glorying to professe he knew no other God then the King, nor beleeving nor fearing none), sitting dallying with his women, one of them plucked a haire from his brest; which being fast rooted, plucked off a little of the skinne, that bloud appeared.

---

[1] Terry, *op. cit.*, 1655 edn., p. 88. Although Terry was in India from September 1616 until February 1619, he himself saw only parts of Malwa and Gujarat; many details in his book were obtained from Coryate. [2] *Ibid.*, p. 86.

[3] *S.P.* 14/105, No. 18. This letter, dated 19 February 1618–19, is calendared in *Cal. S.P. Colonial, ast Indies, China & Japan*, 1617–21, No. 594, and in *Cal. S.P. Dom. Jac. I*, vol. CV, No. 118.

46. Sir Thomas Roe. From the painting by an unknown artist in the National Portrait Gallery, after the portrait painted *circa* 1640 probably by M. J. van Miereveldt.

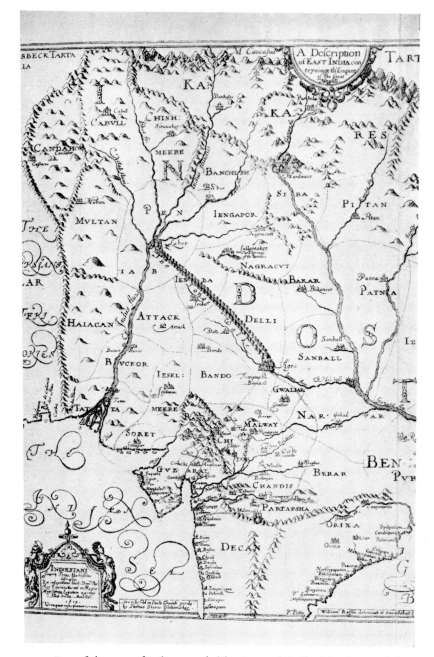

47. Part of the map of India compiled by Roe and Baffin. The first English attempt to map the Mogul Empire, including information supplied to Roe by Coryate.

This small skarre[1] festered and gangrened incurably; so that in a few dayes he despaired of life. And beeing accompanied with all his friends and divers courtiers, he brake out into these excellent words: Which of you would not have thought that I, being a man of warre, should have dyed by the stroke of a sword, speare, or bow? But now I am inforced to confesse the power of that great God whom I have so long despised: that Hee needs no other lance then a little haire to kill so blasphemous a wretch and contemner of His majestie as I have beene.'[2] The Archbishop expressed himself to be much edified by this marvellous example of the power of God upon rebellious atheists.

The Archbishop was writing to Roe in the knowledge that Coryate was dead: 'We could all have wished to have seene Thomas Coryat returned into his Country, because wee do conceive he would have made reports of the furthest Easterne Countries in a better fashion then any Englishman hitherto hath bene able. You shall do well to gett together all the papers which hee had written if they bee delivered in any intelligible fashion.'

There seems to be no doubt that copious notes existed. George Gerrard[3] wrote to Sir Dudley Carleton, then Ambassador at The Hague, on 9 January 1619: 'Here is lately a Ship come from Surratt in the East Indyes which hath brought news of Sir Thomas Roe ... He hath written of Coryates death, who dyed in those parts, and hath left enough written to fill the world with new relationes.'[4] What mischance caused the great bulk of them to disappear is unknown.

Nevertheless, Roe, like Terry, acquired much knowledge from Coryate. Some of Coryate's information can be traced in Roe's correspondence and dispatches, and some appears in pictorial form on the map of India which Roe compiled in collaboration with Baffin. Hardwar is correctly shown at the foot of the mountains where the Ganges issues from the mouth of a gorge and enters the plains. Coryate seems to have told Roe that one of the rocks in the Ganges was thought to be shaped like a cow's head, and a cow's head is marked on the map.

Another famous place of pilgrimage prominently shown on the

---

[1] Crack or incision, obs., *O.E.D.*
[2] Foster gives an account of other versions of this story in *Embassy*, p. 311, n.
[3] Greeted by Coryate in Letter No. 4 as George Garrat, q.v., p. 277.
[4] *S.P.* 14/105, No. 8.

map as a result of Coryate's reports is Jawala Mukhi (she of the flaming mouth), about twenty miles south-east of Kangra. This Hindu temple, standing at the base of a high range of hills, is built over some natural jets of inflammable gas. The issue of flames and cold water from the same fissure in the rock has been regarded for centuries as a miracle, and the flames are considered to be a manifestation of the goddess Devi. Coryate appears to have been the first European ever to visit the spot; he is certainly the first ever to have described it, though we have only his description as he gave it to Terry: 'In this province likewise there is another famous pilgrimage to a place called Jallamakee, where out of cold springs that issue out from amongst hard rocks, are daily to be seen continued eruptions of fire before which the idolatrous people fall down and worship. [This was] seen and strictly observed by Mr. Coryat.'[1]

Having got as far North as Kangra it would have been natural for him in pursuance of his last announced plan to push on to the Persian frontier. But for some unknown reason he did not do so. Instead he appears to have returned to the Company's factory at Agra, possibly having visited Delhi on the way. While in Agra he broke one more lance for his faith in a typically showy and audacious manner. One day he climbed up into a turret from which he faced a minaret near by; when the mullah mounted the minaret to call the people to prayer with the familiar cry 'No God, but one God, and Mohammed the ambassador of God', Coryate shouted him down with '*Lā ilāha illa-l-lah Ḥaẓarat Īsā Ibn Allāh*' —'No God but one God, and Christ the Son of God'.

He must have arrived back in Agra by early July 1617 at the latest, since on 20 July Roe, hearing that he was there, wrote from the Emperor's court at Mandu to one of the Agra factors expressing a desire to learn Coryate's purpose, 'for England or stay; or if I take any new course whither hee will goe with mee'.[2]

The new course to which Roe referred was to proceed to Persia by sea—a mission he half expected to receive instructions to carry out by the next fleet. If he was not sent to Persia Roe hoped to receive permission to sail for England early in 1618. Coryate was thus offered the alternative of travelling to Persia by sea, and thence resuming his journey overland, or of taking a passage home in the same ship as the Ambassador. That he found the

---

[1] Terry, *op. cit.*, 1777 edn., p. 83.    [2] Brit. Mus. Addl. Ms. 6115, f. 205.

invitation attractive may indicate that his health had begun to fail. From Ajmer he had been able to write: 'I do enjoy at this time as pancreaticall and athleticall a health as ever I did in my life; and so have done ever since I came out of England, saving for three dayes in Constantinople, where I had an ague, which with a little letting blood was clean banished; the Lord be humbly thanked for His gracious blessing of health that Hee hath given me.' But three summers in India in those days was a tax on even the strongest constitution. Whatever the reasons, he made his way down to Mandu—a march of some four hundred miles to the south-west.

Here he found the Ambassador and his household installed in a deserted mosque and tomb, within a spacious, well-walled court-yard. A century earlier Mandu had been the capital of the Mo-hammedan kingdom of Malwa, but now the jungle was en-croaching upon the once proud city and most of its splendid buildings were in ruins. The Ambassador's makeshift head-quarters lay on the southern side of the town on the edge of the precipitous slope leading down to the river Narbada. To com-pensate for the inconvenience of being two miles distant from the specially renovated stone building which served as the imperial palace, it had a pleasant airy prospect and, unlike most of the other buildings, required little repair to make it weatherproof. There remained the problem of water.

When the Emperor moved about the country he took a vast concourse of people and animals with him. Roe estimated that there were no less than two hundred thousand men, women, and children in the camp, besides countless elephants, horses, and camels, all requiring food and water. This may have been an overestimate, but the extent of the problem can be gauged by the fact that in Europe at about this time great difficulty was ex-perienced in supplying armies one-tenth the size. Usually the commissariat arrangements were remarkably well organized, but sometimes the Emperor set his staff impossible problems, and his decision to settle at Mandu produced a water famine. The unfortunate inhabitants of the city were ordered to leave, and a proclamation was issued forbidding anybody to keep animals in the vicinity of the camp. It was the custom, as Coryate notes, that 'whatsoever fountaine or tanke is found by any great man in time of drought, hee shall keepe it proper and peculiar to himselfe, without the interruption of any man whatsoever', thus the most economical use was not made of such water as existed. 'The misery', wrote Roe, 'is pitifull; water sould in the streete at an incredible rate; many Perishing for want; all begging that only as almes.' Coryate says that water was so dear that a little skinful was sold for eight pence and he commends the charity of two nobles who daily at their own expense sent ten camels fifteen miles down to the river and distributed water to the poor. Coryate also relates how and by whom the household's water supply was finally secured. A young man named Thomas Herbert,[1] risking his neck, climbed down the hillside near the Ambassador's house and found a spring. The following day a member of the Emperor's Body-guard came across the same spring and laid claim to it. There was a scuffle, the guard was overpowered and bound hand and foot. This incident threatened to cause some unpleasantness but all was eventually smoothed over, and it seems that the Ambassador was left in possession.

The easing of the water shortage enabled Roe to bring back some sheep and goats which he had been compelled to send away into the country. At night these were penned in the courtyard where a fire was kept blazing to scare off the wild beasts of the jungle which prowled outside. Nevertheless a lion not only got in but leapt out again over the high wall with its prey in its mouth. No man might kill a lion without the Emperor's per-mission, which Roe obtained. A few nights later, hearing the commotion caused by the lion's next visit, the Ambassador ran out into the courtyard, preceded by his little white pet dog, barking defiance. Before he could fire, the lion seized the dog and disappeared over the wall. So Roe missed the lion and lost his dog, and returned sorrowfully to bed.

Roe was still in poor health, and still beset with troubles at

---

[1] Born 1597, died (?)1642, sixth and youngest brother of Edward Herbert, first Lord Herbert of Cherbury. Herbert is interesting as being the prototype of many young gentlemen who were rather too wild for the comfort of their families in England, and were shipped off to India to make good or perish. On the voyage out he had behaved so badly that he was turned before the mast; he had been a plague to the factors at Surat, and on his way to the Court he endangered the safety of the party by beating and then firing at a native, to the alarm of his travelling companion the mild Mr. Terry, who described him as 'the most hasty and cholerick young man that ever I knew'. However, he seems to have mended his behaviour during the short time he stayed with Roe, and survived to lead an eventful life as seaman and author. See *Dictionary of National Biography*.

Court. If it had not been for his faith and the spiritual comfort administered to him by his chaplain, Edward Terry, he would have found life quite insupportable. Terry had originally accepted an engagement to travel out to the Indies and back as one of the chaplains in the East India Company fleet which arrived in Surat in September 1616. Roe's chaplain had died in August, and Terry agreed to fill the vacancy. He had joined the Ambassador towards the end of February on the march to Mandu.

Terry first met Coryate when the latter arrived at Mandu, and they saw each other for only ten or twelve weeks. Coryate found in the young chaplain a willing listener to the story of his adventures, while Terry conceived an admiration for Coryate which did not blind him to his faults. Despite its brevity, there is no doubt about the intimacy of their acquaintance. At Mandu they shared a room in the Ambassador's house, and they were tentmates when the Court continued its progress, as it was soon to do.

One reason for the move to Mandu had been to lend moral support to the imperial forces under the command of Jahangir's third and favourite son, Prince Khurram, during a campaign against the Deccan princes. Hostilities had ended with the submission of the King of Bijapur and the surrender of Ahmadnagar and other territory. On 2 October Prince Khurram made a triumphal entry into Mandu to be invested with the title of Shah Jahan. The Emperor now gave orders to leave Mandu for some undeclared destination farther north. Some said he would make for Ahmadabad in Gujarat, others that his councillors, who had the difficult task of attending to administration on the move, would persuade him to make for Agra, the capital, where they could be at rest.

On 5 October a messenger arrived from Surat bearing news which was bitterly disappointing to Roe, and which probably caused Coryate to re-shape his plans once more. The East India Company's fleet of five ships had arrived, but there were no instructions for Roe to proceed to Persia, and no permission for him to sail for home. However, some good news was mixed with the bad. The messenger also brought tidings and letters from home, and details of the presents and merchandise which the fleet carried. The presents included some extremely valuable pearls with which Roe hoped to secure important concessions for the English. He gave special instructions that they should be brought

ashore secretly, sewn into clothes or hidden in a hole bored in a
musket stock, lest they should be seized by the local authorities,
and that some very reliable person should convey them to the
Court.

When the Emperor moved off on 24 October the pearls had not
arrived. The Ambassador being, as he says, 'very weake and not
like to recover upon daily travell in the fields with cold raw
muddie water', nevertheless had no option but to follow. He
managed to obtain a warrant for ten camels at the price fixed by
the Emperor, and on 29 October he and his attendants, including
Coryate, followed after the king 'forced away by the desolations
of the place' which a few days earlier had been so full of activity.

There seems to be no doubt that by this time Coryate's health
was seriously impaired. Terry reports that one day at Mandu
when Coryate was 'there standing against a stone pillar, where the
Embassadour was and myself present with them, upon a sudden
he fell into such a swoon that we had very much ado to recover
him out of it. But at last come to himself, he told us that some sad
thoughts had immediately before presented themselves to his
fancy, which (as he conceived) put him into that distemper; like
Fannius in Martial[1]: *Ne moriare mori*, to prevent death by dying.
For he told us that there were great expectations in England of
the large accounts he should give of his travels after his return
home; and that he was now shortly to leave us, and he being at
present not very well, if he shoulde dye in the way toward Surat,
whither he was now intended to go . . . he might be buried in
obscurity and none of his friends ever know what became of him,
he travelling now, as he usually did, alone.'

Terry makes it appear as though Coryate had already decided,
before leaving Mandu, to go to Surat. But it seems probable that
so long as the Emperor's destination remained undeclared he
decided to stick with the Ambassador in the hope that Agra
would be their goal, whence if his health improved he could once
again resume the journey to Europe overland. Another reason
which may have prompted him to continue for a while with Roe
was that this would give him the opportunity of seeing the
Imperial Court on the move for the first time.

For the march from Mandu a road was cut straight through the

[1] *Epigrammata*, Bk. II, No. 80, 'Because he was flying from an enemy, Fannius
slew himself. Is not this, I ask, madness—to die to avoid death?'

jungle; progress could be as much as ten or twelve miles a day, but there were frequently halts of several days while the Emperor went off on a hunting expedition with a few chosen followers. The camp was about twenty miles in circumference and could be pitched in four hours. In the centre the great mass of the Emperor's lofty red pavilions was encircled by a red calico screen nine feet high patrolled by sentries. Beyond the screen lay a sea of variegated tents pitched in orderly streets according to the rank and function of the owner, great nobles nearest to the Emperor's tents, shopkeepers on the outer fringe.[1]

But when Roe and his suite overtook the Court on 31 October it had not yet resumed this orderly routine. The Emperor had gone off for ten days' hunting leaving the camp 'divided and scattered into many parts; ill water, deare provisions, sicknesse and all sorts of calamitie accompanying so infinite a multitude'.[2]

Two days later the pearls which Roe had been so anxiously awaiting arrived safely. The bearer turned out to be none other than Richard Steel whom Coryate had met between Kandahar and Multan when Steel was on his way home with a letter from the Emperor to King James. On his arrival in England Steel had tried to get the East India Company interested in several schemes, including one of erecting waterworks at Agra to supply the city with water from the river Jumna. The Company were unwilling to participate in this extraordinary project despite the fact that Steel was willing to put up £300 towards it out of his own pocket. Nevertheless they agreed to employ him in a general capacity and allowed him to take out a number of workmen on the chance of being able to interest the Emperor. So here he was once again in India, full of enthusiasm for his new venture. It was left to Roe to explode his flights of fancy by pointing out that the scheme entirely disregarded local religious custom which compelled some to drink only rain-water, others only water which had come from a holy river, and yet others only that which they themselves had drawn or fetched at their own cost; furthermore in the unlikely event of the undertaking being a success, the British would not be allowed to reap the profit since the Emperor would soon have his own people taught how to work it.

This was not the only matter on which Roe had to take issue

---

[1] See Foster, *Embassy*, Vol. II, p. 363; Terry, *op. cit.*, 1777 edn., pp. 398–405.

[2] Foster, *Embassy*, vol. II, p. 438.

with Steel. To the Ambassador's horror Steel had brought with him his wife who had given birth to a son at Surat.[1] Roe told him flatly that her presence was a menace to them all, that she should neither travel nor live at the expense of the Company ('I know the charge of women'), and that if he refused to send her home he would have to 'take a course with both both against my nature'.

Altogether Roe formed a very unfavourable impression of Steel. That he was a thoughtless trouble maker is borne out by his treatment of Coryate who questioned him eagerly for news of home. Steel described how he had seen the King and had told him that he had met Coryate in India. To hear that he had thus been brought to his Sovereign's attention was music to Coryate's ears, but his feelings of pride and pleasure were shattered in a moment when Steel cruelly told him that the King's comment had been 'Is that fool still living?' 'Which when our pilgrim heard it seemed to trouble him very much, because the King spake no more nor no better of him; saying that kings would speak of poor men what they pleased.'[2]

A few days later he discovered that ambassadors could be equally tactless. It became known that the Emperor was definitely making for Ahmadabad and thereupon it seems that Coryate decided to make his way down to Surat, where he was sure of hospitality at the Company's factory. He had, however, still not abandoned his intention of returning overland, for shortly before his departure he obtained from Roe a letter addressed to the British Consul[3] at Aleppo containing a bill for ten pounds. Coryate's delight with Roe's gift turned to indignation when he read the letter. Roe had written 'When you shall hand these letters, I desire you to receive the bearer of them, Mr. Thomas Coryat, with curtesy, for you shall find him a very honest poor wretch'. He complained to Terry that such a description quite spoilt the generosity of the Ambassador's gesture and recalled

[1] Much to Roe's annoyance the Company had agreed to Capt. Gabriel Towerson and his wife and their friend Mrs. Hudson coming out with the fleet. It was Mrs. Towerson's maid whom Steel had secretly married either before or during the voyage. Their son had the distinction of being the second British child born in India. The first was the son of Sir Thomas and Lady Powell who had travelled out with Robert Sherley in 1613. See Foster, *Embassy*, vol. II, p. 439, n.

[2] Terry, *op. cit.*, 1777 edn., p. 70.

[3] The letter was addressed to Libbeus Chapman who had replaced Coryate's friend Bartholomew Haggett.

how a person of honour had written for him a letter of introduction to Sir Henry Wotton, Ambassador at Venice: 'My
Lord, Good wine needs no bush, neither a worthy man letters
commendatory, because whither soever he comes he is his own
epistle.' 'There', said he, 'was some language on my behalf; but
now for my Lord to write nothing of me by way of commendation but Honest poor wretch is rather to trouble me than to
please me with his favour.' He did not hesitate to lay his complaint before Roe who good-naturedly agreed to re-phrase his
letter in a form which was acceptable.

So now he made his farewells and set out on his last tramp. He
seems to have left the camp on or about 18 November 1617, since
on this date he paid in to the East India Company's factors at
Court thirty-five rupees in cash and received in exchange a bill
on the factors at Surat for the same amount.[1] Nothing more is
known about this last lonely journey except that he arrived safely
at his destination and was hospitably received by the English
factors. Indeed, according to Terry, who is the only source of
information, their hospitality was too liberal and hastened his
end: 'But there being over-kindly used by some of the English,
who gave him sack which they had brought from England;
he calling for it as soon as he heard of it, and crying: Sack, sack;
is there such a thing as sack? I pray give me some sack; and
drinking of it, though, I conceive, moderately (for he was a very
temperate man), it increased his flux which he had then upon him.
And this caused him within a few daies, after his very tedious and
troublesome travels . . . at this place to come to his journies end;
for here he overtook Death in the month of December, 1617,
and was buried under a little monument, like one of those are
usually made in our church-yards.'

Terry wrote a twenty-line epitaph which he would have liked
to see inscribed upon the tomb if that had been possible, but
evidently it was not—perhaps the verses were composed only
after Terry had come home. In any case his poetical capabilities
were unworthy of his subject, and the verses are not worth
quoting here. But Terry's prose assessment of his friend, formed
on first-hand impressions, sums up very fairly both Coryate's
virtues and his failings: 'As he was a very particular, so was he
without question a very faithful, relator of things he saw; he

[1] India Office, *Factory Records, Miscellaneous*, vol. XXV, f. 9.

ever disclaiming that bold liberty which divers travellers have and do take by speaking and writing any thing they please of remote parts, when they cannot easily be contradicted . . . He was a man of a very coveting eye, "that could never be satisfied with seeing" (as Salomon speaks, Eccles. i, 8), though he had seen very much; and I am perswaded that he took as much content in seeing as many others in the enjoying of great and rare things. He was a man that had got the mastery of many hard languages to the Latine and Greek he brought forth of England with him; in which if he had obtained wisdome to husband and manage them as he had skill to speak them, he had deserved more fame in his generation. But his knowledge and high attainments in several languages made him not a little ignorant of himself; he being so covetous, so ambitious of praise that he would hear and endure more of it than he could in any measure deserve; being like a ship that hath too much sail and too little ballast. Yet if he had not fall'n into the smart hands of the wits of those times, he might have passed better . . . 'Twas fame, without doubt, that stirred up this man unto these voluntary but hard undertakings, and the hope of that glory which he should reap after he had finished his long travels made him not at all to take notice of the hardship he found in them. That hope of name and repute for the time to come did even feed him and feast him for the time present . . .

'*Sic exit Coryatus*: Hence he went off the stage, and so must all after him, how long soever their parts seem to be: for if one should go to the extremest part of the world East, another West, another North, and another South, they must all meet at last together in the Field of Bones, wherein our Traveller hath now taken up his lodging, and where I leave him.'

But where exactly Terry did leave him is a matter for conjecture. He certainly visited his friend's grave, and according to him this was not at Surat, where the regular English burying-ground had not then been established, but at the town's seaport, the village of Swally, or Suvali, twelve miles away at the mouth of the river Tapti. 'At the East India shore at Swally, on the banks thereof, amongst many more English that lie there interred is laid up the body of Mr. Thomas Coryat.'

Yet there is strong evidence that the body was carried only a little way beyond the walls of Surat, and buried on the western side of the road leading to Broach. Ten years after Coryate's

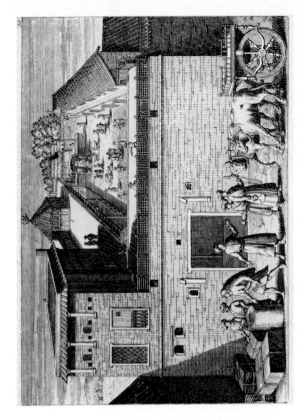

49. The East India Company's factory at Surat in 1638. From Von Mandelslo, *Les Voyages*, 1719 edn. (first published 1658). The warehouses were on the ground floor. In the upper storey were the living quarters (left), and chapel (centre background).

48. Rev. Edward Terry. From the engraving in his *Voyage to East India*, 1655.

50–51. 'Tom Coryat's Tomb.' The Mohammedan-style tomb a mile north of Suvali, popularly known as 'Tom Coryat's Tomb' and marked as such on current Admiralty charts. *Photographed by Rev. H. P. Cromie in 1958*

death an East India Company fleet arrived in Swally roads bringing Sir Dodmore Cotton on his way to Ispahan as Charles I's Ambassador. In the same fleet were Robert Sherley returning from his second mission to England, and a rival Persian Ambassador who had appeared in London and endeavoured to discredit Sherley. This man, Nagd Ali Beg, committed suicide on the fleet's arrival off Surat, and Thomas Herbert, a member of Cotton's suite, records that on 30 November 1627 the Persian Ambassador's body was conveyed 'to Surat where they entombed him not a stone's cast from Tom Coryate's grave, known but by two poor stones that speak his name, there resting till the resurrection.'[1] Furthermore in 1675 Dr. John Fryer says he was shown, just outside the Broach-gate, the tomb of the Persian Ambassador 'not far from whence, on a small hill on the left hand of the road, lies Tom Coriat, our English fakier (as they name him), together with an Armenian Christian, known by their graves lying east and west'.[2]

Were Herbert and Fryer misinformed, or is this one more example of Terry's memory playing him false? Several attempts have been made to solve the mystery. In 1863 A. F. Bellasis published a survey of the tombs at Surat; he could find no trace of the grave there and inclined to the view, on no convincing evidence, that it must have been at Swally.[3] Some years later a further unsuccessful search was made by Sir William Morison who came to the conclusion that the grave had been either swept away or silted over by the periodical floods of the river Tapti.[4] Finally in 1958 the Rev. H. P. Cromie made an investigation at the request of the author which only served to confirm that all traces of his resting place have disappeared.

Nevertheless popular legend identified his place of burial with a large domed tomb in the Mohammedan style, which stands near the shore a mile north of Swally. Though there are instances of similar Christian tombs around Surat, there is no evidence that later generations replaced the original two simple stones with an imposing and expensive monument. But legend once established

[1] Thomas Herbert, *Travels in Persia, 1627–29*, ed. Sir William Foster, London, 1928, p. 31. Thomas Herbert (later knighted) was no relation of his namesake who discovered the spring at Mandu.
[2] John Fryer, *A New Account of East India and Persia*, London, 1698, p. 100.
[3] *An Account of the Old Tombs in the Cemeteries of Surat*, Bombay, 1868, pp. 12–14.
[4] Foster, *Early Travels in India*, p. 240.

is difficult to eradicate. This tomb, which is in the general area indicated by Terry, is a landmark for mariners and at least as early as 1837 was marked on the East India Company's chart of the area as 'Coryottes Tomb'. For nearly a hundred years past the Admiralty has published charts of the Gulf of Cambay, and to this day 'Tom Coryat's Tomb' is shown in position 21° 11′ 0″ N, 72° 38′ 18″ E.

Coryate's fascination for tombs and epitaphs, which had early earned him the nickname of 'a tombstone traveller', was a manifestation of his own yearning for recognition, both in his lifetime and thereafter. This obsession with earthly fame made him prey to a haunting dread that he might lie in an unmarked grave. In a sense his dread became fact, but by this quirk of fortune the supposed site of his interment has been both durably commemorated and widely advertised. How pleased his ghost must be!

# Biographical Notes on Coryate's Circle

The following abbreviations have been used:

| | |
|---|---|
| *Alum. Cantab.* | J. and J. A. Venn, *Alumni Cantabrigienses*, Cambridge, 1922. |
| *Alum. Oxon.* | J. Foster, *Alumni Oxonienses*, Oxford, 1891. |
| B.M. | British Museum. |
| *Cal. S.P. Dom.* | *Calendar of State Papers, Domestic.* |
| *Dict. P. & B.* | R. B. McKerrow and others, *Dictionary of Printers and Booksellers 1557–1640*, London, 1910. |
| *D.N.B.* | *Dictionary of National Biography.* |
| *Harl. MSS.* | *Harleian Manuscripts*, British Museum. |
| Hist. MSS. Comm. | Historical Manuscripts Commission. |
| *M.L.R.* | *Modern Language Review.* |
| MS. | Manuscript. |
| *N. & Q.* | *Notes and Queries.* |
| *O.E.D.* | *Oxford English Dictionary.* |
| P.C.C. | Prerogative Court of Canterbury. |
| *P.M.L.A.* | *Publications of the Modern Language Association,* (U.S.A.). |
| P.R.O. | Public Record Office. |
| *S.T.C.* | A. W. Pollard and G. R. Redgrave, *Short Title Catalogue of English Books 1475–1640*, London, 1926. |
| *T.L.S.* | *The Times Literary Supplement.* |

These notes comprise all those who contributed verses to the *Crudities* and *Crambe*, those who were expected as guests at the Mitre Convivium (see p. 142 above), and those mentioned in Coryate's six extant letters.

References to the *Crudities* are to vol. I of the 1905 edition, as being the most accessible. The ordinal in brackets after a reference indicates the order of precedence in which that contributor's verses are printed in the *Crudities*. The inferences to be drawn from this order of precedence are discussed on pp. 126 and 138 above.

ADAMS, THOMAS (?–1620). See 'Protoplast'.

ALLEY, PETER. His verses, *Crudities*, pp. 75–76 (36th), indicate that he had probably seen the illustrated frontispiece and may even have read the MS. Captain Peter Alley accompanied Sir Walter Ralegh on his last voyage to Guiana and, owing to a head injury, was sent back early to England with letters. 'This bearer, Captain Alley, for his infirmitie of his head I have sent back; an honest, valiant man, he can deliver you all that is past.' (Ralegh to his wife from the Cayenne River, 14 Nov. 1617, see V. T. Harlow, *Ralegh's Last Voyage*, London, 1932, p. 159.) See also *Cal. S.P. Dom.*, vol. XCVI, 7 Feb. 1617–18, Chamberlain to Carleton, and 10 Feb. 1617–18, Sir Wm. Lovelace to Carleton, both reporting Alley's arrival from Guiana with letters.

Ἀποδημουντόφιλος = 'friend of the sojourner abroad'. I suggest he may be Sir Edward Phelips of Montacute (1560?–1614) (q.v.). His 136 lines of verse head the panegyric contributions in the *Crudities*. The succeeding twelve contributors are all knights which suggests that he must have held that rank at least. He proclaims that he is no literary expert, which is borne out by his doggerel; seems to have been acquainted with Coryate during his early years in Somerset, and mentions the Whitsun church-ale of 1606 (see p. 5 above).

ATKINS. 'Master Atkins and his wife at Norton [sub Hamdon]', two miles from Odcombe, are among the local friends whom Coryate greets in Letter No. 6.

AUSTIN, WILLIAM (1587–1634). See *D.N.B.* Contributed ninety-eight lines of verse to the *Crudities*, pp. 83–86 (44th), from which it seems that he may have read the book in MS., and seen the illustrated frontispiece; he was aware that the book would be published at Coryate's expense. Barrister of Lincoln's Inn and miscellaneous writer.

BADLEY, RICHARD. His verses, *Crudities*, pp. 107–10 (52nd) indicate that he had read the book in MS. Possibly the Richard Badley, B.A., from St. John's College, Cambridge, 1611–12. Mr. Shapiro and Professor Williams suggest that he is Richard Baddeley, author of *The Boy of Bilson*, 1622, *S.T.C.*, No. 1185.

BAKER, WILLIAM. His verses, *Crudities*, pp. 79–80 (40th) suggest that he knew Coryate as an entertaining dinner companion. Possibly the son and heir of Richard Baker of Abergavenny, matric. St. Alban Hall, Oxford, 20 April 1604, aged 18 and adm. Middle Temple, 24 Jan. 1606–7. However, there were also Bakers living at Hinton St. George, 5½ miles from Odcombe; a Christopher Baker of this family was adm. Middle Temple, 15 May 1599.

BALCH, ELIZABETH. '... reade this letter [No. 2, to Laurence Whitaker] to Mistris Elizabeth Balch, if shee continueth with your lady.' Mr. Shapiro in *M.L.R.*, 1950, p. 9, suggests that she was an attendant of the wife of Sir Edward Phelips, presumably on the grounds that Whitaker was Sir Edward's secretary. If Whitaker was married she may have been a member of his household.

BARBER, NED. He and his wife are among Coryate's Yeovil friends greeted in Letter No. 6.

BARRAT, WILLIAM (?-1624). See *Dict. P. & B.* as Barrett. Greeted in Letter No. 4. Bookseller in St. Paul's Churchyard, at the sign of the Green Dragon, 1608, and of the Three Pigeons, 1614. Was associated with Edward Blount (q.v.), and the *Crudities* was entered in the Stationers' Company Register in their joint names. From 1608 onwards he published several books of travel, including George Sandys *Relation of a Journey*, 1615. Though apparently a man of some capital, he evidently felt that the financial risk of publishing the *Crudities* had better be borne by the author.

BASTARD, THOMAS (1566-1618). See *D.N.B.* Contributed verses, *Crudities*, pp. 78-79 (39th). Satirist and Divine; born at Blandford, Dorset; educated Winchester and New College, Oxford; adm. perpetual fellow 1588, but, according to Wood, 'being much guilty of the vices belonging to poets and given to libelling, was in a manner forced to leave his fellowship in 1591. So that for the present being put to his shifts, he was not long after made Chaplain to Thomas Earl of Suffolk, lord treasurer of England.'

BERIB. 'Master Berib, his wife and all his family' are among Coryate's Odcombe friends greeted in Letter No. 6.

BING, ROBERT. In Letter No. 4 Coryate asks to be remembered to 'Robert Bing, at Yongs ordinarie, neere the Exchange'. Mr. Shapiro, *M.L.R.*, 1950, suggests that he may be the same Robert Bing whom the Lord Keeper objected to including in the Commission for Virginia in 1642, because he was 'a mere good fellow, a man of no estate, who, for saucy conduct before the Council table, and offensive behaviour to Lord Southampton, had been committed to the Marshalsea'. See *Cal. S.P. Colonial*, 1574-1660, p. 65.

BLOUNT, EDWARD (1564-1632). One of the most enterprising booksellers of his day. Friend of Christopher Marlowe, and published several of his works. In 1608 he moved to The Black Swan, St. Paul's Churchyard; was associated with William Barrat (q.v.). The *Crudities* was entered in the Stationers' Company Register under the joint names of Blount and Barrett (q.v. as Barrat). Greeted in Letter No. 4.

In association with others, issued the First Folio of Shakespeare, 1623. See *Dict. P. & B.*

BOND, JOHN. In Letter No. 4 Coryate asks to be remembered to 'John Bond, my countreyman, chiefe Secretarie unto my Lorde Chancellour [Sir Thomas Egerton, Baron Ellesmere].' Mr. Shapiro, *M.L.R.*, 1950, points out that *D.N.B.* has confused him with a schoolmaster of the same name who died in 1612, and quotes George Garrard (q.v. as Garrat), writing on 1 March 1635: 'Mr. Bond, quondam secretary to Chancellor Ellesmere, now in his old Age, is married to a very handsome young woman' (*Strafforde Papers*, vol. I, p. 373). It seems probable that Ellesmere had two secretaries named Bond, since on 3 Aug. 1604 'Thomas Bonde, Secretary of Thomas, Lord Ellesmere, Lord Chancellor' was adm. to the Middle Temple together with another of Ellesmere's secretaries, and two of his ushers. A 'John Bonde of Cornwall gen.' was adm. to Lincoln's Inn 8 Aug. 1602.

BROOKE, CHRISTOPHER (?–1628). See *D.N.B.* Contributed verses *Crudities*, pp. 56–57 (21st), and under the anagram Richer For Books = Chris. [for] Brooke in *Crambe*, sig. b3 verso. As 'Christoferus Torrens' was one of the guests expected at the Mitre Convivium. Greeted in Letters No. 3 and No. 4. He was an intimate friend of John Donne, John Hoskins, and Richard Martin (q.v. omnes). Gosse sums him up as 'the man in whom contemporary eyes detect endless promise of genius and in whom posterity can scarcely see anything to arrest attention' (*Life & Letters of John Donne*, vol. II, p. 249).

CAMPIAN, THOMAS (?–1620). See *D.N.B.* as Campion. Contributed verses in Latin, *Crudities*, p. 73 (33rd). Musician, poet, and also a doctor of medicine; composer and producer of masques at Court.

CHAPMAN, JOHN. Contributed verses, *Crudities*, pp. 72–73 (32nd). Cannot be identified with certainty. (1) *Middle Temple Register of Admissions* gives: Feb. 14, 1591–2, John Chapman, late of New Inn, gent., son & heir of Henry C. of Godmersham, Kent, gent., called to the Bar 2 May, 1600. (2) *Alum. Oxon.* records a John Chapman of Salop, son of a clergyman; matric. Broadgates Hall, 20 Oct. 1598, aged 17; B.A. 7 July 1602; M.A. 23 June 1605; rector of Donington, Salop, 1607.

CHUNT, WILLIAM. An Odcombe friend greeted in Letter No. 6.

CLARKE, JOSIAS (1579–?). Contributed Latin verses, *Crudities*, p. 82 (42nd). Son of a Dorset clergyman, Coryate's contemporary at

Gloucester Hall, where he matric. 5 Mar. 1595–6, aged 16, graduated
B.A. 31 Jan. 1599–1600; M.A. 6 July, 1603.

CLAVEL, SIR WILLIAM (1568–1644?). Contributed verses, *Crudities*,
pp. 35–36 (13th). Of Dorset; matric. Oriel College, Oxford, 24 Nov.
1581; fellow 1583; B.A. 6 Feb. 1583–4; M.A. 4 May 1587. Adm.
Middle Temple 28 Nov. 1588. Knight banneret.

CONNOCK, RICHARD. As 'Cuniculus Quercianus' expected as a guest at
the Mitre Convivium. Appointed Auditor of Prince Henry's household Dec. 1610 (*Sackville: Cranfield Papers*, p. 271; Birch, *op. cit.*, p.
218). He may be the Richard Connocke, late of New Inn, gent., third
son of John C. of Leskard, Cornwall, gent., who was adm. Middle
Temple 11 Feb. 1582–3. Perhaps the same 'Mr. Connocke' who was a
Gentleman of the Privy Chamber Extraordinary in Prince Henry's
Household (*Harl. MSS.*, vol. 252, f. 8.40/89).

COOKE, ——. Rev. Samuel Purchas's assistant. In Letter No. 4 from
India Coryate writes: 'Pray commend me unto [Rev. Purchas] and
his παραϛάτης [assistant] Master Cooke.' Coryate states that Cooke
gave him a copy of Pierre Gilles's *De Bosphoro Thracio*, which he lost
in Constantinople. Nothing more seems to be known about Cooke.

CORBET, RICHARD (1582–1635). See his *Poems*, ed. J. A. W. Bennett and
H. R. Trevor-Roper, 1955, and *D.N.B.* Contributed verses in Latin
and English, *Crudities*, pp. 70–71 (30th). Contemporary of Coryate's
at Oxford (Broadgates Hall, later Pembroke College) where he was
'esteemed one of the most celebrated wits of the University, as his
poems, jests, romantic fancies and exploits, which he made and perform'd extempore, shew'd'. (Wood, *Athenae*.) Throughout life he
was famed for conviviality; in youth a merrymaker with the wits in
London taverns; a life-long friend of Ben Jonson. He took holy
orders, became chaplain to King James I, and Bishop successively of
Oxford and Norwich. Stories, several too bawdy to be included in
the early editions of Aubrey, are told of the practical jokes he played
even when he was Bishop of Oxford. Aubrey says 'he was a very
handsome man, but something apt to abuse, and a coward'.

COTTON, SIR ROBERT BRUCE (1571–1631). See *D.N.B.* Antiquary.
Greeted in Letter No. 4. Cotton was intimate with most of the leading statesmen and writers of the day. He claimed to trace his ancestry
back to Robert Bruce; King James called him 'cousin'. Coryate had
some knowledge of Cotton's collection of antiquities and may have
benefited, as Ben Jonson did, from Cotton's generous sharing of his
magnificent library which ultimately formed the basis of the British
Museum.

COTTON, SIR ROWLAND (?–1634). Verses, *Crudities*, pp. 32–33 (10th). In *Alum. Cantab.* described as of Bellaport, Salop. Matric. St. John's College, *c.* 1596; adm. Lincoln's Inn June 1599. Author of *Parentalia Spectatissimo R. Cottono Equiti Aurato Salopiensi*, 1635, *S.T.C.*, No. 5870. M.P. for Newcastle-under-Lyme, 1605, 1628; for Salop 1626. Knighted 1608. Will (P.C.C) 1634.

CRANFIELD, LIONEL (1575–1645). See *D.N.B.* and R. H. Tawney, *Business & Politics under James I*, C.U.P., 1958. In the Epistle Dedicatory, *Crudities*, p. 5, Coryate says 'my most sincere and entire friend, M. Lionel Cranfield was the originall and principall animator of me . . . to publish the Observations of my travels'. Cranfield's verses, *Crudities*, pp. 63–64 (24th), are truly laudatory. In 1605 he purchased the Receivership of Crown Revenues in Somerset and Dorset; named as a Member of the Levant Company in the Charter granted to it by James I in 1605 (P.R.O. MSS. F.A. Levant Company No. 107, reproduced in M. Epstein, *The Early History of the Levant Company*, p. 159). In 1611–12 acted as Coryate's banker (see p. 140 above). As 'Gruicampus' was one of the guests expected at the Mitre Convivium. Knighted 1613, and appointed Surveyor General of the Customs. As Buckingham's favour and power increased, Cranfield's rise became even more rapid until in Sept. 1622 he was created Earl of Middlesex, and appointed Treasurer. Not mentioned in any of Coryate's extant letters from India, but it is possible that correspondence with Coryate still lies unrevealed in the vast mass of unstudied and unpublished Cranfield Papers held by the *Hist. MSS. Comm.*

DARBY. 'The poore Widow Darby' is among Coryate's Yeovil friends greeted in Letter No. 6.

DAVIS, JOHN OF HEREFORD (1565?–1618). See *D.N.B.* as Davies. Poet and writing-master. His verses, *Crudities*, pp. 101–7 (51st), confirm his reputation for prolixity and tediousness as a poet, but as a penman he was, according to Fuller, the most skilful of his age, and Prince Henry was one of his pupils. He supplied commendatory verses to a number of works published between 1601 and 1616 (listed in *D.N.B.*).

DIGGES, SIR DUDLEY (1583–1639). See *D.N.B.* His verses, *Crudities*, pp. 31–32 (9th), open with:

> 'Our Author will not let me rest, he sayes,
> Till I write somewhat in his labours praise.'

Entered University College, Oxford, 1598; B.A. 1601; is said to have spent some years thereafter in foreign travel. Joint author with his father of *Foure Paradoxes or Politique Discourses*, 1604. Knighted 1607.

One of the early shareholders in the East India Company, and a founder of the company formed in 1612 to trade with the East by the supposed North-West passage. Later became M.P., and in 1636 Master of the Rolls.

DONES, JOHN. Author of verses, *Crudities*, p. 71 (31st). Not satisfactorily identified, but as Mr. Shapiro argues (*T.L.S.*, 1 Feb. 1936) he is certainly not John Donne (q.v.), because, firstly, John Dones' poem is not included in any seventeenth-century edition of Donne's poems, and secondly, John Donne's contribution to the *Crudities* is shown elsewhere among the Panegyrick Verses, with his name correctly spelt and although several contributors sent a number of poems the work of each is always gathered into a single group. Furthermore, Shapiro points out that two similar but distinct surnames are found in sixteenth and seventeenth century records: (*a*) Dun spelt also Dun(n)e, Don(n)e, Doun, Doon &c., (*b*) Dunch or Dunsh(e), Dun(ne)s, Don(n)es &c. Thus both John Done, author of *Polydoron*, 1631 (*S.T.C.*, No. 1720), and John Done, adm. Lincoln's Inn 3 Nov. 1596, can be ruled out. *Alum. Cantab.* records a John Dunch of Lancashire, matric. sizar, Queens' College, Lent, 1584–5; B.A. from St. John's 1587–8, as Duntch; M.A. from Queens' 1593; B.D. 1606; Vicar of Lakenheath, Suffolk, 1592–8; Vicar of Dullingham, Cambs., 1598–1639; where he was buried 16 Dec. 1639; but there appears to be no obvious connexion.

DONNE, HUGH, of Odcombe, greeted in Letter No. 6. No known connexion of John Donne.

DONNE, JOHN (1575–1631). See *D.N.B.* His 76 lines of verse and quatrain in macaronic language, *Crudities*, pp. 37–39 (15th), epitomize the cutting scorn of the wits. He and Coryate had many mutual acquaintances. At Oxford when he was admitted to Hart Hall, Oct. 1584, he shared rooms with Sir Henry Wotton, and was contemporary with John Hoskins (q.v.). He was adm. Lincoln's Inn 6 May 1592, and occupied the same chambers as Christopher Brooke (q.v.). Took part in Essex's expedition to Cadiz. About 1598 was appointed Secretary to Sir Thomas Egerton, Keeper of the Great Seal. His secret marriage in 1601 to Anne More, Lady Egerton's niece, wrecked his career as a civil servant. His father-in-law contrived to imprison not only Donne, but Christopher Brooke who witnessed the marriage, and his brother Samuel Brooke who performed it. Donne was particularly friendly with Christopher Brooke, Richard Martin, John Hoskins, and Hugh Holland, all of whom, with Donne himself, were among the guests expected at the Mitre Convivium. Coryate greets him from India in Letter No. 4.

DRAYTON, MICHAEL (1563–1631). See *D.N.B.* His verses, *Crudities*, pp. 97–98 (47th), open with:

> 'Dear Tom, thy Booke was like to come to light
> Ere I could gaine but one halfe howre to write.'

Their tardy appearance may explain why so popular and distinguished a poet was placed so late in the order of contributors. His longest and most famous poem, *Poly Olbion*, 1613, was dedicated to Prince Henry, and illustrated by William Hole who executed the illustrations for the *Crudities*.

DYER. 'Old Master Dyer, and his sonne John' are among Coryate's Yeovil friends greeted in Letter No. 6.

EMLEY, LAURENCE. His verses, *Crudities*, pp. 99–100 (49th), are prefaced by Coryate's note: 'These verses immediately following were lately sent me by a learned Gentleman of Magdalen College in Oxford: who though he never saw me, hath vouchsafed to grace my books with his Encomiasticks.' Professor Williams points out (*N. & Q.*, 1956, p. 236) that Laurentius Emley, as Coryate calls him, is almost certainly an error for Theophilus Emilie or Emlie who graduated B.A. from Magdalen 21 Oct. 1605, and was appointed vicar of Matherne, Glamorgan, 1608. (*Alum. Oxon.*) His verses are of interest because they prove that he had seen and studied William Hole's frontispiece to the *Crudities*, indicating that copies of this were run off and circulated prior to the book's publication.

EWINS. 'Master Ewins, old & young, with their wives' are among Coryate's Yeovil friends greeted in Letter No. 6.

FARNABY, THOMAS (1575?–1647). See *D.N.B.* Son of a London carpenter; matric. Merton College, Oxford, June 1590. Coryate may have known him in Somerset, since some time after 1596 he taught under the anagrammatic alias Bainrafe at Martock grammar school, 3½ miles from Odcombe. Later he opened his own school in London and had 300 pupils, mostly sons of noblemen. He was the chief classical scholar as well as the leading schoolmaster of his time in England, and his editions of the classics with elaborate Latin notes were extraordinarily popular throughout the seventeenth century. The first of these, an edition of Juvenal's and Perseus's satires, 1612, was dedicated to Prince Henry and included commendatory Latin elegiacs by Ben Jonson. His verses in Greek and English, *Crudities*, pp. 82–83 (43rd), give no clear indication of his relationship with Coryate.

FENTON, WILLIAM, OF KNOCKFERGUS. Author of quatrain in gibberish, possibly intended to be 'fake-Irish', with an English 'translation', *Crudities*, pp. 73–74 (34th). Professor Williams identifies him as Sir William Fenton, only son of Sir Geoffrey (1539?–1608), the translator and statesman who appears in *D.N.B.*

FIELD, JAMES. Author of verses, *Crudities*, pp. 115–16 (55th). Not satisfactorily identified as spelt or in the variants Feild(e), Fylde, Feld(e). *Alum. Oxon.* records Feilde, James, of Co. York., pleb. Magdalen College, matric. 24 Jan. 1605–6, aged 20, but there is no obvious connexion.

FORD, WILLIAM (1559–?). See *D.N.B.* under Foord. Chaplain to the Levant Company in Constantinople at the time of Coryate's stay there. Greeted in Letter No. 4.

GARRAT, GEORGE (1580–?). In Letter No. 4 to the High Seneschal of the Mermaid Club Coryate greets 'Master George Garrat; of whose beeing you shall understand by Master [John] Donne'. The link with Donne indicates that Coryate refers to George Garrard or Gerrard, son of Sir William Gerrard of Dorney, Bucks; matric. Merton College, Oxford, Nov. 1594; fellow of Merton 1598; Master of Sutton's Hospital; Chaplain to Earl of Northumberland; intimate friend and correspondent of Donne. A number of his letters to Carleton are calendared in *S.P. Dom.*, they are full of Court and political news; that dated 6 Jan. 1618–19 reports Coryate's death in India. Mr. Shapiro, *M.L.R.*, 1950, states that he was a civil servant who 'to the end of his long life seems to have been concerned with good living rather than with literature'. Possibly the same 'Mr Gerrarde' who was a Gentleman of the Privy Chamber Extraordinary in Prince Henry's Household (*Harleian MSS.*, vol. 252, f. 8.40/89).

GOLLOP, GIBBS (1567–after 1624). Succeeded Coryate's father as Rector of Odcombe. In Letter No. 6 Coryate writes to his Mother: 'I pray you recommend me first in Odcombe to Master Gollop & every good body of his family, if he liveth yet.' Matric. Gloucester Hall, Oxford, Nov. 1586; B.A. from Magdalen Hall, June 1489; M.A. from Gloucester Hall, June 1592. See Wood, *Athenae*, as Gallop.

GOODIER, SIR HENRY (1571–1627). See *D.N.B. Suppl.* vol. II, as Goodyer. His father Sir Henry (1534–95) was the early friend and patron of Michael Drayton (q.v.), and the son likewise acquired fame as a patron of literary men. Probably knighted in Ireland 1599. Attended Court 1604 and participated in the festivities of the first year of James I's reign (see Nichols, *Progresses*, passim). Appointed a gentleman of the privy chamber, 1605. His verses, *Crudities*, p. 28

(5th), suggest that he took part in the prank of carrying Coryate on to the stage of a masque hidden in a trunk:

> If any thinke him dull or heavy, know
> The Court and cities mirth cannot be so.
> Who thinks him light, aske them who had the taske
> To beare him in a trunke unto the maske.

Ben Jonson has an epigram to him, No. 85, and he was the friend of Inigo Jones, but he is best known as the closest and most intimate friend of John Donne; commencing soon after 1600 Donne seems for a long time to have written him a weekly letter. As 'Henricus Bonum-annum' was one of the guests expected at the Mitre Convivium.

GRANDI-BOSCO, JOHANNES À. Contributed verses to the *Crudities* which arrived too late and were printed in the *Crambe*, Sig. first A3. I suggest he may possibly be John Hayward = 'High Wood' (1564?–1627) the historian patronized by Prince Henry, knighted 1619. See *D.N.B.*

GRIFFIN, GEORGE. Author of Latin anagram and verses, *Crudities*, p. 101 (50th). Unidentified either as spelt or in the variants Griffith(s), Griffith(e), Grefyth, Gruffith, Gryffythe, Gryphes.

GYFFORD, JOHN. Contributed two sets of verses, *Crudities*, pp. 67–69 (29th); in the superscription alludes to Coryate as 'mine old friend'; it is evident that Gyfford had read the text of the *Crudities* before publication, and had himself travelled in France. I suggest he is John Giffard, second son of Walter Giffard of Chillington, 8 miles S.W. of Odcombe; adm. Inner Temple Nov. 1599.

HACKWELL, WILLIAM (1574–1655). See *D.N.B.* as Hakewill. In Letter No. 3 to Sir Edward Phelips (q.v.) Coryate asks to be remembered to 'M. William Hackwell: and the rest of the worthy gentlemen frequenting your honourable table'. Again in Letter No. 4 Coryate greets 'Master William Hackwell, at his Chamber in Lincolns Inne' where he was one of the chief benchers for nearly thirty years. Besides being a notable legal antiquarian, he was M.P. for various constituencies between 1601 and 1629. Friend of John Donne (q.v.); kinsman and executor of Sir Thomas Bodley.

HALSWELL, ROBERT (1586?–1626). Contributed quatrain, *Crudities*, p. 67 (28th). Professor Williams identifies him as one of the six sons of Sir Nicholas Halswell of Somerset; B.A. from St. Edmund Hall, Oxford, 1605; student of Lincoln's Inn 1607; M.P. for Bridgwater 1614.

HANCOKE, REV. ——. He and his family are greeted in Letter No. 6.

HARRINGTON, SIR JOHN OF BATH (1561–1612). See *D.N.B.* as Harington. Verses, *Crudities*, p. 27 (3rd), referring to Coryate as 'my new-come Odcombe-friend'. The fact that the verses appear third in order of precedence among the knighted contributors confirms that he, not his son, is the author. Both father and son were students of Lincoln's Inn. He was a godson of Queen Elizabeth, who twice banished him from the court for uttering indecent writings. He returned to court at the close of the Queen's reign and in 1602 sent James VI a New Year's gift of a lantern constructed to symbolize the waning light of Elizabeth and the brilliant splendour that was to come. The lantern bore a representation of the crucifixion for the sake of the words of the penitent thief, 'Lord, remember me when thou comest into thy kingdom.' He received no favours on James's accession, but later the king allowed him to undertake some part of Prince Henry's education. To instruct the young Prince and counteract the influence of the Puritans he made him study Bishop Godwin's *De Praesulibus Angliae*, 1601, to which he appended for the Prince's private use his own racy remarks on the characters of Elizabethan bishops.

HAYWARD, SIR JOHN (1564?–1627). See Grandi-Bosco, Johannes à.

HICKS, SIR MICHAEL (1543–1612). See *D.N.B.* The original Letter No. 1 which Coryate wrote him on 15 Nov. 1610 is inserted into Prince Henry's presentation copy of the *Crudities* in B.M. From this letter we know that Coryate had met him at dinner, but was clearly not intimately acquainted with him. Student of Lincoln's Inn 1564; became one of the two chief secretaries to Lord Burghley, and continued as secretary to Lord Treasurer Salisbury, in which latter capacity Coryate wrote to him for help in obtaining a licence to publish the *Crudities*. His brother, Baptist Hicks, later Lord Campden, was a business associate of Lionel Cranfield (q.v.).

HOLLAND, HUGH (?–1633). See *D.N.B.* Author of extensive, ironical verses in Greek, English, Italian, and Welsh, *Crudities*, pp. 43–49 (18th). Also contributed verses to the *Crambe*, printed on an extra leaf following Sig. b4 which is omitted from many copies of the book. As 'Hugo Inferior-Germanus' was one of the guests expected at the Mitre Convivium. In Letter No. 2 to Laurence Whitaker Coryate writes: 'Commend mee likewise to Master H. Holland & Inigo Jones.' Holland was a native of Denbigh; educated Westminster and Trinity College, Cambridge. On leaving Cambridge he went abroad and travelled as far as Jerusalem; is said to have turned Catholic for a time. On return to England he expected preferment and not getting it Fuller says 'he grumbled out the rest of his life in visible discontentment'. Close friend of Christopher Brooke, John Donne, John Hoskins, and Richard Martin (q.v. omnes). Contributed commendatory verses to *Canzonets*, 1598, by Thomas Farnaby (q.v.) and *Sejanus*, 1605, by Ben Jonson (q.v.). Now best known as the author of the sonnet prefixed to the First Folio of Shakespeare. Friend of Sir Robert Cotton (q.v.) with whom he corresponded. Buried in Westminster Abbey.

HOSKINS, JOHN (1566–1638). See *D.N.B.*, and L. B. Osborn, *Life, Letters and Writings of* . . . Educated Westminster, Winchester, and New College, Oxford. At New College was contemporary of John Owen (q.v.) and Henry Wotton. Schoolteacher, 1592, at Ilchester, 4½ miles from Odcombe. Student of the Middle Temple 1593, called to the Bar. In 1601 married a rich widow at Bath. M.P. for Hereford 1603, re-elected 1614 and 1628. Contributed not unfriendly verses in English, some set to music, and Latin to *Crudities*, pp. 58–61 (22nd). As 'Janus Caligula' was one of the guests expected at the Mitre Convivium; the authorship of the Latin poem describing this Convivium has been ascribed to him, probably incorrectly (see I. A. Shapiro, *M.L.R.*, 1950, p. 7, n). In Letter No. 3 to Sir Edward Phelips Coryate asks to be remembered, among others, to 'M. Equinoctiall Pasticrust, of the Middle Temple . . . and the rest of the worthy gentlemen frequenting your honourable table'. Again in Letter No. 4 Coryate greets 'Master John Hoskins, alias Aequinoctiall Pasticrust . . .' This nickname probably originated from Hoskins' nonsense verses, *Crudities*, p. 58:

> 'Or as your equinoctiall pasticrust
> Projecting out a purple chariot wheele,
> Doth squeeze the spheares, . . .'

Author of *Direccons For Speech and Style*, written between 1598 and 1603. When Hoskins' son Benedict asked Jonson to adopt him as one of his 'sons', Jonson replied, 'No I dare not 'tis honour enough for me to be your brother: I was your father's sonne, and 'twas he that polished me.' (See Clark's edn. of Aubrey, vol. I, p. 418.) Among his chief friends were Donne, Brooke, Martin, and Holland (q.v. omnes).

HUGHES, RICHARD. Contributed quatrain in Welsh, *Crudities*, p. 119 (56th). Poet from Caernarvonshire. One of Queen Elizabeth's attendants or 'pedisequi'; later served James I in same capacity (he is described as 'Regi à Pedibus' in the superscription to his quatrain); died 1618 (see *Dict. Welsh Biography*). He may be 'Richard Hughes of Anglesey, gen.' adm. Lincoln's Inn 9 Feb. 1602–3.

INGRAM, SIR ARTHUR (*c.* 1565–1642). See *D.N.B.* and A. F. Upton, *Sir Arthur Ingram*, Oxford 1961. Close business associate of Lionel Cranfield (q.v.); 1604 appointed Comptroller of the Customs of the Port of London; M.P. for various constituencies between 1606 and 1628. Coryate dined at his home (Letter No. 1); was one of the guests expected at the Mitre Convivium. Knighted 1613. An interesting sketch of this rapacious, flamboyant character is given in R. H. Tawney's *Business & Politics under James I.*

JACKSON, JOHN. Author of panegyric verses printed in the shape of an egg, *Crudities*, p. 96 (46th): 'Thy hungry prayses in his [?this] Egge I sing. At thy request, . . .' Leslie Hotson, *Shakespeare's Sonnets dated*, London, 1949, identifies him as John Jackson (*c.* 1575–*c.* 1625), property owner, possibly a freeman of the East India Company and lessee of part of the farm of wine duties into East coast ports. Hotson's researches prove that this Jackson joined with John Hemmyngs, the actor and editor of the Shakespeare First Folio 1623, and William Johnson the owner of the Mermaid Tavern, to act as trustees for Shakespeare in his purchase of a house in Blackfriars in 1613.

An alternative identification, suggested by Professor Williams, is that he was the son of Sir John Jackson of Edderthorpe, Yorks., who went up to Magdalen Hall, Oxford, Oct. 1612, and graduated B.A. in July 1615; student of the Inner Temple 1615; knighted 1619; M.P. for Pontefract 1624–9; died 2 July 1637 (*Alum. Oxon.*). Williams's suggestion is based on the grounds that this Jackson was the friend of Rowland Cotton (q.v.) and editor of Cotton's book *Parentalia* . . . If correct Jackson must have been a precocious versifier and a very youthful member of the London set, since his verses suggest that he was well acquainted with various circumstances connected with Coryate and his book. Hotson's identification appears more probable, though his suggestion that Jackson was a member of the Mermaid Tavern Club seems not proven.

JENINGS, WILLIAM. One of Coryate's Yeovil friends greeted in Letter No. 6.

JONES, INIGO (1573–1652). See *D.N.B.* As a young man travelled extensively in Europe and spent much time in Venice. His association with Ben Jonson (q.v.) in the production of masques at Court began in the winter of 1604–5, Jones designing the scenes, machines, and dresses. Appointed Surveyor of the Works to Prince Henry, Dec. 1610. His verses, *Crudities*, pp. 64–65 (26th), make it clear that he knew about a number of incidents described in the book. As 'Ignatius Architectus' was one of the guests expected at the Mitre Convivium. Adm. Middle Temple Feb. 1612–13. Greeted in Letter No. 2.

JONSON, BENJAMIN (1573?–1637). See *D.N.B.* Author of *An explica-tion of the Emblemes of the Frontispiece*, in rhyming couplets, *Crudities*, pp. xix, xx. He also contributed *The Character of the Author* in prose, and an Acrostic on the author's name, *Crudities*, pp. 16–19. Thus Jonson went to considerable trouble to promote the success of Coryate's book. A further 60 lines of verse arrived too late for in-clusion, but made a handsome opening to the *Crambe*, Sig. first A2. Coryate greets him in Letters No. 2 and No. 4. For Jonson's relation-ship with Coryate and allusions to Coryate in Jonson's works see Chapter X above.

KNIGHT. 'All the Knights' are among the friends living in and near Odcombe whom Coryate greets in Letter No. 6 to his Mother. May be a reference to Sir Edward and Sir Robert Phelips (q.v.).

LEWKNOR, SIR LEWIS (?–1626). Author of verses, *Crudities*, pp. 27–28 (4th); M.A. of Cambridge; student of the Middle Temple 1579; M.P. for Midhurst 1597–8, for Bridgnorth 1604–11. Knighted 1603. Master of the Ceremonies to James I. Author and translator (*S.T.C.*, *Alum. Cantab.*, Wood, *Fasti*, pp. 229 and 270).

LOISEAU DE TOURVAL, JEAN, OF PARIS. Contributed verses in French, *Crudities*, pp. 111–13 (53rd). Born in Paris between about 1573 and 1583; died 1631. Came to England in the suite of the French Am-bassador on the occasion of James I's accession. He remained to embark on a period of activity in the field of Protestant-Jesuit controversy at considerable risk to himself and largely in the service of King James, being often employed on errands across the Channel. He appears in Prince Henry's pension list as receiving £20 in 1612 (Birch, *op. cit.*, p. 467). Several of his letters are calendared in *S.P. Dom.* His grant of denization is recorded in *Cal. S.P. Dom.*, vol. CIX, 23 July 1619. By 1623 had become chaplain to James I and later continued as chaplain to Charles I. Friend of John Donne who as Dean of St. Pauls was one of his patrons when he was inducted as incumbent of St. Martin Orgar, London, on 11 April 1625. In Donne's will he left to 'Mr Tourvall a French minister (but by the ordination of the English church) any picture which he will choose of those which hang in the little dining room & are not bequeathed' (Gosse, *op. cit.*, vol. II, p. 360). He translated James I's *Apologie for the Oath of Allegiance*, printed in Paris 1609; his unpublished MS. translation of Sidney's *Arcadia* is in the Bodleian. For most of the above see article by A. Clarke in *Proceedings of the Huguenot Society of London*, vol. XX, No. 1, 1960.

LOWNES, MATTHEW (?–1625). See *Dict. P. & B.* Although listed by Coryate among the booksellers of St. Paul's Churchyard to whom he

particularly wished to be remembered (Letter No. 4 from India),
Lownes's place of business seems to have been in St. Dunstan's
Churchyard, Fleet Street.

MARTIN, RICHARD (1570–1618). See *D.N.B.* Student at Broadgates
Hall (later Pembroke College), Oxford, but left without a degree.
Adm. Middle Temple 7 Nov. 1587, and temporarily expelled Feb.
1591 for a riot at the prohibited festival of the Lord of Misrule.
M.P. for Barnstaple 1601, for Christchurch 1604–11. Business associate of Lionel Cranfield (q.v.) and legal adviser to several of Cranfield's syndicates (R. H. Tawney, *Business & Politics under James I*,
p. 87). It therefore seems probable that he is the Richard Martin
named as a Member of the Levant Company in the Charter granted
in 1605 (see under Cranfield above). Provided Coryate with a letter
of introduction to Sir Henry Wotton, the Ambassador in Venice
(*Crudities*, vol. I, pp. 377–9). Contributed Sonnet to the *Crudities*,
p. 39 (16th). As 'Richardus Guasta-Stannum' was one of the guests
expected at the Mitre Convivium. In Letter No. 2 to Laurence
Whitaker (q.v.) Coryate writes: 'Commend me also I pray to M.
Martin, though at a man's house in Woodstreet he used mee one
night very perversely before I came away; but you see that my being
at Jerusalem dooth make me forget many injuries.' Coryate also
commends himself to Martin in Letter No. 3 to Sir Edward Phelips,
and again in Letter No. 4 to the High Seneschal of the Mermaid
Club asks to be remembered 'to Master Richard Martin, Counsellor,
at his Chamber in the Middle Temple, but in Terme-time, scarce
else'. Close friend of Christopher Brooke, Hugh Holland, John
Hoskins, Ben Jonson, and John Donne (q.v. omnes). Organized the
splendid masque in the Middle Temple on the occasion of Princess
Elizabeth's marriage, Feb. 1612–13. Elected Recorder of London
Oct. 1618, but died within the month of, according to Aubrey, 'a
symposiaque excesse with his fellow-witts'.

MOCKET, RICHARD (1577–1618). See *D.N.B.* Fellow of All Souls,
Oxford, 1599; D.D. 1609. Was for a time domestic chaplain to
George Abbot, then Bishop of London, subsequently Archbishop
of Canterbury. From March 1610 to June 1614 employed in licensing
books for entry at Stationers' Hall. Laurence Whitaker (q.v.) and
Rev. John Seward (q.v.) wrote to Mocket on Coryate's behalf
seeking a licence for the publication of the *Crudities*. Elected Warden
of All Souls 1614. In Letter No. 4 to the High Seneschal of the Mermaid Club Coryate asks to be remembered 'to Master Doctor
Mocket, resident perhaps in my Lord of Canterburies house at
Lambeth, where I left him'.

MOMFORD, THOMAS. Verses, *Crudities*, pp. 77–78 (38th). Professor Williams identifies him as Thomas Moundeford (*c.* 1550–*c.* 1630), see *D.N.B.* Physician to Queen Elizabeth and King James I. Adm. fellow of the College of Physicians 1594, and its president seven times between 1612 and 1623. His daughter married, 1606, Sir John Bramston, later Chief Justice of the King's Bench, and this marriage resulted in Moundeford having a large legal acquaintance. Momford, Momforth, Mountforth, Moundeford, are all recognized variants of the same name. A Thomas Momford, Doctor of Medicine, was admitted to the Middle Temple 8 March 1606–7, at which date Moundeford would have been in his late fifties at least. Seniority was however no bar, see James Montague below; see also *Middle Temple Register of Admissions* for 17 March 1605–6, when a father and his son were simultaneously admitted.

MONTAGUE, JAMES (1568?–1618). See *D.N.B.* First Master of Sidney Sussex College, Cambridge, 1595; as 'Bishop of Bath & Wells [from 1608 to 1616], Dean of the Chapel of the Kings Household' he was admitted student of the Middle Temple 1 Nov. 1608. Contributed verses to the *Crudities*, p. 81 (41st), under the pseudonym Τὸ Ὀρὸς-ὀξὺ = sharp mountain = mont aigu. In a postscript to Letter No. 4 to the High Seneschal of the Mermaid Club, Coryate writes: 'Pray remember my very humble dutie to my Lord Byshop of Bathe and Welles, generous M. Doctor Montacute; and tell his Lordship, that . . . I resolve (by God's permission) to write such a letter unto him (after I have throughly surveighed so much of this country as I meane to do) as shall not bee unworthy to be read to the Kings most excellent Majesty.' This letter, if written, remains untraced.

NEVILL, SIR HENRY (*c.* 1570–1641). Son of Edward, Lord Abergavenny; knighted at Cadiz 1596; succeeded as 9th Baron 1622. His verses, *Crudities*, p. 26 (2nd), which are not uncomplimentary, occupy second place in the order of precedence. As 'Nevile . . . Henricus' (an allusion to the family motto *Ne vile velis*) was one of the guests expected at the Mitre Convivium.

NORTON, JOHN (?–1612). See *Dict. P. & B.* In Letter No. 4 Coryate greets 'all the Stationers in Paules Church-yard; but especially those by name, Mast. Norton . . .' His bookshop was frequented by the chief book collectors and literary men. He himself made regular visits to the Frankfurt Fair. Master of the Stationers' Company 1607, 1611, and 1612. Coryate was evidently unaware when he wrote from India that Norton had died in the month after he sailed for Constantinople.

OWEN, JOHN (1560?–1622). See *D.N.B.* Contributed two epigrams in English and one in Latin, *Crudities*, p. 74 (35th). Educated Winchester and New College, Oxford. From about 1594 headmaster of King Henry VIII's school, Warwick. Author of eleven books of Latin epigrams, translations from which were made into English, French, German, and Spanish. His first collection of three books of epigrams were dedicated to the first wife of Henry Nevill (q.v.); his third collection published 1612 also consisted of three books, the first two dedicated to Prince Henry, and the third to Charles, Duke of York. Sir John Harrington (q.v.). and John Hoskins (q.v.) are among those to whom he addressed epigrams. In the matter of epigrams he was the rival of Ben Jonson, who described him as 'a pure pedantic schoolmaster, sweeping his living from the posteriors of little children & hath no good thing in him'. Nevertheless he was buried in St. Paul's Cathedral.

PAGE, SAMUEL (1573–1630). See *D.N.B.* His verses, *Crudities*, pp. 76–77 (37th), which are not uncomplimentary, end with

'Thou didst but shave the lands thou saws't of late,
Thy future walkes will them ex-coriate.'

Fellow of Christ Church, Oxford; served as naval chaplain; D.D. 1611. Poet and author of numerous sermons and religious tracts.

PAWLET, JOHN (*c.* 1585–1649). Son and heir of Sir Anthony Pawlet(t) or Poulet(t) of Hinton St. George, 5½ miles from Odcombe. Matric. University College, Oxford, 1601; adm. Middle Temple 1610; M.P. for Somerset 1610–11 and 1614, for Lyme Regis 1621–2. Contributed verses, *Crudities*, p. 62 (23rd). Created Baron Poulett of Hinton St. George 1627; became a distinguished royalist commander. Perhaps the same 'Mr. Pawlett' who was a Gentleman of the Privy Chamber Extraordinary in Prince Henry's Household. (*Harleian MSS.*, vol. 252, f. 8.40/89.)

PAYTON, SIR JOHN (1579–1635). See *D.N.B.* as Peyton. Verses, *Crudities*, p. 29 (6th). Son of Sir John Peyton (1544–1630) who was Governor of Jersey; knighted 1603; friend and neighbour of Sir Robert Cotton (q.v.). His MS. account of his travels in Europe in 1598–9 is in Cambridge University Library (2044 K.k., v.2).

PEACHAM, HENRY (1576?–1643?). See *D.N.B.* B.A. from Trinity College, Cambridge, Jan. 1594–5; became a schoolmaster of varied accomplishments. His first book, *Graphice, or the most auncient & excellent Art of Drawing with the Pen & Limning in Water Colours*, London, 1606, was dedicated to Sir Robert Cotton (q.v.) and passed through many editions under the new title *The Gentleman's Exercise*.

Translated King's James's *Basilicon Doron* into Latin verse, 1610, and presented it to Prince Henry. Contributed verses in Latin, English, and 'Utopian', *Crudities*, pp. 113–15 (54th). The English verses list a number of popular sights:

'Drakes ship at Detford, King Richards bed-sted i'Leyster
The White Hall whale bones, the silver Bason i'Chester'

and proclaim how much they are less worthwhile seeing than Coryate's shoes, of which he provides an illustration. Best known as the author of *The Compleat Gentleman*, 1622.

PHELPES. 'Master Phelpes and his wife' are among Coryate's Yeovil friends whom he asks his Mother to greet in Letter No. 6.

PHILLIPS, SIR EDWARD (1559?–1614). See *D.N.B.* Also spelt Phelips. Fourth and favourite son of Thomas Phelips, Coryate's godfather, from whom in 1588 he inherited Montacute, two miles from Od- combe. Adm. Middle Temple Feb. 1571–2; called to the Bar 1578; Bencher 1596; entered Parliament as knight of the shire of Somerset 1601; King's serjeant-at-law and knighted 1603; Speaker of House of Commons 1604; Chancellor to Prince Henry Dec. 1610; Master of the Rolls 1611. Coryate refers both to him and to his son Sir Robert (q.v.) as 'my Maecenas' and it is almost certainly through them that he was introduced to London and court life. Sir Edward may be *Ἀποδημουντόφιλος* (q.v.) whose verses appear first before those of all other contributors, *Crudities*, pp. 22–26. His secretary, Laurence Whitaker (q.v.), was Coryate's particular friend. In Letter No. 2 to Whitaker Coryate asks to be remembered to him. Letter No. 3 from India is addressed to him, 'at his house in Chancery Lane or Wanstead' (Wanstead House where he entertained the King, 1612), but when it was written he was already in his tomb at Montacute.

PHILLIPS, SIR ROBERT (1586?–1638). See *D.N.B.* Son of Sir Edward Phelips (q.v.). Page to Queen Elizabeth; Gentleman of the Privy Chamber Extraordinary in Prince Henry's Household; knighted 1603; M.P. for East Looe 1603–4, 1610–11, and subsequently for Saltash and Bath. Adm. Middle Temple Feb. 1605–6. Author of condescending verses, *Crudities*, pp. 30–31 (8th). As 'Robertus Equorum Amicus' was one of the guests expected at the Mitre Convivium. In Letter No. 2 to Laurence Whitaker (q.v.) Coryate asks to be remembered to him 'once my Mecaenas, but how affected to me at this time I know not'. Again, in Letter No. 3, addressed to Sir Edward Phelips, Coryate greets 'your well-beloved sonne & heire-apparant, Sir Robert (to whom I have written a few times [lines?] also) and his sweet lady'.

POOLE, SIR HENRY (*c.* 1564–after 1626). Matric. Trinity College, Oxford, Jan. 1579–80; knighted 1603; adm. Lincoln's Inn Feb. 1607–8; M.P. for various constituencies between 1604 and 1626. His verses, *Crudities*, pp. 29–30 (7th), begin with:

'Don Coryate once I saw, but his booke never,
Yet meane I to commend them both together.'

'PROTOPLAST'. 'Pray commend me to M[aster] Protoplast and all the Sirenaicall gentlemen' (Letter No. 2 from India to Laurence Whitaker). Taking 'protoplast' as meaning 'the first created of the human race' = Adam, I suggest this might possibly be the nickname of Thomas Adams (?–1620), bookseller, first at The White Lion 1591–1604, and thereafter at The Bell, both in St. Paul's Churchyard. He was adm. freeman of the Stationers' Company Oct. 1590; liveryman July 1598; junior warden 1611; warden 1614 and 1617. In 1611 he acquired the copyrights of his late master, which included shares in Hakluyt's *Voyages*, Camden's *Britannia*, Holinshed's and Stow's *Chronicles*, and many Greek and Latin classics. See *Dict. P. & B.* and *D.N.B.*

PURCHAS, SAMUEL (1575?–1626). See *D.N.B.* Graduated from St. John's College, Cambridge; took holy orders; curate at Purleigh, Essex; vicar of Eastwood, Essex, 1604–13. Coryate made his acquaintance before leaving England in 1612, by which time Purchas was already working on his collections of travels (*Purchas his Pilgrimage*, the first of three works, was published 1613) made up partly from MS. accounts which he inherited from Hakluyt and partly from travellers' journals which he himself collected. The fact that so little remains of Coryate's Middle East descriptions is due to Purchas's injudicious editing, but he cannot be blamed for the disappearance of Coryate's notes on Persia and India, whose loss he regrets. In Letter No. 4 Coryate asks to be remembered 'to M. Samuel Purkas, the great collector of the Lucubrations of sundry classical authors, for the description of Asia, Africa, and America'. The letter was addressed to the High Seneschal of the Mermaid Club. Purchas states in a side-note that Mr. Rogers, the chaplain who carried it from India, delivered it to him, which suggests that at that time Purchas himself may possibly have been the High Seneschal.

QUIN, WALTER (1575?–1634?). See *D.N.B.* Born in Dublin; travelled abroad and became learned in French, Italian, and Latin. Settled in Edinburgh before 1595, in which year he was presented to James VI, who appointed him tutor to Prince Henry before 1600; came to England with James, 1603. Employed as teacher of music in Prince Henry's household at a salary of £50 p.a. (*Harleian MSS.*, vol. 252,

f. 9.40/90). Contributed verses in Italian, *Crudities*, pp. 54–56 (20th). After Prince Henry's death in 1612 he became tutor to Prince Charles, later Charles I.

RICH, WILLIAM. Contributed verses, *Crambe*, Sig. b4 verso, where he is described as 'of the Middle Temple'. A William Riche of New Inn, gent., was adm. to Middle Temple 1 May 1605.

RICHMOND, ROBERT. As 'Robertus Riccomontanus' contributed ninety-eight lines of verse, *Crudities*, pp. 50–54 (19th), which indicated that he was conversant with the MS. and with Coryate's future plans. May be the author of verses signed R.R. preceding and following Coryate's letters from India in the 1616 pamphlet *Thomas Coriate, Traveller for the English Wits: Greeting.*

SALMON, JOHN. Coryate's stepfather, whom his Mother married in 1608. In the list of friends whom Coryate asks his Mother to greet (Letter No. 6 from India) he adds 'I had almost forgotten your husband'. Coryate does not mention Salmon by name.

SCORY, JOHN. Contributed scornful verses, *Crudities*, p. 36 (14th). Son and heir of Silvan Scory of Wormesley, Herefordshire, and grandson of John Scory, Bishop of Hereford, see *Alum. Cantab.*, which records his admission at Queens' College, Nov. 1592.

SELLY, JOHN. An Odcombe friend greeted in Letter No. 6.

SEWARD, REV. JOHN. Of Yeovil; wrote to Dr. Mocket (q.v.) on Coryate's behalf requesting a licence to publish the *Crudities*, see *Crudities*, vol. 1, p. 149. In Letter No. 6 to his Mother Coryate asks to be commended, first among various Yeovil friends, to 'old Mr. Seward, if he liveth, his wife and children'.

SMITH, NICHOLAS. Author of verses, *Crudities*, p. 98 (48th). Two identifications are possible: (1) Son and heir of Sir George Smith of Exeter; matric. Exeter College, Oxford, Nov. 1590; B.A. June 1594; adm. Lincoln's Inn May 1595; perhaps knighted July 1603. See *Alum. Oxon.* and *Lincoln's Inn Register of Admissions*, also H. J. C. Grierson's edition of *Donne's Poetical Works*, 1912, vol. II, p. 263, n. (2) Son and heir of Nicholas Smith of Theddlethorpe, Lincs.; adm. Gray's Inn March 1605–6; married Mary, daughter of Sir Richard Pell of Dembleby, and may be he who matric. pensioner from Clare College, Cambridge, Easter 1604, see *Alum. Cantab.*

SPEAKE, GEORGE (1591 ?–after 1650). Greeted in Letter No. 4; son and heir of Sir George Speake, who lived at White-Lackington, eight miles from Odcombe. After leaving Magdalen College, Oxford, was adm. Middle Temple Jan. 1610–11.

STANSBY, WILLIAM (?–1639?). See *Dict. P. & B.* In Letter No. 4 Coryate asks to be remembered 'to M. William Stansby, the Printer of my *Crudities* and *Crambe*, at his house in Thames Street: also to his childlesse wife'. He was a bookseller as well as a printer and a man of position in the trade, though he never held any office in the Stationers' Company.

STARRE, ? JOSEPH. 'Master Starre and his wife' are among Coryate's Yeovil friends whom he greets in Letter No. 6. Master Starre may be Joseph Starre, with whom Coryate had a lawsuit in 1608–9, see pp. 118–20 above.

STRANGWAYES, SIR JOHN (1585?–1665). His verses, *Crudities*, pp. 34–35 (12th), make it clear that they were written at Coryate's request. Lived at Melbury, Dorset, 7 miles from Odcombe; matric. Queen's College, Oxford, Oct. 1601; knighted some time prior to admission to Middle Temple, Jan. 1610–11. Between 1614 and 1665 was M.P. for various Dorset constituencies.

SUTCLIN, JOHN (1569–1627). See *D.N.B.* as Suckling, Sir John. Donne called him Sutclin, see Gosse, *Life & Letters of John Donne*, vol. II, p. 149. Contributed verses, *Crudities*, p. 64 (25th). Entered Gray's Inn, May 1590; married Martha Cranfield, sister of Lionel Cranfield (q.v.), by whom he had a son John, the poet. M.P. for Dunwich, 1601, and subsequently for other constituencies. Secretary to Lord Treasurer Cecil 1602; knighted Jan. 1615–16.

SYDENHAM, GEORGE (1589?–1615). Son and heir of Sir John Sydenham, of Brympton, one mile from Odcombe. Mentioned, *Crudities*, vol. II, p. 101, as 'a kinde friend' and lender of a book, though his verses, *Crudities*, pp. 65–67 (27th), are not particularly friendly. Matric. Queen's College, Oxford, July 1606; adm. Middle Temple 1609.

T———, N———. Contributed three sets of verses to the *Crudities*, one in Latin, which arrived too late and were printed in the *Crambe*, Sig. first A4, under the signature N.T. I suggest he may possibly be Sir Nicholas Tufton (1577?–1631); matric. Hart Hall, Oxford, Oct. 1591; adm. Lincoln's Inn Feb. 1595–6; M.P. for Peterborough 1601, and for Kent 1624–5; knighted Apl. 1603; created Baron Tufton Nov. 1626—an honour involving a financial transaction with the King; created 1st Earl of Thanet Aug. 1628. See *Alum. Oxon.*, *Complete Peerage*.

Tὸ 'Oρὸς-ὀξὺ = 'sharp mountain'. Contributed verses, *Crudities*, p. 81 (41st). He is almost certainly James Montague (q.v.); a much less likely identification is Edward Sharphell, obscure friend of John Davis (q.v.). The latter suggestion, made by Mr. John Crow of

King's College, London, is mentioned by Professor Williams, *P.M.L.A.*, vol. LXIX, 1954, p. 319.

TOURVAL. See Loiseau de Tourval, Jean.

VADIANUS, GLAREANUS. Author of several sets of verses in Latin, English, French, Italian, and Spanish, including some excellent nonsense, contributed in two batches, the second so late that it had to be printed with the supplemental verses, *Crudities*, pp. 86–95 (45th) and 116–19. Glareanus was used by writers from the Swiss canton of Glarus, and one of them, Joachim de Watt (1484–1551), styled himself Vadianus (see Didot, *Nouvelle Biographie Universelle*). Professor Williams, in *P.M.L.A.*, vol. LXIX, 1954, p. 322, considers the author to be English and suggests that the signature may be an anagram. He states that attempted solutions such as Dewes, Wade, Ford, Walker, and Watt have proved fruitless. Dr. Hotson tells me that he considers it to be a latinization of San(d)ford (glarea = gravel or sand, vadum = ford) and suggests John Sanford, the witty chaplain who appears in *Downshire (Trumbull) MSS*.

VARNEY, LADY MARY AND LADY URSULA. In a postscript to Letter No. 4 to the High Seneschal of the Mermaid Club Coryate sends greetings to 'all those whose names I have heere expressed, being the lovers of Vertue, and Literature . . . Imprimis, to the two Ladies Varney, the Mother and the Daughter, at Boswell House without Temple-barre.'

The Mother was Mary, née Blakeney (1547?–1642), third wife of Sir Edmund Verney (d. 1599, see *D.N.B.*). Coryate's acquaintance with her and her daughter probably arose through her son Edmund (1590–1642, see *D.N.B.*), who in 1610 was taken into Prince Henry's household as Chief Sewer. She died aged ninety-five, a fortnight after Edmund, then the King's Standard-bearer, had been killed at Edgehill.

The daughter was Ursula, née St. Barbe (1586?–1668), the child of Mary Blakeney's second marriage. She was married aged twelve, with Sir Edmund Verney's consent, to his son Francis (1584–1615, see *D.N.B.*), then aged fourteen. When Francis came of age he brought an action against his stepmother regarding his inheritance, which resulted in an unsatisfactory compromise, whereupon in 1606 he sold his estates, deserted his wife, and went abroad. Eventually he became a buccaneer in the Mediterranean and died at Messina September 1615.

During the period when Coryate probably knew them, 1608–12, Ursula and her mother lived in Drury Lane. See *The Verney Memoirs*, by F. P. and M. M. Verney, 3rd edn., 1925. The first edn.,

1892, vol. II, p. 93, reproduces Mary Verney's portrait at Claydon with a facsimile of her signature, 'Mary Varney'.

WASHBORNE, ANTONY (1573?–?). Contributed verses to *Crambe*, Sig. b4. Second son of John Washborne of Wichenford, Worcs. Matric. St. Mary Hall, Oxford, Aug. 1593; adm. Middle Temple June 1597; called to the Bar Feb. 1603–4.

WATERSON, SIMON (?–1634). See *Dict. P. & B.* 'Mast. Waterson' is among those singled out by name in the greeting 'to all the Stationers in Paules Church-yard', Letter No. 4 from India. His publications included many of Samuel Daniel's works and the *Epigrams* of John Owen (q.v.).

WEST, JOHN (?–1638). As 'Johannes Occidens' was one of the guests expected at the Mitre Convivium. Matric. pensioner from Christ's College, Cambridge, 1598–9; adm. Middle Temple June 1597; of the King's Privy Chamber and a Deputy Remembrancer of the Exchequer, see *Alum. Cantab.* and *Sackville Papers*, vol. I, *Cranfield Papers*, p. 271.

WHITAKER, LAURENCE (1578?–1654). One of Coryate's closest friends; born in Somerset; matric. sizar St. John's College, Cambridge, *c.* 1593; B.A. 1596–7; M.A. 1600. Secretary to Sir Edward Phelips (q.v.). Was responsible with Lionel Cranfield (q.v.) for persuading Coryate to publish the *Crudities*, to which he contributed an explanation of the illustrated frontispiece in rhyming couplets, pp. xv–xix, verses in Greek, Latin, English, and French, pp. 41–43 (17th), and a prose eulogy, p. 149. He also contributed verses to the *Crambe*, Sig. b2. Adm. Middle Temple, 24 March 1613–14. Letter No. 2 from India is addressed to him. In Letter No. 4 to the High Seneschal of the Mermaid Club Coryate makes it clear that Whitaker himself at one time occupied that post. Became one of the clerks of the Privy Council; M.P. for Peterborough 1624–9, and Okehampton, 1641–3.

WILLIAMS, JOHN (*c.* 1572–1636). The King's Goldsmith. Greeted in Letters No. 2 and No. 4. He was 'the sonne of William ap John of Dolowthelane [? Dolwyddelan] in the county of Carnavon, Jentellman' (*Goldsmiths' Company Apprenticeship Book I*, 1584, p. 55); received freedom of the Company by service 7 Sept. 1593; assumed duties of King's Goldsmith, 1603. (P.R.O. Chanc. Misc. 3/41 and P.R.O. Index 6801, March 1603–4 (Docquets)). Charged, 1617, with having supplied the King and the Dean of Westminster with plate made of metal below standard; vindicated 1632. Prime Warden of the Goldsmiths' Company 1620. See Sir Ambrose Heal, *The*

*London Goldsmiths, 1200–1800;* for the P.R.O. references I am indebted to Maj.-Gen. H. D. W. Sitwell, Keeper of the Jewel House, who informs me that though as King's Goldsmith he had the virtual monopoly of supplying the Royal Household with plate, he was allowed only 6*d*. per oz. for fashion, so if he did debase the standard he could hardly be blamed for it.

WILLIAMS, CORYATE'S UNCLE. It seems clear that Coryate's Uncle Williams and John Williams, the King's Goldsmith (q.v.), are two distinct persons. Coryate asks Laurence Whitaker to read Letter No. 2 to John Williams; in the same letter he asks Whitaker 'to conveigh these twoe letters that I have sent to you, to the parties to whom they are directed: my poore mother and mine unckle Williams. You may do me a kind office to desire him . . . to remember me as his poore industrious peregrinating kinsman, neerest unto him in blood of all the people in the world [John Williams was married and had a son]; to remember me, I say, with some competent gratuitie if God should call him out of the world before my returne . . . [implying that he was already an old man, whereas John Williams was still in his early forties]. I praie you if hee be living, and doth use to come to London as he was wont to doo [John Williams lived permanently in London], that you would deliver my letter with your owne hands, and not send it unto him.' In Letter No. 6 to his Mother Coryate writes: 'I have written two letters to my Uncle Williams since I came forth of England, and no more; whereof one from the Mogol's court the last yeere [i.e. the letter he asked Whitaker to forward] and another now.' Both these letters have disappeared.

YAXLEY, SIR ROBERT (?–1628). Courtier; contributed verses, *Crudities*, p. 34 (11th). Second son of William Yaxley of Boston, Lincs.; knighted at Dublin, Sept. 1599; a Gentleman of the Privy Chamber Extraordinary in Prince Henry's Household; adm. Lincoln's Inn, March 1613–14. See *Lincolnshire Pedigrees*, ed. A. R. Maddison, London, 1904, vol. III, p. 1124, also *Lincoln's Inn Admission Register*, London, 1896, p. 165, and Birch, *op. cit.*

# Bibliographical Notes

## A List of Coryate's Known Extant Writings

THE DATES PRECEDING EACH ITEM INDICATE THE DATE OF COMPOSITION

1. 1608–10 *CORYATS/CRUDITIES/Hastily gobled up in five/ Moneths travells in France,/Savoy, Italy, Rhetia commonly/called the Grisons country, Hel/vetia alias Switzerland, some/parts of high Germany, and the/Netherlands:/Newly digested in the hungry aire/of Odcombe in the County of/Somerset, & now dispersed to the/nourishment of the travelling Mem/bers of this Kingdome./*

Printed by W. S. [William Stansby], London, 1611. 4to. Among various inaccuracies in Dr. Jessopp's article on Coryate in *D.N.B.* is the statement: 'perhaps of no book in the English language of the same size and of the same age is it possible to say that there are not two perfect copies in existence'—that in the Chetham Library being said to be the only perfect copy. According to Prof. Wm. A. Jackson, *The Carl H. Pforzheimer Library*, New York, 1940, p. 217, perfect copies with the plates intact are not common, but he has examined four copies in original binding, either calf or vellum, all immaculate, and has heard of several others. Prof. Jackson informed me in Sept. 1959 that he had located some forty copies in all, including a particularly large one, 8¾ in. × 6½ in. bound with the arms of James I, owned by Mr. Arthur Amory Houghton, Jr., formerly owned by Mr. F. B. Bemis. This is presumably King James's presentation copy. Prince Henry's presentation copy is in the B.M. The Folger Library has a copy bound in vellum with the Prince of Wales's feathers on it, which is probably the copy presented by Coryate to Prince Charles. The copy which Coryate presented to the Bodleian (listed as 4to C94 in the 1635 Appendix to the Bodleian catalogue) was displaced by John Selden's copy in 1654 or soon after, it being the then general rule for the Selden copy to displace the copy of a work already in the library, even if the book turned out was a direct present from an individual, or was bought with a benefaction of money. The Sir Lewis Sterling copy in London University is a very fine copy. The copy which belonged to Thomas, 1st Baron Fairfax (1560–1640) is in the London Museum; on the blank leaf following the Panegyricke Verses, Sig. l.4 verso, Fairfax has written his own unpublished contribution: eighteen lines of scurrilous verse with his signature.

2. 1606–11 *CORYATS/CRAMBE,/OR/HIS COLWORT/TWISE SODDEN, AND/Now served in with other/Macaronicke dishes, as the/second course to his/Crudities.*/LONDON/*Printed by* William Stansby/ 1611. 4to.

Many copies lack the extra leaf following Sig. b4, bearing the commendatory verses by Hugh Holland.

3. 1610 LETTER No. 1. Dated 15 Nov. 1610. 'From my chamber in Bowe-Lane' to Sir Michael Hicks, Secretary to Lord Treasurer Salisbury.

The original letter, the only known example of Coryate's handwriting and signature, is inserted into the back of Prince Henry's presentation copy of the *Crudities* in B.M. This letter is referred to by Thomas Birch in his *Life of Prince Henry*, 1760, p. 216, but the text remained unpublished until 1789, see below.

4. 1613–14 *Master Thomas Coryates travels to, and Observations in Constantinople, and other places in the way thither, and his Journey thence to Aleppo Damasco and Jerusalem.*

This is Samuel Purchas's drastically edited version of Coryate's diary and notes which he left at Aleppo before setting out for India in Sept. 1614. It was first published in *Purchas his Pilgrimes*, Pt. II, 1625, fol. (Book X, chap. 12, pp. 1811–31). The original diary and notes have disappeared.

5. 1615 LETTER No. 2. Dated Michaelmas Day (29 Sept.) 1615. 'From the court of the Great Mogul, resident at the towne of Asmere . . .' to 'Most deare and beloved Friend, Maister L[aurence] W[hitaker], animae dimidium meae' from 'Your assured loving friend till death, THO. CORYATE'.

6. 1615 LETTER No. 3. Dated Michaelmas Day (29 Sept.) 1615. 'From the court of the Great Mogul, resident in the towne of Asmere . . .' to 'The Right Honourable Sir Edward Phillips, Knight, and Maister of the Rolles, at his house in Chancery-Lane, or Wanstead' from 'Your Honors most obsequious beadsman Thomas Coryate'.

7. 1615 LETTER No. 4. The postscript is dated 8 Nov. 1615. The Letter is 'From the court of the Great Mogul, resident at the towne of Asmere . . .' to 'the High Seneschall of the Right Worshipfull Fraternitie of Sirenaical Gentlemen, that meet the first Fridaie of every month at the signe of the Mere-Maide in Bread-streete in London, give these'. Coryate signs himself:

'Your Generosities most obliged countreyman, ever to be commanded by you, the Hierosolymitan-Syrian-Mesopotamian-
Armenian-Median-Parthian-Persian-Indian Leggestretcher of Od-
comb in Somerset, Thomas Coryate'.

8. 1615 LETTER No. 5. Undated and drastically cut, but clearly
written and dispatched at the same time as Nos. 2, 3, and 4,
'To his Loving Mother' from 'Your loving sonne THO. COR-
YATE'.

Letters 2, 3, 4, and 5 were printed in 1616 soon after their arrival
in England in a pamphlet entitled *Thomas Coriate, Traveller for
the English Wits: Greeting. From the Court of the Great Mogul.* S.T.C.
No. 5811. There are twenty-two lines of prefatory verses purport-
ing to be spoken by Coryate but clearly, from their satirical content, not composed by him. The pamphlet is illustrated with four
woodcuts, the only one of interest being that of Coryate riding on
an elephant, which appears on the title page and is twice repeated
later. At the end of the pamphlet are ninety-six lines of verse
addressed 'To his loving Friend, Thomas Coryate', and signed
'R.R.' These initials may stand either for Robert Richmond, who as
'Robertus Riccomontanus' contributed extensive verses to the
*Crudities* (see p. 138 above), or for Robert Rugge, who dubbed
Coryate a Knight of Troy (see p. 169 above). The pamphlet was
not entered in the Stationers' Company Register. It is interesting to
note that it was printed by W. Jaggard and Henry Fetherston—
not by any of the printers and booksellers to whom Coryate
specifically wished to be remembered in his letters. There seems
to be no doubt that it had a very considerable success. Another
issue with altered title, *Thomas Coriate, travailer for the English
wits, and the good of this kingdom* (S.T.C. No. 5812), was issued in the
same year, 1616, indicating that one issue was quickly sold out.
S.T.C. No. 5812 seems to be very rare indeed; S.T.C. lists only
the copy owned by the late Captain William Jaggard.

A further indication of the pamphlet's popularity are the
allusions in plays of the period. In Fletcher's *Queen of Corinth*,
first produced some time before March 1618–19, Neanthes ex-
claims, 'on my conscience this is the Ulissean Traveller that sent
home his Image riding upon Elephants to the great Mogul'
(Act III, Sc. 1). In Nabbes' *The Bride*, 1638, Horten says, 'This
stone of a strange form and colour was brought by the learned
traveller of Odcombe from the Great Mogull' (Act V, Sc. 7).
Another allusion to Coryate in Act II, Sc. 1 of *The Ball*, by James
Shirley, printed in 1639, indicates that his travels nearer home were
not forgotten. Freshwater says he has sold his estate and wagered

it at five to one against his return from Venice; he contemplates repeating this for seven years, by which time he will be able to buy Constantinople and give it to the Emperor. Barker suggests that if he should purchase Jerusalem and bring it nearer, the Christian pilgrims would be much obliged, and adds 'You remember Coriate', to which Freshwater replies 'Honest Tom Odcombe'. In Act I, Sc. 4 of William Cartwright's *The Ordinary*, published in 1651 but written and acted some years earlier, Coryate, William Lithgow, and Sir John Mandevile are bracketed together as intrepid travellers.

9. 1616 LETTER No. 6. Dated 31 Oct. 1616. 'From Agra, the capitall city of the dominion of the Great Mogoll, in the Easterne India.' To his mother.

Somehow John Taylor obtained possession of this letter or a copy of it. It was published as a pamphlet in 1618 entitled *Mr. Thomas Coriat to his Friends in England sendeth Greeting: from Agra* (S.T.C. No. 5809), with satirical verses by J.T. (i.e. John Taylor) and a woodcut of Coryate riding a camel. It was entered to 'Master Beale' in the Stationers' Company Register on 2 Oct. 1617 under the title *A Letter from Thomas Coryate to his Mother*, and printed by I.B. (John Beale).

10. 1615–17 NOTES MADE IN INDIA. These few fragments are all that survive of the mass of notes made in India, and on the way thither from Aleppo. 'Great pitie it is', writes Purchas, *Pilgrimes*, 1625, Pt. I, p. 597, 'that his voluminous Observations of his foot Pilgrimage, longer then perhaps of any man ever hath bin in that kind, are either lost, or at least not come to some discreet hand, which might, no doubt, distill good instructions thence for the publike, as sweet fresh water out of the huge salt Ocean. Some written Notes of his, it pleased Sir Thomas Roe to give me, whence (omitting such things as before you have had in Sir Thomas Roes owne Observations) I have inserted a few . . .' They appear on pp. 600–2 of the *Pilgrimes*, 1625, Pt. I, Bk. 4, chap. 17.

## A Chronological List of Subsequent Editions
## of Coryate's Writings

1625 Purchas, *Pilgrimes*, Pt. I, Bk. 4, chap. 17, reprinted large portions of Letters No. 2, 3, and 6.

1630 Letter No. 6 with its prefatory verses was included in *All the Workes of John Taylor the Water-Poet*, 1630, fol., thereby conclusively identifying Taylor as the author of the verses.

1707 *De reys van Thomas Coryat na Asmere, zijnde de Hof-stad van den Grooten Mogol in't jaar 1615* in *Naaukeurige Versameling der gedenkwaardigste zee en land-reysen na oost en west-indien,* Leyden, 1707. 8vo.

A translation of the selections contained in *Purchas his Pilgrimes,* Pt. I (i.e. large parts of *Letters No. 2, 3, and 6* and the *Notes made in India*).

1727 The same text as *De reys van Thomas Coryat* . . . in another edition entitled *De wijd-beroemde voyagien na oost en west-indien,* collected by J. L. Gottfried, Leyden, 1727, fol.

1776 *CORYAT'S CRUDITIES; reprinted from the Edition of 1611. To which are now added His Letters from India, &c. and extracts relating to him, from various authors: being A more particular Account of his Travels (mostly on Foot) in different Parts of the Globe, than any hitherto published. Together with his Orations, Character, Death, &c.* 3 vol. W. Cater, Samuel Hayes, J. Wilkie: London; E. Easton: Salisbury, 1776. 8vo.

[Another issue] W. Cater, J. Wilkie: London; E. Easton: Salisbury, 1776. 8vo.

The price of the three volumes in boards was fifteen shillings (see advertisement at end of Appendix dated 1777 in the B.M. copy of *Antiquitates Sarisburienses,* 1771). Some large paper copies of this edition were issued. Besides the *Crudities* in full (except for the author's interesting note on the errata at Sig. Eee3), including *Posthuma fragmenta poematum Georgii Coryate,* there are reprinted in vol. III:

(*a*) *Thomas Coriate, Traveller for the English Wits,* London, 1616. Sig. K2.

(*b*) *Coryat's Crambe,* 1611, excluding the prefatory verses and excluding *To the Reader,* Sig. H to H3. Sig. N.

(*c*) All the material used by Samuel Purchas from *Pilgrimes,* Pt. I, Bk. 4, chap. 17, and Pt. II, Bk. 10, chap. 12. Sig. Q.

(*d*) Most of John Taylor's works relating to Coryate. Sig. Y6.

(*e*) Extract relating to Coryate from the 1655 edn. of Rev. Edward Terry's *A Voyage to East India.* Sig. Dd7.

In a preface the publishers write: 'The Fame of this "Odcombian Legstretcher", and the favourable Reception his Book has always met with, rendered it so very scarce and valuable, that it was thought adviseable to reprint it, with all the original Copper-Plates . . . As all the different Publications concerning Coryat, are very rarely (if at all) possessed by one Person, it was imagined, that if every Thing material relating to him were extracted from the different Authors, and subjoined to his Crudities, it would be

a very acceptable Present to the Public.—This is done in the present
book, in which nothing of Consequence, that could be procured
is omitted.'

The immediate cause of a revival of interest in Coryate was
probably the appearance in 1767 of a book by Samuel Paterson
(1728–1802, see *D.N.B.*), written under the pseudonym Coriat
Junior. This book, entitled *Another Traveller! or Cursory Remarks
and Tritical Observations made upon a Journey through Part of the
Netherlands in the latter End of the Year 1766*, was well received.
The notice in the *Monthly Review*, vol. 39, July–December 1768, p.
434, reads: 'Coriat *Junior*! Our Readers will exclaim, pray who was
Coriat Senior? why, truly, he was so odd a character, that our
Author's owning him for a relation, gives us a favourable opinion
of his modesty and humility. Tom was really a droll genius, a great
traveller, and published his *Crudities*, as he facetiously styled his
works, with the good natured view of making his Readers as
merry as he was himself. His wit and pleasantry however, were of
the lower rates, bordering a little on buffoonery, or so; but he was
nevertheless often very diverting, and would make you laugh . . .'
The reviewer goes on to quote from Paterson's chap. 13 (vol.
I, p. 112), which is entitled '*Somewhat about Tom Coriat: and of the
Advantage of talking Latin*': I am but a poor scholar, God
help me!—my old namesake, honest Tom Coriat, was a very great
one—honest Tom! who was certainly a wiser man than the world
thought him; and a better than many of those that laughed at
him . . . Tom possest one part of Falstaffe's character in a very
eminent degree; and if he was not over-witty himself, he was the
true cause *that wit was in other men* (see the verses, some of which
are incomparably humorous, prefixed to his Crudities . . .) . . .
Poor Tom! as many of us know, lived about a hundred and fifty
years since—when, or where, or in what manner he died, nobody
can tell with any certainty.'

Not even Dr. Johnson (godfather to 'Coriat Junior's' son)
knew the answer—though he thought he did. When Paterson's
book came up in discussion in April 1772 he announced firmly
to Boswell that Coryate had died at Mandu. 'Tom Coriat, (said
he) was a humourist about the Court of James the First. He had a
mixture of learning, of wit and of buffoonery. He first travelled
through Europe, and published his travels. He afterwards travelled on foot through Asia, and had many remarks; but he died at
Mandoa and his remarks were lost.' (See Boswell's *Life of Johnson*,
ed. G. B. Hill, revised by L. F. Powell, Oxford, 1934, vol. II,
pp. 176–7.)

1789 LETTER No. 1, printed for the first time in the article on Coryate in 2nd edition of *Biographia Britannica*, vol. IV, which appeared in 1789. Coryate did not appear in the 1st edition of 1747–76. The article in the 2nd edition by 'R' (? Abraham Rees 1743–1825, see *D.N.B.*) is the fullest and most accurate account of his life that has hitherto appeared.

1798 *Thomas Coriat's/Cruditäten,/oder/Beschreibung seiner Reise durch Frank=/reich, Italien, die Schweiz, Deutschland/und die Niederlande. Nebst Nachrichten von seinem Aufenthalt/in Ostindien./* . . . Erster Theil [First Part] . . . Berlin, 1798.

A translation, with many passages omitted, of the *Crudities*, vol. I, pp. 152–376. The name of the translator, Matthias Christian Sprengel (1746–1803, see *Allgemeine Deutsche Biographie*, vol. XXXV, pp. 299–300) does not appear in the book, but that of the publisher, W. Öhmigke, Jun., does. Sprengel was clearly inspired by, and worked from, the 1776 edition of the *Crudities* since he gives a translation of the publishers' introduction to that edition. The title indicates that he intended to publish subsequent parts, but there is no evidence that these ever appeared.

It is a rare book. One copy exists in the Universitäts-Bibliothek, Marburg, and another in the Universitäts-und-Staatsbibliothek, Cologne.

1808 LETTER No. 1 TO SIR MICHAEL HICKS, reprinted in Sir Samuel Egerton Brydges's *Censura Literaria*, London, 1808, vol. VIII, pp. 73–77, together with a covering letter from Robert Triphook, bookseller of Bond Street, London, in whose possession the letter then was. Triphook believed that it had never before been printed and 'considering the very singular and extraordinary character of the writer' presumed it might 'be sufficiently curious to lay before the readers of the *Censura*'.

?1810 *Thomas Coriate Traveller for the English Wits: Greeting.* A type facsimile of the 1616 pamphlet with title and spelling as in S.T.C. No. 5811, except that the imprint reads 'Featherston', not Fetherston. The woodcuts have been recut and are very inferior to the originals. According to a note in the copy which was in the Wilmerding collection, this reprint was made by Woodman & Lyon in Russel Street, Covent Garden in 1725. However, the British Museum catalogue gives the date of publication as ?1810 on the grounds that the watermark and ornaments point to that date approximately. A number of such type facsimiles were produced at the beginning of the nineteenth century.

1880  R. de Lasteyrie, *Voyage à Paris de Th. Coryate* (*Mémoires de la Société de l' Histoire de Paris et de l'Ile de France*, Paris, 1880, vol. VI, p. 28 et seq.). A carefully annotated translation of pp. 167–95 (1905 edn.) of the *Crudities*, vol. I. See p. 19, n above.

1880  A. de Montaiglon, *Un Voyageur Anglais à Lyon sous Henri IV.* (*Collection des Opuscules Lyonnais No.* 2), Lyon, 1880. A translation, with interesting notes, of pp. 201–15 (1905 edn.) of the *Crudities*, vol. I. De Montaiglon admits that he owes his acquaintance with Coryate to his friend de Lasteyrie.

1905  *Coryat's Crudities Hastily gobled up in five Moneths travells etc.* [With *Posthuma fragmenta poematum Georgii Coryate*], 2 vols., James MacLehose & Sons, Glasgow, 1905. 8vo. A reprint of the 1611 edition excluding the author's note on the errata at Sig. Eee3, and without any of the additional material included in the 1776 edition. The same publishers reprinted Purchas, Moryson, and other books of early travels.

1921  Sir William Foster, *Early Travels in India*, Oxford, 1921, reprints *Letters No. 2, 3, 4, 5, and 6* using the texts of the 1616 and 1618 pamphlets, (but excluding the verses, all but one of the illustrations, and some of the greetings to individuals) together with *Notes made in India* from Purchas, and Edward Terry's *Account of Coryate* from the 1655 edition of the *Voyage to East India*, p. 57 et seq. There is an excellent short preface on Coryate, and the texts are admirably annotated.

## Works Attributed to Coryate

1. VERSES IN SOMERSET DIALECT ON THE FOUNDATION OF BATH.

Henry Chapman in a pamphlet, *Thermae Redivivae: or the City of Bath described*, London, 1673, pp. 16–17, makes the unsupported statement that Coryate 'Having read much of Jeoffrey Monmouth (the single Author that Bladud found out these Waters and Bath, the City), especially in that which had reference to what was concerned in the Great Table hung up against the Wall in the King's Bath, dedicating it to old Jeoffrey's Ghost, he bolts out in this Poetical Rapture:

'Ludhudibras a Meazel Voule, did zend his zun a graezing,
Who Vortuend hither vor to cum, and geed his Pigs sum peazun;
Poor Bladud he was Manger grown, his Dad, which Zum call Vaether,
Zet Bladud Pig, and Pig Bladud, and so they ved together,
Then Bladud did the Pigs invect, who, grunting ran away,
And vound whot waters prezently, which made um vresh and gay.

Bladud was not so grote a Vool, zeeing what Pig nid doe,
He beath'd and wash'd, and rins'd and beath'd, from Noddle
   down to toe
Bladud was now (Gramercy Pig) a delicate Vine boy,
So whome he trudges to his Dad, to be his only Joy.
And then he bilt this gawdy Town, and sheer'd his beard Spade-
   wayes,
Which Voke accounted then a Grace, though not so, now a days.
Two Thowsand and vive hundred Years, and thirty vive to that,
Zince Bladud's zwine did looze their Greaze, which we Moderns
   cal Vat.
About that time, it was alzo, that Ahob's zuns were hanged,
And Jezabel, their Mam, (curz'd deel) caus'd Naboth be Stone
   banged.
Chee cud zay more, but cham A veard, Voke will account this
   Vable,
O Invidles! if yee woon not me, yet chee pray believe the Table.
        Miscenter Saeria Nugis.'

If Coryate wrote these verses they would almost certainly have been composed before he left England for the last time in 1612. The author states that they were written 2,535 years after Bladud and his pigs fell ill and were cured by the Bath waters. The problem therefore is to determine what the author took to be the date of this incident.

The earliest extant version of the legend attributing Bath's foundation to Bladud, son of Hudibras and father of King Lear, occurs in Geoffrey of Monmouth's *Historia Regum Britanniae* written about the middle of the twelfth century. In the matter of dates Geoffrey gives no nearer indication than that Bladud became King 1,415 years after the flood (see John Jay Parry, *Brut y Brenhinedd*, Cambridge, Mass., 1937, p. 33).

In any case Geoffrey says nothing about Bladud being cured by the waters, so the author must have been using one of the many later embroideries of the story. Holinshed states that Bladud 'began to rule . . . in the yeare of the world 3085', which he equates with 882 B.C. (see *Chronicles*, London, 1807 edn., vol. I, p. 446). As the founding of Bath is supposed to have taken place shortly before Bladud's accession this would make the date of the verses shortly before 1653.

Chapman, it will be noted, states that the author had in mind 'what was concerned in the Great Table hung up against the Wall in the Kings Bath'. This 'Great Table' is not mentioned in John Leland's *Itinerary*, nor in William Camden's *Britannia*, nor in any of the several seventeenth-century descriptions of Bath which I have consulted. In 1699, however, a statue of King Bladud was erected in the King's Bath with an inscription stating that Bladud discovered and founded the baths in 863 B.C. It seems probable that the date 863 B.C. was copied from the 'Great Table' for which the inscription beneath the statue was substituted. On this basis the verses were written in 1672, fifty-five years after Coryate's death, and the year before Chapman's pamphlet was published. This suggests that Chapman himself may have been the author, and that he attributed the verses to Coryate as a joke.

2. *The/Odcombian/Banquet:/Dished foorth/by/Thomas the Coriat,/and/ Served in by a number of Noble Wits/in prayse of his/CRUDITIES and CRAMBE too./Asinus portans mysteria/Imprinted for Thomas Thorp/ 1611.*

This pamphlet consists of an Anagram and couplet; Laurence Whitaker's prose eulogy of the *Crudities*; Ben Jonson's Character of the Author; all the panegyric verses which appear in the *Crudities* except the Greek anagram by Farnaby at Sig. g4; and a final page headed NOVERINT UNIVERSI explaining in an insulting manner why the text of the *Crudities* is omitted.

It is frequently listed as one of Coryate's works whereas in fact he had nothing to do with its publication. The circumstances of its appearance are described on pp. 134–7 above.

3. CONVIVIUM PHILOSOPHICUM AT THE MITRE TAVERN—A COMIC LATIN POEM

There are several manuscripts of this poem:

(*a*) In P.R.O. among John Chamberlain's papers, S.P. 14/66/2. This MS. states that the author is Dominus Radulphus Colphabius, and is endorsed on the reverse side 'Latin Rimes of Tom Corriat'.

(*b*) In the Library of Lincoln College, Oxford, in an old commonplace book, folio 185ᵛ, Radulphus Colphabius is again shown as the author. This MS. was printed by Andrew Clark in the notes of his edition of *Aubrey's Brief Lives*, Oxford, 1898, vol. II, pp. 50–53, side by side with a contemporary English version lent to him by the late Falconer Madan and ascribed to John Reynolds.

(*c*) Clark states, *op. cit.*, vol. I, pp. 50 and 53, that the same Latin poem in an old copy owned by Falconer Madan is headed 'Mr. Hoskins, his Convivium Philosophicum' and is marked at the end 'per Johannes Hoskins, London'.

(*d*) In the Bodleian in *MS. Rawl. Poet 117, ff. 192a–191b* (reading in reverse order). The author is given as Dr. Rodolphus Colfabius.

(*e*) At Belvoir Castle among the MSS. of the Duke of Rutland. The author is styled Dr. Rodolfus Calfaber (see Gosse, *Life & Letters of John Donne*, London, 1899, vol. I, p. 279).

L. B. Osborn includes version (*b*) and the English translation in her *Life, Letters & Writings of John Hoskyns*, pp. 196 and 288. She points out that the endorsement of version (*a*) '*of* Tom Corriat' can be construed in the sense of *about* or *belonging to* him. The poem is certainly more about Coryate than anyone else; he figures in nine of the nineteen stanzas, seven of which are wholly concerned with him. I. A. Shapiro points out, *M.L.R.* 1950, p. 7, n, that Coryate would not have written mocking verses about himself and that he cannot be identified with Radulphus Colphabius of Brasenose College since Coryate was at Gloucester Hall, and his name is latinized in the poem as 'Coriatus'. Shapiro also suggests that the ascription to John Hoskins can be ruled out both because he was at New College and because in the poem he is named 'Janus Caligula'. The identity of Radulphus Colphabius remains an enigma. The occasion for which the poem was composed is discussed on pp. 142–4 above.

### A Note on Manuscripts in the Bodleian Library

None of the manuscripts catalogued as concerning Coryate contains any new biographical information.

*Rawl. Poet 117, ff. 192a–191b* is a less good text of the poem on the Convivium Philosophicum than that in the P.R.O.

*Rawl. Poet 120, ff. 31*<sup>v</sup> ⎫
*Eng. Poet e 14*  ⎬ These sets of verses on Coryate and his travels
*Malone 19* ⎭ are of no particular merit or interest.

*Rawlinson B. 259* consists of a transcription of the eulogistic verses prefacing the *Crudities* and some biographical notes, culled from Anthony à Wood, Edward Terry, Samuel Purchas, and from Coryate's own writings, by Thomas Hearne (1678–1735), the historical antiquary.

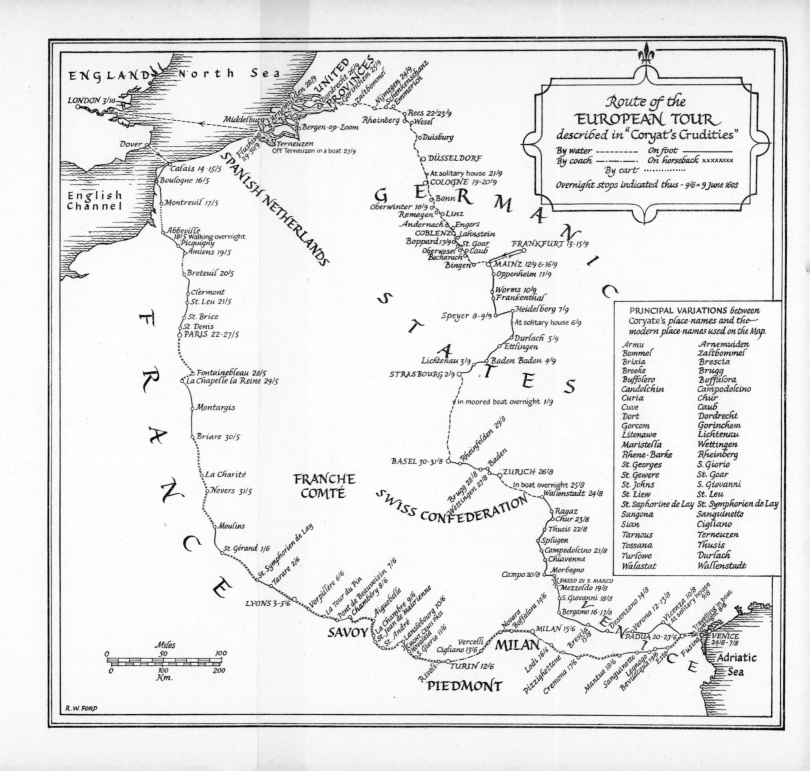

Route of the
EUROPEAN TOUR
described in "Coryat's Crudities"

By water ----------  On foot ———————
By coach ———————  On horseback ×××××××
By cart ··············

Overnight stops indicated thus - 9/6 = 9 June 1603

PRINCIPAL VARIATIONS between
Coryate's place-names and the
modern place-names used on the Map.

| | |
|---|---|
| Armu | Arnemuiden |
| Bommel | Zaltbommel |
| Brixia | Brescia |
| Brooke | Brugg |
| Buffolero | Boffalora |
| Candolchin | Campodolcino |
| Curia | Chur |
| Cuve | Caub |
| Dort | Dordrecht |
| Gorcom | Gorinchem |
| Litenawe | Lichtenau |
| Maristella | Wettingen |
| Rhene-Barke | Rheinberg |
| St. Georges | S. Giorio |
| St. Gewere | St. Goar |
| St. Johns | S. Giovanni |
| St. Liew | St. Leu |
| St. Saphorine de Lay | St. Symphorien de Lay |
| Sangona | Sanguinetto |
| Sian | Cigliano |
| Tarnous | Terneuzen |
| Tossana | Thusis |
| Turlowe | Durlach |
| Walastat | Wallenstadt |

ENGLAND — North Sea
LONDON 3/10
Middelburg
Dover
Calais 14·15/5
Boulogne 16/5

English Channel

Montreuil 17/5

Abbeville 18/5 Walking overnight
Picquigny
Amiens 19/5

Breteuil 20/5

Clermont
St. Leu 21/5

St. Brice
St. Denis
PARIS 22-27/5

Fontainebleau 28/5
La Chapelle la Reine 29/5

Montargis

Briare 30/5

La Charité
Nevers 31/5

Moulins

St. Gérand 1/6

FRANCHE COMTÉ

St. Symphorien de Lay
Tarare 2/6
Vorpillère 6/6
LYONS 3-5/6

SAVOY

Aiguebelle
La Chambre 9/6
St. André
Lanslebourg 10/6
St. Jean de Maurienne
La Tour du Pin
Pont de Beauvoisin 7/6
Chambéry 8/6
MONT CENIS PASS
Novalesa
S. Giorio 11/6
TURIN 12/6
Rivoli
Vercelli
Cigliano 13/6
PIEDMONT

Lodi 16/6
Pizzighettone
Cremona 17/6

UNITED PROVINCES
Arnemuiden 28/9
Dordrecht 26/9
Gorinchem 25/9
Zaltbommel
Nijmegen 24/9
Schenckenschanz
Emmerich
Rees 22/23/9
Rheinberg
Wesel
Flushing 29/30/9
Terneuzen
Off Terneuzen in a boat 27/9
Bergen-op-Zoom

SPANISH NETHERLANDS

Duisburg

DÜSSELDORF

At solitary house 21/9
COLOGNE 19-20/9
Bonn
Oberwinter 18/9
Remagen  Linz
Andernach  Engers
COBLENZ  Lahnstein
Boppard 17/9  St. Goar
Oberwesel  Caub
Bacharach
Bingen

GERMANIC STATES

FRANKFURT 13-15/9

MAINZ 12/9 & 16/9
Oppenheim 11/9

Worms 10/9
Frankenthal
Heidelberg 7/9
Speyer 8-9/9
At solitary house 6/9
Durlach 5/9
Ettlingen
Lichtenau 3/9  Baden Baden 4/9
STRASBOURG 2/9

In moored boat overnight 1/9

Rheinfelden 29/8
BASEL 30-31/8  Baden
Brugg 28/8  ZURICH 26/8
Wettingen 27/8  In boat overnight 25/8
Wallenstadt 24/8

SWISS CONFEDERATION

Ragaz
Chur 23/8
Thusis 22/8
Splügen
Campodolcino 21/8
Chiavenna
Campo 20/8  Morbegno
PASSO DI S. MARCO
Mezzoldo 19/8
S. Giovanni 18/8
Bergamo 16-17/8
Novara  Desenzano 14/8
Boffalora 14/6  Verona 12-13/8  Vicenza 10/8
MILAN 15/6  At solitary house 9/8
Brescia  Travelling in boat
15/8  PADUA 20-23/6  9/8
MILAN  Mantua 18/6  Sanguinetto  VENICE
Legnago 19/6  Fusina, overnight 8/8  24/6 - 7/8
Bevilacqua  Este  24/6 - 7/8
Adriatic Sea

Miles
0    50    100
0    100    200
Km.

R.W. FORD

# Index

PRINTED AND BOUND IN ENGLAND BY
HAZELL WATSON AND VINEY LTD
AYLESBURY AND SLOUGH